T0374774

THE

PUBLICATIONS

OF THE

Lincoln Record Society

FOUNDED IN THE YEAR

1910

VOLUME 34

FOR THE YEAR ENDING 30TH SEPTEMBER, 1937

THE

Registrum Antiquissimum

OF THE

Cathedral Church of Lincoln

Volume V

EDITED BY

KATHLEEN MAJOR

M.A., B.LITT.

ON THE PLAN LAID DOWN BY THE LATE

CHARLES WILMER FOSTER

PRINTED FOR

THE LINCOLN RECORD SOCIETY

BY

THE HEREFORD TIMES LIMITED, HEREFORD

1940

PREFACE

The thanks of the Society, as well as my personal gratitude, are again due to the Dean and Chapter for permitting my access to their muniments, which has been possible even since war began, through the kindness of the Chancellor of the Cathedral in allowing the MSS. necessary for this volume to be kept in an accessible place. They have once more contributed to the cost of the volume.

The fifth volume of REGISTRUM ANTIQUISSIMUM appears without the facsimiles of charters, which contributed both to the interest and value of the preceding volumes. Owing to the war it was impossible to take the charters to London to be reproduced, and it is therefore intended to include the plates both for this volume and the next in a portfolio to be issued when conditions are once more normal. In view of the prevalence of seals of quite small land-owners, as well as of several women of only moderate rank, this postponement is much to be regretted, but we may hope that the seals of John son of Stepi, Robert of Raithby, Avina and Richenilda daughters of Athelstan and many others may eventually be produced in all their fineness.

In the course of preparing the South Riding charters it was found that the number was so great that to include them all in one volume would have been to produce a book so unwieldy as to be inconvenient to the user ; for this reason the present volume contains the charters of the wapentakes of Wraggoe and Louthesk ; those of Calcewaith, Candleshoe, Bolingbroke, Hill, Gartree, and Horncastle will appear in the subsequent one. The numbering of the charters in the REGISTRUM ANTIQUISSIMUM is confusing. At the end of the thirteenth century a scribe filled several folios with copies of charters which had already been entered at the time of the original compilation. His object was not clear, as the earlier copies were all transcribed in the clear and correct style of the first scribe. This, together with the modern numbering by a duplication of numbers distinguished by *a* and *b*, gives the Wraggoe charters a somewhat confused appearance, as in few cases has it been possible to run them consecutively, if all those relating to one village were to be brought together.

The documents cover that part of Lincolnshire from within a few miles to the East of Lincoln over the wolds to the marshland of the north-east coast of the county. The landowners of Wraggoe wapentake make grants of much the same type as those of the North and the West Riding. The units are usually a toft and a croft or a bovate or half bovate of land. There are, however, fewer grants of pasture rights than in the other two Ridings. In Louthesk the grants are frequently on a smaller scale, and are of three or four acres or even less, rather than a bovate or half bovate. In this area are indications of the saltworks which were of importance (nos. 1603, 1718–9, 1721), and the particular problems of the region as regards drainage are indicated in references to the sea dyke (nos. 1719, 1721, etc.). The Louthesk charters are of overwhelming interest and importance in their illustration of the survival of the free peasantry and of the very strong Scandinavian element in that region.[1] The prevalence of Old English and Scandinavian names is such that the original forms of the Anglicised or Latinised versions found in the charters are given for the benefit of those who, like myself, are ignorant of the Norse and Danish languages. For this valuable list I am indebted to Miss Dorothy Whitelock, of St. Hilda's College, Oxford. The influence of the Breton element which in this area had its centre in Gayton le Wold, the head of the soke of the Count of Brittany and Earl of Richmond, is shown in the appearance of such names as Conan, Coste, Tenggi and Wimarc.

In respect of place names it is interesting to notice in Holton by Beckering the use of the English form Bradegate (p. 17) and the Scandinavian form Bretthegate (p. 20) for that road referred to on other occasions by a classically minded scribe as *Via Lata* (pp. 13–14).

Several grants of men with chattels and children (*secta* or *sequela*)

[1] The peculiarities of the agricultural economy and of the Scandinavian traditions of this region are described in Professor Stenton's introduction to the *Documents Illustrative of the Social and Economic History of the Danelaw*, a study of which is an indispensable preliminary to the understanding of the extraordinary interest of the marsh areas. The charters here printed form an addition to that series and to the *Transcripts of Charters of Gilbertine Houses*, L.R.S. xviii.

are to be found, one so late as 1251 ; in the last case two of the sons, Gilbert and Richard, were expressly exempted from the grant (no. 1459). Sybil of Benniworth bought Robert son of Rannulf son of Seward of Hainton from Thomas son of William for twenty shillings and two talents of silver and could dispose of him as she wished at her death (no. 1503). William son of Godric, granted with his wife Eda, by Rannulf of Withcall to the church of Lincoln (no. 1580), seems to have obtained his freedom and prospered, as his son Walter married Matilda daughter of Ralf son of Ernis who was a person of some substance (nos. 1593–4). An interesting arrangement was made by which William handed over his property to his son and daughter-in-law, saving possession in his lifetime to himself and reasonable dower to his wife, with the promise that he would maintain the young couple in his house to the best of his ability.

Another grant of interest is one made by Humphrey son of Walter and Alice his wife partly for the soul of their dead son Robert, partly because Humphrey was unable to fulfil a vow of pilgrimage through old age and ill-health (no. 1639). In one case the dean and chapter made a grant with the proviso that, should the elder brother return and wish to claim it, the grantee must resign the land to the grantors (no. 1470). This seems a clear instance of a state of affairs which, in days when news of those who had gone on crusade or pilgrimage or to war was difficult to get, must have been of no infrequent occurrence. Another grant was made of land which had escheated through felony (no. 1600), while in no. 1697 it is clearly stated that the grantee shall hold, not of the grantor, but of his lords, the dean and chapter.

There are few deeds dealing with parish churches, but no. 1572 is interesting as an example of obstruction by the dean and chapter during the vacancy of the see when the prior and convent of Sixle wished to enter into the church of South Cadeby. No. 1509 provides a residence for the homeless vicar of Hainton, and the last charter in the volume records the appropriation of Kelstern parish church to Thornton Abbey for the rebuilding of the conventual church.

A grant by Basilia wife of John of Carlton is notable for the attestation of the ruridecanal chapter of Louthesk and of ten women (no. 1688). Otherwise there is little of note in the diplomatic of the charters.

No. 1459 contains an acquittal from suit in the Riding court: a reference to this obscure institution is always of interest. In Hainton occurs a reference to the perch of sixteen feet, apparently the local measure (No. 1507).

Once again I am deeply indebted to Professor and Mrs. Stenton for unlimited assistance whenever it was asked for, as it was on many occasions. Not only have they given me the benefit of their knowledge on general problems but both of them have also read the proofs. To Mr. George Dixon, whose kindness was previously acknowledged under his former name of Gibbons, I am once more indebted for the service of proof-reading. The *corrigenda* for Volume III were sent by Dr. H. E. Salter to Canon Foster before his death, but were not found among his papers until lately. The Chancellor of the Cathedral has supplied me with *corrigenda* for Volume IV: other *corrigenda* were sent by Mr. Charles Johnson, who also kindly allowed me to consult him on certain obscure words. My thanks are also due to the staff of The Hereford Times Ltd. for their admirable work in the preparation of the volumes.

My final thanks are once more recorded to Canon Foster, who gave me the inestimable privilege of continuing his edition of this superb collection of charters. It is indeed unfortunate that Lincolnshire should have suffered the loss of his immense knowledge of its history and topography before he could complete the edition of its finest collection of twelfth- and thirteenth- century records.

KATHLEEN MAJOR.

July, 1940.

CONTENTS

In the following table the twelfth century charters are separately enumerated.

The South Riding

Wraggoe Wapentake

ABBREVIATIONS AND NOTES

General Abbreviations

Abs.	Abstract.
Marg.	Margin.
Pd	Printed.
Q	Quis, the Redactor of the Registrum Antiquissimum now identified with Master John of Schalby. See vol. i, pp. xxviii ff.
Q2	The redactor's scribes. See vol. i, p. xxxivn.
Rubric	A rubricated title in the several cartularies.
Texts : MS—	Under this head are specified the several texts used for each charter in this edition, the text from which a charter is printed having the first place assigned to it.
Var. R.	Various reading (*or* readings).
*	This sign is used to indicate the beginning of a new page of the Registrum Antiquissimum, when it comes in the middle of a charter.
Witn.	Witness.
1, 2, 3, etc.	Indicate the numbers of the charters in the Registrum Antiquissimum. See vol. i, p. xiv.

Manuscripts

A.	Registrum Antiquissimum (D. and C., A/1/5). See vol. i, p. xiii ff.
Add. Chart.	Additional charter. See vol. i, p. xiv.
D. and C. (in references)	Muniments of the Dean and Chapter of Lincoln.

Orig. – – – – – Original charter in the muniment room of the Dean and Chapter of Lincoln.

R. – – – – – Registrum (D. and C., A/1/6). See vol. i, pp. xli, xlii.

R.A., Reg. Ant. – – – Registrum Antiquissimum.

PRINTED BOOKS

Ass: Arch: Rep. – – *Associated Architectural Societies' Reports and Papers.*

Book of Fees – – – *The Book of Fees, commonly called Testa de Nevill* (Rolls Series).

C.P.R. – – – – *Calendar of Patent Rolls.*

C.R.R. – – – – *Curia Regis Rolls*, vols. i–vii.

Excerpta e rotulis finium – *Excerpta e rotulis finium in turri Londonensi asservatis, Henrico tertio regi.* Two vols. 1886.

Final Concords I. – – *Abstracts of final concords (Lincolnshire) temp. Richard I, John and Henry III*, ed. W. Boyd and W. O. Massingberd. (Privately published.)

Free Peasantry – – – *The Free Peasantry in the Northern Danelaw*, by F. M. Stenton. *Kungl. Humanistiska Vetenskapssamfundet i Lund* 1926 (pp. 73–183).

Liber Antiquus – – – *Liber Antiquus Hugonis de Welles*, ed. A. Gibbons, privately printed 1888.

L.R.S.– – – – – The Publications of the Lincoln Record Society.

The Lincolnshire Domesday – *The Lincolnshire Domesday and the Lindsey Survey*, ed. C. W. Foster and T. Longley (Lincoln Record Society, vol. xix).

Lincs. N and Q. – – – *Lincolnshire Notes and Queries.*

Selden Society liii – – *Rolls of the justices in eyre for Lincolnshire* 1218–9 *and Worcestershire* 1221, edited by Doris Mary Stenton.

Stenton, Danelaw Charters – *Documents illustrative of the social and economic history of the Danelaw*, edited by F. M. Stenton. (London, Milford, for the British Academy.)

V.C.H. – – – – *Victoria County History.*

Notes

The Registrum Antiquissimum has supplied the plan or framework of this volume, that is, that cartulary is printed consecutively, except in the instances specified in the Preface, while charters which are not included in it are interpolated in the appropriate places. Each charter from the Registrum Antiquissimum is distinguished by having its serial number in the cartulary printed in Old English type in the middle of the page. The interpolated charters are marked by the words Add. Chart. (Additional Charter) printed in the middle of the page. If there is an original charter the document has been printed from that text, and if there is no original document the text of the Registrum Antiquissimum has been preferred to any other. To the text from which a document is printed is assigned the first place under the head of 'Texts'; and important various readings in the other texts are given under 'Var. R.'

The text of these volumes attempts to reproduce the documents letter for letter, with all marks of accentuation. Endorsements of original charters earlier than the seventeenth century have been printed. The abbreviated Latin forms have been extended, and where there might be any doubt in regard to the form intended italics have been used. The compendium which frequently occurs at the end of a name has been retained unless it has seemed likely that an extension was contemplated, and for such extensions italics have been used. Since the use of capitals in medieval texts is arbitrary, the modern use has been adopted, a course which may serve as a guide to the sense, and also help the student more readily to catch sight of names. The punctuation of the documents, though sometime capricious, has been adhered to. Since print can never be a perfect substitute for an original document, facsimiles of some of the most important original charters are provided.

The historical year, beginning 1st January, is used throughout this edition, except that in the texts of documents the original has been adhered to.

LIST OF CHARTERS

PRINTED IN THIS VOLUME WHICH ARE INCLUDED IN THE REGISTRUM ANTIQUISSIMUM

Reg. Ant.	Original texts	R.	This vol.
355	–	1476	1458
356=380	–	1477	1459
357	–	1475	1460
359	Dij/72/3/26	1452	1463
360=419	Dij/72/3/29	1450	1464
361=363=415	Dij/72/3/23	1443	1465
362	Dij/72/3/25	1453	1466
363=361=415	Dij/72/3/23	1443	1467
364=417	Dij/72/3/24	1445	1468
365=416	Dij/72/3/21	1444	1469
366	Dij/72/3/22	1446	1470
367	–	1434	1491
368	–	1485	1510
368a=413	Dij/72/3/30	1449	1473
369	–	1473	1511
369a	Dij/71/3/56	1429	1493
370	–	1472	1512
370a=389	–	1433	1495
371	–	1474	1513
371a	Dij/71/3/58	1427	1496
372=423	–	1471	1514
372a	–	–	1497
373a=392	Dij/71/3/65	1426	1498
374a=426	–	1430	1499
375a	–	1428	1500
375b=393	Dij/71/3/52	–	1501
376a=391	Dij/71/3/55	1432	1502
377a	–	1437	1503
378=401	Dij/87/1/35	1480	1522
378a=402	Dij/87/1/36	1481	1523
379=422	–	1479	1524
380=356	–	1477	1526

Reg. Ant.	Original texts	R.	This vol.
381=397	Dij/83/1/36	1456	1527
382	–	1457	1530
383=425	–	1458	1531
384=395	–	1465	1537
385=394	–	1467	1538
386=396	–	1466	1539
387	–	1470	1540
388=409	–	1484	1543
389=370a	–	1433	1544
390	–	–	1503a
391=376a	Dij/71/3/55	1432	1546
392=373a	Dij/71/3/65	1426	1547
393=375b	Dij/71/3/52	–	1548
394=385	–	1467	1549
395=384	–	1465	1550
396=386	–	–	1551
397=381	Dij/83/1/36	1456	1552
398	–	–	1532
399	–	–	1533
400	–	–	1534
401=378	Dij/87/1/35	1480	1522
402=378a	Dij/87/1/36	1481	1523
403	Dij/83/1/27	1459	1553
404	Dij/83/1/23	1461	1554
405	Dij/83/1/25	1462	1555
406	Dij/83/1/26	1463	1556
407	Dij/83/1/24	1464	1557
408	–	1646	1564
409=388	–	1484	1565
410	–	1482	1566
411	–	1483	1567
412	–	–	1474
413=368a	Dij/72/3/30	1449	1475
414	–	–	1476
415=361=363	Dij/72/3/23	1443	1477
416=365	Dij/72/3/21	1444	1478

Reg. Ant.	Original texts	R.	This vol.
417=364	–	–	1479
418	Dij/72/3/28	1447	1480
419=360	Dij/72/3/29	1450	1481
420	Dij/72/3/31	1448	1482
421	–	–	1483
422=379	–	1479	1524
423=372	–	1471	–
424	Dij/71/3/68a	1440	1504
425=383	–	1458	1531
426=374a	–	1430	1499
433	–	1332	1570
434	–	1333	1571
435	Dij/68/2/45	1650	1573
436	–	1642	1574
437	–	1643	1575
438	Dij/88/3/29	1623	1578
439	Dij/88/3/27	1624	1579
440	–	1625	1580
441	–	1627	1581
442	Dij/88/3/26	1626	1582
443	Dij/88/3/28	1628	1583
444	–	1632	1584
445	–	1633	1585
446	–	1631	1586
447	–	1629	1587
448	Dij/88/3/25	1630	1588
449	–	1634	1589
450	Dij/88/3/30	1635	1590
451	Dij/71/2/35	1641	1595
452	Dij/71/2/34	1640	1596
453	Dij/66/1/2	1488	1597
454	Dij/66/1/1	1489	1598
455	Dij/66/1/3	1490	1599
456	–	1516	1602
457	–	1510	1603
458	–	1500	1604

Reg. Ant.	Original texts	R.	This vol.
459	–	1512	1605
460	–	1508	1606
461	–	1514	1607
462	–	1513	1608
463	–	1511	1609
464	–	1506	1610
465	–	1499	1611
466	–	1498	1612
467	–	1502	1613
468	–	1507	1614
469	–	1504	1615
470	–	1501	1616
471	–	1492	1621
472	–	1494	1622
473	–	1493	1623
477	Dij/86/2/25	1594	1630
478	Dij/86/2/34	1617	1631
479	–	1595	1632
480	Dij/86/2/37	1615	1633
481	–	1614	1634
482	Dij/86/2/24	1596	1635
483	Dij/86/2/27	1597	1636
484	Dij/86/2/26	1601	1637
485	Dij/86/2/33	1602	1638
486	Dij/86/2/38	1605	1639
487	Dij/86/2/32	1607	1640
488	Dij/86/2/31	1609	1641
489	Dij/86/2/30	1608	1642
490	Dij/86/2/29	1610	1643
491	Dij/86/2/1	1603	1644
492	Dij/86/2/28a	1598	1645
493	Dij/86/2/28b	1611	1646
494	–	–	1647
495	–	–	1648
496	–	1541	1656
497	–	1524	1657

Reg. Ant.	Original texts	R.	This vol.
498	–	1527	1658
499	–	1538	1659
500	–	1543	1660
501	–	1525	1661
502	–	1526	1662
503	–	1533	1663
504	–	1542	1664
505	–	1530	1665
506	–	1529	1666
507	–	1528	1667
508	–	1552	1668
509	–	1549	1669
510	–	1548	1670
511	–	1553	1671
512	Dij/87/1/1	1556	1672
513	–	1554	1673
514	–	1544	1674
515	–	1534	1675
515a	–	1532	1676
516	–	1551	1677
517	–	1531	1678
518	–	1547	1679
519	–	1557	1680
520	–	1546	1681
521	–	1522	1682
522	–	1523	1683
523	–	1539	1684
524	–	–	1685
525	–	–	1686
526	–	–	1687
527	–	1545	1688
528	–	1590	1698
529	–	1555	1699
530=696	Dij/87/1/22a	1899	1700
531	–	1586	1701
532	–	1563	1702

Reg. Ant.	Original texts	R.	This vol.
533	–	1592	1703
534	Dij/87/1/18	1559	1704
535	Dij/87/1/2	1562	1705
536	–	1585	1706
537	Dij/87/1/19	1574	1707
538	Dij/87/1/20	1575	1708
539	–	1576	1709
540	Dij/87/1/5	1573	1710
541	Dij/87/1/4	1572	1711
541a	–	1589	1712
542	Dij/87/1/13	1569	1713
543	–	1587	1714
544	Dij/87/1/22	1564	1715
545	Dij/87/1/12	1558	1716
546	–	1571	1717
547	–	1578	1718
548	–	1580	1719
549	–	1581	1720
550	–	1579	1721
551	–	1582	1722
552	–	1583	1723
553	–	1577	1724
696=530	Dij/87/1/22a	1899	1700

PRINTED IN THIS VOLUME WHICH ARE NOT INCLUDED IN THE REGISTRUM ANTIQUISSIMUM

Original texts	R.	This vol.
–	1478	1461
Dij/72/3/27	1451	1484
Dij/72/3/34	–	1485
Dij/72/3/32	–	1486
Dij/72/3/33	–	1487
–	1454	1488
Dij/72/3/20	–	1489
Dij/72/3/18	–	1490
–	1441	1505
Dij/71/3/68b	1439	1506
Dij/71/3/64	–	1507
–	1438	1508
–	1442	1509
Dij/88/1/25	1800	1515
Dij/88/1/24	1801	1516
Dij/87/1/34	–	1525
Dij/83/1/38	–	1528
Dij/83/1/35	1455	1529
–	1460	1535
Dij/66/3/26	–	1536
–	1468	1541
–	1469	1542
Dij/83/1/33	–	1558
Dij/83/1/34	–	1559
Dij/83/1/34a	90	1560
Dij/83/1/29	98	1561
Dij/88/1/30	99	1562
Dij/70/1/27	78	1563
–	1486	1568
Dij/86/3/37	–	1569
Dij/68/2/46	–	1572
–	1644	1576
–	1645	1577
Dij/88/3/31	1638	1591
Dij/88/3/32	1639	1592

Original texts	R.	This vol.
Dij/88/3/33	1637	1593
Dij/88/3/34	1636	1594
Dij/66/1/4	–	1600
–	1491	1601
–	1503	1617
–	1505	1618
–	1509	1619
–	1515	1620
–	1495	1624
–	1496	1625
Dij/88/3/54	1497	1626
Dij/86/2/8	1604	1649
Dij/86/2/20	1616	1650
Dij/86/2/19	1613	1651
Dij/86/2/21	1599	1652
Dij/86/2/9	1600	1653
–	1606	1654
–	1612	1655
–	1518	1689
–	1519	1690
–	1520	1691
–	1521	1692
–	1535	1693
–	1536	1694
–	1537	1695
–	1540	1696
–	1550	1697
Dij/87/1/3	1567	1725
Dij/87/1/6	1568	1726
Dij/87/1/16	1566	1727
Dij/87/1/17	1561	1728
Dij/87/1/21a	1560	1729
–	1565	1730
–	1570	1731
–	1584	1732

Original Texts	R.	This Vol.
–	1588	1733
–	1591	1734
–	1593	1735
Dij/69/2/41	1647	1736
–	1648	1737
Dij/69/3/20	1649	1738
Dij/83/1/3	–	1739
Dij/83/1/5	–	1740
Dij/83/1/7	–	1741
Dij/83/1/2	–	1742
Dij/83/1/4	–	1743
Dij/83/1/12	–	1744
Dij/83/1/21	–	1745
Dij/83/1/8	–	1746
Dij/73/1/4a	–	1747

CORRECTIONS FOR VOLUME III

p. 7, l. 16—*for* nobis *read* vobis.

p. 9, l. 2—*for* huic *read* hinc.

p. 12. This refers to Grove in Sandford St. Martin (co. Oxford) and the holding is given in *Rotuli Hundredorum*, ii, p. 844; all the names are of that part of the county. The endorsement must have been a fourteenth century guess.

p. 28, l. 3—*for* obediencia *read* obedienciam.

p. 45, l. 50—*for* dietia *read* dietis.

p. 91, l. 50—*for* tandem *read* eandem.

p. 286, l. 39—*for* huic *read* hinc.

p. 273, no. 934. The earliest date is 1273, when Oweyn became mayor of Oxford for the first time.

p. 290, no. 951. The date must be after 1226, the year in which Pandulph died, as he is referred to as " of happy memory ".

CORRECTIONS FOR VOLUME IV

p. 2, l. 15—*for* suspiciam *read* suscipiam.

p. 65, no. 1180 title—*for* facto *read* facta.

p. 81, l. 3—*for* enacted *read* exacted

p. 86, in Note to no. 1201—*for* 1199 *read* 1189.

p. 214, l. 9—*for* tofit *read* tofti.

p. 272, in Note to no. 1448—*for* excerpts *read* excerpta.

INDEX

p. 287 and p. 334—*for* Avalon (Yonne, France) *read* Avalon (Isère, France).

p. 293—Claxby, William son of Henry of. *This man was of Claxby Pluckacre, not of Claxby by Normanby as he is identified in the index. He was also known as William of Wyham* (*see below*, p. 28).

p. 310—*for* Lincoln (10), chancery of, *read* chancellorship of.

p. 321, *for* Saham co. Norfolk *read* co. Camb.

p. 337, s.v. Faith—*for* fida interposita *read* fide interposita.

NOTE FOR VOLUME V

The dedications of the churches of North and South Somercotes were originally St. Mary and St. Peter respectively. Owing to a mistake in the Duchy of Lancaster Office in 1681, the dedications were reversed and North Somercotes is now attributed to St. Peter and South to St. Mary. The parish of the Blessed Mary referred to in no. 1685 is therefore North Somercotes.

[Registrum Antiquissimum]

The South Riding

Wraggoe Wapentake

BURGH ON BAIN

355

1458. Grant by Hugh of Burgh and Beatrice his wife, to the church of Lincoln and the Common, of all the land in Burgh [on Bain] which Alan Crapus had given them in frank marriage with Beatrice his daughter, and a toft of the fee of John de Gerumwill'. (Circa 1230–1240.)

Carta Hugonis de Burgo de terra quam Alanus Crapus tenuit in eadem (A rubric).

Omnibus Christi fidelibus ad quos presens scriptum peruenerit ∴ Hugo de Burgo 7 Beatricia uxor eius salutem . Noueritis nos dedisse concessisse 7 hac presenti carta nostra confirmasse deo 7 beate Marie 7 commune canonicorum Linc' ecclesie totam terram illam cum pertinentiis in territorio de Burgo quam Alanus Crapus de Burbo[1] nobis dedit cum me Beatricia filia sua in libero maritagio cum vno tofto de fesido[2] Johannis de Gerumwill'[3] 7 iacet inter terram Gilberti Gep 7 terram Roberti filii Gilberti tenendum[4] 7 habendum[4] imperpetuum in puram 7 perpetuam elemosinam [5]liberam[5] 7 quietam ab omni seruicio 7 exaccione seculari . cum omnibus pertinenciis suis libertatibus 7 asiamentis infra uillam 7 extra . Nos uero 7 heredes nostra[6] warantizabimus 7 defendemus totum dictum tenementum cum pertinenciis libertatibus 7 asiamentis tamquam [7]puram[7] 7 perpetuam elemosinam liberam 7 quietam dictis canonicis contra omnes homines imperpetuum . 7 in huius rei testimonium presens scriptum sigillo nostro confirmauimus . Hiis testibus .E. succentore Linc' . Ricardo Abraham . Phillppo[8] de Tumba . Atam[9] de Feretro . Johanne de Nettelton'[10] . Willelmo Goscelini[11] . G. de Sancto Andrea . capell*anis* . Johanne de Sancto Edwardo . Roberto Scoto 7 aliis.

Marginalia in A: (1) Burgo. (2) .a.
Texts: MS.—A. R 1476.
Var. R.: [1] *sic:* Burgo *in* R. [2] *sic:* feudo *in* R. [3] Gertumvill' R. [4] *sic.* [5]–[5] R *omits.* [6] *sic:* nostri *in* R. [7]–[7] R *omits.* [8] *sic:* Philippo R. [9] *sic:* Adam R. [10] R *adds* magistro Willelmo *after* Nettelton. [11] Gocelyn R.
Note: These charters are incorrectly placed in Walshcroft wapentake in A but are included in the Wraggoe charters in R. For Elias the succentor see vol. iv, p. 280. The other witnesses occur about this time.

356 and 380

1459. Grant by Reginald de Jarpenuill', to the church of Lincoln and the Common, of a toft and two bovates in Burgh [on Bain] which Ivo of Burgh held of him: also of the said Ivo with all his chattels and issue except his sons, Gilbert and Richard. In the event of his death before that of Alice his wife, he has arranged, with her consent, that his heirs will not assign this land to her as dower. Moreover, he and his heirs will acquit this land from all suits in the county, riding, wapentake, and all other secular courts, as well as from sheriff's aid and all other secular service. (1251.)

De vno tofto 7 .ij. bouatis 7 Yuone cum sequela (A356 rubric: by Q).

Omnibus Christi fidelibus ad quos presens scriptum peruenerit ·/ Reginaldus de Jarpenuill' eternam in domino salutem . Nouerit vniuersitas vestra me diuine caritatis intuitu 7[1] pro salute anime mee 7 animarum antecessorum 7 omnium heredum meorum . dedisse . concessisse 7 hac presenti carta mea confirmasse deo 7 beate Marie 7 commune canonicorum Linc' ecclesie . in liberam . puram . 7 perpetuam elemosinam . vnum toftum . 7 duas bouatas terre in villa de Burgo . quas Yuo de Burgo tenuit de me cum pratis pascuis [2]7[2] pasturis . 7 omnibus aliis aysiamentis . 7 libertatibus ad dictum toftum 7 duas bouatas terre cum pertinenciis infra villam . 7 extra [3]pertinentibus[3] . Et predictum Yuonem natiuum meum cum omnibus catallis suis 7 tota sequela sua . excepto Gilberto 7 Ricardo filiis eiusdem Yuonis . Habendum 7 tenendum dicte ecclesie Linc' . in liberam puram 7 perpetuam elemosinam . Et sciendum quod si humanitus de me contingat ante mortem Alicie vxoris mee . de consensu eiusdem Alicie volo quod heredes mei eidem Alicie vxori mee de dote sua alibi prouideant ad valenciam tercie partis sue quam* illuc[4] debent[5] recipere . ita quod in nullo dicte ecclesie preiudicium generetur ·/ aut grauamen . Et ego Reginaldus 7 heredes mei totam predictam terram 7 toftum cum . prato[6] Yuone 7 tota sequela sua ut predictum est memorate ecclesie Linc' tanquam liberam puram 7 perpetuam [3]elemosinam[3] contra omnes homines 7 feminas warantizabimus defendemus 7 acquietabimus inperpetuum de omnibus sectis in comitatu[7] thrythingis[8] wapentagiis . 7 de[1] omnibus aliis curiis secularibus . 7 vicecomitis auxilio . 7 omni alio seruicio seculari 7 demanda quocunque nomine censeatur . Et in huius rei robur 7 testimonium presenti scripto sigillum meum apposui . Hiis testibus . magistro Radulfo de Luda . Petro de Wysebech' . Hugone de Burgo capellano . Alexandro de Luda cementario . Mikaele de de[9] Lincolnia aurifabro . Johanne seruiente . Radulfo clerico . 7 aliis.

Marginalia in A: 356 .c. 380. (1) Burgo. (2) Burgo.

Texts: MS—A356 (in the lower margin of ff. 65*d* and 66*d* by Con: rubric by Q). A380 (by Q2). R1477.

Var. R.: [1] A380 *omits.* [2–2] A380 *and* R *omit.* [3–3] R *omits.* [4] illic *in* A380. [5] *sic*: deberet *in* A380 *and* R. [6] *sic*: prefato *in* A380 *and* R. [7] comitatibus R. [8] Thrithingis A380: Trithingis R. [9] *sic.*

Note: Reginald swore to observe this grant 3rd February, 1251 (see no. 1461 below).

**Folio* 66 in no. 356.

Hdl. WALESECROFTE. . 6 . 6 .

357

1460. Grant by [William son of] Alan Crapus of Burgh [on Bain], to the church of Lincoln and the Common, of the land given by his father to Hugh of Burgh with Beatrice his daughter in frank marriage. (Circa 1230–1240.)

Carta Alani de Burgo . de terra in Burgo (A rubric).

Omnibus sancte matris ecclesie filiis Alani[1] Crapus de Burgo salutem . Noueritis me dedisse concessisse 7 hac presenti carta mea confirmasse deo 7 beate Marie 7 commune canonicorum Linc' ecclesie totam terram illam quam Alanus pater meus dedit Hugoni de Burgo cum Beatricia filia sua in libero maritagio . tenendum[2] 7 habendum[2] imperpetuum cum omnibus pertinentiis libertatibus 7 asiamentis infra uillam 7 extra . in puram 7 perpetuam elemosinam . liberam 7 quietam ab omni seruicio 7 exaccione seculari . Hec autem terra iacet in territorio de Burgo ex aquilonari[3] parte uille . Hee sunt partes . quatuor selliones apud Gatefurlang' . unus sellio sub Litteldikes cum terra de Meitenwelle[4] . forarium de Stainholm' . vnus sellio super Stainholm' . unum forarium ex orientali parte de Grussegate[5] cum duobus sellionibus . vnus sellio ad Storkesdale[6] . duos[7] selliones super Strete-furlang' . duo selliones ad[8] Calkehill'[9] . duo selliones ad Mikeldale . duo foraria iuxta Scharhou[10] . Isti uero duo selliones cum duobus forariis sunt ex australi parte uille cum partibus sequentibus preter unum [11]sellionem[11] ex orientali parte de Flaxewelle cum uno sellione seorsum Flaxewell' . duo selliones in Bohiwang'[12] . duo selliones super Stretefurlang' . duo selliones in Smathcorydale . unus sellio ad Stainhollelangd' vnus sellio ad Riland'[13] . duo selliones super Rugholm' duo selliones super Bainfurland' cum prato ad vadum de Becune[14] . Ego uero Willelmus 7 heredes mei warantizabimus 7 defendemus totum dictum tenementum cum omnibus pertinenciis suis 7 libertatibus dictis canonicis tanquam puram 7 perpetuam elemosinam . liberam 7 quietam ab omni seruicio 7 exaccione contra omnes homines inperpetuum . 7 in huius rei testimonium huic scripto sigillum meum apposui . Hiis testibus . E. succentore Linc' . Ricardo Abraham . Philippo de Tumba . Ada de Feretro . Johanne de Nettelton' . magistro Willelmo . Willelmo Gocelin .G. de Sancto Andrea . capellanis . Johanne de Sancto Edwardo[15] . Roberto Scoto . Ricardo de Leycestr' . Gileberto clerico . 7 aliis.

Marginalia in A: (1) .b. (2) Burgo.
Texts: MS—A. R1475.
Var. R.: [1] *sic :* R *has* Willelmus filius Alani. [2] *sic.* [3] aquilonali R. [4] Meidenwell R. [5] Grissegate R. [6] Stockesdale R. [7] duo R. [8] super R. [9] Kaltehill' R. [10] Scarhou R. [11]–[11] R *omits.* [12] Boihiwang R. [13] Richeland R. [14] Beinne R. [15] R *adds* clerico.

Add. Chart.

1461. Memorandum that Reginald de Jarkemull' swore in the chapter house at Lincoln to observe the terms of his grant of land and of Ivo his villein, to the Common. 3rd February, 1251.

Memorandum quod anno gracie . M° . CC . Quinquagesimo . incrastino Purificacionis beate virginis dedit 7 concessit dominus Reginaldus de Iarkemull'[1] miles per cartam suam commune canonicorum Lincoln' duas bouatas terre 7 vnum toftum in villa de Burgo 7 Yuonem natiuum suum cum omnibus catallis suis 7 tota sequela sua in capitulo Linc' 7 tactis sacrosanctis iurauit pro se 7 heredibus suis se omnia in carta predicta fideliter obseruaturum Presentibus ibidem dominis .H. decano .R. precentore .R. thesaurario magistro .S. de London Serlone .R. Auus[1] .R. de Pertona . 7 .N. Greco dominis .W. de Well .R. de Wysebech .R. de Bollesouer Galfrido de Thame canonicis Linc' Galfrido de Bannebyr' Alexandro de Wẏncumbe Simone de Saham Nicholao de Wassingburgh Roberto Scoto Roberto de Bekeford Galfrido de Misterton vicariis eiusdem ecclesie . Et in huius rei testimonium predicte carte appensum est hoc memorandum.

Text: MS—R1478.
Var. R.: [1] *sic.* [2] *sic : possibly recte* R Amis *who occurs about this time.*

358

1462. This charter relates to Walesby and is printed in volume iv at no. 1370 above.

Folio 66*d*.

The greater part of folio 66*d* is blank. At the foot there occurs in the hand of Q. CARTE DE JORDEBURG' DEBENT HIC SCRIBI.

Folio 67.

Hdl. WRAGHOU (by Q). . 6 . 7 .

HOLTON BY BECKERING

359

1463. Grant by Thomas of Bleasby, to the church of Lincoln and the Common, of a toft in Holton by Beckering. (Circa 1220–1230.)

De terris ⁊ redditibus extra villam (A heading).

Omnibus Christi fidelibus ad quos presens scriptum peruenerit . Thomas de Blesby[1] salutem in domino . Nouerit vniuersitas uestra me dedisse . concessisse . ⁊ hac presenti carta mea confirmasse . pro salute anime mee ⁊ antecessorum ⁊ successorum meorum deo . ⁊ beate Marie ⁊ commune canonicorum Linc' ecclesie in liberam puram ⁊ perpetuam elemosinam quoddam toftum in uilla de Houtun'[2] cum omnibus pertinenciis suis . Illud uidelicet toftum quod iacet inter regiam stratam . ⁊ toftum Rogeri in angulo . ⁊ vndecim acras ⁊ dimidiam terre arabilis . ⁊ duas acras prati in teritorio de Houtun'[2] . quarum tres selliones jacent sub Littelgate inter terram ecclesie de Houtun'[2] ⁊ terram Willelmi Wryde . ⁊ tres selliones . iacentes inter terram dicte ecclesie .; ⁊ terram Bartholomei . ⁊ quatuor selliones ex parte boreali de Barnhougathe[3] . inter terram Radulphi prepositi . ⁊ terram Alicie vxoris Reyneri . ⁊ vnum sellionem per medium Langholm' inter terram Henrici filii Reyneri . ⁊ terram Thome Mustel . ex parte orientali ville . Item . ex parte occidentali ville tres selliones abbuttantes super villam . ⁊ jacent inter terras Willelmi filii Ranulphi . Super Toftes deyl[4] tres selliones jacentes inter terram Willelmi filii Ranulphi .; ⁊ pratum Johannis clerici . ⁊ super eodem furlang' unum sellionem jacentem inter terram Willelmi Wryde . ⁊ terram Willelmi filii Ranulphi . Item vnum forarium abbuttantem super regiam stratam juxta terram ecclesie . ⁊ alium forarium abbuttantem super terram ecclesie . ⁊ iacet iuxta terram Willelmi filii Ranulphi . Item vnum sellionem abbuttantem super eundem forarium inter terram Thome Mustel . ⁊ terram

Ranulphi . Item duas percatas prati in Thorneng . inter pratum Johannis prepositi 7 pratum Willelmi filii Gilberti . Item in Esteng in Lange . tres percatas prati . inter pratum Henrici filii Reyneri 7 pratum domine de Rande . Et duas percatas prati in Scortes jacentes inter pratum Willelmi filii Ranulphi 7 pratum Walteri Brand'[5] . Item duas percatas prati jacentes inter[6] pratum Rogeri in angulo :' 7 pratum Bartholomei . Tenend*os* 7 habend*os* prefatis canonicis in puram liberam 7 perpetuam elemosinam liberam 7 quietam ab [7]omni[7] seruicio 7 exaccione seculari :' 7 demanda . Et ego Thomas de Blesby[1] . 7 heredes mei warantizabimus adquietabimus 7 defendemus . predictum toftum cum tota predicta terra arabili 7 prato prescripto cum omnibus pertinenciis suis libertatibus 7 aysiamentis prefatis canonicis contra omnes homines in perpetuum tanquam puram liberam 7 perpetuam elemosinam . [8]Et in huius[8] rei testimonium presens scriptum . fide pro me 7 heredibus meis interposita :' sigillo meo confirmaui . Testibus . Ricardo . capellano de Houtun'[2] . domino Thoma de Bekering milite . Radulfo de Hauley . Roberto filio Helti . Johanne filio capellani de Lyssinton' . Radulpho de Kotes[9] . Simone [10]le[10] Fraunceys.

Endorsed: (1) Houton' .j. toft'. (13 cent.). (2) Lindes' . (13 cent.). (3) Thom' de Beseby (13 cent.). (4) .viij. (13 cent.).

Slit for seal-tag. Size: 7¼ x 7¼ inches.

Marginalia in A: (1) Howton (by Q2). (2) Howton (by Q2).

Texts: MS—Orig. Dij/72/3/26. A. R1452.

Var. R.: [1] Bleseby A *and* R. [2] Howton' A. [3] Barnhovgate A. Barnhougate R. [4] dayl A. [5] Braund R. [6] in (*sic*) R. [7–7] A *omits*. [8–8] In cuius A. [9] Cotes A. [10–10] A *omits*.

Note: In 1212 the heirs of Jocelin of Bleasby [in Legsby] were holding three carucates in Bleasby and Holton of Reginald Crevequer's heirs (*Book of Fees*, i, pp. 171–2). Thomas Mustel and Ralf de Hauley were jurors for the wapentake of Wraggoe in 1242 (*ibid.* ii, p. 1061). Thomas of Beckering and Robert son of Helto occur in 1219 (Selden Society, vol. liii, nos. 87, 335, 671).

360 and 419

1464. Confirmation by Martin son of Wycius of Beesby, to the church of Lincoln and the Common, of a half bovate and a toft in Holton [by Beckering] which they had of the gift of William son of William the palmer of Holton [by Beckering]. (Circa 1200.)

Confirmatio eiusdem (A419 rubric).

Sciant presentes 7 futuri quod ego Martinus filius Wÿcii de Besebi[2] concessi 7 hac carta mea confirmaui deo 7 beate Marie 7 commune canonicorum Lincol' ecclesie . illam dimidiam bouatam terre cum pertinentiis suis 7 cum tofto in Houton'[3] . quam habent de dono Willelmi filii Willelmi palmeri de Houton'[3] . Scilicet ex orientali parte ville :' v. acras . videlicet .ij. selliones ex occidentali parte de Galtereng .

⁊ .ij. selliones sub Barnhow [⁊[1]] ij. selliones sub Hildekinlandes . ⁊ .ij. sellio[nes ex[1]] aquilonali parte de Barnhowgate[4] . ⁊ duas per[ticatas[1]] prati in Esteng . Et ex occidentali parte [uille .v.[1]] acras . scilicet . super Northolm' .ij. selliones . ⁊ super [Sanholm.[5]] .j. sellionem ⁊ super Thornfurlangs[6] .ij. selliones . ⁊ [apud[1]] Stein .j. sellionem [7]⁊ inter vias .j. sellionem[7] . ⁊ .ij. pertica[tas[1]] prati in Westeng . ⁊ toftum[8] illud quod u[ocatum est[1]] Grescroft quod durat in longitudine a uia [que ducit[1]] per medium uille . usque . ad Barnhowgate[4] [cu[1]]m omnibus pertinentiis[9] ⁊ aisiamentis infra uillam ⁊ ex[tra ad[1]] terram illam pertinentibus . in puram ⁊ perpetuam elemosinam liberam ⁊ quietam ab omni seculari [ser[1]]uitio ⁊ exactione ∴ sicut carta dicti Willelmi quam inde habent ∴ testatur . Et ut hec mea concessio rata ⁊ stabilis permaneat in perpetuum . eam sigilli mei appositione duxi roborandam[10] . Hiis testibus . Eudone preposito .W. Blundo . Johanne de Wikeford' . Matheo de Lond' . ⁊ G. Lorimer . capellanis .P.[11] de Bekering .T. filio eius .T. de Scotyni[12]. Willelmo Mustel'.

Endorsed : (1) Houtona di[midiam bou]atam . cum .j. tofto . . . . . . (13 cent.). (2) Walscroft (by Q). (3) .xxxix. (13 cent.). (4) .xliij. (cancelled. 13 cent.). (5) .viij (13 cent.).

Tag for seal. Size : 6 x 3⅞ inches.

Marginalia in A : 360. Howton. 419 Confirmatio.

Texts : MS—Orig. Dij/72/3/29. A360 (by Q2). A419. R1450.

Var. R. : [1] *supplied from* A419 : *the charter is injured.* [2] Bleseby A360. Beseby R. [3] Hovton A360. [4] Barnhovgate A360. Barnhongate A419 *and* R. [5] Sandholm R. [6] Thornfurlanges A360. Tornfurlanges A419. Thornfurlang R. [7–7] R *omits.* [8] totum (*sic*) A360. [9] A360 *substitutes* suis. [10] roboratum (*sic*) A360. [11] Petro R. [12] Scotenye A360. Scotiny A419. Scoteny R.

Note : For the dates of Eudo the provost see volume iv, p. 283, above. Walter Blund and John of Wigford witness with him about this date (see vol. iv, nos. 1298, 1332 and 1361 above). Peter of Beckering occurs 1200 (C.R.R., 1, p. 259). William Mustel occurs in 1202 (L.R.S. xxii., no. 1132).

361

1465. Two numbers have been given to the same charter which is printed at 1467 below.

362

1466. Grant by Simon of Beckering, to the church of Lincoln and the Common, of a bovate in Holton [by Beckering] containing ten acres on each side of the village. (Circa 1220–1230.)

Omnibus Christi fidelibus Simon de Bekering' salutem . Noueritis me pro salute anime me[1] . antecessorum . ⁊ successorum meorum dedisse ⁊ concessisse . ⁊ hac presenti carta mea confirmasse deo et beate Marie et comune canonicorum

Linc' ecclesie vnam bouatam terre arabilis interitorio de Houton'[2] . que continet decem acras ex orientali parte ville . et decem acras ex occidentali parte eiusdem ville . Scilicet sex selliones super Aldfeld inter terram Walteri de Brinkel . ⁊ terram Leticie . vnum sellionem [3]super[3] Barnehou inter terras eiusdem Walteri vnum sellionem super Barnehou inter terram Roberti Strith[4] . ⁊ terram Reineri . duos selliones ibidem inter terram eiusdem Roberti . ⁊ terram Radulfi Swetebitheban[5] . super Norlandes[6] vnum sellionem inter terram Alani filii Lamberti ⁊ terram Henrici Fichet . super Northolm'[7] vnum sellionem inter terram Galfridi Mustel ⁊ terram Ricardi clerici . super Langholm' vnum sellionem inter terram Johannis filii Emme . et terram Henrici filii Reinneri . et vnum sellionem in Langholm' inter terram Reineri de Houton' et terram Alani filii Lamberti . Item in Langholm' vnum sellionem inter terram Willelmi de Houton' ⁊ terram Radulfi prepositi . item super Langholm' vnum sellionem inter terram Sibille . ⁊ terram Walteri filii Luce . super Siluerholm' duos selliones inter terram Simonis filii Hingelais . ⁊ terram Leticie . super Sandholm' duos selliones inter terram monachorum de Parco ⁊ terram Galfridi Mustel . In Sandholm' vnum sellionem inter terram Jordani Rath . ⁊ terram Radulfi Swetebitheban[5] . Item ibidem vnum sellionem inter terram Sibille . ⁊ terram [7]Roberti[7] Stirth[4] super Norholm'[8] . vnum sellionem . inter terram Radulfi Swethebitheban[5] ⁊ terram Ricardi clerici . vnum sellionem in Northolm'[8] inter terram monachorum de Parco . ⁊ terram Ricardi clerici . Item in Northolm'[8] duos selliones . inter terram Leticie ⁊ terram Roberti Stirth[4] . Et vnum sellionem ibidem inter terram ecclesie . ⁊ terram Roberti . Stirth[4] . cum omnibus pertinenciis tam in pascuis quam [9]aisiamentis aliis[9] ad dictam bouatam terre pertinentibus tam infra villam quam extra . Tenendam ⁊ habendam in puram ⁊ perpetuam elemosinam liberam ⁊ quietam ab omni exaccione[10] seculari . Et ego ⁊ heredes mei defendemus ⁊ warantizabimus dictam bouatam terre cum pertinenciis tanquam puram ⁊ perpetuam ⁊ liberam elemosinam deo ⁊ beate Marie ⁊ dicte comune canonicorum Linc' ecclesie . contra omnes homines imperpetuum . Et ad maiorem huius rei securitatem presenti scripto sigillum meum apposui . Hiis testibus . Thoma de Riggesbẏ . Willelmo de Blesebẏ . Waltero de Brink' . Gilberto Fluri[11] . Johanne de Lissington' . Radulfo de Cotes . Henrico de Wragbẏ . Reinero de Houton' . Ricardo de Leycestr' . Johanne de Merston' . Winemero de Burwell' . vicariis Linc' ecclesie.

Endorsed : (1) xlvj (13 cent. cancelled). (2) xj (13 cent.) (3) Simon de Bekeringh'. Houton' .j. bouat' (13 cent.). (4) .xxxvij. (13 cent.).
Slit for seal-tag. Size : 9⅜ x 3½ inches.
Marginalia in A : Houton'.

Texts: MS—Orig. Dij/72/3/25. A362. *This is a part only and ends at Houton'* (*see* Var. R.2). *Underneath the scribe has written* Plus non scribitur de ista carta quia tertia pars est deleta per infusionem incausti quod non potest legi. *The charter has suffered injury from some acid but not to the extent suggested by the scribe, and even the injured part can be read against the light.* R1453.

Var. R.: [1] *sic:* mee R. [2] *The copy of this charter in* A *ends here.* [3]–[3] R *omits.* [4] Strich R. [5] Swetebiteban R. [6] Northlandes R. [7]–[7] R *omits.* [8] Northholm R. [9]–[9] R *has* in aliis aisiamentis. [10] R *has* actione (*sic*). [11] Flury R.

Note: William of Bleasby occurs 1218 (Selden Society, vol. liii, no. 44), as does Gilbert Flury (*ibid.*, no. 424). John of Marston, Richard of Leicester and Winemer of Burwell all witness several charters about this date (e.g. nos. 1172, 1175, 1180, 1281 in vol. iv. above). Simon of Beckering was dead by 1234 when his widow Margery was suing for dower. (*Final Concords*, i, p. 269.)

361 and 363 and 415

1467. Grant by Henry son of Richard the clerk of Holton [by Beckering], to the church of Lincoln and the Common, of a toft and a croft in Holton [by Beckering]. (Circa 1210–1220.)

De .j. tofto in Houtona (A415 rubric).

Notum sit omnibus tam presentibus quam futuris quod ego Henricus filius Ricardi clerici de Houton'* dedi 7 concessi 7[1] presenti carta mea confirmaui deo 7 beate Marie 7 commune canonicorum Lincoln' ecclesie totum toftum in villa de Houton' . quod Robertus filius Tocke[2] aliquando de me tenuit . cum crofto quod iacet inter idem toftum 7 horreum meum . quod quidem croftum continet in longitudine .' quadraginta 7 octo pedes . 7 in latitudine quater viginti 7 tres pedes . Habendum 7 tenendum in puram 7 perpetuam elemosinam . liberum solutum 7 quietum ab omni seculari seruitio exaccione 7 demanda . Et ego Henricus 7 heredes mei warentizabimus eisdem canonicis predictum toftum cum crofto . defendemus 7 adquietabimus erga omnes homines imperpetuum . In huius autem donationis robur 7 testimonium .' presens scriptum sigilli mei appositione corroboraui . Hiis testibus . Conano sacrista . Henrico de Altari . Willelmo de Midl'[3] . Ricardo [4]de[4] Neuport . Petro de Cheuermund' . Johanne filio Walteri de Normanneb'[5] . Sỳmone de Torp'[6] . Philippo Hors . presbitero[7] Johanne de Bukenham' 7 aliis.

Endorsed: (1) Houton' . Lỳnd' j. toft' cum crofto (13 cent). (2) .xj (13 cent.). (3) xxxvj (13 cent.).

Slit for seal-tag. Size: 5⅞ x 4¼ inches.

Marginalia in A: 363. Henricus filius Ricardi (by Q). 415. (1) Houton' (2) .j. toftum.

Texts: MS—Orig. Dij/72/3/23. A 361, 363. *These two numbers have been given to the same charter probably because no.* 362 *has been begun and abandoned after two lines in the margin below. If the latter is ignored the text reads continuously.* A415. R1443.

Var. R.: [1] R *adds* hac. [2] Toke A415. [3] Midlei R. [4]–[4] A363 *omits.* [5] Normanb' A363. Normanneby A415. Normanby R. [6] Thorp' R. [7] *The stop would seem rightly to follow* presbitero, *but the scribe seems to have made an error in punctuation.*

Note: For the dates of Conan the sacrist see volume iv, p. 281, above.

* *Folio 67d* (in no. 361).

364 and 417

1468. Confirmation by Hawis daughter of William of Holton [by Beckering], with the consent of Walter her son and heir, to the church of Lincoln and the Common, of a toft and six acres of land on each side of the village given to them by Henry her free man. (1205–1214.)

Confirmacio eiusdem (A 417 rubric).

Sciant presentes 7 futuri quod ego Hawis filia W[illelmi de[1]] Hout'[2] de co[nsensu[1]] Walteri filii mei [. 7 . her[1]]edis mei concessi 7 hac presenti mea carta confirmau[i deo 7[1]] beate Marie [7 commun[1]]e canonicorum Linc' ecclesie unum toftum in Houtun 7 sex acras terre arabilis ex una parte uille 7 sex acras terre arabilis ex alia parte uille . que Henricus meus liber homo dedit illis cum omnibus pertinentiis suis sicuti carta quam predicti canonici habent de predicto Henrico protestatur . 7 ut hec mea concessio 7 confirmatio rata permaneat eam sigilli mei apposicione corroboraui . Teste . Philippo subdecano . magistro Johanne de Tinemue . Hugone de Sancto Edwardo canonicis Linc' ecclesie . Radulfo de Haint'[3] decano . Willelmo Mustel . Willelmo Brett'[4] . Toma filio eius . Jordano Rat . Willelmo Paumer . 7 multis aliis.

Endorsed: (1) Confirm[acio] . Hauwis de Houtun j. toft' .vj. acr' (13 cent.). (2) xxxviij (cancelled—13 cent.). (3) iij (13 cent.).

Slit for seal-tag. Size: $5\frac{1}{4}$ x $2\frac{1}{8}$ inches.

Marginalia in A: 417 Confirmatio.

Texts: MS—Orig. Dij/72/3/24. A364: 417. R1445.

Var. R.: [1] *supplied from* A417: *the charter is injured.* [2] Houton' *in* A363 *and* R. Houtun' *in* A417. [3] Hainton' A417. Haynton' R. [4] Bretun A417 *and* R.

Note: Philip became subdean before the death of Bishop William of Blois (see above, vol. ii, no. 350). He succeeded William de Bramfeld who was murdered 25th September, 1205. Although William's date of entry on the office is uncertain it is evident that Philip did not precede him as Philip was a witness to William of Blois' grant of the prebend of Decem Librarum to William son of Fulk (above, vol. ii, no. 350): William son of Fulk witnessed a charter (vol. i, no. 293, above) in a group separate from the canons in the time of William the subdean, which proves that he did not receive the canonry until after William's murder. John is found as subdean 27th February, 1214 (*Liber Antiquus*, p. 72). Le Neve's date of 1214 for Richard Kentensis is probably incorrect.

365 and 416

1469. Grant by Henry son of Richard the clerk of Holton [by Beckering], to the church of Lincoln and the Common, of a toft and twelve acres of land, six on each side of the village. (1205–1214.)

De .ij. tofto 7 .xii. acris in Houton' (A 416 rubric).

Sciant presentes 7 futuri quod ego Henricus filius Ricardi clerici de Houtun[1] dedi 7 concessi 7 hac presenti mea carta confirmaui deo [⁊[2]] beate Marie ⁊ commune[3] canonicorum Linc' ecclesie unum toftum in Hout'[1] quod fuit Roberti filii Toke[4] . ⁊ sex acras terre arabilis ex una parte uille eiusdem ⁊ sex acras terre arabilis e[x alia part[1]]e uille cum prato ad eas pertinente ⁊ omnibus aliis pertinentiis suis ⁊ liberam communam in omnibus libertatibus [5]⁊[5] asiamentis infra uillam ⁊ extra[6] [7]ad[7] uillam de Houtun pertinentibus . in puram ⁊ perpetuam elemosinam liberam quietam ⁊ solutam a forinseco ⁊ ab omni [7]alio[7] seculari seruitio ⁊ exactione . ⁊ Ego Henricus ⁊ heredes mei warantizabimus predictam terram supradicte ecclesie contra omnes homines . Teste[8] . Philippo subdecano . magistro Johanne de[9] Tinemue[10] . Hugone de Sancto Edwardo canonicis Linc' ecclesie . Radulfo [7]decano[7] de Haint'[11] . Willelmo Mustel . Willelmo Brettun[12] . Jordano Rat . Willelmo Paumer . Radulfo filio Arnolt de Linc' . ⁊ multis aliis.

Endorsed: (1) Henrici filii Ricardi clerici de Houtun . de .xii. acris (13 cent.). (2) .x. (13 cent.).
Slit for seal-tag. Size: 5½ x 2¼ inches.
Marginalia in A: 365 Hooton. 416. (1) Houton'. (2) .j. toftum ⁊ xii acr'.
Texts: MS—Orig. Dij/72/3/21. A365: 416. R1444.
Var. R.: [1] Houton' A365 *and* R: Hontun A416. [2] *supplied from* A416: *the charter is injured.* [3] ecclesie (*sic*) R. [4] Tocke R. [5–5] A416 *omits.* [6] A416 *adds* villam. [7–7] R *omits.* [8] *sic.* [9] A365 *omits.* [10] Tinnemue A416. [11] Haintun' A416. Haynton R. [12] Bretton A365. Bretun R.
Note: For the date see the note to the previous charter.

366

1470. Grant by William [de Lexington], the dean, and the chapter of Lincoln to William son of Henry of Holton [by Beckering], of three parts of a messuage and five acres of land in Holton [by Beckering], which had previously been of William, Henry's father, and Agnes his wife. The rights of possible claimants are reserved, and William may not pledge, sell or alienate the land without the consent of the dean and chapter. Should Simon the eldest son of Henry, return and wish to sue for the land William shall give it up to the dean and chapter, who shall grant it to Simon. (1263–1272.)

Indented.

Per presens scriptum pateat vniuersis quod [1]nos[1] W. decanus ⁊ capitulum Linc' ecclesie concesserunt ⁊ dimiserunt Willelmo filio Henrici de Houton' tres partes vnius mesuagii . ⁊ quincque[2] acras terre cum pertinenciis in Houton' . Tenend*um* de nobis ⁊ successoribus nostris pro seruicio inde debito ⁊ consueto . videlicet duodecim denarios per annum . scilicet medietatem ad Pascha . ⁊ aliam medietatem ad festum sancti[3] Michaelis . vna cum wardis . releuiis . ⁊ eschaetis . si que contingunt . illas videlicet [4]tres[4] partes tofti . ⁊ illas quincque acras terre cum pertinenciis que fuerunt quondam Henrici patris predicti Willelmi . ⁊ Agnetis vxoris sue in eadem villa saluo iure cuiuslibet in predicto tenemento ius calumpniantis seu exigentis . nec eciam liceat dicto [1]Willelmo[1] nec aliquibus ex parte sua aliquam partem tofti sive dicte terre aliquibus . inuadiare . vendere . seu alienare . in preiudicium nostrum seu alicuius ius seu calumpniam exigentis in predicto tenemento . sine voluntate ⁊ assensu nostro . Et si contingat quod [1]Simon[1] frater predicti Willelmi primogenitus filius eiusdem predicti Henrici veniat ⁊ predictam terram[5] petere velit . Idem Willelmus nobis predictam terram reddet ⁊ . idem[6] decanus ⁊ capitulum predicto Simoni ⁊ heredibus suis [7]predictum toftum[7] cum terra reddent saluo iure suo eisdem contingenti . In cuius rei testimonium mutuis scriptis in modo cirograffi confectis . mutua singna[8] hinc inde sunt apensa . Hiis testibus . domino Simone archidiacono Stowye[9] . domino Godredo . domino Willelmo de Yngham[10] . domino Johanne de Wẏdintona . ⁊ multis aliis.

Endorsed: (1) xxxix (cancelled 13 cent.). (2) iiij (13 cent.). (3) In Houton' tres partes vnius mesuagii ⁊ quinque acr'. (13 cent). (4) .ix. (13 cent.).

Slit for seal-tag. Size: 6 x 4½ inches.

Marginalia in A: (1) Hooton (by Q). (2) xij.

Texts: MS—Orig. Dij/72/3/22. A (by Q2). R1446.

Var. R.: [1–1] A *omits.* [2] *sic.* [3] R *repeats* sancti. [4–4] R *omits.* [5] terre (*sic*) R. [6] *sic :* iidem R. [7–7] predictam terram R. [8] *sic :* signa *in* A *and* R. [9] Stouvie A. Stowe R. [10] Yngam A. Ingham R.

Note: The dates given are those of William de Lexington as dean. Simon de Barton was archdeacon of Stow from 1260 to 1280 (Le Neve, *Fasti Ecclesiae Anglicanae*, vol. ii, p. 77).

367

1471. This charter relates to Hainton and is printed at no. 1491 below.

368

1472. This charter relates to Rand and is printed at 1510 below.

368a and 413

1473. Confirmation by Ralf son of Martin of Beesby, of the gift of William son of William of Holton [by Beckering]. (Circa 1210–1215.)

Confirmacio quinque acrarum ⁊ dimidie in campo de Houton' (A 413 rubric).

Notum sit omnibus tam presentibus quam futuris quod ego Radulfus filius Martini de Besebi[1] concessi[2] ⁊ presenti carta mea confirmaui deo 7 beate Marie 7 commune canonicorum Lincoln' ecclesie .' quinque acras terre 7 dimidiam in territorio de Houton' . quas habent ex dono Willelmi filii Willelmi de Houton' . videlicet ex[3] occidentali parte eiusdem ville .' duas acras apud West[4] Langes subtus villam . 7 dimidiam acram prati . in West[4] Eng . iuxta pratum Willelmi filii Ranulfi uersus occidentem . 7 duas acras 7 dimidiam . ex orientali parte ville inter Viam Latam 7 Viam Paruam . 7 duas perticatas prati in Est Eng . iuxta pratum Alani filii Reineri[5] .' uersus orientem . Has autem . predictas quinque acras 7 dimidiam cum omnibus pertinentiis suis eisdem canonicis concessi 7 confirmaui in puram 7 perpetuam elemosinam perpetuo possidendas . liberas solutas 7 quietas ab omni seculari seruitio 7 . exaccione . Et ego Radulfus 7 heredes mei warentizabimus eisdem canonicis prenominatas[6] quinque acras 7 dimidiam cum omnibus pertinentiis suis contra omnes homines imperpetuum . In huius autem rei robur 7 testimonium .' presens scriptum sigilli mei appositione corroboraui . Hiis testibus . Radulfo de Hainton' decano . Conano[7] 7 Waltero capellanis . Petro de Bekering[8] . Willelmo filio eius . Johanne de Lissington' . Roberto Giffard'[9] . Willelmo de Midlei[10] . Petro de Cheuermund' . Ricardo de Humberstain . Philippo Pullan' . Johanne . Alexandro . 7 Benedicto 7 aliis.

Endorsed: (1) Houton' . Lŷndes' v. acras (14 cent.). (2) Walscroft (by Q). (3) .xxxix. (13 cent.). (4) + (5) xlij (cancelled—13 cent.). (6) vij (13 cent.).

Slit for seal-tag. Size: 7 x 4¼ inches.

Marginalia in A: 368A Howton'. 413 (1) Houton'. (2) Confirmatio.

Texts: MS—Orig. Dij/72/3/30. A368A (by Q2, in the lower margin) 413. R1449.

Var. R.: [1] Beseby R. [2] concessessi (*sic*) A368A. [3] 7 A368A. [4] Vest A368A. [5] Romeri A368A. [6] prenominatis (*sic*) A368A. [7] Canano A368A. [8] Bekerin A368A. [9] Galfrid' R. [10] Midelay A368A.

412

1474. Grant by William son of William of Holton [by Beckering], to the church of Lincoln and the Common, of five and a half acres of arable land and meadow in Holton [by Beckering]. (Circa 1210–1215.)

De .v. acris . 7 dimidia . in Houton' (A rubric).

Sciant presentes 7 futuri quod ego Willelmus filius Willelmi de Houton' dedi 7 concessi 7 presenti carta mea confirmaui deo 7 beate Marie 7 commune canonicorum Linc' ecclesie quinque acras terre 7 dimidiam in territorio de Houton' . Scilicet ex occidentali parte uille predicte duas acras apud Westlanges subtus uillam . 7 dimidiam acram prati in Westeng . iuxta pratum Willelmi filii Ranulfi uersus occidentem . 7 duas acras 7 dimidiam ex orientali parte uille .

inter Viam Latam 7 Viam Paruam . 7 duas perticatas prati in Esteng iuxta * pratum Alani filii Reineri uersus orientem . Habendas 7 tenendas cum omnibus pertinenciis suis in puram 7 perpetuam 7 liberam elemosinam . liberas . solutas . 7 quietas ab omni seculari seruitio 7 exactione . Et ego Willelmus 7 heredes mei warentizabimus eisdem canonicis prenominatas quinque acras 7 dimidiam cum omnibus pertinenciis suis contra omnes homines imperpetuum . In huius autem rei robur 7 testimonium presens scriptum sigilli mei appositione corroboraui . Hiis testibus . Radulfo de Hainton' decano . Conano 7 Waltero capellanis . Petro de Bekering . Willelmo filio eius . Johanne de Lissincton' . Roberto Giffard' . Willelmo de Midlei . Petro de Cheuermund . Philippo Pullano . Alexandro . Johanne . 7 Benedicto . 7 aliis.

Marginalia in A: (1) Houton'. (2) v. acre 7 dimidia.
Text MS—A.

**Folio 78d.*

Hdl. WRAGHOU.

413

1475. A duplicate of 368A which is printed at 1473 above.

Marginalia in A: (1) Houton'. (2) Confirmatio.

414

1476. Release and quitclaim by Mabel, widow of William the palmer, to the dean and chapter of Lincoln, of all her right and claim in the land and meadow which William her husband had given them. (Circa 1215–1220.)

Quietaclamacio de eadem terra (A rubric).

Sciant presentes 7 futuri quod ego Mabilia quondam uxor Willelmi palmar' in libera uiduitate mea remisi 7 quietumclamaui decano 7 capitulo Linc' 7 in eodem capitulo abiuraui totum ius 7 clamium quod habui uel habere potui in terris quas predictus Willelmus maritus meus contulit commune Linc' ecclesie in puram 7 perpetuam elemosinam perpetuo possidendis . Scilicet quinque acris terre arabilis in territorio de Houton' . 7 duabus percatis prati in latitudine in Est Eng . 7 duabus percatis duobus pedibus minus in Westeng . Habendis 7 tenendis imperpetuum . sine omni reclamatione uel contradiccione mei uel heredum meorum . In huius igitur rei robur 7 testimonium presenti scripto sigillum meum apposui . Testibus . Thoma de Norton' . Conano . Henrico de Torpel capellanis . Thoma de Hardres . Osberto de Neuport . Ricardo de Neuport . Rogero de Neuport . ⁊ aliis.

Marginalia: De eadem terra.
Text: MS—A.
Note: This group of witnesses is frequently found about this time: see nos. 1109–10, 1121 etc. in vol. iv. above.

Folio 79.

Hdl. WRAGHOU . 7 . 9 .

415

1477. A duplicate of 363 which is printed at 1467 above.

Marginalia: (1) Houton. (2) .j. toftum.

416

1478. A duplicate of 365 which is printed at 1469 above.

Marginalia: (1) Houton'. (2) .j. toftum ⁊ xii acre.

417

1479. A duplicate of 364 which is printed at 1468 above.

Marginalia: Confirmatio.

418

1480. Grant by William son of William the palmer of Holton [by Beckering], to the church of Lincoln and the Common, of a toft and half a bovate of land of which five acres lie on the east and five on the west of the village. (Circa 1200.)

De .j. tofto ⁊ dimidia bouata terre in Houtona (A rubric).

Omnibus sancte matris ecclesie filiis hanc cartam uisuris uel audituris Willelmus filius Willelmi palmeri[1] de Houton'[2] salutem . Sciatis me dedisse ⁊ concessisse ⁊ hac carta mea * confirmasse deo ⁊ beate Marie ⁊ commune canonicorum Linc' . ecclesie dimidiam bouatam terre in territorio de Houton[2] ⁊ vnum toftum in uilla eadem . Scilicet ex orientali parte ville ∴ v. acras . videlicet iij. selliones ex occidentali parte de Galtereng . ⁊ .ij. selliones sub[3] Barnhow[4] . ⁊ .ij. selliones sub[5] Hildekinlandes . ⁊ ij. selliones ex aquilonali parte de Barnhougate[6] . ⁊ .ij. perticatas prati in Esteng . Et ex occidentali parte uille ∴ v. acras . scilicet super Northolm[7] ∴ ij. selliones . ⁊ super Sanholm'[8] .j. sellionem . Et super . Thornfurlangs .ij. selliones . ⁊ apud Stein .j. sellionem . ⁊ inter uias .j. sellionem . 7 duas perticatas prati in Westeng . Cum toto[9] illo . quod uocatum est Grescroft . quod durat in longitudine a via que [ducit . per[10]] medium uille . usque ad Barnhougate ;· et cum omnibus pertinentiis 7 aisiamentis ad terram illam pertinenti[bus[10]] infra uillam 7 extra . Pro salute anime méé 7 pro animabus antecess[orum[10]] meorum . in puram 7 perpetuam elemosinam liberam 7 quietam ab omni seculari seruicio 7 exactione [Et[10]] ego Willelmus prenominatus 7 heredes mei . warantizabimus predictis canonicis predictam terram cum pertinentiis contra omnes homines ;· 7 de omni seculari seruitio 7 exactione defendemus . Hiis testibus . Eudone preposito . Waltero Blundo . Johanne de Wikeford . Matheo de London' . 7 G. Lorimer' . capellanis . P.[3] de Bekeringes[11] . T. de Bekering' . T. de Scotẏni[12] . Willelmo Mustela[13] . Heltone de Snelleslunde.

Endorsed: (1) Hout' . dim' bouat' . (14 cent.). (2) .xxxix. (14 cent.). (3) xl (cancelled—13 cent.). (4) v (13 cent.).

Slit for seal-tag. Size: 5¾ x 3¾ inches.

Marginalia in A: (1) Houton'. (2) dimidia bovata cum .j. tofto.

Texts: MS—Orig. Dij/72/3/28. A. R1447.

Var. R.: [1] Palmer R. [2] Houtun A. [3] super R. [4] Barnhou A *and* R. [5] *in* R. [6] Barhougate A. [7] Northholm R. [8] Sandholm R. [9] *sic*: tofto *in* A. [10] *Taken from* A: *there are some holes in the charter.* R *has a blank space where* ducit per *should come.* [11] Bekering R. [12] Scoteny R. [13] Mustel' A. Mustel R.

Note: This gift was confirmed by Martin son of Wycius of Beesby in no. 1464 above. The witnesses are the same.

**Folio 79d.*

Hdl. WRAGHOU.

419

1481. A duplicate of 360 which is printed at no. 1464 above.

Marginalia: Confirmatio.

420

1482. Grant by William son of William the palmer of Holton [by Beckering], to the church of Lincoln and the Common, of half of his toft and half a bovate of land in Holton [by Beckering]. Of this half bovate four acres and three perches of arable land and six perches of meadow lie on one side of the village and five acres and one perch of arable land and three perches of meadow on the other side. (Circa 1210–1215.)

De dimidio tofto . 7 dimidia . bouata . in Houtona (A rubric).

[Notum sit omnibus tam presentibus quam[1]] futuris quod ego Willelmus filius Willelmi palmerii de Houton'[2] dedi 7 concessi 7 presenti carta mea [confirmaui deo 7 beate[1]][3] 7 commune canonicorum Lincoln' ecclesie medietatem tofti mei uersus orientem . que quidem me[dietas continet quinque perticatas in[1]] latitu*dine . 7 decem in longitudine .' in villa de Houton' . 7 dimidiam bouatam terre in territo[rio eiusdem uille cum pertinenciis . Scili[1]]cet quatuor acras 7 tres perticatas terre arabilis 7 sex perticatas prati ex una parte ville . 7 [quinque acras 7 unam perticatam terre[1]] arabilis 7 tres perticatas prati ex alia parte ville . Cuius quidem terre .' hee sunt partes . Ex [occidentali parte uille iacent duo selli[1]]ones super Langholm' pro tribus acris inter terram Galfridi Mustell'[4] 7 terram Willelmi filii Ranulfi [7 unus sellio iuxta Bradegate pro una[1]] acra inter terram predicti . G. terram prefati .W. 7 subtus villam[5] de Houton' vnus sellio [pro tribus perticatis inter terram Roberti filii[1]] Reineri .' 7 terram Ade Tysun . Sex uero perticate prati .' iacent in Northholm[6] Sic [proximiores prato Walteri filii Luce uersus occ[1]]identem . Ex orientali uero parte ville .' iacent duo selliones super Langholm'[6] pro duabus [acris 7 una perticata inter terram Walteri filii L[1]]uce . 7 [7]aliis duobus sellionibus[7] quos ibidem in manu mea retinui . 7 ex aquilo[nali parte de Barenhougate duo selliones pro una[1]] acra inter terram Ade Tysun 7 terram Reineri[8] filii Henrici . 7 subtus Litelgate .' [duo selliones pro duabus acris inter terram Johannis le G[1]]rant[9] .' 7 terram Roberti filii Ricardi . Tres quidem[10] perticate prati iacent in Est Eng[11] [. inter pratum Alani filii Reineri[8] . 7 alias tres pertic[1]]atas quas ibidem in manu mea retinui . Habenda 7 tenenda cum omnibus pertinen[ciis 7 cum omnibus libertatibus 7 aisiamentis infra[1]] villam 7 extra villam in puram 7 perpetuam elemosinam . libera soluta 7 quieta ab [omni seculari seruitio . 7 exactione . Et ego Willelmus[1]] 7 heredes mei eisdem canonicis prenominatas terras cum tofto 7 omnibus aliis pertinen[ciis warantizabimus defendemus 7 adquietabimus[1]] contra omnes homines imperpetuum . in huius autem donacionis robur 7 testimonium presens scriptum [sigilli mei appositione corroboraui . Hiis testibus[1] .] Petro de Bekering domino meo . magistro Roberto de Brinkell' . magistro Alano de Rowell' [Petro de Cheuermund . Willelmo de Midl'[12] . Petro de B[1]]ekering . Johanne filio sacerdotis de Lissingtona . Philippo Pullano . Johanne 7 Alexandro 7 aliis.

Endorsed : medietatem tofti 7 dimidiam bouatam terre . in Houtone (14 cent.).
Slit for seal-tag. Size : probably circa 8 x $5\frac{3}{4}$ inches.
Marginalia in A : (1) Houton'. (2) dimid' unius tofti et dimid bovat'.
Texts : MS—Orig. Dij/72/3/31. A. R1448.
Var. R. : [1] *The words in square brackets are supplied from* A, *the left side of the*

charter having been torn away. [2] Houtun' A. [3] *sic :* R *adds* Marie. [4] Mustel' A *and* R. [5] viam R. [6] Northholm A. Norhholm' R. [7]–[7] alios duos selliones A. [8] Raineri R. [9] Graunt R. [10] R *repeats* quidem. [11] Esteng A *and* R. [12] Midley R.

**Folio* 80.

Hdl. . 8 . ϕ .

421

1483. Confirmation of the preceding gift by Peter of Beckering. (Circa 1210–1215.)

Confirmatio eiusdem (A rubric).

Notum sit omnibus tam presentibus quam futuris quod ego Petrus de Bekering concessi 7 presenti carta mea confirmaui deo 7 beate Marie 7 commune canonicorum Linc' ecclesie donationem quam Willelmus filius Willelmi palmer' de Houtun fecit eidem commune in puram 7 perpetuam elemosinam perpetuo possidendam . Scilicet medietatem tofti eiusdem Willelmi uersus orientem . que quidem medietas continet quinque perticatas in latitudine 7 decem in longitudine . in uilla de Houton' . 7 dimidiam bouatam terre in territorio eiusdem uille cum pertinenciis . Scilicet . iiij^{or} . acras 7 tres perticatas terre arabilis 7 sex perticatas prati ex una parte uille . 7 quinque acras 7 unam perticatam terre arabilis 7 tres perticatas prati ex alia parte uille . Cuius quidem terre hee sunt partes . Ex occidentali parte uille iacent duo selliones super Langholm pro tribus acris inter terram Galfridi Mustel 7 terram Willelmi filii Ranulfi . 7 unus sellio iuxta Bradegate pro una acra inter terram predicti .G. 7 terram prefati Willelmi . 7 subtus uillam de Houton' unus sellio pro tribus perticatis inter terram Roberti filii Reineri . 7 terram Ade Tysun' . Sex uero perticate prati iacent in Northolm Sic propinquiores prato Walteri filii Luce uersus occidentem . Ex orientali vero parte uille iacent duo selliones super Langholm pro duabus acris . 7 una perticata inter terram Walteri filii Luce et alios duos selliones quos dictus Willelmus ibidem in manu sua retinuit . 7 ex aquilonali parte de Barnhougate duo sel*liones pro una acra inter terram Ade Tysun 7 terram Reineri filii Henrici . 7 subtus Litelgate duo selliones pro duabus acris inter terram Johannis le Grant 7 terram Roberti filii Ricardi . Tres quidem perticate prati iacent in Esteng inter pratum Alani filii Reineri 7 alias tres perticatas quas memoratus Willelmus ibidem in manu sua retinuit . Habenda 7 tenenda cum omnibus pertinenciis . 7 cum omnibus libertatibus 7 aisiamentis infra uillam 7 extra uillam in puram 7 perpetuam elemosinam . libera . soluta . 7 quieta ab omni seculari seruitio 7 exactione . vt autem hec mea concessio 7 confirmatio rate 7 inconcusse permaneant ∴

eas presenti scripto sigilli mei appositione corroboraui . Hiis testibus . magistris Roberto de Brinkel . Roberto de Grauel' . 7 Willelmo persona de Tuxford . Conano . Waltero . 7 Rumfaro sacerdotibus . Petro de Cheuermont . P. de Bekering de Linc' . Philippo Hors . Ysaac clerico.

Marginalia : Confirmatio.
Text: MS—A.

**Folio* 80*d.*

Hdl. WRAGHOU.

ADD. CHART.

1484. Grant by R[oger de Rolveston], the dean, and the chapter of Lincoln, to Simon of Beckering, of the land mentioned in the two preceding charters. If Simon or his heirs shall lose the land, either through force or judicial process, the dean and chapter will give them nothing in exchange. (Before 1224 : probably circa 1220.)

Omnibus Christi fidelibus ad quos presens scriptum peruenerit .R. decanus 7 capitulum Linc' ecclesie salutem . Noueritis nos concessisse 7 presenti carta nostra confirmasse Simoni de Bekering medietatem vnius tofti in villa de Houton' . 7 dimidiam bouatam terre cum pertinentiis in territorio eiusdem ville . Que quidem habemus ex dono Willelmi filii Willelmi palmer' 7[1] confirmatione Petri de Bekering . Scilicet medietatem tofti predicti Willelmi uersus orientem . que quidem medietas continet quinque perticatas in latitudine 7 decem in longitudine . Et quatuor [2]acras[2] 7 tres perticatas terre arabilis 7 sex perticatas prati ex vna parte ville . 7 quinque acras 7 vnam perticatam terre arabilis 7 tres perticatas prati ex alia parte ville . Cuius quidem terre hee sunt partes . ex occidentali parte ville jacent duo selliones super Langholm' pro tribus acris inter terram Galfridi Mustell 7 terram Willelmi filii Rannulfi . 7 vnus sellio juxta Bradegate pro vna acra ⁏ inter terram predicti .G. 7 terram prefati .W. 7 subtus villam de Houton' vnus sellio pro tribus perticatis inter terram Roberti filii Reineri 7 terram Ade Tisun'[3] . Sex uero perticate prati jacent in Northholm' Sic[4] propinquiores prato Walteri filii Luce uersus occidentem . Ex orientali uero parte ville jacent duo selliones super Langholm' pro duabus acris 7 vna perticata inter terram Walteri filii Luce . 7 alios duos selliones quos dictus Willelmus ibidem in manu retinuit . 7 ex aquilonali parte de Barnhougate duo selliones pro vna acra inter terram Ade Tisun[3] . 7 terram Reineri filii Henrici . 7 subtus Litelgate duo selliones pro duabus acris inter terram

Johannis le Grant[5] ⁊ terram Roberti filii Ricardi . Tres quidem perticate prati jacent in Est Eng inter pratum Alani filii Reineri ⁊ alias tres perticatas quas memoratus Willelmus ibidem in manu sua retinuit . Habenda ⁊ tenenda cum omnibus pertinentiis ⁊ libertatibus ⁊ aisiamentis infra uillam ⁊ extra villam eidem Simoni ⁊ cuicunque assignauerit preterquam domui religiose in feodo ⁊ hereditate libere ⁊ quiete . reddendo inde nobis annuatim duodecim denarios pro omni seruicio ⁊ exactione . Scilicet .vj. denarios ad Pascha ∴ ⁊ .vj. denarios ad festum sancti Michaelis . In huius autem rei robur ⁊ testimonium presens scriptum sigilli nostri appositione corroborauimus . Et si predictus Simon uel heredes eius prefatam terram uel aliquam ejus partem vi uel judicio amiserint ∴ nullum eis dabimus excambium.

Endorsed: (1) Houton' . med' toft' (14 cent.). (2) ix (13 cent.). (3) xliiij (cancelled—13 cent.).

Fragment of seal on tag:—green. Obverse, second seal of chapter. Reverse: **TIA PLE**

Size : 6½ x 6½ inches.

Texts : MS—Orig. Dij/72/3/27. R1451.

Var. R. : [1] ex R. [2–2] R *omits*. [3] Týsun R. [4] si R. [5] Graunt R.

Note : The dean must be Roger de Rolveston as Simon of Beckering was dead by 1234 (*Final Concords*, i., p. 269). Charters no. Dij/72/3/21 to no. Dij/72/3/30 are filed together on a parchment string.

Add. Chart.

1485. Grant by Peter son of Simon of Holton [by Beckering], to the church of Lincoln for the fabric, of ten acres of land, five on each side of the village, and four perches of meadow, two on each side of the village. (Circa 1220.)

Sciant omnes tam presentes quam futuri quod ego Petrus filius Simonis de Houtona pro salute anime mee ⁊ predecessorum meorum dedi ⁊ concessi ⁊ hac mea presenti carta confirmaui deo ⁊ fabrice ecclesie beate Marie Lincolniensis diuine pietatis intuitu in puram ⁊ perpetuam elemosinam quinque acras terre in villa de Hout' ex vna parte ville . et quinque acras terre ex altera parte uille de Hout' . ⁊ duas perticatas prati ex vna parte ville de Hout' ⁊ duas ex altera parte uille cum omnibus pertinenciiis infra uillam ⁊ extra uillam . de quinque acris ex orientali parte uille de Hout' ∴ jacet vna selio sub Litelgate juxta terram ecclesie . ⁊ vna selio jacet inter terram Alani filii Lamberti . ⁊ Roberti filii Ricardi . Et due seliones inter uias . illas scilicet que iacent inter terram Alani filii Lamberti ⁊ Willelmi filii Randolf . Et vna selio sub Bretthegate inter terram Jordani Rat . ⁊ Galefridi Mustel ⁊ vna selio sub ipsa uia inter terram Walteri filii Lucie . ⁊ Alani filii Lamberti . ⁊ vna selio sub Barnkougate[1] inter terram Ade Tisun et Aliz Gregorie . 7 vna selio sub Hildekinlandes inter terram Ricardi Ruffi . 7 Radulfi filii Willelmi . 7 vna selio super Brigdail . il inter terram Radulfi filii Willelmi . 7 Humfridi Pa . et vna perticata prati in Estheng juxta pratum predicti Humfridi Pa . 7 vna perticata prati in Galterheng ex parte occidentali uille de Hout' . ex quibus . v^{que} . predictis acris jacet una selio sub Stangate inter terram Roberti Stoc 7 Ade Tisun . 7 vna selio sub eadem uia inter terram Hauis de Bekering 7 Helewis filie Hugonis . 7 vna selio sub eadem uia iuxta terram Walteri filii Alani 7 Jordani Rat . 7 vna selio sub eadem uia inter terram Alani filii Lamberti 7 Hauis de Beckering . Et vna selio super Tofesdale inter terram Willelmi Palmeri . 7 Alani filii Lamberti . 7 vna selio super Blakebethe iuxta terram Reineri filii Henrici . Et due seliones super Thornefurlanges inter terram Simonis filii Hingleis 7 Henrici de Hout' . 7 vna selio iacet in Watefures inter terram Henrici 7 Johannis Magni . 7 vna selio que iacet ad capud uille inter terram Willelmi filii Randolfi et vna perticata prati in Westheng de duabus quas habeo iuxta pratum Ranulfi bercarii . 7 vna perticata prati iacet sub Crakewad iuxta pratum Radulfi filii Willelmi . Et quod ego predictus Petrus filius Simonis de Hout' 7 heredes mei predictam terram deo 7 fabrice ecclesie beate Marie Lincolniensis contra omnes homines warantizabimus . Hiis testibus . magistro Hugone canonico . Waltero Albo canonico . magistro Roberto de Holme canonico . Petro de Bechering . Waltero de Martun . Gilberto de Hormesbi . Matheo de Wŷhum . 7 multis aliis.

Endorsed : Carte de Houtona (13 cent.).
Slit for seal-tag. Size : 6⅜ x 4¾ inches.
Text : MS—Orig. Dij/72/3/34.
Var. R. : [1] *sic* : Barnhougate *is the usual form.*
Note : This and the two subsequent charters are filed together on a parchment string. Of the persons mentioned in this charter Adam Tisun, Jordan Rat and John le Grant all occur in 1218 and 1219 (Selden Society, vol. liii, nos. 87 and 424). Walter Blund witnesses as canon in 1220 (see vol. iii, no. 919, above) and Robert de Holm witnesses as canon in 1219 (see vol. ii, no. 375, above).

ADD. CHART.

1486. Confirmation by Henry son of Richard of Holton [by Beckering], of the gift made in the preceding charter by Peter son of Simon, his man. (Circa 1220.)

Sciant omnes tam presentes quam futuri quod ego Henricus filius Ricardi de Houtona pro salute anime mee 7 predecessorum meorum concessi et hac mea presenti carta confirmaui deo 7 fabrice ecclesie beate Marie Lincolniensis quinque acras terre ex vna parte uille de Hout' . Et .v. acras terre ex altera parte uille de Hout' . Et duas perticatas prati ex vna parte uille de Hout' . ⁊ duas perticatas prati ex altera parte uille cum omnibus pertinenciis infra uillam ⁊ extra uillam quas Petrus filius Simonis homo meus de Hout' dedit deo ⁊ fabrice ecclesie beate Marie Lincolniensis in puram ⁊ perpetuam elemosinam . Et quod ego Henricus de Hout' ⁊ heredes mei predictam donationem warentizabimus sicut carta ipsius Petri de Hout' testatur. Hiis testibus . magistro Hugone de Sancto Edwardo canonico Linc' . Waltero Albo canonico . magistro Roberto canonico . Petro de Bekering . Waltero de Martuna . Gilberto de Hormesbi . Matheo de Wẏum . et multis aliis.

No endorsement.
Slit for seal-tag. Size : 6½ x 3 inches.
Text : MS—Orig. Dij/72/3/32.

ADD. CHART.

1487. Confirmation by Gilbert of Rigsby of the gift made by Peter son of Simon, from his fee. (Circa 1220.)

Sciant omnes tam presentes quam futuri quod ego Gilbertus de Righesbi pro salute anime mee ⁊ predecessorum meorum concessi ⁊ hac mea presenti carta confirmaui donationem quam Petrus filius Simonis de Hout' dedit de feudo meo scilicet quinque acras terre ex una parte uille de Houtuna . Et quinque acras terre ex altera parte ville de Hout' . et duas perticatas prati ex vna parte uille de Hout' . ⁊ duas perticatas prati ex altera parte ville de Hout' cum omnibus pertinenciis infra uillam ⁊ extra uillam quas Petrus filius Simonis dedit caritatis intuitu deo ⁊ fabrice ecclesie beate Marie Lincolniensis in puram ⁊ perpetuam elemosinam ex consensu ⁊ voluntate ⁊ confirmatione Henrici filii Ricardi sicut carte ipsius Henrici . ⁊ Petri filii Simonis inde confecte testantur . In huius etiam rei robur ⁊ testimonium scriptum presens sigilli mei[1] roboraui . Hiis testibus . Hugone de Sancto Edwardo . Waltero Albo . magistro Roberto de Holme . Petro de Bechering . Waltero de Martun . Gilberto de Hormesbi . Matheo de Wẏhum . et multis aliis.

No endorsement.
Slit for seal-tag. Size : 6 x 3⅝ inches.
Text : MS—Orig. Dij/72/3/33.
Var. R. : [1] *sic* : appositione *presumably omitted.*

ADD. CHART.

1488. Quitclaim by Geoffrey son of William of Rand, to Richard the dean and the chapter of Lincoln, of all the lands which he formerly held of them in Holton [by Beckering]. (1254–1258.)

Omnibus Christi fidelibus ad quos presens scriptum peruenerit Galfridus filius Willelmi de Rande salutem in domino . Nouerit vniuersitas vestra me dedisse concessisse ⁊ presenti carta mea confirmasse (⁊ de me ⁊ heredibus meis resignasse ac inperpetuum quietas clamasse Ricardo decano ⁊ capitulo Linc' terras subscriptas cum omnibus suis pertinenciis quas quidem terras aliquando tenui de eisdem (videlicet tres seliones iacentes ex orientali parte ville de Houton' inter vias scilicet inter terram ecclesie de Houton' ⁊ terram Bartholomei ⁊ tres seliones iacentes ex parte boriali de Barnhougate inter terram quondam Thome filii Ranulphi ⁊ terram Galfridi filii Willelmi de Rande et duos seliones iacentes ex occidentali parte ville de Houton' super Wranglandes inter terram Thome Mustel de Tyrington (⁊ terram domini . . Prioris de Sixell' cum prato eisdem selionibus adiacente . Tenend*as* ⁊ habend*as* predictis . . decano ⁊ capitulo Linc' vel quibuscumque assignare voluerint in liberam puram ⁊ perpetuam elemosinam libere quiete pacifice sine omni contradiccione vel reclamacione mei vel heredum meorum inperpetuum . Ego vero dictus Galfridus ⁊ heredes mei predictum tenementum cum omnibus pertinenciis suis dictis . . decano ⁊ capitulo ⁊ eorum assignatis warantizabimus defendemus ⁊ adquietabimus de omnibus secularibus seruiciis exaccionibus ⁊ demandis . In cuius rei testimonium presenti scripto sigillum meum apposui . Hiis testibus domino Reginaldo de Gerpeuill Thoma Mustel de Tyrington Willelmo de Blesebÿ Johanne de La Grene de Bekering Roberto filio Walteri de Houton Jacobo filio Ranulphi de eadem Simone Frauncеÿs (Rogero de Turuill ⁊ Roberto de Karleton clerico ⁊ aliis.

Text : MS—R1454.

Note : The dates given are those of Richard Gravesend's tenure of the deanery. Reginald de Jarpenvill occurs in 1251 (no. 1459 above) and in 1252 (*Excerpta e rotulis finium*, ii, p. 146).

BECKERING [IN HOLTON PARISH]

ADD. CHART.

1489. Grant by Hode son of Roger of Beckering, to the church of Lincoln and the fabric, of a toft in Beckering which William his uncle had held of Robert son of William the smith of Beckering. (Circa 1200.)

Sciant omnes tam presentes quam futuri quod ego Hode filius Rogeri de Bekering pro salute anime mee ⁊ predecessorum m[eorum dedi con]cessi . 7 hac mea presenti carta confirmaui deo . 7 fabrice ecclesie beate Marie Lincolniensis . in puram 7 perpetuam ele[mosinam[1]] vnum toftum in villa de Bekering quod Willelmus awnculus[2] meus[3] de Roberto filio Willelmi fabri de Bekering . Habendum 7 tenendum d[e me et[1]] heredibus meis libere 7 quiet[e] 7 honorifice ex omni consuetudine . 7 exactione . Et quod ego prefatus Hode 7 heredes mei predictum toftum deo 7 fabrice ecclesie beate Marie Linc' contra omnes homines warantizabimus . In huius eciam rei robur 7 testimonium presens scriptum sigilli mei munimine roboraui . Hiis testibus . Petro de Bekering . Simone filio suo . Willelmo fratre suo . Roberto filio Galfridi de Lissingtun . Evstacio de Bekering' . Galfrido filio Willelmi . et multis aliis.

Endorsed : De tenementis in Bekering' (14 cent.).
Slit for seal-tag. Size : 7$\frac{1}{2}$ x 2$\frac{1}{8}$ inches.
Text : MS—Orig. Dij/72/3/20.
Var. R. : [1] *The words in square brackets are supplied conjecturally as the charter is torn.* [2] *sic.* [3] *sic* : tenuit *presumably omitted.*
Note : Peter of Beckering and William his son witness a charter late Henry II (Stenton, *Danelaw Charters*, p. 71) and Peter with Simon the parson, his son, witness another in the late twelfth century (*ibid.*). There was, however, another Simon of Beckering who was a layman (see note to no. 1466 above).

Add. Chart.

1490. Confirmation by Robert son of William the smith of Beckering, of the preceding grant. (Circa 1200.)

[Sciant[1]] omnes tam presentes quam futuri quod ego Robertus filius Willelmi fabri de Bekering concessi . 7 hac mea presenti carta [confir[1]]maui deo 7 fabrice ecclesie beate Marie Lincolniensis pro salute anime mee 7 predecessorum meorum vnum toftum in villa [de[1]] Bekering in puram 7 perpetuam elemosinam quod Willelmus awnculus[2] Hodonis tenuit de me . Habendum . 7 tenendum de me 7 heredibus meis libere 7 quiete 7 honorifice ab omni consuetudine 7 exactione . Et quod ego predictus Robertus filius Willelmi fabri de Bekering 7 heredes mei predictum toftum deo 7 fabrice ecclesie beate Marie Linc' contra omnes homines warantizabimus ∴ sicut carta ipsius Hodonis testatur . In huius etiam rei robur 7 testimonium presens scriptum sigilli mei munimine roboraui. Hiis testibus . Petro de Bekering . Simone filio suo . Willelmo fratre suo . Roberto filio Galfridi de Lissingtun . Evstacio de Bekering . Galfrido filio Willelmi 7 multis aliis.

Endorsed : de Bekering' (13 cent.).
Slit for seal-tag. Size : 7$\frac{1}{2}$ x 2$\frac{3}{8}$ inches.
Text : MS—Orig. Dij/72/3/18.
Var. R. : [1] *The words in square brackets are supplied conjecturally as the charter is torn.* [2] *sic.*

HAINTON

367

1491. Quitclaim by Henry son of Peter of Hainton, to the church of Lincoln and the Common, of a barn in Hainton, the ground on which it is situated and an adjoining croft, formerly held of the Common by master Odo of Kilkenny. (Circa 1240.)

Omnibus Christi fidelibus ad quos presens scriptum peruenerit ∴ Henricus filius Petri de Haynton'[1] . salutem in domino . Noueritis me concessisse . dedisse . ⁊ quietum clamasse de me ⁊ heredibus meis in perpetuum . deo ⁊ beate Marie . ⁊ commune canonicorum Linc' . ecclesie . grangiam illam in villa de Heynton'[2] cum tota placea in qua sita est . cum crofto versus boream ∴ eidem adiacente . Quam quidem grangiam cum crofto predicto magister Odo de Kilkenny[3] aliquando tenuit de memorata communa canonicorum Linc' . ecclesie . Habendum . ⁊ tenendum . dictis canonicis in perpetuum . integre . libere[4] . quiete . ⁊ pacifice* . in liberam puram ⁊ perpetuam elemosinam . quietam ab omni seruicio seculari . Ita quod nec ego vel heredes mei vel aliquis ex parte nostra . in dictis grangia[4] . placea vel crofto . aliquo vnquam tempore . in posterum aliquid iuris ∴ nobis vendicare possimus . In cuius rei robur ⁊ testimonium presens scriptum sigilli mei apposicione roboraui . Testibus . Ricardo Tuschet . Ricardo filio Thome . Villelmo[5] le Abbe . Ricardo Frende . Ricardo le Abbe . Villelmo[5] le Markaund . Radulpho Bynd[6] . Matheo filio Thome de Heẏnton'.

Marginalia in A: Haynton'.
Texts: MS—A (by Q2). R1434.
Var. R.: [1] Heynton R. [2] Haynton R. [3] Kilkenn' R. [4] R *adds* et. [5] *sic*: Willelmo R. Q2 *frequently uses* V *where* W *is more usual.* [6] Bid R.

Note: Richard Tuschet was holding a knight's fee of Geoffrey of Benniworth in Hainton in 1242–3 (*Book of Fees*, ii, p. 1002). Master Odo of Kilkenny was party to a fine levied concerning some land in Holton by Beckering in 1250 (L.R.S. xvii, p. 59) and granted land there to Sixle about the same time (L.R.S. xviii, pp. 8–9). Richard son of Thomas of Hainton and Richard Frend witnessed a charter 1232–35 (*ibid.*, p. 27). The former, with William Abbot, attests 1228–32 (*ibid.*, p. 11). Petronilla widow of Henry son of Peter quitclaimed her right in a toft in Hainton given to the dean and chapter by her husband. (See no. 1497 below; her quitclaim is Dij/71/3/57.) The date of her quitclaim is not earlier than 1264 as it is attested by Reginald the vicar, who was instituted in that year (L.R.S., xx, p. 14).

**Folio* 68.

Hdl. . 6 . 8 .

368

1492. This charter relates to Rand and is printed at 1510 below.

369a

1493. Grant by Roger the dean, and the chapter of Lincoln, to Richard son of Alan of Hainton, of half a toft in Hainton, formerly of Walter the weaver, which they had of the gift of Richard son of Ralf; and a bovate in the same village which they had of the gift of Ralf son of Richard of Hainton. For these Richard shall pay a yearly render of twelvepence. (Before 1219.)

Omnibus Christi fidelibus ad quos presens scriptum peruenerit ; Rogerus decanus ⁊ capitulum ecclesie Lincoln' salutem eternam in domino . Nouerit vniuersitas uestra nos concessisse ⁊ presenti carta nostra confirmasse Ricardo filio Alani de Hainton'[1] ; medietatem tofti quod fuit Walteri tixtoris in villa de Hainton'[1] continentis dimidiam acram terre ex orientali parte . Quod quidem habemus ex dono Ricardi filii Radulfi de Haint'[2] . et vnam bouatam terre in territorio eiusdem ville de Hainton'[2] ; quam habemus ex dono Radulfi filii Ricardi . Habendas ⁊ tenendas cum omnibus pertinenciis suis . libertatibus ⁊ aisiamentis infra villam ⁊ extra ; eidem Ricardo filio Alani ⁊ heredibus suis . in feodo ⁊ hereditate . libere ⁊ quiete . Reddendo inde nobis per annum duodecim denarios pro omni seruitio ⁊ exaccione . Scilicet sex denarios ad festum sancti Michaelis . ⁊ sex denarios ad Pascha . In huius autem rei robur ⁊ testimonium ; presenti scripto sigillum nostrum apposuimus.

Endorsed: (1) iiij. (2) Hainton' (13 cent.). (3) x.
Slit for seal-tag. Size: $6\frac{1}{2}$ x $4\frac{3}{4}$ inches.
Marginalia in A: (1) Haynton'. (2) .xij.d'.
Texts: MS—Orig. Dij/71/3/56. A (by Q2) R1429.
Var. R.: [1] Heynton A. Haynton R. [2] Haynton A *and* R.
Note: The grantor is dean Roger de Rolveston, and the date is probably about 1215 (see note to no. 1498 below). Richard son of Alan with his issue and chattels was given to the chapter by Adam de Nevill' (no. 1506 below) and rights in him were released by Norman de la Charité in 1200 (no. 1505 below).

370

1494. This charter relates to Thorpe and is printed at 1512 below.

370a and 389

1495. Grant by Robert son of Ernis of Hainton, to the church of Lincoln and the Common, of a toft and four acres of arable land in Hainton. (Late Henry II.)

De .i. tofto ⁊ .iiii^{or} . acris terre in Hainton'. (A 389 rubric.)

Universis sancte matris ecclesie filiis ad quos presens scriptum pervenerit ; Robertus de Haington'[1] filius Hernisii salutem . Noverit universitas vestra me dedisse et concessisse et hac presenti carta mea confirmasse deo et beate Marie et commune Lincolniensis ecclesie toftum illum qui iacet inter toftum Willelmi[2] de Carlet' ∴ 7 [3]toftum[3] Alani filii Johannis . et quatuor acras terre arabilis in territorio de Haington[1] ∴ scilicet in orientali parte ville quatuor selliones in Dunnesholm[4] et unum sellionem in Scortdaleholm . 7 in occidentali parte ville . quatuor selliones qui porriguntur super Lacredic . 7 duos selliones super Stainwelleholm[5] in puram et perpetuam elemosinam cum omnibus aisiamentis ad illas pertinentibus Et hanc donationem ego et heredes mei warantizabimus predicte commune contra omnes homines . 7 ut hec mea donatio illibata permaneat ∴ eam sigilli mei appositione roboravi . Testibus . Alano persona de Cheuermund[6] . Hugone de Mustrel[7] . Radulfo de Barkewrd[8] Ricardo Abbate Ricardo filio Radulfi Ricardo de Herewelle.[9]

Marginalia in A 389: (1) Hainton'. (2) .j. toftum .7. iiii[or] acras.
Texts: MS—A389. 370A. R1433.
Var. R.: [1] Haignt' A370A: Haynton R. [2] Villelmi A370A. [3]–[3] R *omits*. [4] Dounnesholm A370A: Dunesholm R. [5] Stainvelholm A370A. Staynwelleholm R. [6] Ceuerind A370A. [7] Mustel R. [8] Barcworth' R. [9] Herwelle A370A: Berwelle R.
Note: Alan parson of Kirmond witnessed charters *temp.* Henry II (L.R.S. xviii, pp. 10, 13): another witness to the second of these was Richard son of Ralf of Hainton, presumably to be identified with the fifth witness of this charter. Richard son of Ralf Abbot of Hainton witnessed late Henry II (*ibid.*, p. 2): for the family of Abbot, descended from Ralf of Grimblethorpe, son of Hacon of Hainton, see C. W. Foster, *A history of the villages of Aisthorpe and Thorpe in the Fallows*, p. 37, and L.R.S. xviii, index.

371a

1496. Quitclaim by William of Wyham, with the consent of his heirs, to Alan son of Richard of Hainton, of all his right and claim in the bovate of land in Hainton which Alan holds of the dean and chapter of Lincoln and which they had of the gift of Ralf son of Richard. William had previously held this bovate of Ralf, but had freely resigned it into his hand. Should any charter or other deed prejudicial to Alan be produced on behalf of William or his heirs, it shall be null and void. (Before February, 1219.)

Sciant presentes 7 futuri quod ego Willelmus de Wẏhum[1] assensu 7 consensu heredum meorum dedi 7 quietum clamaui Alano filio Ricardi de Hainton'[2] 7 heredibus uel[3] assignatis suis de me 7 heredibus meis totum jus 7 clamium quod habui uel habere possem in illa bouata terre cum pertinenciis in territorio de Hainton'[2] quam predictus Alanus tenet de communa Lincoln' ecclesie ex dono Radulfi filii Ricardi qui illam dicte commune in puram 7 perpetuam elemosinam contulit post meam quietam clamacionem 7 resignationem uoluntariam ∴ qui illam aliquando de dicto Radulfo tenui . set postea in manu[4] eiusdem Radulfi reddidi 7 resignaui Habendam 7 tenendam predicto Alano 7 heredibus uel asignatis suis inperpetuum de communa Lincoln' ecclesie absque impedimento uel calumpnia mei uel heredum meorum . Sciendum est itaque quod si de cetero aliqua carta uel aliquod scriptum ex parte [5]mea[5] uel heredum meorum proferatur uel exhibeatur ∴ quod preiudicium uel grauamen uel calumpniam dicto Alano 7 heredibus uel asignatis suis inferre uideatur ∴ nullum obtineat robur nullaque habeatur firmitas . hoc autem firmiter obseruandum ∴ pro me 7 heredibus meis iuraui . 7 huic scripto in testimonium 7 robur facti mei sigillum meum apposui . Hiis testibus . Henrico tunc decano de Hainton'[6] . Alano capellano . Osberto de Neuport . Johanne de Essex . Mauricio clerico . Roberto filio decani . Ricardo le Abbe . [5]Willelmo le[7] Abbe[5] . Ricardo filio Thome . Petro de Tẏringtun[8] . Alano clerico . 7 aliis.

Endorsed: (1) ij (13 cent.). (2) Hainton' (13 or 14 cent.). (3) + (13 or 14 cent.).

Slit for seal-tag. Size: 7 x 4½ inches.

Marginalia in A: Haynton'.

Text: MS—Orig. Dij/71/3/58. A. R1427.

Var. R.: [1] Wyum R. [2] Haynton' A *and* R. [3] 7 R. [4] viam (*sic*) A. [5–5] R *omits*. [6] Haynton' R. [7] A *adds* ab. [8] Tirington' A. Tyrington' R.

Note: William of Wyham, who was also known as William of Claxby Pluckacre, was dead before February, 1219, when his widow Isabel was party to pleas of dower (Selden Society, vol. liii, nos. 673, 691 and 696). As William of Claxby he granted land in Spridlington circa 1200 (see vol. iv, nos. 1144–5 above: in the index Claxby is wrongly identified as the village of that name in Walshcroft wapentake). Osbert of Newport occurs frequently as a witness circa 1210–1220 (see vol. iv, nos. 1148, 1160, 1171 above).

372a

1497. Sale and quitclaim by Henry son of Peter of Hainton, to the dean and chapter of Lincoln, of a toft and buildings in Hainton, for which they gave him twelve marks of silver in his great necessity. (Circa 1240–1250.)

Sciant presentes 7 futuri quod ego Henricus filius Petri de Haynton' vendidi 7 quietum clamaui venerabilibus viris . dominis . decano . 7 capitulo Lincoln' ecclesie pro duodecim marcis argenti quas mihi in magna necessitate mea numerauerunt 7 tradiderunt . vnum toftum vnum toftum[1] cum pertinenciis suis 7 edificiis in eodem . inuentis . quod est inter terram Reginaldi de Karleton' . 7 terram Ricardi filii Johannis de Haynton' . Habendum 7 tenendum predictis dominis . libere . pacifice . integre . 7 quiete ab omni exaccione seculari in perpetuum . Et ego predictus Henricus 7 heredes mei predictis dominis decano 7 . capitulo . Linc' predictum toftum cum pertinenciis suis sicut predictum est ⁊ contra omnes homines varentizabimus[1] . adquietabimus . 7 defendemus inperpetuum . In cuius rei testimonium presenti scripto sigillum meum apposui . Hiis testibus . Ricardo Tuschet . Ricardo filio Thome . Willelmo le Abbe . Ricardo de Marisco . Radulfo Biddes.

Marginalia: Haynton'.
Text: MS—A (by Q2, in the margin).
Var. R.: [1] *sic*.
Note: The date is probably about the same period as no. 1491 above.

Folio 68d.

373a and 392

1498. Grant by Ralf son of Richard of Hainton, to the church of Lincoln and the Common, of a bovate of land in Hainton. (Before February 1219.)

De una bouata terre in Haynton'. (A rubric.)

Uniuersis[1] Christi fidelibus ad quos presens scriptum peruenerit Radulfus filius Ricardi de Haintun[2] salutem . Nouerit uniuersitas uestra me pro salute anime mee 7 antecessorum 7 successorum meorum dedisse . 7 hac presenti carta[3] confirmasse deo 7 commune ecclesie beate Marie Lincoln' vnam bouatam terre in territorio de Haintun[4] cum omnibus pertinenciis 7 aisiamentis suis infra villam de Haintun[5] 7 extra . in puram 7 perpetuam * elemosinam ⁊ in hiis subscriptis partibus . Scilicet ex orientali parte predicte ville ad Dunesholm tres seliones ex occidentali parte terre [6]Briani de Insula . Et in eodem[7] Dunesholm 7 in alio loco tres seliones ex occidentali parte terre[6] predicti Briani . Et ad Foxeholes[8] tres seliones . Et ad Baden Welleholm tres seliones . Et ad Sandholm[9] tres seliones inter terram Willelmi le Abe 7 terram Ricardi fratris sui . [6]Et[6] ex australi parte [10]de[10] Sandholm[9] duos seliones . Et ad Mashingdale duos seliones iuxta terram ecclesie . Et ad Mikeldale ler[11] duos seliones ex occidentali parte terre Willelmi Wyther[12] . Et ad le Panne vnum selionem ex occidentali parte terre Sewardi filii Alani . Et ad Scale Hil[13] duos seliones ex australi parte terre Symonis de Dribi[14] . Et ad Strete furlanges[15] duos seliones ex aquilonari parte terre Willelmi filii Hemerici . Ex[16] duos seliones ex australi parte [6]terre[6] predicti Willelmi . Et ad Wymer Hauhes[17] duos seliones 7 dimidiam . Et ex occidentali parte predicte ville ad Brodland quatuor seliones . Et ad Pirtingraues[18] tres seliones . Et ad Hairic holm duos seliones inter terram monialium de Syxle[19] . 7 terram Radulfi carpentarii . Et in eodem Hairic holm[20] 7 in alio loco tres seliones iuxta terram monialium de Syxle[21] scilicet ex orientali parte . Et ad Suines Stighes[22] tres seliones . Et ad eandem Suines Stighes[23] 7 in alio loco quatuor seliones ex orientali parte terre predictarum monialium . Et duos seliones ex australi parte de Suines Stighes[24] ex occidentali parte terre predictarum [25] monialium[25] . Et ad Huel[26] quatuor seliones iuxta[27] terram earundem monialium . Et ad eandem Huel 7 in alio loco tres seliones ex occidentali parte terre Willelmi filii Hemerici . Et ad Stanwelle[28] Holm duos seliones ex australi parte terre predictarum monialium . Et ad Barcwrd Gate[29] tres seliones inter terram earundem monialium . 7 terram Michaelis . Et ad Barcwrd Gate[30] 7 in alio loco vnum selionem ad Mirepit . Et ad Franewang duos seliones ex occidentali parte terre Willelmi mercenarii . Ego itaque dictus Radulfus 7 heredes mei warantizabimus dictam bouatam terre cum pertinenciis suis predicte commune inperpetuum . Hiis testibus . Hugone de Duningtun[31] capellano . Willelmo le Abe de Haintun[32] . Ricardo fratre suo . Osberto de Neuport . Mauricio de Neuport clerico . Ricardo filio Sewardi . Ricardo filio Thome de Haintun[33] . Alano de Haintun[33] clerico . Symone Kat . Willelmo mercenario de Haintun[33] . 7 aliis.

Endorsed: (1) j (13 cent.). (2) Hainton' (13 or 14 cent.). (3) .vij. (13 cent.). Slit for seal-tag. Size: 7 x $4\frac{5}{8}$ inches.

Marginalia in A392: (1) Hainton'. (2) .j. bovat' terre.

Texts: MS—Orig. Dij/71/3/65. A373A (by Q2). 392. R1426.

Var. R.: [1] Wniversis A373A. [2] Hainton A373A *and* 392. Haynton R. [3] R *adds* mea. [4] Haynton A373A *and* R. [5] Hainton' A373A. Haint' A392. Haynton R. [6]–[6] A373A omits. [7] eo R. [8] Foxoles A373A *and* R. [9] Sandeholm A373A. Sanholm A392. [10]–[10] A392 *omits*. [11] Mikeldale A392. [12] Vither A373A. Wither R. [13] His 373A. [14] Driby A392. [15] Stretfurlanges A392. [16] *sic* : et *in* A392 *and* R. [17] Wymerhaues A373A. Wimerhauhes A392. [18] Pintingraves A373A. [19] Sixle A392. Sixel R. [20] Hauicholm A392. [21] Sixle A373A. Sixele A392 *and* R. [22] Suinestighes R. [23] Suines stiges A373A. Suinestighes R. [24] Suines stiges A373A. Suine Stihes A392. Suinestighes R. [25] A373A *omits*. [26] Heuel A373A. [27] inter R. [28] Stanuelle A373A. [29] Bracvordgate A373A. Barchwrdgate A392. Barcworthgates R. [30] Bracvrdgate A373A. Barchwrdgate A392. Barcworthgates R. [31] Dunigton' A373A. Dunyngton R. [32] Haynton' A373A. R. [33] Hainton A373A. Haynton R.

Note: The charter cannot be later than 1219 as the land was released to Alan son of Richard in no. 1496 above. Alan is probably son of Richard son of Alan who received the grant in 1493 above. Richard son of Seward makes a grant in 1226 (see no. 1499 below). Osbert and Maurice of Newport witness frequently circa 1210–1220 (see note to previous charter). Richard and William Abbot witness early Henry III (L.R.S. xviii, p. 26).

**Folio 74d* (in A392).

Hdl. WRAGHOU

374a and 426

1499. Notification by Richard son of Seward of Hainton of the settlement of a dispute begun by writ of right in the shire court. He had claimed to hold of William the dean, and the chapter of

Lincoln, two parts of a bovate and a half, and of a messuage and a half and nineteen pence rent, in Hainton by the free service of two parts of three shillings and sixpence for all service. But he has now quitclaimed to William the dean, and the chapter of Lincoln, all the right and claim which he had in all the land which Richard son of Alan of Hainton held of the dean and chapter, two parts of which he had claimed in the court. For this the dean and chapter have given him eight and a half marks of silver. (Probably 1226.)

Carta Ricardi filii Sewardi de Hainton' de .ij. bovatis 7 dimidia . 7 .j. tofto 7 dimidia in Hainton. (A426 rubric.)

Omnibus Christi fidelibus ad quos presens scriptum peruenerit Ricardus filius Seward' de Haynton' salutem . Nouerit vniuersitas vestra quod cum ego vendicassem in comitatu Linc' a decano 7 capitulo Linc' per breue domini regis de recto duas partes [[1]vnius bouate terre 7 dimidie 7 vnius mesuagii . 7 dimidii . 7 decem 7 nouem denarios redditus cum pertinenciis in villa [2]de[2] Haynton'[1]] que[3] clamaui tenere de dictis decano 7 capitulo Linc' per liberum seruicium duarum parcium trium solidorum 7 sex denariorum per annum pro omni seruicio . tandem facta est [1]finalis[1] pax 7 concordia in pleno commitatu Linc' inter nos in huc[4] modum .' Videlicet quod ego Ricardus quietum clamaui de [2]me[2] 7 heredibus meis in perpetuum . Willelmo decano Linc' ecclesie 7 successoribus suis 7 eiusdem loci capitulo absque ullo penitus retinemento totum ius 7 clamium quod habui uel habere potui in tota terra 7 mesuagiis cum pertinenciis que Ricardus filius Alani de Haynton'[5] tenuit de decano 7 capitulo Linc' . de quibus duas partes vendicaui sicut supradictum est . Ego autem Ricardus tactis sacrosanctis ewangeliis pro me 7 heredibus meis iuraui . quod ego uel heredes mei nuncquam in dicta terra uel pertinenciis aliquid vendicabimus . Et pro ista[6] quieta clamacione dederunt mihi prefati decanus 7 capitulum ad manus .' octo marcas argenti 7 dimidiam . Et in huius rei testimonium 7 robur .' presenti scripto sigillum [2]meum[2] apposui . Hiis testibus . Radulfo filio Reginaldi tunc vicecomite Linc' . Philippo de Kim'[7] . Henrico de Braybroc . Willelmo de Well'[8] . Teobaldo[9] Houtayn[10] . Gilberto de Treyly[11] senescallo episcopi Linc' . Ricardo de Salfledb'[12] . Alexandro de Lafford' . Warnero de Engayn[13] . Ricardo Mauclert[14] . Eustachio 7 Galfrido seruientibus domini episcopi Linc' . Gilberto de Parten'[15] . Weomaro[16] de Burvell'[17] 7 aliis.

Marginalia in A: 373A (1) iij*s.* 7 vi*d.* (2) Haynton' 426. (1) Haÿnton. (2) .ij. bo' 7 dim' 7 unum toftum 7 dim'.

Texts: MS—A426 and 374A. R1430.

Var. R.: [1–1] R *omits.* [2–2] A426 *omits.* [3] quas R. [4] *sic* : hunc *in* A426 *and*

R. [5] Haintone A426. [6] illa A426. [7] Kýma R. [8] Welle R. [9] Theobaldo A426 *and* R. [10] Hauthen A426. Hauteyn R. [11] Treyli A426. Treillý R. [12] Salfledby A426. Salfleteby R. [13] Engain A426. [14] *sic*: Mauclerc A426. Mauclerk R. [15] Partenay R. [16] Wiomaro A426, *probably* recte Winemer *as* Winemer of Burwell *often witnesses about this time.* [17] Burewell' A426. Berewell' R.

Note: Ralf son of Reginald was sheriff in 1226, but there is a possibility he may also have held office in the preceding year (Lincolnshire Notes and Queries xxiv, no. 189, supplement, p. 7).

375a

1500. Confirmation by Richard Tuschet of Hainton, to the church of Lincoln and the Common, of a gift of a bovate of land in Hainton made by William of Wyham. (Query circa 1240.)

Omnibus Christi fidelibus presens scriptum visuris vel audituris Ricardus Tuschet de Haynton' salutem in domino . Noueritis me ratam 7 gratam[1] habere concessionem 7 donacionem quam Willelmus de Vyum[2] fecit decano 7 capitulo Lincoln' 7 commune canonicorum ibidem de vna bouata terre cum prato . 7 omnibus aliis pertinenciis ad dictam bouatam terre spectantibus in villa de Hainton'[3] . que est de feodo meo . Et dictam bouatam terre cum prato 7 aliis pertinenciis . eisdem decano 7 capitulo ∴ sigillo meo confirmo . Et ego predictus Ricardus 7 heredes mei . predictis decano 7 capitulo . predictam bouatam terre cum prato 7 aliis pertinenciis suis contra omnes homines 7 feminas warentizabimus inperpetuum . In cuius rei testimonium huic scripto sigillum meum apposui . Hiis testibus . Ricardo filio Thome . Radulfo Byddes[4] . Willelmo le Abbe . Henrico de Solario . Rogero . Willelmo filiis Maurici[5] clerici.

Texts: A. R1428.

Var. R.: [1] ratam (*sic*) R. [2] Wyhum R. [3] Haynton' R. [4] Biddes. [5] Mauricii R.

Note: It is not clear whether this William is the grantor of no. 1496 above or his grandson, who succeeded Ralf son of the first William in July, 1233, as a minor *Excerpta e rotulis finium,* i, p. 246). Nor is it clear whether this bovate is the ame as that of no. 1496. The witnesses suggest a date similar to no. 1491 above, although two of them witness no. 1496 above.

375b and 393

1501. Grant by William Abbot of Hainton, to the church of Lincoln and the Common, of part of his toft in Hainton containing half a perch of land. (Circa 1215–1220.)

De .j. tofto . 7 dimidia perticata . in Hainton'. (A393 rubric.)

Omnibus Christi fidelibus ad quos presens scriptum peruenerit Willelmus Abbot de Haynton'[1] ∴ salutem . Nouerit uniuersitas uestra me diuine pietatis intuitu 7 pro salute anime mee . 7 pro animabus omnium antecessorum 7 successorum meorum dedisse 7 concessisse 7 presenti carta mea confirmasse deo 7 beate Marie 7 commune canonicorum Linc' ecclesie .' quandam partem tofti mei in villa de Hainton'[2] uersus aquilonem . que continet dimidiam percatam terre . Tenendam 7 habendam eisdem canonicis cum libero introitu 7 exitu 7 pertinenciis suis . in puram 7 perpetuam elemosinam . liberam . solutam . quietam . ab omni seculari seruicio 7 exaccione uel demanda . Ego etiam Willelmus 7 heredes mei warantizabimus illam dimidiam percatam terre cum pertinenciis . prefatis canonicis defendemus 7 adquietabimus erga omnes homines imperpetuum . In huius autem rei robur 7 testimonium presenti scripto sigillum meum apposui . Hiis testibus . Thoma de Norton' . Henrico de Torpell' . 7 Johanne fratre eius .' capellanis . Osberto . Mauricio . Rogero de Neuport[3] .' clericis . Ricardo de Hainton'[2] . Ricardo Abbot . Petro de Tyrington'[4] . Willelmo[5] de Barton' . Alano clerico . 7 multis aliis.

Endorsed: (1) .j. (13 cent.). (2) ix (13 cent.). (3) Hainton' de parte toft' (13 cent.). *Written on the fold of the charter at the front* Ricardus Skurloc de Hainton (13 cent.).

Broken seal on tag: green, round, diameter probably $1\frac{3}{4}$ inches, a fleur de lis; legend

.... WILELMI LE

Size: $6\frac{7}{8}$ x $4\frac{3}{8}$ inches.

Marginalia in A393: (1) Hainton'. (2) .j. toftum dimidie percate.

Texts: MS—Orig. Dij/71/3/52 . A.

Var. R.: [1] Hayton' A393. [2] Haynton' 375B. [3] Neupor A393. [4] Tirington' A393. [5] Willelmus (*sic*) A375B.

Note: For the witnesses see note to no. 1147 in vol. iv above.

376a and 391

1502. Grant by Richard son of Ralf of Hainton, to the church of Lincoln and the Common, of half a toft in Hainton, which was of Walter the weaver. (Circa 1200.)

De dimidio tofto . in eadem villa. (A391 rubric.)

Vniuersis sancte matris ecclesie [1]filiis[1] ad quos presens scriptum peruenerit Ricardus filius Radulfi de Haintun[2] salutem . Nouerit uniuersitas uestra me dedisse 7 concessisse 7 hac presenti carta mea confirmasse deo 7 beate Marie 7 commune canonicorum Linc' ecclesie pro salute anime mee 7 antecessorum meorum in puram et perpetuam elemosinam medietatem thofti[3] qui fuit Walteri[4] tixtoris in uilla de Haintun continentis dimidiam acram terre ex orientali parte . Et ego 7 heredes mei warantizabimus predictum thoftum[5] predicte commune contra omnes homines . Hiis testibus . Radulfo [6]decano[6] de Haintun[7] . Matheo de Lund' . Waltero Blundo [6]iuniori[6] . Willelmo Abbate de Haintun[7] . Ricardo

Abbate . Willelmo filio Ricardi de Haintun[8] . Michaele filio Hosberti[9] pistoris[10] . Johanne clerico.

Endorsed: (1) vij (13 cent.). (2) Ricardi filii Radulfi de Heintun . med' toft' . (13 cent.). (3) .iij. (13 cent.).
Slit for seal-tag. Size: 5⅞ x 3 inches.
Marginalia in A: 376A Haynton'. 391 Hainton' dimidium toftum.
Texts: MS—Orig. Dij/71/3/55. A. R1432.
Var. R.: [1] A391 *omits*. [2] Hainton A376A *and* R. [3] tofti *in* A376A *and* 391 *and in* R. [4] Valteri A376A. [5] toftum *in* A376A *and* 391 *and in* R. [6–6] R *omits*. [7] Hainton' A376A. Haynton R. [8] Haynton A376A *and* R. [9] Osberti R. [10] R *adds* 7.
Note: Richard son of Ralf son of Warin witnessed with his father late Henry II (L.R.S. xviii, p. 2). He occurs again about the same time (*ibid.*, p. 4) and about 1196–1200 in the next charter below. William Abbot was seized of land in Hainton 1204–5 (Foster *op. cit.*, p. 37). Ralf dean of Hainton occurs in 1200 (see no. 1505 below).

377a

1503. Sale and quitclaim by Thomas son of William, to the lady Sybil of Benniworth, of Robert son of Rannulf son of Seward of Hainton, for twenty shillings and two talents of silver. (1196–1198.)

Omnibus sancte dei matris ecclesie filiis . Thomas filius Willelmi salutem . Nouerit vniuersitas uestra me dedisse 7 quietum clamasse Robertum filium Ranulfi filii Sewardi de Heintona[1] natiuum meum domine Sibille de Beningword'[2] 7 ei cui sibi melius placueerit[3] post decessum suum dare sine ullo retinemento michi 7 heredibus meis pro uigintis[4] solidis 7 duobus talentis quos michi inde dedit . et ut ista donacio 7 quieta clamacio rata 7 inconcussa permaneat .˙ 7 ne heredes mei hanc donacionem 7 quietam clamacionem possint inpedire . hanc cartam meam presentem feci ei in testimonio . Hiis testibus . magistro Willelmo cantore . magistro Radulfo de Virem[5] . magistro Valtero[6] Blundo . magistro Ricardo de Kym' . magistro Petro de Hungrie[7] . magistro Roberto secretario . Symone capellano meo . Willelmo nepote Varneri[8] . Ricardo Vylein . Radulfo clerico de Cucuvald'[9] . Rogero dyspensario[10] meo . Ricardo filio Radulfi de Heynt'[11] . Roberto de Hotham . Waltero Grim.

Marginalia in A.: De natiuo.
Texts: MS—A (by Q2). R1437.
Var. R.: [1] Haynton R. [2] Beningworth R. [3] *sic*. [4] viginti R. [5] Vireni R. [6] Willelmo (*sic*) R. [7] Hungry R. [8] Warneri R. [9] Cucuwald R. [10] *The scribe has written in* A dysynerio, *in* R disnerio: dyspensario *seems to be the most probable reading.* [11] Haynton' R.
Note: William of Blois was precentor 1196–1203. Thomas son of William was also known as Thomas of Saleby: he was the grandson of Hacon the Doomsday tenant of Hainton. He died before Hubert Walter ceasedto be Justiciar in 1198. *Magna Vita Sancti Hugonis* (Rolls Series), p. 175. See also C. W. Foster, *A history of the villages of Aisthorpe and Thorpe in the Fallows*, 1927, pp. 36, 72–3, and genealogical table to face p. 70.

390

1503A. Grant by Thomas son of William son of Hacon of Saleby to the church of All Saints, Hainton, of a toft on the south side of the cemetery in Hainton. (Before 1198.)

De uno tofto in Hainton' (A rubric).

Universis sancte matris ecclesie filiis ad quod presens scriptum pervenerit ⁖ Thomas filius Willelmi filii Haconis de Salebi . Noverit universitas vestra me dedisse 7 concessisse 7 hac presenti carta mea confirmasse deo 7 ecclesie Omnium Sanctorum de Hainton unum toftum in Haintun quod iacet in australi parte cimiterii ecclesie de Haintun scilicet illud quod iacet inter toftum prefate ecclesie 7 inter toftum Sigwardi filii Angeri in puram 7 perpetuam elemosinam . liberum 7 quietum ab omni seculari servitio 7 exactione . Et ego Thomas 7 heredes mei warantizabimus predictum tenementum predicte ecclesie de Haintun contra omnes homines . Hiis testibus . magistro Johanne de Mersco Gilberto de Benigwrd . David de Totingtun . Hugone clerico de Radthebi . Roberto de Hotham . Symone capellano ipsius Thome . Matheo serviente ipsius Thome.

Marginalia in A: Hainton .1. toftum.
Text: MS—A.
Note: For Thomas son of William see note to the preceding charter.

Folio 81.

Hdl. WRAGEHOU . 8 . 1 .

424

1504. Notification by Norman de la Charité that he will ratify whatever William de Karletune does in his name in a suit with the dean and chapter, concerning Richard son of Alan of Hainton. (1200.)

Carta ratihabicionis (A rubric).

Uniuersis sancte matris ecclesie filiis ad quos presens scriptum peruenerit Normannus de la Charite salutem . Nouerit uniuersitas uestra me ratum habere quicquid Willelmus de Karletune[1] seneschallus meus fecerit de Ricardo [filio Alani[2]] de Haint'[3] . uersus capitulum Linc' ecclesie . Hiis testibus . Simone de Pateshille . Eustachio de [Faucun-]be[rge[2]][4] . Henrico de Hwichet' . Huberto vicecomite Linc' . Ricardo de Camuill'[5] . 7 multis aliis.

Facsimile.
Endorsed: (1) Normanni de la Charite (13 cent.). (2) Hainton (13 cent.).
Slit for seal-tag. Size: 7¼ x 2⅛ inches.

Texts: MS—Orig. Dij/71/3/68*a*. A. R1440.
Var. R.: [1] Karletone A. Carletun R. [2] *Supplied from* A: *there is a hole in the charter.* [3] Haut' A. Haẏnton' R. [4] Faucumberge R. [5] Caumuill' R.
Note: The suit with the dean and chapter over Richard son of Alan was heard in Michaelmas Term 1200 (C.R.R. I, p. 263). Norman is there called *de Camera*. He was the second husband of the much married Grace daughter of Thomas son of William of Saleby (see note to no. 1503 above). Her first husband was Adam de Nevill to whom she was married when scarcely four years old shortly after her father's death. Adam quitclaimed Richard son of Alan in no. 1506 below. On his death about January, 1200, Grace was married before Ascension Day in that year to Norman de la Charité (*Magna Vita Sancti Hugonis* (Rolls Series), p. 176 and n). Her subsequent husbands were Brian de Insula, to whom she was married in 1205, and Geoffrey de Worth, whom she married after 1234. (See R. C. Dudding, *History of Saleby*, pp. 13–20.)

ADD. CHART.

1505. Sale and quitclaim by Norman de la Charité, to the church of Lincoln and the Common, of Richard son of Alan of Hainton, with all his issue and chattels. (1200.)

Vniuersis sancte matris ecclesie filiis ad quos presens scriptum peruenerit Normannus de la Charite salutem . Nouerit vniuersitas vestra me dedisse ⁊ hac presenti carta mea confirmasse deo ⁊ beate Marie ⁊ commune canonicorum Linc' ecclesie Ricardum filium Alani de Haẏnton ⁊ totam sectam suam ⁊ omnia catalla sua ⁊ totum ius ⁊ totum clamium quod habui in eodem Ricardo ⁊ pro ista donacione ⁊ quieta clamacione dederunt michi prenominati canonici nouem marcas argenti in primo aduentu regis Johannis apud Linc' post coronacionem suam scilicet coram Simone de Pateshill ⁊ Eustachio de Faucumberg ⁊ Henrico de Hwithene domini Regis justiciariis tenentibus placita in bancco . Hiis testibus Osberto de Hwitington clerico magistro Simone de Derby Hugone de Rolueston Radulfo de Haint' decano Willelmo de Carleton Thoma seruiente de Haẏnton ⁊ multis aliis.

Text: MS—R1441.
Note: John was in Lincoln 21st November, 1200.

ADD. CHART.

1506. Grant and quitclaim by Adam de Nevill, to the chapter of Lincoln, of Richard son of Alan and all his chattels. (1198-1200.)

Vniuersis sancte matris ecclesie filiis ad quos [hoc scri[1]]ptum peruenerit Adam de Nouill' salutem Nouerit vniuersitas vestra me dedisse ⁊ c[oncessis[1]]se ⁊ penitus quietumclamasse de me ⁊ de heredibus meis in puram ⁊ perpetuam elemosinam pro salute anime mee ⁊ pro animabus antecessorum meorum deo ⁊ ecclesie beate Marie ⁊ capitulo eiusdem ecclesie Ricardum filium Alani ⁊ omnia catalla sua ⁊ totum jus ⁊ totum clamium quod habui in eodem Ricardo Et vt donacio rata permaneat ; eam presenti scripto 7 s[igill[1]]i mei apposicione confirmaui . Hiis testibus Radulfo decano de Tiringtona Ada Týsun Willelmo de Faldigwrd[2] Ricardo filio Radulfi de Haýnton Ricardo Abbate [3]Willelmo Abbate[3] Willelmo filio Orgari Roberto de Scalebi Hugone de [B[1]]all.'

Endorsed: (1) Carta Ade de Novilla pro humagio Ricardi (early 13 cent.) filii Alani de Heinton' (13 cent., but later than the other endorsement).

Tag for seal. Size: 6 x $3\frac{1}{2}$ inches.

Texts: MS—Orig. Dij/71/3/68*b*. R1439.

Var. R.: [1] *supplied from* R: *the charter is torn and faded.* [2] Faldingworth R. [3]-[3] R *omits.*

Note: See note to no. 1504 above.

ADD. CHART.

1507. Grant by R[oger] the dean and the chapter of Lincoln, to Richard son of Alan of Hainton, of a toft and land in Hainton for a yearly render of two shillings and sixpence. (Circa 1200.)

Uniuersis Christi fidelibus ad quos presens scriptum peruenerit .R. decanus . 7 capitulum Linc' . ecclesie salutem . Nouerit uniuersitas uestra nos concessisse 7 hac presenti carta nostra confirmasse Ricardo filio Alani de Haintun 7 heredibus suis unum toftum continens dimidiam achram[1] terre . pergate . xvj . pedum . 7 octo acras terre arabilis in territorio de Haintun . Scilicet quatuor acras ex parte orientali eiusdem uille . 7 quatuor acras ex parte occidentali . Tenend' de nobis in feudo 7 hereditate sibi 7 heredibus suis Reddendo nobis annuatim pro prenominata terra 7 pro prato terre pertinenti . 7 pro quodam prato ad Swineham 7 pro quodam prato ad Swinestiges duos solidos 7 vi . denarios . Scilicet . xv . denarios . ad Pasca . 7 xv . denarios ad festum sancti Michaelis . Huius autem terre prenominate hee sunt partes . Due selliones ad Staindales . 7 quatuor selliones inter Hukehou 7 Lefwinehou . 7 una sellio ad Kalkewelle . In occidentali uero parte una sellio iuxta uiam apud Barchwrthe 7 una sellio contra Swortemoldes . 7 una sellio ad Tranepit . 7 una sellio in mora . 7 uia sellio super Airichholm . 7 tres selliones ad Wdegate Et ut hec nostra concessio in perpetuum rata permaneat sigilli nostri munimine coroborauimur.[1]

Endorsed: Hainton' . j . toft' . viii . acr' (13 cent.).

Slit for seal-tag. Size: $5\frac{3}{4}$ x $4\frac{1}{4}$ inches.

Text: MS—Orig. Dij/71/3/64.

Var. R.: [1] *sic.*

Note: This grant was probably made either at the conclusion of the suit with Adam de Nevill or Norman de la Charité. From the hand it appears to be much earlier in date than no. 1493 above.

ADD. CHART.

1508. Grant by Robert son of Richard of Hainton, to the church of Lincoln and the Common, of Richard son of Ralf and Agnes his wife, daughter of Eudo of Hainton, his *nativi*, with all their issue and chattels. (Circa 1215–1220.)

Omnibus Christi fidelibus ad quos presens scriptum peruenerit Robertus filius Ricardi de Haẏnton salutem . Nouerit vniuersitas vestra me diuine pietatis intuitu (⁊ pro salute anime mee (⁊ pro animabus omnium antecessorum ⁊ successorum meorum dedisse ⁊ concessisse (⁊ presenti carta mea confirmasse deo ⁊ beate Marie ⁊ commune canonicorum ecclesie Linc' Ricardum filium Radulfi ⁊ Agnetem vxorem eius filiam Eudonis de Haẏnton natiuos meos cum tota sequela sua ⁊ cum omnibus catallis suis in puram ⁊ perpetuam elemosinam perpetuo possidendos (liberos (solutos ⁊ quietos de me ⁊ de heredibus meis inperpetuum . In huius autem rei robur ⁊ testimonium presens scriptum sigilli mei apposicione corroboraui . Hiis[1] Thoma de Norton Simone de Cancia ⁊ Roberto de Balderton capellanis Willelmo de Mannecestr' Simone de Thorp' Willelmo de Midleẏ Ricardo de Neuport Winemero Petro de Cheuermund Mauricio de Neuport Thoma de Waltham ⁊ aliis.

Text: MS—R1438.
Var. R.: [1] *sic*: testibus *omitted*.
Note: The witnesses are practically the same as in nos. 1147–8 in vol. iv above: see note to no. 1147.

ADD. CHART.

1509. Grant by Philip the dean and the chapter of Lincoln, at the instance of the Archdeacon of Lincoln, to William de Leython, vicar of Hainton, so long as he remains vicar, of the houses on the west of the church which the Archdeacon held of the chapter at a yearly rent, because William has no house of the chapter's assignment in Hainton. They will reduce the annual rent to forty pence and the vicar shall keep the buildings in a state as good or better than when he received them. The dean and chapter do not bind themselves to make a similarly liberal concession to William's successor. 2nd March, 1290.

Pateat vniuersis per presentes quod nos Philippus decanus ⁊ capitulum Linc' considerantes diligenter quod dilectus nobis in Christo Willelmus de Leẏthon' capellanus perpetuus vicarius ecclesie nostre de Haẏnton :/ licet eidem W. ratione dicte vicarie sue cura ⁊ sollicitudo totius parochie iniureat ⁊ regimen animarum nullas domos seu edificia ibi habeat ex assignacione nostra ad inhabitandum ad huius curam que ei vt predicitur incumbit peragendam .' concessimus eidem . W. quamdiu ibidem vicarius permanserit ac prehabito in hac parte diligenti tractatu 7 deliberacione pleniori concorditer ad instanciam venerabilis confratris nostri 7 concanonici domini Willelmi Archidiaconi Linc' qui nobis 7 capitulo nostro deuotus extitit 7 de expresso consensu eiusdem concedimus per presentes quod idem vicarius domos 7 edificia cum tota placea que idem Archidiaconus apud Haẏnton ex parte occidentali ecclesie de nobis ad firmam pro annuo censu tenuit .' teneat 7 inhabitandum habeat exnunc inposterum de nobis .' quam diu ibidem vicarius permanserit remisso interim prefato vicario dicto censu annuo quem dictus dominus . . Archidiaconus nobis pro illis reddere solebat vsque ad quadraginta denarios annuos nobis seu clerico prepositure commune nostre nomine nostro per dictum vicarium annis singulis soluendos videlicet ad festum sancti Martini in yeme 7 ad natiuitatem sancti Johannis Baptiste pro equalibus porcionibus (primo termino solucionis faciende incipiente .' in festo dicti sancti Martini proximo in ẏeme venturo 7 altero termino in festo Natiuitatis sancti Johannis tunc proximo sequenti vt predicitur 7 sit deinceps annis singulis quam dictus vicarius dictas domos 7 placeam tenuerit 7 ibidem vicarius permanserit pro omnibus terrenis demandis . Et est sciendum quod idem vicarius interim dictas domos seruabit 7 manutenebit in adeo bono statu quos eas modo recepit vel meliori . Cum autem idem .W. ibidem vicarius esse desierit .' licebit nobis 7 successoribus nostris non obstante hac liberali concessione nostra .' dictas domos 7 edificia cum placea memorata in manum nostram resumere 7 de illis facere 7 disponere prout nobis opertunum videbitur 7 crediderimus expedire . Nos vero super premissis dicto domino Willelmo has litteras fieri fecimus sigillo capituli nostri 7 sigillo domini . . Archidiaconi tunc firmarii apud Haẏnton roboratas litteris consimilis tenoris penes nos sub sigillo dicti domini Willelmi vicarii remanentibus in memoriam rei geste Datum 7 actum in capitulo nostro Linc' die Mercurii proxima post Dominicam in passione domini videlicet .xj. Kalendas Aprilis . Anno domini M° . cc° . Octogesimo Nono .

Text: MS—R1442.

Folio 69*d*.

RAND

368

1510. Grant by Ralf of Rand, son of John the clerk of Rand, to the church of Lincoln and the Common, of sixty acres of land, of which thirty are on the east and thirty on the west of the village, a toft, and all the meadow and pasture appurtenant to the arable land. (Circa 1240–1250.)

Omnibus Christi fidelibus presens scriptum visuris uel audituris . Radulfus de Rande filius Johannis clerici de Rande salutem in domino . Nouerit vniuersitas vestra me dedisse 7 concessisse 7 hac presenti carta mea confirmasse deo 7 ecclesie beate[1] Marie Linc' 7 canonicis deo ibidem seruientibus ac eorundem[2] assignatis pro salute anime mee 7 antecessorum meorum in puram 7 perpetuam elemosinam triginta acras terre arabilis iacentes ex orientali parte uille de Rande 7 alias triginta acras terre arabilis iacentes ex occidentali parte uille eiusdem et totum illud toftum[3] quod ego tenui in villa de Rande 7 totum pratum subscriptum cum patura[4] ad predictam terram 7 totum pratum pertinentem . videlicet . ex orientali parte ville de Rande . super Westholm' tres selliones . Item super Northolm[5] tres selliones . Item super Peselandes 7 Peselandil[6] 7 Peselandale quatuor selliones Item super Cranholm' quatuor selliones Item super Trethornes vnum sellionem Item intra vias septem selliones Item super Louhougate[7] duas[8] selliones Item [9]iuxta Abyrdic[9] sex selliones Item in Bulington[10] Sike[11] vnum sellionem . Item in[12] Sutholm duas[8] selliones . Item iuxta [13]Estward Esdland[13] vnum sellionem . Item super Waterfores vnum sellionem . 7 totam terram cum prato 7 omnibus pertinenciis suis quam Galfridus le Franceys[14] aliquando tenuit in eadem uilla . Item in Neucroft' quatuor perticatas prati in latitudine . Item in Braystares[15] duas perticatas in latitudine . Item in Westeng' decem perticatas[16] in latitudine . Item in Calue-croft[17] quatuor perticatas in latitudine . Item[18] Bules tres perticatas in latitudine Item in Esteng' septem perticatas in latitudine 7 in Warlotes vnam perticatam in latitudine . Item in Mikyleng'[19] super Hÿlles[20] duas perticatas in latitudine . Item pratum illud quod abuttat super terram Ade de Fulnetby contra Brayestares[15] 7 quoddam[21] pratum quod est contra curiam domine Item in occidentali parte ville de Rande de terra arabili iuxta uiam Linc' vnum selionem . Item super Langingdale tres selliones . Item super Calfcroft[17] duas[8] selliones Item super Rogerriskes duas[8] selliones . Item super Lestandlandes[22] vnum sellionem . Item 7 foreram de Lefstanlandes[23] . Juxta Crucem tres selliones Item iuxta Strete vnum sellionem Item super Wodeil[24] quatuor selliones . Item super Sandes tres selliones Item super Waterforis[27] tres selliones . Item super Aselacsic tres butas 7 tres selliones . Item uersus curiam Ade de Fulnetby quatuor selliones . Item super Akyrdic[26] 7 [27]super[27] Styakyr[28] quatuor selliones . Item in Lynlandes[29] duas[8] selliones . Tenend' 7 habend' sibi

7 cuicunque dare ac assignare voluerint libere 7 quiete pacifice 7 honorifice cum libero introitu 7 exitu 7 omnibus aliis quibuscunque pertinenciis libertatibus aysiamentis 7 liberis consuetudinibus in pratis in pascuis in aquis in semitis sicut aliqua elemosina liberius 7 quietius teneri potest ac[30] poterit . Et ego predictus Radulfus de Rande 7 heredes mei dictis matrici ecclesie beate uirginis Marie Linc' 7 canonicis ibidem deo seruientibus 7 eorum asignatis supra[31] scriptam terram cum tofto 7 prato 7 omnibus aliis supradictis pertinenciis contra omnes homines inperpetuum sicuti aliqua elemosina liberius 7 quietius warantizari 7 defendi poterit .' warantizabimus 7 de omnibus adquietabimus 7 defendemus 7 si in predictis terra arabili 7 prato plus uel minus quam supra scriptum est contineatur pro tanta dicta ecclesia 7 canonici et eorum assingati[32] eam tenebunt cum prato supra supra[33] scripto . Et ut hec mea donacio 7 concessio robore firmitatis perpetuetur presenti scripto sigillum meum apposui in testimonium . Hiis testibus . domino Henrico le chanberleng'[34] . domino Radulfo de Normanuill' . domino Willelmo Burdeth[35] . domino Henrico le Bek[36] . Thoma Mustel . Willelmo de Bleseby . Roberto de Snellislund[37] . Reynero de Sotteby . Hugone de Helewell' . Roberto de Wyuelingham[38] clerico . Roberto Mus . . .[39]

Marginalia in A: (1) Rande. (2) Rand'.
Texts: MS—A (by Q2). R1485.
Var. R.: [1] R *adds* virginis. [2] eorum R. [3] toftum illud R. [4] *sic*: pastura R. [5] Northholm R. [6] Peselandhil R. [7] Sonhougate R. [8] duos R. [9–9] super Akerdic R. [10] Bolington R. [11] sic R. [12] bi R. [13–13] Erward Esdland. [14] Fraunceys R. [15] Brayscares R. [16] perticate R. [17] Kaluecroft R. [18] R *adds* in. [19] Mikeleng R. [20] Hilles R. [21] R *adds* parvum. [22] Lefstanlandes. [23] R *adds* item. [24] Wodehil R. [25] Waterfores R. [26] Akerdic R. [27–27] R *omits*. [28] Stiacr' R. [29] Linlandes R. [30] 7 R. [31] super R. [32] *sic*: assignati R. [33] *sic*. [34] Chaumberlayn R. [35] Burreth R. [36] Beck' R. [37] Snelleslund' R. [38] Wollingham R. [39] Mustrel R.
Note: Henry the Chamberlain was holding land in various places in Lincolnshire 1242 (*Book of Fees*, ii, pp. 1017, 1054, 1062, etc.): he died in 1256 (*Excerpta e rotulis finium tempore Regis Henrici*, ii, p. 229). Sir Ralf de Normanvill was party to a fine concerning land in Stainton by Langworth in 1250 (L.R.S. xvii, p. 54). William Burdet was party to a fine 21st May, 1245 (*ibid.*, p. 7). Thomas Mustel held land in Alvingham in 1242 (*Book of Fees*, ii, p. 1053).

Folio 70.
Hdl. WRAGHOU . 7 . ϕ

THORPE LE VALE

369

1511. Grant by Roger de Mureyis of Thorpe le Vale, to the church of Lincoln and the Common, of six acres of land in Thorpe le Vale. (Circa 1240–1250.)

Omnibus Christi fidelibus ad quos presens scriptum peruenerit Rogerus de Mureyes[1] de Frimthorp[2] salutem in domino . Nouerit vniuersitas vestra me dedisse concessisse 7 hac presenti carta mea confirmasse deo 7 beate Marie 7 commune canonicorum Linc' ecclesie pro salute anime mee 7 antecessorum 7[3] successorum meorum sex acras terre arrabilis in territorio de Frimthorp[2] cum omnibus pertinenciis suis in liberam puram 7 perpetuam elemosinam . Quarum scilicet quatuor acre 7 tres percate jacent super Blamhild'[4] inter terram prioris de Markeby . 7 terram Aluredi hominis [5]prioris[5] de Sixil[6] a via scilicet usque ad diuisam de Binbrock'[7] . 7 quinque percatas terre in magna cultura versus austrum que jacent inter terram Willelmi filii Agnetis 7 terram meam propriam . Tenend*as* 7 habend*as* prefatis canonicis in liberam puram 7 perpetuam elemosinam liberam 7 quietam ab omni seruicio . 7 exaccione seculari ·/ 7 demanda . Et ego Rogerus de Moreyes[1] 7 heredes mei warantizabimus adquietabimus 7 defendemus predictas sex acras terre arrabilis cum omnibus pertinenciis suis prefatis canonicis contra omnes homines inperpetuum . tanquam puram[8] 7 perpetuam elemosinam Et in huius rei testimonium presens scriptum sigillo meo roboraui . Testibus . domino Roberto de Bollesouer . Stephano rectore ecclesie de Keuermound'[9] . Egidio fratre suo . Ricardo de Stretton' . Rogero carpentario de Keuermound[9] . Willelmo filio Gilberti . Johanne filio eius . Willelmo filio Roberti . Stephano de Ireford'[10] . Willelmo filio Martini . 7 aliis.

Marginalia in A: (1) Frimthorp. (2) Frymthorp.
Texts: MS—A (by Q2) R1473.
Var. R.: [1] Morers R. [2] Frumpthorp' R. [3] ac R. [4] Blaẏnhild' R. [5–5] R *omits*. [6] Sixel R. [7] Binnebrok' R. [8] R *adds* liberam. [9] Keuermund R. [10] Yreford R.
Note: Thorpe le Vale, formerly Frunthorpe, is a hamlet in the parish of Ludford Magna, which has lost its separate status (L.R.S. xix, p. lxx). In A it is spelt Frimthorpe by Q2, but Frunthorpe or Frumthorpe is more usual in other records. Roger de Mureres levied a fine with Richard de Mureres concerning land in Thorpe le Vale 19th May, 1240 (*Final Concords*, i, p. 308). The witnesses are much the same as those to the next charter, which cannot be earlier than 1239–40 (see note to it below). On the other hand, Stephen had ceased to be rector of Kirmond before the end of Grosseteste's sixteenth year (1250–1251) as Simon of Baumber was instituted (L.R.S. xi, p. 125).

370

1512. Grant by Roger de Mureyis, to the church of Lincoln and the Common, of one whole *cultura* and five perches lying in the great *cultura*, both on the north side of the village. (Circa 1240–1250.)

Omnibus Christi fidelibus ad quos presentes littere peruenerint Rogerus de Moreyis[1] salutem in domino . Nouerit vniuersitas vestra me dedisse concessisse 7 hac presenti carta mea confirmasse pro salute anime mee 7 antecessorum 7[2] successorum meorum deo 7 beate Marie 7 commune canonicorum Linc' ecclesie vnam culturam terre arrabilis integram cum omnibus pertinenciis suis in territorio de Frimthorp[3] ex parte aquilonali eiusdem ville que iacet super Balamhild'[4] inter terram prioris de Markeby ⁊ terram prioris de Sixil[5] a via scilicet usque ad diuisam de Binbrock'[6] . ⁊ quinque percatas terre ex eadem parte ville . que iacent in magna cultura ex parte australi inter terram Willelmi filii Agnetis ⁊ terram meam propriam . Habend*as* ⁊ tenend*as* predictis[7] canonicis in puram liberam ⁊ perpetuam elemosinam liberam ⁊ quietam ab omni seruicio ⁊ exaccione seculari ⁊ demanda . Et ego Rogerus de Mureis[1] ⁊ heredes mei warantizabimus (adquietabimus ⁊ defendemus totam predictam culturam cum prescriptis quinque percatis ⁊ omnibus pertinenciis suis . prefatis canonicis contra omnes homines inperpetuum tanquam puram liberam ⁊ perpetuam elemosinam . Et in huius rei testimonium presens scriptum fide media pro me ⁊ heredibus meis interposita sigillo meo confirmaui . Testibus dominis[8] priore de Irford'[9] . Willelmo rectore ecclesie de Lutheford' . Adam vicario ecclesie eiusdem . Henrico filio Willelmi de Lutheford' . Willelmo filio Ricardi . Stephano de Irford'[9] . Rogero carpentario . de Keuermound'[10] . Willelmo fratre eius . Willelmo filio Gilberti . Johanne filio suo . Willelmo filio Alani . Petro de Hautley[11] ⁊ aliis.

Marginalia in A: Frunthorp. (16 cent.)
Texts: MS—A (by Q2) R1472.
Var. R.: [1] Morers R. [2] ac R. [3] Frumptorp' R. [4] Blaynhyld R. [5] Sixel R. [6] Bynnebrok' R. [7] prefatis R. [8] domino R. [9] Yreford R. [10] Keuermund R. [11] Hauley R.
Note: Adam was instituted vicar of Great Ludford 1239–1240 (L.R.S. xi, p. 40). See also the note to the preceding charter.

371

1513. Confirmation by Peter son of Roger de Mureyis, of his father's gift, no. 1511 above. (Circa 1240–1250.)

Omnibus Christi fidelibus ad quos presens scriptum peruenerit Petrus filius Rogeri de Mureyis[1] salutem in domino . Noueritis me ratam ⁊ gratam habere illam donacionem concessionem ⁊ confirmacionem quam Rogerus de Mureyis[1] pater meus fecit deo ⁊ beate Marie ⁊ commune canonicorum Linc' ecclesie in puram . liberam . ⁊ perpetuam elemosinam de sex acris terre arrabilis in territorio de Frimthorp[2] cum omnibus pertinenciis suis ex parte aquilonali ville sicut in carta dicti Rogeri patris mei quam supradicti canonici Linc' ecclesie inde habent continetur . quam videlicet cartam presenti scripto . ⁊ sigilli [3]mei[3] munimine duxi confirmandam . Testibus Stephano rectore ecclesie de Keuermound'[4] . Ricardo de Stretton' . Rogero carpentario de Keuermound'[4] . Willelmo filio Gilberti . Johanne filio eius . Willelmo filio Roberti . Stephano de Yrford'[5] . Willelmo filio Martini . 7 aliis.

Marginalia in A: Frunthorp. (16 cent.)
Texts: A (by Q2) R1474.
Var. R.: [1] Murers R. [2] Frumpthorp' R. [3–3] R *omits*. [4] Keuermund R. [5] Yreford R.
Note: The witnesses are the same as in no. 1511 above.

372 and 423

1514. Grant by T. son of Jollan of Thorpe le Vale, to the church of Lincoln and the Common, of William son of Godric, two bovates of land on one side of the village, and two bovates *ad arandum* on the other side, a toft and six acres of land. (Circa 1160–1170.)

De .ij. bovatis .i. tofto 7 vi acris in Fruntorp' (A423 rubric) .T. filius Gollani de Fruntorp'[1] omnibus hominibus suis 7 amicis Francis et Anglis salutem . Noverit universitas vestra me dedisse 7 concessisse 7 presenti carta mea confirmasse deo 7 sancte Marie et commune canonicorum Linc' in puram et perpetuam elemosinam 7[2] liberam ab omni seculari servitio Willelmum filium Godrici 7 duas bovatas terre in Fruntorp'[1] ex una parte ville 7 duas bovatas ad arandum ex altera parte eiusdem ville cum tofto quod fuit Leverici 7 sex acras terre . quatuor versus virgultum ex parte orientali . 7 duas acras in cultura que dicitur Firmeracre cum pratis 7 omnibus pertinentibus ad predictam terram . 7 hoc pro anima patris mei 7 predecessorum meorum . Hanc vero donacionem guarantizabo et ego et heredes mei contra omnes homines . Hiis . testibus . domino decano . Pagano canonico . Radulfo subdecano magistro Petro de Melide[3] Rogero Parvo Roberto constabulario . Rogero de Derby . Fulchone de Casneto . Alexandro Malbisse Galfrido Torp'[4] Ivone 7 Aluredo[5] sacerdotibus . Ada 7 Thoma diaconis . Roberto clerico domini Ade . Ernulfo filio Ernaldi . Aluredo clerico de Ludeford'[6] 7 Gotheo filio eius . Petro clerico magistri Petri.

Marginalia in A: (1) Fruntorp. (2) .ii. bovat' .i. toft' 7 vi acr'.
Texts: A423 and 372; R1471.
Var. R.: [1] Frimtorp' A372. Frumpthorpe R. [2] R *omits*. [3] Derml' (*sic*) A372. Demel' R. [4] Thorp' R. [5] Aldredo A372 *and* R. [6] Lutheford R.
Note: Ralf witnesses as subdean Oct., 1162 (see vol. iv, no, 1292 above) and in 1167 (*ibid.*, no. 1293). Alexander Malbisse also witnesses on the first occasion. Master Peter de Melide witnesses with Alexander Malbisse and Pain 1173–1182 (Stenton, *Danelaw Charters*, p. 9).

Add. Chart.

1515. Grant by Hugh son of William of Thorpe [le Vale] to Richard Sely of Willingham of half of his toft in Thorpe [le Vale] and as much more within the toft as equals the half part in Wellehole outside the west ditch, together with two acres of arable land. (Circa 1230–1240.)

[Sciant] presentes et futuri quod ego Hugo filius Willelmi de Torp[1] dedi et concessi et hac presenti carta mea confirmavi Ricardo [Seli] de Wiflingham et heredibus suis mediam partem tocius tofti mei in Torp versus austrum . ⁊ tantum plus infra toftum [quantum] est media pars in Wellehole extra foveam occidentalem ⁊ duas acras terre arabilis in territorio de Torp[1] unam scilicet acram ex parte australi eiusdem ville ultra Depedale iuxta terram Gocelini . ⁊ unam acram terre ex parte aquilonali ville ultra domum Petri iuxta terram prioris de Markebi[2] cum omnibus pertinenciis ⁊ aisiamentis ⁊ libertatibus infra villam ⁊ extra ad tantum feudum[3] pertinentibus . Illi et heredibus suis habenda ⁊ tenenda de me et heredibus meis libere ⁊ quiete iure hereditario . Reddendo inde annuatim mihi ⁊ heredibus meis unum obulum ad festum sancti Michaelis pro omni servicio et consuetudine seculari . Et ego et heredes mei warantizabimus predicto Ricardo ⁊ heredibus suis toftum nominatum ⁊ terras prenominatas cum pertinenciis pro predicto servicio contra omnes homines in perpetuum . Et ut hec mea donacio ⁊ concessio rata ⁊ stabilis in perpetuum permaneat presens scriptum [sigilli mei apposicione] roboravi . Hiis testibus . Rogero de Murers[4] . Willelmo filio Gileberti de Ludeford . Gileberto filio Alani de Ludeford [Andrea filio Alani de Ma]lbertorp . ⁊ multis aliis.

No ancient endorsement.
Slit for seal-tag. Size: $6\frac{3}{8}$ x 3 inches.
Texts: MS—Orig. Dij/88/1/25. R1800.
Var. R.: *The words in square brackets are supplied from* R: *the charter is damaged.* [1] Thorp R. [2] Markeby R. [3] feodum R. Muters (*sic*) R.
Note: This charter seems to be earlier than the following one, which is certainly before 1247. The first two witnesses are grantor and witness in nos. 1511 and 1512 above.

Add. Chart.

1516. Grant by Thomas son of Richard Sely, to the church of Lincoln and the Common, of the land mentioned in the preceding grant which had been of Richard his father. (Circa 1230–1245.)

Omnibus Christi fidelibus Thomas filius Ricardi Selẏ[1] salutem . Noveritis me dedisse . concessisse . de me et de heredibus meis quietum clamasse . ⁊ hac presenti carta mea confirmasse deo ⁊ beate Marie ⁊ commune canonicorum Linc' ecclesie illam medietatem thofti que fuit Ricardi patris mei in villa de Thorp' versus austrum ⁊ tantum plus infra thoftum quantum est media pars in Wellehole extra foveam occidentalem . ⁊ duas acras terre arabilis in territorio eiusdem ville . unam scilicet acram ex parte australi ville ultra Depedale iuxta terram Gocelini ⁊ unam acram ex parte aquilonali ville ultra domum Petri iuxta terram prioris de Markeby Tenend' et habend' dictis canonicis in puram ⁊ perpetuam elemosinam liberam ⁊ quietam ab omni servicio cum omnibus pertinenciis . libertatibus ⁊ aisiamentis infra villam ⁊ extra sine omni reclamacione mei vel heredum meorum . Et ego ⁊ heredes mei defendemus ⁊ warantizabimus dictam terram cum pertinenciis . libertatibus ⁊ aisiamentis dictis canonicis contra omnes homines in perpetuum . ⁊ in huius rei robur ⁊ testimonium presens scriptum sigillo meo juramento a me corporali prestito interveniente . confirmavi . Hiis testibus . Elya succentore . Henrico sacrista Ricardo capellano ⁊ Ada clerico custodibus altaris Linc' ecclesie R[icardo] de Straton' . Achardo . Thoma . ⁊ Roberto clericis ⁊ aliis.

Endorsed: Thorp' (13 cent.).
The bottom of the charter where the slit for the seal-tag should be is torn away.
Size: 6⅜ x 5 inches.
Texts: MS—Orig. Dij/88/1/24. R1801.
Var. R.: [1] Seli R.
Note: For the dates of Elias the succentor and Henry the sacrist see vol. iv, pp. 280–1, above.

373

1517. Printed in volume IV at no. 1390 above.

Marginalia in A: (1) Croxeby. Debent scribi in Walescroft sunt scripta et ideo vacant hic (by Q). (2) Croxeby.

374

1518. A duplicate of 352 which is printed in volume IV at no. 1387 above.

Marginalia: (1) Croxby. (2) Scribatur in Walsecroft . fuit scripta et ideo vacat (by Q).

375

1519. Printed in volume IV at no. 1392 above.

376

1520. A duplicate of 353 which is printed in volume IV at no. 1388 above.

Marginalia: Croxby.

377

1521. A duplicate of 354 which is printed in volume IV at no. 1389 above.

Marginalia: Croxby.

SNELLAND

378 and 401

1522. Grant by Geoffrey son of Bertram, to the church of Lincoln and the Common, of a toft and a bovate containing ten acres on each side of the village of Snelland together with two acres of increment (*de accremento*). (Circa 1210–1220.)

De .i. tofto . 7 vna bouata terre in Snelleslund. (A 401 rubric.)

Sciant presentes 7 futuri quod ego Galfridus filius Bertram dedi 7 concessi 7 presenti carta mea confirmaui deo 7 beate Marie 7 commune canonicorum Lincoln' ecclesie pro salute animarum patris 7 . matris mee 7 omnium antecessorum 7 successorum meorum .' vnum toftum in villa de Snelleslund[1] .' quod Willelmus frater Bertram tenuit . 7 vnam bouatam terre in territorio eiusdem ville cum pertin*entiis continentem decem acras terre arabilis ex una parte ville . 7 decem ex alia[2] parte Scilicet quinque acras que iacent proxime[3] curie mee uersus occidentem . 7 quatuor acras que abutissant super diuisam de Fulneteb' . 7 vnam acram in Clackesdale[4] . que jacet proxima terre que fuit Radulfi de Hoiland' . 7 duas acras in Lund de accremento . Item ex alia[5] parte ville . duas acras 7 dimidiam in Gosdam . ex parte occidentali de Scuruodal'[6] .' quatuor acras . ex parte occidentali de Mor Gate[7] . vnam acram . In Kirkefurlang duas acras 7 dimidiam 7 vnam acram prati in West Eng . Habenda 7 tenenda cum pertinenciis omnibus . libertatibus 7 aisiamentis infra uillam 7 extra villam .' in puram 7 perpetuam elemosinam . liberam solutam 7 quietam ab omni seculari seruitio [8]7[8] exaccione 7 demanda . Et ego 7 heredes mei prefatum toftum 7 terram cum pertinentiis warentizabimus predictis canonicis . defendemus 7 adquietabimus erga omnes homines imperpetuum . In huius autem donacionis robur 7 testimonium . presens scriptum sigilli mei appositione corroboraui . Hiis testibus . Conano sacrista Lincoln' 7 Nicholao de Hainton'[9] capellanis . Willelmo de Tuxford' . Roberto camerario . Petro de Bekering . Rogero camerario . Adam de Brigeford[10] . Ricardo Abbe de Hainton' . Petro de Estgate . Petro de Cheuermund'[11] . Ricardo de Neuport . Philippo Hors . presbitero . Johanne 7 Benne[12] . 7 aliis.

Endorsed: (1) xxxiiij (13 cent.). (2) +. (3) Galfridi filii Bertram dat Communi .j. Toftum 7 .j. Bouatam terre in Snelleslund' (13 cent.).
Tag for seal. Size: 6¼ x 5¼ inches.
Marginalia in A: 378 Snellesloung. 401 Snelleslund .j. toftum 7 .j. bovat'.
Texts: MS—Orig. Dij/87/1/35. A378 by Q2 *and* 401. R1480.
Var. R.: [1] Snelleslunde A378. [2] altera R. [3] proximo A378. [4] Clackedale A378. Clakesdale R. [5] altera A378. [6] Scurnodal' R. [7] More gate. Morgate R.

A378. [8]–[8] R *omits.* [9] Hampton' R. [10] Brigesford R. [11] Scheuermound A378. [12] Benno A378 *and* 401.

Note: Conan is found as sacrist in 1214 and at a date circa 1218–20. He had ceased to hold office before 1221 (see vol. iv, p. 281, above).

* *Folio* 77*d* (in A401).

Hdl. Wraghou.

378a and 402

1523. Confirmation by Robert the Chamberlain of the preceding grant. (Circa 1210–1220.)

Confirmacio eiusdem terre . per . Robertum. (A 402 rubric.)

Omnibus Christi fidelibus ad quos presens scriptum peruenerit ; Robertus Camerarius salutem . Nouerit vniuersitas uestra me concessisse 7 presenti carta mea confirmasse deo 7 beate Marie 7 canonicis Lincoln' ecclesie ; donationem 7 concessionem quam Galfridus filius Bertheram[1] fecit eisdem canonicis de vno tofto in villa de Snelleslund'[2] quod Willelmus frater[3] Bertram tenuit . 7 vna bouata terre in territorio eiusdem ville ; continente decem acras terre arabilis ex una parte ville . 7 decem ex alia[4] parte . Scilicet quinque acras que iacent proxime curie eiusdem Galfridi uersus occidentem . 7 quatuor acras que abutissant super diuisam de Fulneteb'[5] . 7 vnam acram in Clackesdale[6] . que iacet proxima terre que fuit Radulfi de Hoiland' . 7 duas acras in Lund de accremento . Item ex alia parte ville ; duas acras 7 dimidiam in Gosdam . ex parte occidentali de Scuruedale[7] ; quatuor acras ex parte occidentali de Morgate (vnam acram . In Kirkefurlang'[8] ; duas acras 7 dimidiam . 7 vnam acram prati ; in West Eng . Habendis 7 tenendis cum pertinentiis in puram 7 perpetuam elemosinam . Liberam solutam 7 quietam ab omni seculari seruitio 7 exaccione 7 demanda . In huius autem rei robur 7 testimonium ; presens scriptum sigilli mei appositione corroboraui . Hiis testibus . Conano sacrista Linc' 7 Nicholao de Hainton' capellanis . [9]Willelmo[9] rectore ecclesie de Tuxford' . Petro de Bekering' . Adam de Brigeford' . Petro de Cheuermund'[10] . Ricardo de Neuport . Rogero Camerario . Ricardo Abbe[11] . Petro de Estgate . 7 aliis.

Facsimile.

Endorsed: (1) xxxv (13 cent.). (2) +. (3) Confirmatio Roberti Camerarii de .j. tofto . 7 .j. Bouata terre in Snelleslund' (13 cent.). (4) .j.

Fragment of seal on tag: probably round with diameter about 1½ inches, green; device probably a bird,

ERTI CA

Size: 5¼ x 6¼ inches.

Marginalia in A: Confirmatio.

Texts: MS—Orig. Dij/87/1/36. A378A (by Q2) 402. R1481.

Var. R.: [1] Bertram A378A *and* 402 *and* R. [2] Snelleslound A378A. [3] filius R. [4] altera R. [5] Fulnettby A378A *and* 402: Fulneteby R. [6] Clakesdale A402 *and* R. [7] Sturnedale A378A *and* R. [8] Kyrke furlang A402. [9]–[9] R *omits.* [10] Cheuermound A378A. [11] Albe A378A *and* R. Albo A402.

379 and 422

1524. Grant by Helto (Hent) of Snelland, to the church of Lincoln and the Common, of a toft in Snelland. (Circa 1210.)

De uno tofto in Snelleslund. (A422 rubric.)

Notum sit tam presentibus quam futuris quod ego Hent de Stenleslund[1] dedi et concessi et hac presenti carta mea confirmavi deo et beate Marie et commune canonicorum Linc' ecclesie unum toftum in villa de Stnelleslund[2] qui iacet medius inter toftum Willelmi persone 7 toftum Hugonis de Merles . quem Reinerus[3] tenuit . qui porrigitur usque in finem longitudinis eorundem toftorum versus aquam in Wespart[4] . 7 versus orientem usque ad viam que est * inter eundem toftum et toftum Willelmi aduunculi[5] mei . in puram liberam et perpetuam elemosinam pro animabus patris mei et matris mee et omnium antecessorum[6] meorum . necnon 7 pro salute mea et omnium heredum meorum . Hanc autem terram ego et heredes mei warantizabimus predictis canonicis imperpetuum contra omnes homines . Et ut ista donatio firma permaneat ·/ hanc cartam sigilli mei appensione[7] corroboravi . Hiis testibus . Willelmo persona de Stnelleslund[8] . Hugone de Merle . Thoma clerico de Stnelleslund[9] . Galfrido filio Bertram . Willelmo filio Ivonis de Reresbi[10] . Joseph[11] filio Radulfi templarii . Thoma filio Willelmi persone . Serlone Ruffo de Linc' . Willelmo filio Heut' et multis aliis.

Marginalia in A: 422 (1) Snelleslund. (2) .j. toftum. 379 Snellesland.
Texts: MS—A422 *and* 379. R1479.
Var. R.: [1] Snelleslaund A379. Snelleslund R. [2] Snelleslound A379. Snellelund R. [3] Reynerus A379. [4] Westpart A379. Wespare R. [5] auunculi A379. [6] successorum A379. [7] apposicione A379. [8] Snelleslound' A379. Snelleslund' R. [9] Snelleslounde A379. Snelleslund R. [10] Reresby A379 *and* R. [11] *sic*: Josepho A379.

Note: Hent as given in A is a scribe's error for Heut, a contemporary variant spelling of Helto. Helto was dead before 1219, when a dispute arose between the Abbot of Barlings and Robert son of Helto over the advowson, which the Abbot pleaded had been given by charter to the Abbey since the presentation of the last rector, William, by Helto. The Abbot also produced the confirmation of Helto's grant by William bishop of Lincoln (Selden Society, vol. liii, no. 234). William must therefore have been instituted to Snelland before May, 1206. The Abbot won his case and James was instituted on his presentation in the tenth year of Hugh of Wells (L.R.S. iii, p. 175). Geoffrey son of Bertram and Hugh de Merle occur in 1202 (L.R.S. xxii, nos. 382 and 418).

*_Folio_ 72 (in no. 375).

Hdl. . 7 . 2 .

ADD. CHART.

1525. Grant by Roger, the dean, and the chapter of Lincoln, to John son of Geoffrey of Snelland, of the land in Snelland which they had of the gift of Geoffrey son of Bertram. (Before 1224.)

Vniuersis Christi fidelibus ad quos presens scriptum peruenerit :' Rogerus decanus 7 capitulum ecclesie Lincoln' salutem eternam in domino . Nouerit vniuersitas uestra nos concessisse 7 presenti carta nostra confirmasse Johanni filio Galfridi de Snelleslund' . vnum toftum in villa de Snelleslund' quod Willelmus frater Bertram tenuit . 7 vnam bouatam terre in territorio eiusdem ville :' continentem decem acras terre arabilis ex una parte ville . 7 decem ex alia . Scilicet quinque acras que iacent proxime curie eiusdem Galfridi uersus occidentem . 7 quatuor acras que abutissant super diuisam de Fulneteb' . 7 vnam acram in Clackesdale . que iacet proxima terre que fuit Radulfi . de Hoiland' . 7 duas acras in Lund de accremento . Item ex alia parte ville . duas acras 7 dimidiam in Gosdam . ex parte occidentali de Scuruedale :' quatuor acras . ex parte occidentali de Mor gate :' vnam acram . in Kÿrkefurlang . duas acras . 7 dimidiam . 7 vnam acram prati in West eng . Habenda 7 tenenda de nobis cum pertinentiis eidem Johanni 7 cuicunque assignauerit exceptis viris religiosis 7 Iudeis :' in feodo 7 hereditate libere 7 quiete . Reddendo inde nobis per annum duos solidos . pro omni seruitio 7 exaccione . Scilicet duodecim denarios ad Pascha . 7 duodecim denarios ad festum sancti Michaelis . In huius autem concessionis robur 7 testimonium :' presens scriptum sigilli nostri appositione corroborauimus.

Endorsed: Snelleslund' (13 cent.).
Fragment of second seal of the Chapter on tag (see vol. ii, frontispiece, and p. 343 above).

IA PLE

Size: 6 x 4⅜ inches.
Text: MS—Orig. Dij/87/1/34.
Note: Roger had ceased to be dean in 1224. John son of Geoffrey seems to have been the son of Geoffrey son of Bertram.

380

1526. A duplicate of 356 which is printed at no. 1459 above.

LUDFORD

381 and 397

1527. Grant by Henry son of Thomas of Duggleby [in Kirkby Grindalythe par., Co. York], to the church of Lincoln and the Common, of half a toft in Ludford. (Circa 1210–1215.)

De dimidio tofto in Lufford (A397 rubric).

Sciant presentes 7 futuri quod ego Henricus filius Thome de Diuekelbi[1] :' dedi 7 concessi 7 presenti carta mea confirmaui deo 7 beate Marie 7 commune canonicorum Lincoln' ecclesie :' medietatem illius tofti uersus orientem in quo mansit Bertram . 7 post eum Goda uxor eius .ʼ in villa de Lufford'[2] . Habendam 7 tenendam cum pertinentiis in liberam puram 7 perpetuam elemosinam . liberam solutam 7 quietam ab omni seculari seruitio 7 exaccione Et ego Henricus 7 heredes mei warentizabimus predictis canonicis prenominatam tofti medietatem . defendemus 7 adquietabimus erga omnes homines inperpetuum .ʼ cum suis pertinentiis . In huius autem rei robur 7 testimonium .ʼ presens scriptum sigilli mei appositione corroboraui . Hiis testibus . Conano . Rumfaro 7 Waltero capellanis . Sẏmone[3] de Cancia[4] . Willelmo de Midlei[5] . Ricardo de Humberstain[6] . Petro de Cheuermund'[7] . Roberto Blundo de Lincoln' . Philippo Hors . Johanne presbitero . Symone[8] de Torp' . Hugone . 7 Benedicto . 7 aliis.

Endorsed: (1) +. (2) xiiij. (13 cent.). (3) Henricus filius Thome dat unam medietatem cuiusdam tofti in Lufford' (13 cent.). (4) +. (5) .xxij. (13 cent.). (6) .xxij. (13 cent.).

Tag for seal. Size: 6 x 5⅝ inches.

Marginalia in A: 381 Lufford (13 cent.). Ludford (16 cent.). 397. Luford'. dimidium toftum.

Texts: MS—Orig. Dij/83/1/36. A381 (by Q2). 397. R1456.

Var. R.: [1] Diuekesby R. [2] Lutheford R. [3] Simone R. [4] Kantia A397. [5] Midley A381 *and* R. [6] Humberstaẏn R. [7] Cheuermound'A381 *and* R. [8] Simone A381 *and* R.

Note: The first, third, fourth, sixth, seventh and thirteenth witnesses all attest a charter which cannot be later than 1219 (*see* vol. iv, no. 1305 above).

Add. Chart.

1528. Grant by Andrew son of William of Welton, to Jocelin son of Bertram of Ludford, of three bovates of land and a toft in Ludford, for a render of forty pence at the feast of St. Martin, thirty-one and a half pence at Easter, and forty pence at Pentecost. (Late twelfth century.)

Sciant presentes 7 futuri quod ego Andreas filius Willelmi de Welletona dedi 7 concessi 7 hac presenti carta mea confirmaui Goselino filio Bertram de Luddeford 7 heredibus suis[1] in uilla de Ludford[2] . tres bouatas terre 7 unum toftum cum omnibus pertinentiis . illi 7 heredibus suis tenendas de me 7 de heredibus meis libere 7 quiete pro omni seculari seruitio reddendo annuatim michi uel heredibus meis ad festum sancti Martini .xl. denarios . et ad Pascha .xxxi. denarios . 7 obolum . et ad Pentecosten . xl. denarios . Et ego Andreas 7 heredes mei warantizabimus totam predictam terram predicto Goselino 7 heredibus suis in perpetuum contra omnes homines . Hiis testibus . domino Roberto de Greli . Ricardo de Stures . Thoma de Sotbi . Willelmo filio

Gilberti de Ludford . Gilberto filio Alani clerici . 7 Aufredo fratre suo . Willelmo filio Gosse. Willelmo filio Ricardi . 7 Jocio fratre suo . Willelmo de Welletun' . 7 aliis.

No ancient endorsement.
Fragment of seal on tag :—round, green, a conventional device
SIGILL' . . . .

Size : 7⅜ x 3½ inches.
Text : MS—Orig. Dij/83/1/38.
Var. R. : [1] An erasure about an inch in length. [2] An erasure about half an inch in length.

Note : The hand is an early one and suggests a date not later than 1200. Robert de Grelley was aged eleven in 1185 (H. and K. F. ii, p. 251) : in 1212 he held land in Nettleton and Bigby (*Book of Fees*, i, p. 157) and the vill of Swineshead (*ibid.*, p. 194). Richard de Sturs occurs circa 1200 (*see* vol. iv, no. 1236 above). Thomas of Sotby and William of Ludford occur in 1202 (L.R.S. xxii, nos. 1456 and 656).

ADD. CHART.

1529. Grant by Henry son of Thomas of Duggleby to the church of Lincoln and the Common, of Joce son of Bertram his *nativus*, with his issue and chattels. (Circa 1200–1210.)

Omnibus Christi fidelibus ad quos presens scriptum peruenerit ∴ Henricus filius Thome de Diuegilb'[1] salutem . Noueritis me dedisse 7 concessisse 7 presenti carta mea confirmasse deo 7 beate Marie 7 commune canonicorum Lincoln' ecclesie Jocium filium Bertram de Lufford'[2] natiuum meum cum tota sequela sua 7 cum omnibus catallis suis in puram 7 perpetuam elemosinam liberum solutum 7 quietum de me 7 heredibus meis inperpetuum pro salute anime mee 7 pro animabus omnium antecessorum 7 successorum [3]meorum . Et[3] ego 7 heredes mei warentizabimus eisdem canonicis predictum Jocium cum tota sequela sua 7 cum omnibus catallis suis ∴ contra omnes homines inperpetuum . In huius autem rei robur 7 testimonium presens scriptum sigilli mei appositione corroboraui . Hiis testibus . Willelmo de Cancia . Roberto de Stowe clerico . Willelmo filio Willelmi de Malbertorp'[4] . Roberto Blundo de Lincoln' . Willelmo pistore de Lincoln' . Radulfo Stampard'[5] . [3]de Linc'[3] . Philippo . 7 Petro clericis 7 aliis.

Endorsed : xiij. (13 cent.).
Tag for seal. Size : 8 x 2¾ inches.
Texts : MS—Orig. Dij/83/1/35. R1455.
Var. R. : [1] Diuegesby R. [2] Lutheford R. [3–3] R omits. [4] Malberthorp R. [5] Scampard R.

Note : Joce and Joscelin are probably identical although the grant by Andrew of Welton which seems to be made to a free man, has every appearance of being earlier than the grant of the *nativus* by Henry son of Thomas of Duggleby. This charter seems to be of the same date as no. 1527, which is a considerably later type of hand than 1528. One of the witnesses, Robert Blund, occurs in both no. 1527 and in no. 1529.

BENNIWORTH

382

1530. Grant by William son of Gilbert, lord of Benniworth, to the church of Lincoln and the Common, of a toft with a house thereon, with its appurtenances and trees in Benniworth. (1224–1242.)

Omnibus sancte matris ecclesie filiis ad quos presens scriptum peruenerit Willelmus filius Gilberti de Benigwrth[1] dominus ville de Benigwrth'[1] salutem . Noueritis me dedisse concessisse 7 hac presenti carta mea confirmasse deo 7 beate Marie 7 commune canonicorum Linc' ecclesie vnum toftum in Benigwrth'[1] cum domo in eodem tofto constructa cum omnibus pertinenciis suis 7 arboribus illud scilicet toftum quod Radulfus filius Bone aliquando tenuit 7 iacet inter toftum Brictiue . 7 toftum quod Gilbertus pater meus dedit dictis canonicis 7 extendit a via que est uersus aquilonem usque ad toftum Elye quod est uersus austrum * Tenendum 7 habendum in puram 7 perpetuam elemosinam liberam 7 quietam ab omni seruicio . 7 exaccione seculari . Et ego 7 heredes mei warantizabimus 7 defendemus dictum toftum cum pertinenciis tanquam puram 7 perpetuam elemosinam liberam 7 quietam ab omni seruicio 7 exaccione dictis canonicis contra omnes[2] in perpetuum . 7 in huius rei robur 7 testimonium huic scripto media iuramenti interposicione sigillum meum apposui . Hiis testibus Elya succentore . Philippo de Tumba . Adam de Feretro . [3]Abraham[3] . Ricardo . Willelmo de Alta Ripa . Johanne de Nettelton' 7 Ricardo [3]de[3] Louneh'[4] capellanis . Johanne de Sancto Edwardo . Roberto Scoto . Gilberto vicario . Gilberto clerico . 7 aliis.

Marginalia in A: (1) Beningwrth. (2) Benyngworth.
Texts: MS—A. R 1457.
Var. R.: [1] Beningworth R. [2] R *adds* homines. [3] R *omits*. [4] Louueth' R.
Note: William of Benniworth succeeded his father about 1224. He was alive in 1239, but seems to have been succeeded by his son Geoffrey before 1242 (H and K.F., ii, pp. 135–6). Elias is not known to have become succentor before 1223–4.

* *Folio* 72*d*.

383 and 425

1531. Grant by William of Benniworth, son of Gilbert of Benniworth, to the church of Lincoln and the Common, of a bovate with pasture in Benniworth. (1224–1242: possibly before 1235.)

De .i. bovata terre cum pertinenciis in Beningwrth (A 425 rubric).

Omnibus Christi fidelibus ad quos presens scriptum pervenerit ∴ Willelmus de Benigwrd'[1] filius Gilberti de

Benigwrd'[2] salutem . Noveritis me dedisse ⁊ hac presenti carta mea confirmasse . deo ⁊ beate Marie ⁊ commune canonicorum Linc' ecclesie in puram ⁊ perpetuam elemosinam unam bovatam terre arabilis in teritorio de Benigwrd'[1] . cum communi pastura ubique in campis et aliis aisiamentis infra villam et extra cum omnibus pertinenciis [3]suis[3] . Illam videlicet bovatam terre[4] quam Arnisius[5] Harald filius Walteri Harald quondam [6]tenuit[6] . in predicto teritorio . Hanc donacionem feci eis pro salute anime mee ⁊ patris mei ⁊ antecessorum meorum . Et ego Willelmus predictus et heredes mei warantizabimus defendemus ⁊ acquietabimus prefate ecclesie ⁊ prefatis canonicis prefatam bovatam terre cum omnibus pertinentiis suis contra omnes homines imperpetuum . Hiis testibus domino Philippo de Benigword'[2] milite . Hugone Munne[7] . Willelmo de Manneby [6]Radulfo filio Thome[6] . Radulfo filio Bone . Michaele de Staintone[8] . Thoma filio Alicie . Alano de Beckefeld[9] Berengario filio Hugonis et aliis.

Marginalia in A: 425 Benigworthe.
Texts: MS—A425. 383. R 1458.
Var. R.: [1] Benigwrth' A383. Beningworth R. [2] Benigwrth' A383. Benigworth' R. [3]–[3] A383 *omits*. [4] A383 *adds* arrabilis. [5] Harnisius A383. [6]–[6] R *omits*. [7] Musse A383. [8] Staynstun' A383. Staynton R. [9] Betefeld R.
Note: This charter is in the hand of the Continuator, and it therefore seems probable that it may have been granted before 1235. The hand is circa 1225–35.

Folio 73 (after no. 383).
Hdl. . 7 . 3.

398

1532. Grant by Gilbert of Benniworth, to the church of Lincoln and the Common, of a piece of land in Benniworth. (Early thirteenth century.)

De quadam porcione terre in Beningworthe. (A rubric.)

Vniuersis sancte matris ecclesie filiis ad quos presens scriptum peruenerit ⸵ Gilebertus de Benigwrdhe salutem . Nouerit uniuersitas uestra me dedisse ⁊ concessisse ⁊ hac presenti carta mea confirmasse deo ⁊ beate Marie ⁊ commune canonicorum Lincoln' ecclesie pro salute anime mee ⁊ omnium antecessorum meorum in puram ⁊ perpetuam elemosinam terram quandam in Beningwrthe duarum perticarum ⁊ octo pedum in latitudine uersus septemtrionalem partem . versus meridiem trium perticarum . ⁊ sex pedum . ⁊ quindecim perticarum in longitudine . illam uidelicet que iacet proxima tofto Henrici filii Hugonis presbiteri ex orientali parte . Tenendam ⁊ habendam imperpetuum . libere ⁊ quiete ab omni seculari seruitio ⁊ exaccione . Ego autem predictus Gilebertus ⁊ heredes mei warantizabimus predictam terram prefate commune contra omnes homines . Hiis testibus. Thoma de Muletun . Alano fratre eius . Roberto de Bussaihe . Rogero de Stikeswold . Roberto de Canuilla . Waltero Blundo iuniore . Eudone preposito . ⁊ aliis.

Marginalia : (1) Beningworth'. (2) portio cuiusdam terre.
Text : MS—A.
Note : Gilbert of Benniworth was holding land in the early thirteenth century (H. and K.F., ii, p. 135). He had succeeded his father Roger before 1189 : he died before 1224 (H. and K.F., ii, pp. 179–80). Eudo was provost in the late twelfth and early thirteenth centuries (*see* vol. iv, p. 283). Walter Blund witnesses with him (*see* nos. 1332, 1333 in vol. iv, above). Thomas of Moulton occurs frequently 1202–1209 (L.R.S. xxii, 395, 1147, etc.). The probable date of this charter is circa 1200.

399

1533. Grant by Bona daughter of Ralf of Benniworth, to the church of Lincoln and the Common, of a toft and half a bovate in Benniworth. (Circa 1200.)

De .j. tofto . ⁊ dimidia in Beningworth'.* (A rubric.)

Vniuersis sancte matris ecclesie filiis ad quos presens scriptum peruenerit .· Bona filia Radulfi de Beningwrth salutem . Nouerit uniuersitas uestra me dedisse ⁊ concessisse ⁊ hac presenti carta mea confirmasse deo ⁊ beate Marie ⁊ commune canonicorum Lincoln' ecclesie in puram ⁊ perpetuam elemosinam pro salute anime mee ⁊ antecessorum meorum unum toftum continens in latitudine quinque percatas ⁊ quatuor pedes . ⁊ in longitudine sicut iacet iuxta ecclesiam Omnium Sanctorum ex parte orientali . ⁊ vnam dimidiam bouatam terre in territorio de Beningword . Scilicet ex occidentali parte uille . vnam selionem super Pesholm . ⁊ unam selionem inter uias . ⁊ unam selionem super Stokesdale . ⁊ unam selionem super Farwelles . ⁊ unam selionem super Scardaile ex australi parte uie ⁊ unam selionem super Pantune gate . ⁊ unam selionem iuxta uiam Linc' apud Hamme . ⁊ unam perticatam iuxta toftum Radulfi filii Thome .· uersus North . ⁊ totum pratum pertinens ad terram que fuit Ernaldi filii Radulfi in Reinerbuc . ⁊ duas perticatas prati in Northeng . ex transuerso Rubergtunge . Et ex orientali parte uille unam selionem super Scortruberge ⁊ unam perticatam ex parte orientali uille ex transuerso uia de Duningtuna . ⁊ unam selionem in Thormedoholmdale . scilicet heuedland . ⁊ unam selionem apud Simundesti . ⁊ unam selionem apud Grenedic . ⁊ unam perticatam ex transuerso Kitehou . ⁊ unam perticatam ad caput de Skitehov . ⁊ unam perticatam apud Steinwellebech . ⁊ unam perticatam apud Aluerhou . ⁊ septem pedes in latitudine super Witehille cum communi pastura ubique in campis . ⁊ aliis aisiamentis infra uillam ⁊ extra uillam . Et ut hec donatio ⁊ concessio rata ⁊ stabilis permaneat ∴ ne inposterum alicuius malignitate possit in irritum prouocari ∴ presentis scripti seriem sigilli mei attestatione corroboraui . Hiis testibus . Petro de Bekeringge . Nigello de Beninwrd . Willelmo nepote Warneri . Johanne fratre eius . Willelmo filio Warneri . Henrico filio Warini.

Marginalia : .j. toftum 7 dimidiam bovatam.
Text : MS—A.
Note : Peter of Beckering occurs 1190 and in the late twelfth century (Stenton, Danelaw Charters, pp. 6, 70) ; he occurs also in 1206 (L.R.S. xxii, no. 1451). William son of Warner and William *nepos* of Warner both occur among the chief citizens of Lincoln in 1206 (*ibid.*, no. 1448).

* *Folio* 76.

Hdl. Wraghou . 7 . 6 .

400

1534. Confirmation by Gilbert of Benniworth of the toft and land mentioned in preceding charter. (Circa 1200.)

Confirmatio terre eiusdem. (A rubric.)

Universis sancte matris ecclesie filiis ad quos presens scriptum pervenerit Gilebertus de Beningwrd salutem . Noverit universitas vestra me concessisse 7 hac presenti carta confirmasse deo 7 beate Marie 7 commune canonicorum Linc' ecclesie in puram 7 perpetuam elemosinam pro salute anime mee 7 omnium antecessorum meorum illam dimidiam bovatam terre cum tofto habentem in latitudine quinque percatas 7 quatuor pedes 7 cum omnibus pertinentiis 7 aisiamentis infra villam 7 extra villam . quam Ernaldus frater Bone de Benigwrd dedit Henrico filio Bone de Beningwrd . Cuius scilicet Henrici servitium eadem Bona deo 7 sancte Marie 7 predicto commune canonicorum contulit in elemosinam . Hanc autem elemosinam 7 concessionem deo 7 predicte ecclesie collatam ego 7 heredes mei warantizabimus eis contra omnes homines . Et ut hec concessio rata 7 stabilis permaneat ∴ eam sigilli mei attestatione corroboravi . Hiis testibus . Petro de Bekering . Nigello de Beningwrd . Willelmo nepote Warneri . Johanne fratre eius . Willelmo filio Warneri . Jordano filio Suaue . 7 multis aliis.

Marginalia : Confirmatio.
Text : MS—A.

Add. Chart.

1535. Grant by R., the dean, and the chapter of Lincoln, to Henry son of Bona of Benniworth, of a toft and half a bovate in Benniworth which they had of the gift of the said Bona. For this Henry shall pay twelve pence yearly. (Before 1224.)

Vniuersis sancte matris ecclesie filiis ad quos presens scriptum peruenerit R. decanus ⁊ capitulum Lincoln' ecclesie salutem . Nouerit vniuersitas vestra[1] concessisse ⁊ hac presenti carta nostra confirmasse Henrico filio Bone de Benyngworth ⁊ heredibus suis . vnum toftum continens in latitudine quinque percatas ⁊ quatuor pedes ⁊ in longitudine sicut iacet iuxta ecclesiam Omnium Sanctorum ex parte orientali ⁊ vnam dimidiam bouatam terre in territorio Benyngwrd quam predicta Bona mater predicti Henrici contulit deo ⁊ beate Marie ⁊ commune canonicorum in elemosinam . pro salute anime sue ⁊ antecessorum suorum cum omnibus pertinenciis ⁊ communi pastura vbique in campis ⁊ aliis eisiamentis infra villam ⁊ extra . villam sicut carta predicte Bone matris predicti Henrici testatur . Tenend' de nobis libere ⁊ quiete ⁊ honorifice sibi ⁊ heredibus suis in puram ⁊ perpetuam elemosinam Reddendo nobis annuatim pro omni seruicio seculari exaccione duodecim denarios scilicet sex denarios . ad Pascha ⁊ vj denarios ad festum sancti Michaelis Et ut hec nostra concessio rata ⁊ stabilis perseueret ne in posterum alicuius contrauersia possit in irritum prouocari eam sigilli nostri attestacione communimus &c.[2]

Marginalia: (1) Benyngworth. (2) Robertus Scamelesby iam tenet . ⁊ tenet unam bovatam terre et .i. mesuagium reddendo pro eisdem eciam xii[d] que fuerunt Johannis Donyngton' . ⁊ Roberti Otteby.

Text: MS—R 1460 (in the margin in a 15th century hand).

Var. R.: [1] *sic* nos *presumably omitted*. [2] *sic*.

Note: Although this gift survives only in transcript it seems reasonable to assume that the dean is Roger de Rolveston, since the grant of Bona's gift, to be held by her son, would probably be made shortly after the gift itself.

ADD. CHART.

1536. Grant by Roger, the dean, and the chapter of Lincoln, to master William of Benniworth, the subdean, of the toft and croft in Benniworth, which they had of the gift of Geoffrey son of William of Benniworth. For this master William shall give each year for all service a wax candle of a pound's weight to burn on the high altar of the church of Lincoln. (1241–1243.)

[Omnibus Christi] fidelibus ad quos presens scriptum peruenerit . Rogerus decanus ⁊ capitulum Linc' ecclesie salutem in domino . Nouerit [universitas vestra] nos dedisse . ⁊ hac presenti carta nostra confirmasse . dilecto fratri . ⁊ concanonico [nostro] magistro Willelmo de Bening[worth] . . . . ⁊ assignatis suis quoddam toftum nostrum cum crofto . in villa de Beningwrthe cum omnibus [pertinenciis suis] . . . . [f]ilius Roberti quondam tenuit . qui scilicet fuit pater domini

Walteri abbatis de Bardeneẏa [quod toftum habuimus ex d]ono Galfridi filii Willelmi de Beningwirth' . Tenendum ⁊ habendum dicto magistro Willelmo de Benigworth . . . . [subde]cano ⁊ assignatis suis . libere . integre . ⁊ pacifice in perpetuum . Reddendo inde singulis annis nobis . . . . beate virginis Marie . vnum cereum vnius libre ardentem super magnum altare Lincolniens' ecclesie . . . . mor . . . . omni seruicio . exaccione . ⁊ demanda seculari . Et in huius rei robur ⁊ testimonium presens scriptum [sig]illi nostri munimine duximus roborandum . Testibus Ricardo de Wẏsebech' . Thoma de Askebẏ canonicis Linc' ecclesie . Radulpho de Ver . Henrico sacrista . Elẏa succentore . Roberto Basset . Ricardo de Stretton' . Johanne filio Fulconis.

No ancient endorsement.

Seal on parchment tag. An almost perfect specimen of the second chapter seal (*see* vol. ii frontispiece and p. 343 above), in green wax.

Obverse + SIGILLUM CAP . . . . LINCOLNIENSIS ECCLESIE
Reverse + AVE MARIA GRACIA PLENA DOMINUS TECUM

Size : $8\frac{3}{8}$ x $3\frac{1}{2}$ inches.

Text: MS—Orig. Dij/66/3/26.

Var. R. : *The charter is much damaged and the words in square brackets have been supplied conjecturally.*

Note : The dates given are those of Roger de Weseham as dean. William of Benniworth became sub-dean of the cathedral in 1231. The abbot of Bardney is Walter of Benniworth 1241–3 (V.C.H. Lincs. ii, p. 103).

KIRMOND LE MIRE

384 and 395

1537. Grant by Alan son of Alfred of Kirmond le Mire, to the church of Lincoln and the Common, of the third part of his toft, croft, garden and meadow in Kirmond le Mire. (Circa 1210–1220.)

Confirmatio de eadem. (A 395 rubric.)

Sciant presentes ⁊ futuri quod ego Alanus filius Aluredi de Cheuermund dedi ⁊ concessi ⁊ presenti carta mea confirmaui deo ⁊ beate Marie ⁊ commune canonicorum Linc' ecclesie terciam partem tofti mei ⁊ crofti ⁊ gardini ex parte aquilonali proximam tofto Alani filii sacerdotis . in quo quidem tofto ego mansi . ⁊ terciam partem prati mei similiter . versus aquilonem . quod iacet subtus croftum meum versus orientem inter duos riuuolos . Habenda ⁊ tenenda integre ⁊ plenarie cum omnibus pertinenciis suis in puram ⁊ perpetuam elemosinam liberam[1] solutam ⁊ quietam ab omni seculari servitio . consuetudine ⁊ exactione . Et ego Alanus et heredes mei memoratis canonicis prenominatam terciam partem tofti[2] . crofti . gardini . ⁊ prati integre ⁊ plenarie cum pertinenciis[3] warentizabimus defendemus ⁊ adquietabimus erga omnes homines imperpetuum . In huius[4] autem rei robur ⁊ testimonium .˒ presens scriptum sigilli mei apposicione corroboraui . Hiis testibus . Conano sacrista . Rumfaro ⁊ Waltero capellanis . Alano diacono . Ricardo de Humberstain[5] . Alano persona de Cheuermund . Roberto fratre eius . Petro clerico de Cheuermund . Alano filio Rogeri capellani . Hugone de Toppeclive[6] . Philippo Hors . Johanne . Alexandro . ⁊ Benedicto ⁊ aliis.

Marginalia : in A395 De eadem. In A384 Cheuermond'.
Texts : MS—A395, 384. R 1465.
Var. R. : [1] A384 *has* in puram *with cancellation marks below.* [2] A384 *adds* ⁊. [3] A384 *adds* suis. [4] A384 *has* cuius. [5] Humberstayn A384 *and* R. [6] Toppeclif A384.
Note : For the dates of Conan as sacrist *see* vol. iv, p. 281, above.

385 and 394

1538. Confirmation by Alan de Scrutevill', to the church of Lincoln and the Common, of the third part of the toft, croft, garden and meadow in Kirmond le Mire formerly held of him by Alan son of Alfred of Kirmond. (Circa 1210–1220.)

De tercia parte unius tofti in Cheuermont' (A 394 rubric).

Omnibus Christi fidelibus ad quos presens scriptum pervenerit .˒ Alanus de Scrutevill[1] salutem . Noveritis me dedisse ⁊ concessisse ⁊ presenti carta mea confirmasse deo ⁊ beate Marie ⁊ commune canonicorum Lincolniensis ecclesie terciam partem tofti ⁊ crofti ⁊ gardini ⁊ prati subtus croftum quod Alanus filius Aluredi aliquando tenuit de me in villa de Cheuermund . Illam scilicet partem versus aquilonem proximam[2] tofto Alani filii sacerdotis . Habendam ⁊ tenendam cum omnibus pertinenciis suis in puram ⁊ perpetuam elemosinam liberam solutam ⁊ quietam ab omni seculari servitio ⁊ exacione pro salute anime mee ⁊ pro animabus omnium antecessorum ⁊ successorum meorum . Hanc autem predictam terram cum pertinenciis ego Alanus ⁊ heredes mei warantizabimus eisdem canonicis contra omnes homines inperpetuum . Ut igitur hec mea donatio firma ⁊ stabilis permaneat .˒ eam presenti scripto ⁊ sigilli mei appositione corroboravi . Hiis testibus . Conano . Rumfaro ⁊ Waltero capellanis . Roberto de Campuilla[3] . Henrico de Houton .˒ Willelmo de Scruteluill[4] .˒ Alano persona de Cheuermund . Roberto fratre eius . Petro de Cheuermund clerico . Alano filio Rogeri capellani . Philippo Hors . Johanne . Benedicto . Alexandro[5] ⁊ aliis.

Marginalia in A : 394 (1) Keuremund. (2) iii*a* pars unius tofti. 385 Ceuermund.
Texts : A 394 and 385. R 1467.
Var. R. : [1] Strutevillis A385. Stuteuill' R. [2] proximo (*sic*) in R. [3] Campvill' A385. Campuill' R. [4] *sic* : Scruteuill A385. Stuteuill R. [5] Alexander (*sic*) A385.

386 and 396

1539. Renewal by Emma widow of Alan son of Alfred, before the dean and canons of Lincoln, of the release and quitclaim of all her right and claim in the land mentioned in the two preceding charters which she had sought as dower by writ of the lord king. For this quitclaim the dean and chapter have given her four marks of silver. (Circa 1220.)

Quieta clamacio de eadem (A 396 rubric).

Sciant presentes ⁊ futuri quod ego Emma quondam uxor Alani filii Aluredi* de Cheuermund in libera viduitate mea remisi ⁊ quietum clamaui in comitatu Linc' decano et canonicis[1] Linc' totum ius ⁊ clamium quod habui vel habere possem in quadam terra[2] in villa de Cheuermund quam predictus Alanus quondam vir meus eisdem canonicis contulit in elemosinam perpetuo possidendam . Videlicet in tercia parte tofti ⁊ crofti ⁊ gardini ⁊ prati subtus croftum quod aliquando fuit eiusdem Alani illam scilicet partem versus aquilonalem proximam tofto Alani filii sacerdotis . De qua quidem tercia parte petebam rationabilem partem meam nomine dotis per breue domini Regis . Et eandem remissionem et quietam clamacionem innouaui coram eodem capitulo Linc' ⁊ ibidem totum ius ⁊ clamium quod in eadem terra petebam tactis sacrosanctis euangeliis abiuraui . Pro hac autem remissione ⁊ quieta clamantia[3] dederunt mihi prefati decanus ⁊ capitulum Linc' quatuor solidos argenti . In huius igitur [4]rei robur[4] ⁊ testimonium presenti scripto sigillum meum apposui . Testibus . Thoma de Norton' . Henrico de Torpell ∴ Helya capellanis . Osberto . Rogero de Neuport . Widone de Keles' clericis . Alano filio sacerdotis.

Marginalia in A: 396 De eadem.

Texts: A 396 and 386. R 1466.

Var. R.: [1] capitulo A386. [2] terram (*sic*) in A386. [3] quieta clamacione R. [4–4] A386 *omits*.

Note: This charter must be later than no. 1537 above, but the witnesses suggest that it is not much later than 1220. *Cf.* no. 1147 in vol. iv, above, which cannot be later than 1219 and is witnessed by Thomas of Norton, Henry de Torpell and Roger of Newport: also no. 1132 which must be earlier than 1224. An Alan of Kirmond occurs in 1219 (Selden Society, liii, no. 8), but he seems to be more probably Alan son of Robert, than the husband of Emma.

**Folio* 75*d*.

Hdl. Wraghou.

387

1540. Grant by Alan son of Robert of Kirmond le Mire, to the church of Lincoln and the Common, of a bovate and a toft in Kirmond le Mire, which he had of the gift of the lord Hugh de Malebisse. (Circa 1230.)

Omnibus Christi fidelibus ad quos presens scriptum peruenerit . Alanus filius Roberti de Keuermund salutem Noueritis me dedisse . concessisse 7 hac presenti carta mea confirmasse deo 7 beate Marie 7 commune canonicorum Linc' ecclesie vnam bouatam terre in territorio de Keuermund cum vno tofto ad illam partem[1] . Quam quidem bouatam [2]terre[2] habui de dono [3]de[3] domini Hugonis de Malisbyse[4] 7 iacet ex parte aquilonali cuiusdam alius * bouate quam habui de dono eiusdem Hugonis . Tenendum 7 habendum dictis decano 7 canonicis in puram 7 perpetuam elemosinam liberam 7 quietam ab omni seruicio 7 exaccione seculari cum omnibus pertinenciis suis libertatibus 7 asyamentis infra villam 7 extra . Et ego 7 heredes mei defendemus 7 warantizabimus totum prefatum tenementum cum suis pertinenciis [3]suis[3] 7 libertatibus prefatis decano 7 canonicis contra omnes homines inperpetuum . Et ad hoc fideliter tenendum ego pro me 7 heredibus meis tactis sacrosanctis ewangeliis corporale prestiti sacramentum . Et insuper presens scriptum sigillo meo confirmaui . Hiis testibus . Johanne capellano de Keuermund . Thoma persona de Parua Luford'[5] . Rogero carpentario de Keuermund' . Petro de Hauley . Hugone de Burgo . Roberto Musters de Wllingham . Reinero de Stoteley[6] . Hugone de Helewelle . Radulfo filio Thome de Benigwrth[7] 7 aliis.

Marginalia in A: Ceuermond'.
Texts: MS—A (by Q2) R 1470.
Var. R.: [1] *sic*: pertinente R. [2–2] R *omits.* [3–3] *sic*: R. *omits.* [4] Malebise R. [5] Lutheford R. [6] Scoteby R. [7] Beningworthe R.
Note: Alan son of Robert of Kirmond levied a fine with Hugh Malbisse concerning two bovates of land in Kirmond 30th September, 1226 (*Final Concords*, i, pp. 193–4) and another with Richard de Scrotevill' on 8th July, 1230 (*ibid.*, p. 225). Thomas rector of Little Ludford witnessed a charter of Thomas de Scoteni to Sixle between 1228 and 1232 (L.R.S. xviii, p. 11). He had ceased to be rector 1238–9 when his successor William of Kelstern was instituted (L.R.S. xi, p. 35).

* *Folio* 73*d*.

ADD. CHART.

1541. Note that William Suth of Kirmond le Mire now holds the third part of the croft, toft, garden and meadow in Kirmond which the chapter had of the gift of Alan son of Alfred, for a yearly render of sixpence. (Early fourteenth century.)

Memorandum quod Willelmus Suth de Keuermund tenet terciam partem vnius crofti / tofti / gardini 7 prati subtus croftum quod capitulum habuit ex dono Alani filii Alueredi in Keuermund prout carte supra scripte testantur . Reddendo annuatim sex denarios ad Pentecostem sicut satis apparet per cartam capituli ostensam in curia per dictum Willelmum qui eam habet.

Text: MS—R 1468.
This note is apparently about the same period as the compilation of the cartulary: the charter referred to is no. 1538 of this edition.

Add. Chart.

1542. Note that William Suth of Kirmond holds the six acres of land in the charter immediately above written (no. 1540 above). (Early fourteenth century.)

Memorandum quod Willelmus Suth de Keuermund tenet sex acras terre de quibus sit mencio in carta proxima prescripta . Reddendo inde annuatim sex denarios prout per cartam quam inde ostendit in curia dictus Willelmus satis apparet.

Text: MS—R 1469.

388

1543. A duplicate of 409 which is printed at 1565 below.

389

1544. A duplicate of 370a which is printed at 1495 above.

390

1545. This charter related to Hainton and is printed at 1503a above.

391

1546. This charter relates to Hainton and is printed at 1502 above.

392

1547. A duplicate of 373a which is printed at 1498 above.

393

1548. A duplicate of 375b which is printed at 1501 above.

394

1549. A duplicate of 385 which is printed at 1538 above.

395

1550. A duplicate of 384 which is printed at 1537 above.

396

1551. A duplicate of 386 which is printed at 1539 above.

397

1552. A duplicate of 381 which is printed at 1527 above.

LISSINGTON

403

1553. Grant by Beatrice Flury, to the church of Lincoln and the Common, of a toft, four acres of arable land in Lissington and two acres of meadow in Lissingleys. (Circa 1200.)

De .i. tofto .iiij^{or}. acris terre . ⁊ ij. acris prati in Lissingtona. (A rubric.)

Omnibus Christi fidelibus ad quos presens scriptum peruenerit . Beatricia Fluri[1] salutem . Sciatis me dedisse ⁊ concessisse ⁊ hac carta mea confirmasse ⸵ deo ⁊ beate Marie ⁊ commune canonicorum Linc' ecclesie ⸵ pro salute anime mee ⁊ pro animabus antecessorum meorum . vnum toftum in Lissington' . ⁊ quatuor acras terre arabilis cum pertinentiis .* ⁊ duas acras prati . in territorio eiusdem uille . Scilicet toftum quod Fulco de Bekering' tenuit quod jacet juxta toftum Gileberti Fluri[1] proximum apud occidentem . ⁊ .ij. acras terre ⸵ ex orientali parte uille que simul jacent super Blesebẏhill'[2] . iuxta terram Sẏmonis Legrant[3] apud orientem . ⁊ .ii. acras terre ex occidentali parte uille . scilicet .j. acram subtus Nortgate[4] ⸵ inter terram Roberti de Trihampton'[5] ⸵ ⁊ terram Gocelini filii Pagani . ⁊ dimidiam acram super Watheslanges[6] inter terram Johannis filii Helewisie ⁊ Amice de Lindewde[7] . ⁊ dimidiam acram super Thislilandes inter terram Roberti Giffard . ⁊ terram Amice de Lindewd'[8] . ⁊ duas [9]acras[9] prati in Lissinglea[10] . scilicet duas forensiores uersus orientem ⸵ in cultura Gileberti fratris mei . In puram ⁊ perpetuam elemosinam liberam ⁊ quietam de omni seculari seruicio ⁊ exactione . Ego uero . B. ⁊ heredes mei . warantizabimus predictam terram cum pertinentiis ⁊ cum prato ⸵ predictis canonicis ⸵ contra omnes homines . Hanc autem donationem ⁊ concessionem feci illis in libera potestate mea . Hiis testibus . Radulfo decano de Heinton'[11] . Eudone capellano . Heltone de Snelleslund' . Willelmo persona de Snellund'[12] . Gocelino filio Pagani . Roberto Giffard . Johanne filio sacerdotis de Lissigton'[13] . Henrico filio Jordani.[14]

Endorsed : (1) .v. (13 cent.). (2) Wraghou (13 cent.). (3) Lissinton' (13 cent.). (4) scribatur (? by Q). (5) xvi. (13 cent.).

Tag for seal. Size : 6 x 4½ inches.

Marginalia in A : (1) Lissingtona. (2) .j. toftum ⁊ .iiii. acras ⁊ .ii. prati.

Texts : MS—Orig. Dij/83/1/27. A. R 1459.

Var. R. : [1] Flurẏ R. [2] Belesbihill' A. [3] Le Grant A. Le Graunt R. [4] Northgate R. [5] Threhampton' R. [6] Wateslanges A. [7] Lindwode R. [8] Lindewde A. Lindwode R. [9–9] R *omits.* [10] Lissingleia R. [11] Haynton' R. [12] Snelleslund A. *and* R. [13] Lissington' A. *and* R. [14] Jordanis (*sic*) A.

Note : Beatrice daughter of Walter Flury brought an assise of novel disseisin against Gilbert Flury in 1202. She was apparently living in his house at that time, presumably unmarried (L.R.S. xxii, no. 477). Eudo witnesses the next charter as provost, an office which he held in the time of William of Blois as precentor 1196–1203. William the parson of Snelland was instituted before May, 1206, and died before 1219 (see note to no. 1524 above). Helto of Snelland occurs 1202 (L.R.S. xxii, no. 475).

* *Folio* 77.

Hdl. Wraghou. . 7 . . 7 .

404

1554. Confirmation of the preceding grant by Gilbert Flury, brother of Beatrice Flury. (Circa 1200.)

Confirmacio eiusdem. (A rubric.)

Omnibus Christi fidelibus ad quos presens scriptum peruenerit ∴ Gilebertus Fluri[1] salutem . Sciatis me concessisse 7 hac carta mea confirmasse deo 7 sancte Marie 7 commune canonicorum Linc' ecclesie .j. toftum in Lissington' . 7 quatuor acras terre arabilis . cum pertinentiis . 7 duas acras prati ∴ in territorio eiusdem uille . que ∴ Beatricia soror mea dedit eis . in puram 7 perpetuam elemosinam liberam 7 quietam ab omni seculari seruicio 7 exactione . prout carta sua quam eis inde contulit ∴ testatur . Ego uero Gilebertus 7 heredes mei) warantizabimus predictis canonicis predictam elemosinam contra omnes homines . Hiis testibus . Radulfo decano de Haintan'[2] . Eudone preposito . Heltone de Snelleslund[3] . Willelmo fratre suo . Gocelino filio Pagani . Roberto Giffard . Johanne filio sacerdotis . de Lissington' 7 Henrico filio Jordani.

Endorsed : xvij. (13 cent.).
Tag for seal. Size : 5½ x 3¼ inches.
Marginalia in A : Confirmatio.
Texts : MS—Orig. Dij/83/1/23. A. R 1461.
Var. R. : [1] Flury R. [2] Hainton A. Haynton R. [3] Snelleslunt A.

405

1555. Notification by Gilbert son of Herbert of Rigsby, that he has granted to the church of Lincoln and the Common, a toft and a bovate of land and a selion in Lissington which Robert Giffard held. He has also released and quitclaimed to the canons the aforesaid Robert Giffard with his homage. (Circa 1200.)

De . una bouata terre . 7 tofto in Lissingtona. (A rubric.)

Notum sit omnibus tam presentibus quam futuris quod ego Gilbertus filius Herberti[1] de Righesbi[2] dedi 7 concessi 7 presenti carta mea confirmaui deo 7 beate Marie 7 commune canonicorum Lincoln' ecclesie vnum toftum in Lissington' 7 vnam bouatam terre in territorio eiusdem ville . Illud scilicet toftum 7 illam bouatam ∴ que Robertus Giffard' tenuit in eadem villa . ⁊ preterea unum sellionem qui jacet inter terram que fuit eiusdem Roberti ⁊ terram Rannulfi filii Jocelini ex aquilonari parte domus ipsius Roberti . Habenda ⁊ tenenda cum omnibus pertinentiis suis in puram ⁊ perpetuam elemosinam . liberam solutam ⁊ quietam ab omni seculari seruitio ⁊ exaccione . Et ego ⁊ heredes mei warentizabimus predictis canonicis predictas terras cum pertinentiis contra omnes homines . ⁊ adquietabimus eas in omnibus inperpetuum erga omnes homines . Preter hec remisi ⁊ quietum clamaui dictum Robertum Giffard[3] ⁊ homagium ipsius predictis canonicis . Ita quod ipse Robertus ⁊ heredes ipsius quieti sint[4] de me ⁊ heredibus meis inperpetuum . In huius rei robur ⁊ testimonium ⁖ presens scriptum sigilli mei apposicione corroboraui . Hiis testibus . Petro de Bekering' . Willelmo de Baiocis . [5]Henrico de Colevill' . Ricardo de Blesebi . Adam de Baiocis[5] . Willelmo de Su*lenni . Galfrido de Torleia . Gilberto [5]Fluri . Johanne[5] filio sacerdotis de Lissinctona[6] . Roberto filio Galfridi de Lissincton'[7] . ⁊ aliis.

Endorsed : (1) xviij. (13 cent.). (2) .iiij. (13 cent.).
Tag for seal. Size : 6½ x 4 inches.
Marginalia in A : (1) Lissington'. (2) .j. bovat' cum tofto.
Texts : MS—Orig. Dij/83/1/25. A. R 1462.
Var. R. : [1] Hereberti A. [2] Rigesbi A. Riggesby R. [3] Giffardum A. [4] sunt A. [5]–[5] R *omits*. [6] Lissington' A *and* R. [7] Lissington' R.
Note : Gilbert of Rigsby was involved in a plea concerning the advowson of Lissington church in 1202 (L.R.S. xxii, no. 89). He was holding land in several places in Lincolnshire, Stallingburgh, Rigsby, Leverton and Leake, in 1212 (*Book of Fees*, ii, pp. 159, 162, 194). Peter of Bekering and William of Bayeux occur in 1202 (L.R.S. xxii, no. 38). Gilbert Flury and Robert Giffard occur in the preceding charter.

**Folio* 77*d*.

Hdl. WRAGHOU'.

406

1556. Grant by Robert Trihaunt, to the church of Lincoln and the Common, of a toft and two selions in Lissington. (Circa 1200.)

De .j. tofto . ⁊ .ij. sellionibus . in Lissington'. (A rubric.)

Vniuersis sancte matris ecclesie filiis ad quos presens scriptum peruenerit ⁖ Robertus Trihaunt[1] salutem . Nouerit uniuersitas uestra me dedisse ⁊ concessisse ⁊ hac presenti carta mea confirmasse deo ⁊ sancte Marie ⁊ commune Linc' ecclesie toftum quendam[2] in Lissingt' quem Walterus Tic tenuit de me iuxta Thomam capellanum . ⁊ duas selliones unam quam Walterus Tic tenuit in orientali parte in Ricroft[3] . ⁊ aliam in occidentali parte sub Norþgat[4] iuxta Sẏmonem magnum cum communi pastura eiusdem uille in puram ⁊

perpetuam elemosinam pro salute anime mee . ⁊ patris mei . ⁊ matris mee . ⁊ antecessorum meorum . ⁊ ego ⁊ heredes mei warantizabimus predictum toftum ⁊ predictas selliones contra omnes homines . Hiis testibus . Ricardo de Kẏm[5] . Rogero Scoto . Eudone preposito . Sẏmone de Kẏm[5] . Roberto Camerario . Willelmo Musteil[6] . Willelmo [7]filio[7] Hermeri . Gileberto Fluri[8] . Johanne magno . Waltero crasso . ⁊ multis aliis.

Endorsed: (1) .iij. (13 cent.). (2) Roberti de trehamtun (probably contemporary). (3) xv. (13 cent.).

Tag for seal. Size: 8 x 2½ inches.

Marginalia in A: (1) Lissington'. (2) .i. toftum . ⁊ .ii. sell'.

Texts: MS—Orig. 83/1/26. A. R 1463.

Var. R.: [1] Trihaunt' R. [2] quemdam R. [3] Ucroft A. Vcroft' R. [4] Northgat A. Northgat' R. [5] Kyme R. [6] Mustel R. [7–7] R *omits*. [8] Flury R.

Note: Robert Trihantun died between 25th November and 9th December, 1218 (Selden Society, liii, nos. 38 and 512). On the name of this family see *Early Yorkshire Charters*, vol. iv, *The Honour of Richmond*, ed. C. T. Clay, *intro.*, p. xxx. The attestation of Eudo the provost (*see* vol. iv, p. 283, above) with Richard of Kyme suggests a date about 1200 or shortly after.

407

1557. Grant by Nicholas son of Wigot of Linwood, to the church of Lincoln and the Common, of the toft and two selions granted in the preceding charter. (Circa 1210–1220.)

De .j. tofto . ⁊ .ij. sellionibus . in eadem. (A rubric.)

Sciant presentes ⁊ futuri quod ego Nicholaus filius Wẏgoti [1]de Lindewode[1] dedi ⁊ concessi ⁊ presenti carta mea confirmaui deo ⁊ beate Marie ⁊ commune canonicorum Lincoln' ecclesie . pro salute anime mee ⁊ pro animabus omnium antecessorum ⁊ successorum meorum ∴ vnum toftum in Lissington' quod Walterus Tic aliquando tenuit iuxta Thomam capellanum . ⁊ duos selliones in territorio eiusdem ville de Lissington' . vnum quem Walterus Tic tenuit in orientali parte in Riecroft[2] . ⁊ alium in occidentali parte subtus Northgate iuxta Sẏmonem magnum . Habend*um* ⁊ tenend*um* cum communi pastura eiusdem ville ⁊ cum omnibus pertinentiis libertatibus ⁊ aisiamentis infra villam ⁊ extra ∴ in liberam . puram . ⁊ perpetuam elemosinam . solutam ⁊ quietam ab omni seruitio seculari ⁊ exaccione . ⁊ ego Nicholaus ⁊ heredes mei warentizabimus prefatis canonicis terras prenominatas cum pertinentiis . defendemus ⁊ adquietabimus erga omnes homines imperpetuum . In huius autem rei robur ⁊ testimonium ∴ presenti scripto sigillum meum apposui . Hiis testibus . Thoma de Norton' capellano . Henrico de Torpell' . Sẏmone de Torp' . Willelmo de Baiocis . Ada de

Baiocis . Ricardo de Neuport . Wẏnemero . Petro de Cheuermund' . Ẏuone Harefot . Johanne Euge[3] ⁊ aliis.

Endorsed : (1) xx. (13 cent.). (2) .iii. (13 cent.).
Tag for seal Size : 6¾ x 3⅞ inches.
Marginalia in A : (1) Lissington'. (2) .j. toftum . ⁊ .ii. sell'.
Texts : MS—Orig. Dij/83/1/24. A. R 1464.
Var. R. : [1] R *omits*. [2] Ryecroft R. [3] *sic* : *often* Enge.
Note : The first, second, third, sixth, seventh, eighth and ninth witnesses attest a deed not later than 1219 (*see* vol. iv, no. 1147, above).

Add. Chart.

1558. Grant by Hugh the bearded, goldsmith, of Lincoln, to Amicia his granddaughter, of all the land in Lissington which Herbert Giffard her father, and later Hugh Giffard her brother had held of the mother church of Lincoln and had sold to Hugh the bearded. During her lifetime Christiana, Amicia's mother, shall enjoy two parts of the land, which on her death shall revert to the latter. A yearly render of twelvepence shall be paid to the mother church of Lincoln. (15th May, 1249–1265.)

Omnibus Christi fidelibus presens scriptum visuris uel audituris Hugo cum barba aurifaber de Linc' . salutem in domino . Nouerit uniuersitas uestra me in libera potestate mea dedisse . concessisse . ⁊ hac presenti carta mea confirmasse Amicie nepte mee ⁊ heredibus suis totam terram illam cum omnibus pertinentiis suis infra villam ⁊ extra que fuit Herberti Giffard' patris eiusdem Amicie in villa de Lessington' quam Hugo Giffard' filius eiusdem Herberti ⁊ heres . frater predicte Amicie de matrice ecclesia Linc'. patre suo Herberto defuncto tenuit ; ⁊ michi vendidit . Tenendam ⁊ habendam illi Amicie ⁊ heredibus suis . libere . ⁊ quiete . Ita tamen quod Christiana mater eius in vita sua tote prenominate terre duas partes percipiet ⁊ post eiusdem Christiane obitum ad dictam Amiciam ⁊ heredes suos sine aliqua contradictione tota dicta terra redeat . Reddendo inde annuatim matrici ecclesie Linc' . duodecim denarios . ad duos terminos videlicet ad Pascha sex denarios . ⁊ ad festum sancti Michaelis sex denarios . pro omni seruicio ⁊ exactione pro ut ego reddere consueui . Hiis testibus . dominis Seẏer de Frewill' . Thoma de Bekering' . Petro rectore ecclesie de Lissington' . Radulfo de Chotes . Thoma filio Johannis . Thoma filio Roberti . Gile de Linc' . Thoma Thog' . Alano aurifabro . Ẏvone aurifabro . Willelmo barbur' . ⁊ multis aliis.

No ancient endorsement.
Tag for seal. Size : 7¾ x 4½ inches.
Text : MS—Orig. Dij/83/1/33.
Note : The limiting dates are fixed by the attestation of Peter rector of Lissington,

who was instituted 15th May, 1249 (L.R.S. xi, p. 111), and whose successor was instituted 1264–5 (L.R.S. xx, p. 18). Christiana seems to have married a Flury alter on, as Christiana Flury in her widowhood grants to Robert West and Amy his wife, Christiana's daughter, probably identical with the Amicia of this charter 1284–5 (Dij/83/1/32). In Dij/83/1/28 Christiana is stated to be the daughter of Hugh the bearded.

The handwriting of this charter is oddly primitive for its date and has been marked by the nineteenth century compiler of the catalogue "early thirteenth century" although on handwriting alone one would assign it to that period, the internal evidence shows that it is impossible.

ADD. CHART.

1559. Grant by John the shepherd and Ysoda his wife, with one will and consent to Robert son of Gilbert West of Lissington, of a toft with buildings on it in Lissington, which John and Ysoda formerly held of Gilbert West. Robert shall pay a yearly render of eight silver pennies to Gilbert. (15th May, 1249–1265.)

Omnibus Christi fidelibus ad quos presens scriptum peruenerit . Johannes bercarius de Lisingtona et Ysoda vxor eius salutem in domino Noueritis nos vna voluntate 7 vno consensu consessisse dedisse Roberto filio Gileberti West de Lisingtona et heredibus suis uel asingnatis[1] suis vnum toftum cum domibus in eodem sitis . quod quondam tenuimus de Gileberto West de Lisingtona 7 totum jus 7 clameum quod in dicto tofto 7 domibus unquam habuimus uel habere poterimus . Illud scilicet toftum quod jacet inter toftum Gileberti West de Lisingtona ex vna parte 7 uiam que uocatur . Rauenesti ex altera uersus orientem . Ita quod nos nec heredes nostri nec aliquis per nos aliquod jus de cetero in dicto tofto nec in domibus uendicare uel exigire poterimus . Thenend[1] . 7 habend' . eidem . Roberto 7 heredibus suis uel asingnatis[1] suis . de nobis 7 heredibus nostris . libere . 7 quiete . bene . 7 in pace . Reddendo inde annuatim pro nobis 7 heredibus nostris Gileberto West de Lisingtona 7 heredibus suis uel asingnatis[1] suis . octo denarios argenti ad duos terminos anni . videlicet . ad festum sancti Botulphi . quatuor denarios 7 ad festum sancti Thome apostoli ante Natale domini . quatuor denarios pro omni seruicio seculari exaccione 7 demanda . Nos uero 7 heredes nostri dicto Roberto 7 heredibus suis uel asingnatis[1] suis dictum toftum cum domibus contra omnes homines pro predicto seruicio sicut predictum est ∴ warantizabimus . defendemus . 7 adquietabimus 7 ut hec nostra concessio 7 carte nostre quieta clamatio rata sit 7 stabillis[1] fide media in perpetuum . In huius reẏ[1] testimonium presenti scripto singna[1] nostra apposuimus . Hiis testibus . Johanne de Riggesbẏ . magistro Petro persona de Lisingtona . Radulfo de Cotes de eadem . Johanne Fluri de eadem .

Johanne del grene de Beckeringe . Johanne del bec de Howtona . Henrico de Friuill' . de Lissingtona . Thoma Fluri de eadem . Johanne Lanceleue de eadem . Gilleberto West de eadem . ⁊ aliis.

Endorsed : Johannis bercarii ⁊ Isode uxoris (13 cent.).
Two tags for seals. Size : 9 x 4½ inches.
Text : MS—Orig. Dij/83/1/34.
Var. R. : [1] *sic.*

LISSINGLEYS

Add. Chart.

1560. Grant by William de Amundavill, to Richard of Friesthorpe, son of Gamel, of a plot of meadow in Lissingleys, for a yearly render of one penny. (Circa 1220.)

Sciant presentes ⁊ futuri quod ego Willelmus de Amundauill' dedi ⁊ concessi ⁊ hac pre[senti carta mea con]firmaui Ricardo de Fristorp' filio Gameli placeam meam prati in Lissingle que iacet inter boscos . ⁊ continet in [latitudine decem pertica[1]]tas Habendam ⁊ tenendam sibi ⁊ heredibus suis uel suis assignatis cui ⁊ quando dare uel assignare [2]uel legare[2] uoluerit . [libere qu[1]]iete ⁊ pacifice . in feodo ⁊ hereditate Reddendo inde annuatim michi ⁊ heredibus meis vnum denarium ad festum sancti Laurentii pro omni seculari seruicio ⁊ exactione ⁊ demanda . Et ego prenominatus Willelmus ⁊ heredes mei . warantizabimus ⁊ defendemus [2]⁊ acquietabimus[2] totam predictam placeam prati cum omnibus pertinenciis predicto Ricardo ⁊ heredibus suis ut[3] suis assignatis cui ⁊ quando dare uel assignare uel legare uoluerit contra omnes homines imperpetuum . Et ut hec mea donatio concessio ⁊ conf[irm[1]]atio rata sit ⁊ stabilis imperpetuum huic presenti scripto sigillum meum apposui . Hiis testibus . Ricardo de Sualecl[if Willelmo[1]] le Chamberlayn . Roberto Wyb . Ricardo de Fristorp' filio Hugonis . Johanne fratre eius . Willelmo[4] Sturs . Ada filio Jolani[5] de [Frestorp' Rober[1]]to Sturs de Faldingwrd'[6] . Ricardo de Neuilla . Philippo Furri . Galfrido fratre eius . Thoma cementario de Fristorp . [Thoma[1]] filio Johannis de Faldingwrd[6] ⁊ aliis.

No ancient endorsement.
Tag for seal. Size : 6⅞ x 4½ inches.
Texts : MS—Orig. Dij/83/1/34*a*. R 90.
Var. R. : [1] *Supplied from* R : *the charter has two large holes.* [2–2] R *omits.* [3] *sic* : *and in* R. [4] R *adds* de. [5] *sic* : Jollani R. [6] Faldingworth R.
Note : Philip and Geoffrey Furry occur 1219 (Selden Society, vol. liii, nos. 62, 502, 776). William de Amundavill occurs late 12th century (see vol. iv, no. 1234 above). Robert Sturs levied a fine in 1245 with John and Edusa who may be identical with Edusa in the next charter (L.R.S. xvii, p. 29).

ADD. CHART.

1561. Grant by Richard of Friesthorpe, son of Gamel, to Edusa his daughter, of a plot of meadow in Lissingleys, to be held of St. Mary and St. John the Baptist, for a yearly render of one penny to the fraternity of St. John the Baptist at Pentecost. (Circa 1220.)

Sciant presentes ⁊ futuri quod ego Ricardus de Fristorp' . filius G[ameli[1]] dedi ⁊ hac presenti carta confirmaui . Eduse filie mee pro seruicio suo vnam placeam prati in Lissin[gele[1]] jacentem [propinquiorem[1]] iuxta Rawyldayl[2] versus orientem . ⁊ que se extendit in longitudine ab Scortwde uersus boream [⁊ continet[1]] in longitudine . sexaginta ⁊ sex perticatas . ⁊ in latitudine . decem perticatas Habendum ⁊ tenendum sibi ⁊ heredibus eius uel eius assingnatis . de deo ⁊ beata Maria . ⁊ beato Johanne Baptista . libere ⁊ quiete . Reddendo inde annuatim [fraternitati[1]] dicti beati Johannis vnum denarium . die Pentecosten . pro salute anime mee . ⁊ antecessorum meorum ⁊ succ[essorum[1]] meorum ⁊[3] fidelium . Et ut hec mea concessio donacio . ⁊ huius carte confirmacio . robur perpetu[e stabilitatis[1]] optineant ∴ presens . scriptum . sigilli mei inpressione roboraui . Hiis testibus . Ricardo de Fristorp' clerico . Ricardo de Sturs . Rogero fratre suo . Thoma filio Ade . Thoma filio Johannis de Fristorp'. Waltero carpentario . Johanne filio Thome ∴ ⁊ aliis.

No ancient endorsement.
Tag for seal Size: $7\frac{1}{4}$ x $2\frac{3}{4}$ inches.
Texts: MS—Orig. Dij/83/1/29. R 98.
Var. R.: [1] *The words in square brackets have been supplied from* R *as the charter is stained and partly illegible through damp.* [2] Rawildayle R. [3] R *adds* omnium.
Note: This charter and the following one are probably slightly later in date than no. 1560.

ADD. CHART.

1562. Grant by Richard of Friesthorpe, son of Gamel, to Stephen his son, of a plot of meadow in Lissingleys, to be held of the lords of Snarford for a yearly render of one penny. (Circa 1220.)

Sciant presentes ⁊ futuri quod ego Ricardus de Fristorp' filius Gameli [1]concessi[1] . dedi . ⁊ hac presenti carta[2] confirmaui Stephano filio meo v[nam pla[3]]ceam prati in Lissingle[4] . que . se extendit . ab Wudebrac in longitudine [versus[3]] austrum . ⁊ continet in longitudine viginti quatuor perticatas ⁊ in latitudine decem perticatas . Habendum ⁊ tenendum . sibi ⁊ heredibus eius uel eius assingnatis[5] de dominis feodi . scilicet de dominis de [Snart[3]]ford' . libere . ⁊ quiete . Reddendo inde annuatim . dictis dominis vnum denarium . die sancti Laurencii . pro omni seruicio 7 demanda . Et ut hec mea concessio . donacio 7 huius carte confirmacio robur perpetue stabilitatis optineant ·/ presens scriptum sigilli mei inpressione roboraui . Hiis testibus . Ricardo de Fristorp' clerico . Ricardo de Sturs . Rogero fratre eius . Thoma filio Ade . Thoma filio Johannis . 7 aliis.

No ancient endorsement.
Tag for seal. Size: 5 x 2¾ inches.
Texts: MS—Orig. Dij/88/1/30. R 99.
Var. R.: [1]–[1] R *omits.* [2] R *adds* mea. [3] *Supplied from* R: *the charter is injured and partly illegible from damp.* [4] Lissingele R. [5] *sic*: assignatis R.

Add. Chart.

1563. Grant by Adam le Fraunceys of Friesthorpe, to the church of Lincoln and the Common, of three acres of meadow in Lissingleys. (Circa 1248–1253).

Omnibus Christi fidelibus presens scriptum inspecturis vel audituris . Adam Le Fraunceys de Frystorp'[1] ·/ salutem in domino . Noueritis me diuine pietatis intuitu . 7 pro salute anime mee 7 antecessorum . 7 heredum meorum dedisse 7 concessisse . 7 hac presenti carta mea confirmasse . deo 7 beate Marie 7 commune canonicorum Linc' ecclesie . in liberam puram 7 perpetuam elemosinam tres acras prati quas habui in Lyssingeleie[2] . Habendas 7 tenendas dictis canonicis libere . quiete . integre . 7 pacifice in perpetuum . Et ego Adam 7 heredes mei predictas tres acras prati tanquam liberam puram 7 perpetuam elemosinam prefatis canonicis Linc' ecclesie contra omnes homines 7 feminas warantizabimus adquietabimus 7 defendemus de omni seruicio seculari 7 demanda . in perpetuum . Et in huius rei robur 7 testimonium presens scriptum sigilli mei apposicione corroboraui . Hiis testibus . dominis .H. subdecano Linc' . Thoma de Askeby . Galfrido de Tham'[3] . canonicis Linc' . Rollano sacrista . Rogero de Thuruill' . Roberto de Feretro . Willelmo de Stures . Johanne filio persone de Frystorp' . Ricardo fratre suo . Ada clerico . Ricardo Ceinbel.

Endorsed: (1) Carta Ade Le Fraunceys de Frystorp' de tribus acris prati in [Lissing]lee (13 cent.). (2) Fristhorp' (13 cent.). (3) . . . tridig (13 or early 14 cent.). (4) contingens capitulum (? 14 cent.).
Tag for seal. Size: 7⅜ x 4¼ inches.
Texts: MS—Orig. Dij/70/1/27. *This charter is filed on a string with the Friesthorpe charters.* R 78.
Var. R.: [1] Fristorp' R. [2] Lissingeleye R. [3] Thame R.
Note: Hugh de Hoketon did not become sub-dean until 1248 at the earliest, as William of Benniworth was still in office on 12th February in that year. *See* vol. ii, no. 364, above. Thomas of Ashby, Rollain the sacrist and Roger de Thurvill witness two charters of Henry Lexington, as dean between 1248 and 1253 (*ibid.*, nos. 622 and 623).

BLEASBY AND WELTON

408

1564. Grant by Alexander of Welton [le Wold], to the church of Lincoln and the Common, of a toft and two bovates in Welton [le Wold] and two tofts and one bovate in Bleasby. (Late twelfth century.)

De terra in Welleton' 7 in Bleseby. (A rubric.)

Omnibus sancte matris ecclesie filiis ad quos presens scriptum peruenerit Alexander de Welleton'[1] salutem . Nouerit uniuersitas uestra me dedisse 7 hac mea presenti carta confirmasse unum toftum 7 duas bouatas terre in Welletun[1] quas Eilricus tenuit . 7 unum toftum 7 unam bouatam terre in Blesebi[2] . quam Hugo de Cheuermund[3] tenuit . 7 unum toftum quod Godwinus tenuit in eadem uilla contra portam meam deo 7 sancte Marie Linc' . 7 commune canonicorum pro salute anime mee 7 animarum antecessorum meorum in puram 7 perpetuam elemosinam 7 liberam ex[4] omni actione[5] 7 seculari seruitio . Hanc autem donationem ego Alexander 7 heredes mei warantizabimus predicte commune contra omnes homines . Hiis testibus . Rogero Scoto . Eudone presbitero . Ranulfo de Withkale[6] . Ricardo Uilen[7] . Yuone de Leghesbi[8] . Roberto filio Eilwardi . Philippo de Leghesbi[8] . Roberto de Heintun[9] . 7[10] aliis.

Marginalia in A: (1) Welleton'. (2) .j. toftum . 7 .ii. bouat'. (3) Bleseby. (4) .ii. bouat' cum tofto.

Texts: A. R 1646.

Var. R.: [1] Welton R. [2] Bleseby R. [3] Keuermund R. [4] ab R. [5] *sic*: exactione R. [6] Withcale R. [7] Vilein R. [8] Legesby R. [9] Hainton'. [10] R *adds* multis.

In R *this charter is entered with the Welton de Wold charters in Louthesk wapentake.*

Note: Roger Scot witnesses between 1196 and 1203 (vol. iv, no. 1140, above) and in the late twelfth century (*ibid.* no. 1362). Eudo the priest is probably identical with Eudo of Boston who attests on both those occasions.

Folio 78.

Hdl. WRAGHOU .7.8.

409=388

1565. Grant by Philip of Timberland, to the church of Lincoln and the Common, of a toft containing four selions, and pasture for two cows, one ox, one horse and twenty sheep in Bleasby. (Circa 1210–1220.)

De .i. tofta (*sic*) cum pastura in Bleseby (A 409 rubric).

Omnibus Christi fidelibus ad quos presens scriptum pervenerit ∴ Philippus de Timberlund[1] salutem . Noverit universitas uestra me pro salute anime mee 7 omnium antecessorum 7 successorum meorum dedisse 7 concessisse[2] 7[3] presenti carta mea confirmasse deo 7 beate Marie 7 commune canonicorum Linc' ecclesie unum toftum in villa de Bleseby in quo continentur .iiii[or]. selliones . videlicet illud toftum quod Thurbertus tenuit . quod iacet contiguum tofto Johannis de Lanum versus austrum . [va] quod iacet contiguum tofto Johannis de Lanum versus austrum[cat] . 7 pasturas[4] ad duas vaccas . unum bouem . unum equum . 7 uiginti oues . Tenend' 7 habend' eisdem canonicis cum libero introitu 7 exitu 7 cum omnibus pertinenciis suis libertatibus 7 aisiamentis infra villam 7 extra in puram 7 perpetuam elemosinam liberam . solutam[5] . quietam ab omni servitio seculari 7 exactione uel demanda . Et ego Philippus 7 heredes mei warantizabimus predictum toftum cum libero introitu [6]7 exitu[6] 7 pasturam prenominatam cum omnibus pertinenciis suis . libertatibus 7 aisiamentis infra villam 7 extra . defendemus 7 adquietabimus erga omnes homines imperpetuum . In huius[7] autem rei robur 7 testimonium presenti scripto sigillum meum apposui . Hiis testibus . Thoma de Norton' ∴ Henrico de Torpell[8] ∴ Henrico de Norhampton[9] ∴ Roberto de Balderton[10] ∴ capellanis . Osberto de Neuport . Roberto[11] Thede . Nicholao de Wicford[12] . Thoma de Waltham . Rogero de Neuport . Widone de Keles[13] ∴ Yvone Harfot[14] . 7 aliis.

Marginalia in A : 409 (1) Bleseby. (2) .i. toftum cum pástura. 388 (1) Bleseby (2) Bleseby.

Texts : A 409 and 388. R 1484.

Var. R. : [1] Tẏmbẏrlund A388. Tymberlund R. [2] concesse A388. [3] A388 *adds*. hac. [4] pasturam A388 *and* R. [5] R *adds* 7. [6]–[6] A388 *and* R *omit*. [7] cuius A388. [8] Thorpell' A388. [9] Norhamton A398. [10] Baldirton' A388. [11] A388 *adds* de. [12] Wykeford A388. Wikeford R. [13] Keleseye R. [14] Harefot A 388 *and* R.

Note : These clerks are found frequently witnessing charters about this time.

Half folio 73*d*, *on which no.* 388 *is written, is blank ; at the foot Q wrote* Carte de Walscroft et de Jordeburg debent hic scribi *but crossed it through.*

Folio 74.

Hdl. Wraghou . 7 . 9 . Communa

410

1566. Grant by Walter son of William of Holton [by Beckering], to the church of Lincoln and the Common, of a toft in Bleasby. (1205–1214.)

De .j. tofto in eadem. (A rubric.)

Sciant presentes 7 futuri quod ego Walterus filius Willelmi de Hout' dedi 7 concessi 7 hac presenti [1]mea carta[1] confirmaui deo 7 beate Marie 7 commune canonicorum Linc' ecclesie unum toftum in Blesebi[2] quod Ailsi tenuit in eadem uilla cum omnibus pertinenciis suis in puram 7 perpetuam elemosinam liberam . [3]quietam . 7 solutam[3] ab omni seculari seruitio 7 exactione . Et ego Walterus 7 heredes mei warantizabimus predicte ecclesie supradictum toftum contra omnes homines . Testibus . Philippo subdecano . Hugone de Sancto Edwardo . Johanne de Tinnemue[4] . Ricardo de Blesebi[2] . Roberto fratre suo . Henrico de Hout' .

Marginalia in A. : (1) Bleseb'. (2) j. toftum.
Texts : A. R 1482.
Var. R. : [1] R *has* carta mea. [2] Bleseby R. [3] R *has* solutam 7 quietam. [4] Tynemue R.
Note : For Philip the subdean see note to no. 1468 above.

411

1567. Confirmation of the preceding grant by Philip of Timberland. (1205–1214.)

Confirmatio eiusdem. (A rubric.)

Sciant presentes 7 futuri quod ego Philippus de Tymberlund' ratam 7 gratam habui . 7 hac mea [1]carta[1] confirmaui donationem quam fecit Walterus filius Willelmi de Hout' [1]scilicet[1] unum toftum in Blesebi[2] quod Ailsi tenuit in eadem villa . deo 7 beate Marie 7 commune canonicorum Linc' ecclesie sicuti [1]carta[1] quam idem canonici habent de Waltero [1]de Houton'[1] protestatur . 7 ego Philippus 7 heredes mei warantizabimus predicte ecclesie predictam confirmacionem contra omnes homines . Teste[3] Philippo subdecano . Hugone de Sancto Edwardo . magistro Johanne de Tinemue[4] . Ricardo de Blesebi[2] . Roberto fratre suo . Henrico de Houtun.[5]

Marginalia in A : Confirmatio.
Texts : A. R 1483.
Var. R. : [1] R *omits*. [2] Bleseby R. [3] *sic* : testibus R. [4] Tÿnemue R. [5] Houton' R.

STAINTON BY LANGWORTH

ADD. CHART.

1568. Release and quitclaim by Simon Savage of Stainton [by Langworth] to Isoreus son of Alexander, his *nepos* and heir, of all his right and claim in the land which Laurence Savage, Simon's brother, had held. For this Isoreus shall give Simon six shillings a year so long as he shall live. (Before 1219.)

Sciant presentes 7 futuri (quod ego Simon Saluag*ius* de Steÿnton remisi 7 quietum clamaui Ÿsoreo filio Alexandri nepoti meo 7 heredi totum jus 7 clamium quod habui in tota terra que fuit Laurencii Saluagii fratri meo illi 7 heredibus suis de me 7 heredibus meis inperpetuum . Et pro hac remissione ⁊ quietaclamacione dedit michi dictus Ysoreus singulis annis (quamdiu vixero sex solidos scilicet tres solidos ad festum sancti Botulphi (⁊ tres solidos ad purificacionem beate virginis . Et vt ista remissio ⁊ quietaclamacio rata perseueret inposterum eam presenti scripto ⁊ sigilli mei patrocinio roboravi . Testibus Thoma de Fiskerton canonico Linc' (Willelmo de Angoteb' Ricardo de Rowell clericis Heltone de Snelleslund Galfrido de Lundo (Ricardo filio Guarneri de Haint' Willelmo filio Eudonis de Reresbẏ (Lamberto fratre suo Germano de Reresbẏ Roberto de Snelleslund (Roberto de Fiskerton et multis aliis.

Text: R 1486.

Note: Helto of Snelland, one of the witnesses, was dead in 1219 (Selden Society, vol. liii, no. 234). Thomas of Fiskerton witnesses as a canon 1203–1206 (*see* above, vol. ii, no. 350).

SIXLE

Add. Chart.

1569. Grant by Robert Grelle, to Roger of Sixle and Agnes his wife, of a toft in Sixle and two bovates there which had previously been held in villeinage. For this they shall pay a yearly render of half a mark for all service, saving the forensic service due from such a tenement and suit of Robert's court in Sixle. (Before 20th December, 1230.)

Sciant presentes ⁊ futuri quod ego Robertus Grelle dedi concessi ⁊ hac presenti carta mea confirmaui Rogero de Sixil ⁊ Agneti vxori sue ⁊ heredibus eorum vnum toftum in villa de Sixil . illud silicet[1] toftum quod Cecilia filia Elie quondam tenuit . Et duas bouatas terre illas silicet[1] quas Alanus Bouer quondam tenuit in teritorio eiusdem ville in vilenagio . Tenend' ⁊ habend' . predicto Rogero ⁊ Agneti vxori sue ⁊ heredibus eorum . libere . quiete . integre . bene ⁊ in pace . Reddendo inde annuatim mihi ⁊ heredibus meis dimidiam marcam argenti ad quatuor terminos constitutos . videlicet ad festum sancti Botulfi .xx. denarios . ad festum Sancti Micahaelis[1] .xx. denarios . ad festum Natalis domini .xx. denarios . ⁊ ad Pascha .xx. denarios . pro omni seculari seruicio ⁊ demanda . saluo mihi ⁊ heredibus meis forinsecum seruicium quantum pertinet ad tantum tenementum in eadem villa . ⁊ sectam curie mee in eadem villa . Et ego Robertus Grelle ⁊ heredes mei . predictum toftum . ⁊ dictas duas bouatas terre cum omnibus pertinenciis suis infra villam ⁊ extra ./ predicto Rogero ⁊ Agneti vxori sue ⁊ heredibus eorum . pro predicto seruicio ./ contra omnes gentes warantizabimus ⁊ adquietabimus imperpetuum . In cuius rei testimonium presenti scripto ./ sigillum meum apposui . Hiis testibus . Nicholao Tucchet . Sewal' de Worz . Willelmo de Benigword' . Willelmo de Blesebẏ . Waltero de Wilingham . Henrico West de Ludeford . Roberto de Timbirlunt in Blesebẏ . ⁊ aliis.

No ancient endorsement.
Tag for seal. Size : 7 x 3⅞ inches.
Text : MS—Orig. Dij/86/3/37.
Var. R. : [1] *sic.*
Note : Robert Grelley died before 20th December, 1230 (*Excerpta e rotulis finium tempore regis Henrici* i, p. 208). William of Benniworth succeeded his father in 1226 (H. and K.F., vol. ii, p. 136).

The Wraggoe charters end on folio 81.

Folio 81d.

Hdl. Communa

This folio is blank.

Folios 82 and 82d contain the charters of the wapentake of Ludborough printed in Volume IV at nos. 1400–1402 and 1423–1425.

Folio 83.

Hdl. . 8 . 3 .

This folio is blank.

Louthesk Wapentake

Folio 83d. Ludesch.

SOUTH CADEBY

433

1570. Grant by William Kitling, to the church of Lincoln and the Common, of a toft and half a bovate of land in South Cadeby, five acres on each side of the village, with the pasture and freedom of common belonging to it. (1205–1214.)

Carta Willelmi Kitling de .j. tofto ⁊ dimidia bouata in Catebẏ. (A rubric.)

Sciant presentes ⁊ futuri quod ego Willelmus Kitling[1] dedi ⁊ concessi ⁊ hac presenti mea carta confirmaui deo ⁊ beate Marie ⁊ commune canonicorum Linc' ecclesie unum toftum in Catebi[2] ⁊ dimidiam bouatam terre in territorio[3] eiusdem uille scilicet quinque acras terre arabilis ex una parte uille ⁊ quinque acras terre arabilis ex alia parte que tenui de Alano Punchardun[4] . ⁊ pasturam ⁊ liberam communam ad dimidiam bouatam terre pertinentem in omnibus libertatibus ⁊ aisiamentis [communibus[5]] ad uillam de Catebi[2] pertinentibus in puram ⁊ perpetuam elemosinam liberam quietam[6] solutam ab omni seculari seruicio ⁊ exactione . Teste[7] Philippo subdecano . magistro Johanne de Tinnemue[8] . Hugone de Sancto Edwardo . canonicis Linc' . Willelmo filio Symonis . Alano capellano . Roberto filio Eustacii[9] . ⁊ multis aliis.

Marginalia in A : (1) Vacat hic quia in Jordeburg (by Q). (2) Cateby (by Q2). (3) i toftum ⁊ dim' bovat' (by Q2).
Texts : MS—A. R1332.
Var. R. : [1] R *adds* de Kateby. [2] Kateby R. [3] campis R. [4] Punchardon' R. [5] *added in the margin in* A. [6] R *adds* ⁊. [7] *sic.* [8] Tinemue R. [9] Eustachii R.
Note : Q thought this and the following charter referred to North Cadeby, but even so that village is in Haverstoe, not in Yarborough wapentake. In R they are among the charters of Grimsby (i.e. Bradley and Haverstoe) wapentake. For Philip the subdean see note to 1468 above.

434

1571. Confirmation by Alan Punchardun of the preceding grant. (1205–1214.)

Confirmacio eiusdem terre per Alanum Punchard. (A rubric.)

Omnibus sancte matris ecclesie filiis ad quos presens scriptum peruenerit : Alanus Punchardun de Catebi[1] . salutem . Nouerit uniuersitas uestra me ratam ⁊ gratam habuisse ⁊ hac mea carta confirmasse donationem quam fecit Willelmus Kitling de Catebi[2] deo ⁊ beate Marie ⁊ commune canonicorum Linc' ecclesie . scilicet unum toftum in Catebi[2] ⁊ dimidiam bouatam terre in campis eiusdem uille . Et ego Alanus ⁊ heredes mei warantizabimus eandem terram predicte ecclesie ⁊ defendemus de forinseco ⁊ de omni alio seruitio ad terram pertinente contra omnes homines . Teste[3] Philippo subdecano . magistro Johanne de Tinemue . Hugone de Sancto Edwardo . Willelmo filio Simonis . Alano capellano . Roberto filio Eustacii[4] . ⁊ multis aliis.

Marginalia in A : Confirmatio (by Q2).
Texts : MS—A. R1333.
Var. R. : [1] Cateby R. [2] Kateby R. [3] *sic* : testibus *in* R. [4] Eustachii R.

Add. Chart.

1572. Notification by R, the prior, and the convent of Sixle that the church of South Cadeby which was confirmed to them by Bishop Hugh I, fell vacant after the death of bishop William of Blois. Owing to the vacancy in the see they could not obtain free entry to the church on account of the opposition of the dean and chapter of Lincoln, who wished, as they said, to preserve the rights of the cathedral and would only allow the priory the custody of the church, with the obligation of paying two marks a year for the fruits to whomsoever the dean and chapter should nominate. The priory received the custody on these conditions, saving all their privileges and indulgences conferred or to be conferred by bishop or Pope and agreed not to make use of any papal letters against the dean and chapter during the vacancy. (Circa 1206–1209).

Omnibus sancte matris ecclesie filiis ad quos littere presentes peruenerint .R. prior 7 conuentus de Sixla eternam in domino salutem . Nouerit vniuersitas uestra quod ecclesia de Katebẏ . quam nobis bone memorie .H. quondam Lincol' episcopus in proprios vsus perpetuo possidendam concessit .' 7 autentico scripto suo confirmauit . post decessum venerabilis patris nostri .W. Lincol' episcopi cepit vacare . Set quia vacante sede Lincol' liber non patebat nobis in predictam ecclesiam ingressus . presertim cum venerabiles viri (decanus 7 capitulum Lincol' pro conseruando jure matricis ecclesie sue Lincol' ut dicebant se nobis ad tempus obicerent .' nos eisdem decano 7 capitulo humiliter supplicauimus . Ipsi autem precibus nostris humiliter condescendentes pro statu ecclesie Lincol' 7 statutis capituli Lincol' vacante sede integre conseruandis .' nobis predicte ecclesie de Katebẏ custodiam concesserunt . Ita quidem quod nos duas marcas pro fructibus eiusdem ecclesie annuatim quamdiu Lincol' ecclesia vacauerit .' ei cui predicti decanus 7 capitulum Lincol' nos assignauerint persoluemus . Nos autem predicte ecclesie custodiam sub predicta forma ab eis recepimus . Saluis nobis omnibus priuilegiis 7 indulgenciis 7 confirmacionibus nostris nobis a domino papa uel episcopis quibuscunque collatis uel conferendis . Preterea promisimus in uerbo ueritatis quod non utemur contra dictos decanum 7 capitulum litteris domini pape impetratis uel impetrandis occasione ecclesie de Katebẏ vacante sede Lincol' . 7 in huius rei robur 7 testimonium presenti scripto sigillum nostrum simul cum sigillo magistri ordinis de Sempingham appendimus.

No endorsement.

Two tags for seals cut from another document . ? account of expenses at Sixle.
Size : 6¼ x 4 inches.

Text : MS—Orig. Dij/68/2/46.

Note : Hugh of Bayeux gave South Cadeby church to Sixle in the reign of Henry II (L.R.S. xviii, p. 4) and the gift was confirmed by Bishop Hugh I, circa 1189–91 (see volume ii, no. 338, viii, above). The vicarage was ordained by master Reginald of Chester, official of bishop Hugh of Wells (*Liber Antiquus Hugonis Wells*, pp. 57, 66). The date of the present deed is after the death of William of Blois in May, 1206, and probably before the consecration of his successor in 1209. The church was finally adjudged to Sixle by Archbishop Langton as papal judge delegate (see vol. ii, no. 354 above).

CALCETHORPE

435

1573. Grant by Robert son of William of Keddington, with the assent of William his heir, to the church of Lincoln, of a toft in Calcethorpe. (Late twelfth century.)

Carta Roberti filii Willelmi . de uno tofto in Chelestorp. (A rubric.)

Omnibus sancte matris ecclesie filiis ad quos presens scriptum peruenerit . Rob[ertus filius Willelmi de Chedẏngtun[2] salutem[1] .] Nouerit uniuersitas uestra quod ego dedi 7 concessi 7 hac carta mea conf[irmaui deo . 7 . sancte[1]] Marie Lincolniensis . in puram 7 perpetuam elemosinam . assensu Willelmi here[dis mei toftum quod[1]] Eustacius filius Godefridi tenuit de me in Chelestorp liberum 7 quietum ab omni seculari seruitio . 7 prefatum toftum eis contra omnes[3] warantizare promisi . His[4] testibus . Gilleberto[5] Pilat[6] . Stephano de Foterbi . Gilleberto[5] Donnai[7] . Lamberto de Chelestorp . 7 multis aliis.

Endorsed: Roberti filii Willelmi de tofto de Kelestorp (13 cent.).
Tag for seal. Size: 5½ x 2½ inches.
Marginalia in A: (1) Tesoltorp' (by Q2). (2) i toftum (by Q2).
Texts: MS—Orig. Dij/68/2/45. A. R1650.
Var. R.: [1] *supplied from* A: the top right hand corner of the charter has been torn away. [2] Chedyngt' R. [3] A *adds* homines. [4] *sic*: hiis A *and* R. [5] Gileberto A. Gilberto R. [6] Pylat' R. [7] Domai R.
Note: Gilbert Pilate occurs frequently 1196–1203. Stephen of Fotherby and Gilbert Dounei or Donnei witness together circa 1200 (see vol. iv, pp. 235–6 above).

WELTON LE WOLD

436

1574. Grant by Hamo son of Rannulf, to the church of Lincoln and the Common, of a toft and half a bovate of land in Welton [le Wold]. (Late twelfth century.)

Carta Hamonis filii Ranulfi . de quodam tofto in Welleton' . 7 dimidia . bouata. (A rubric.)

Vniuersis sancte matris ecclesie filiis ad quos presens scriptum peruenerit Hamo filius Ranulfi salutem . Nouerit uniuersitas uestra me dedisse 7 concessisse 7 hac presenti carta mea confirmasse deo 7 beate Marie 7 commune canonicorum Linc' ecclesie in puram [1]7[1] liberam 7 perpetuam elemosinam toftum qui[2] fuit Ranulfi . 7 dimidiam bouatam terre in territorio de Welletun[3] pro salute anime mee 7 omnium antecessorum meorum . 7 ego 7 heredes mei warantizabimus pr̨edicte ecclesie predictam donationem contra omnes homines .

Et ut hec donatio mea rata permaneat :· eam sigilli mei[4] appositione corroboraui . Hiis testibus . Odone persona ecclesie sancti Clementis de Salfletbi[5] . Ricardo filio Acii . Roberto Vauasur . Willelmo filio Roberti . 7 Johanne fratre suo.

Marginalia in A : Welleton i. toftum dimidia . bovata (by Q2).
Texts : MS—A. R1642.
Var. R. : [1–1] R *omits.* [2] *sic.* [3] Welton' R. [4] me (*sic*) R. [5] Salfleteby R.
Note : The first parson of Saltfleetby St. Clement whose institution is recorded is Philip of Saltfleet in 1224–5 (L.R.S. ix, p. 137). Robert Vavasur witnesses late twelfth century (*Danelaw Charters,* p. 397). William son of Robert and John his brother are probably the sons of Robert of Legbourne (see H. and K.F. ii, pp.106–9).

437

1575. Grant by William son of Warin of Welton [le Wold], to the church of Lincoln and the Common, of a toft and half a bovate of land in Welton [le Wold]. (Late twelfth century.)

Carta Willelmi filii Warini . de .j. tofto . 7 dimidia . bouata in Welleton'. (A rubric.)

Vniuersis sancte matris ecclesie filiis ad quos presens scriptum peruenerit Willelmus filius Warin[1] de * Welletun[2] salutem . Nouerit uniuersitas uestra me dedisse 7 concessisse 7 hac presenti carta mea confirmasse deo 7 beate Marie 7 commune canonicorum Linc' ecclesie in puram 7 liberam 7 perpetuam elemosinam toftum iacentem inter toftum Hosberti[3] filii Arnaldi 7 toftum Walteri filii Godricii[4] . 7 dimidiam bouatam terre que fuit Hugonis filii Eudonis in territorio de Welletun[2] pro salute anime mee 7 omnium antecessorum meorum 7 ego 7 heredes mei warantizabimus predictam donationem predicte ecclesie contra omnes homines . Et ut [5]hec[5] donatio mea rata permaneat :· eam sigilli mei appositione corroboraui . Hiis testibus . Odone persona ecclesie sancti Clementis de Salfletbi[6] . Ricardo filio Acii . Roberto Vauasur . Willelmo filio Roberti . 7 Johanne fratre suo.

Marginalia in A : Welleton' . j. toftum 7 dimidia bovata (by Q2).
Texts : MS—A. R1643.
Var. R. : [1] *sic* : Warini R. [2] Welton' R. [3] Osberti R. [4] Godrici R. [5–5] R *omits.* [6] Salfleteby R.
Note : See the note to the previous charter. A William son of Warin who may be identical with this grantor occurs in 1202 (L.R.S. xxii, no. 1203).

*Folio 84.

Hdl. . 8 . 4– .

ADD. CHART.

1576. Grant by Thomas de Wheldrake [co. York] and (?) Edith his wife of Welton [le Wold], to the church of Lincoln and the

Common, of a toft and a croft with buildings and appurtenances in Welton [le Wold]. (Circa 1230–1245.)

Omnibus Christi fidelibus Thomas de Queldric de Welton' 7 Eduli'[1] vxor eius salutem . Noueritis nos dedisse concessisse 7 hac presenti carta nostra confirmasse deo 7 beate Marie 7 commune canonicorum Lincoln' ecclesie vnum toftum cum vno crofto cum edificiis 7 pertinenciis in Welton quod iacet inter terram Alani filii Alexandri 7 terram Johannis filii Ernisii et extendit se in longitudine a via que est ad capud australe vsque ad forarium Johannis filii Arnulfi versus partem aquilonalem Tenenda 7 habenda in puram 7 perpetuam elemosinam liberam 7 quietam ab omni seruicio 7 exaccione seculari sine omni reclamacione vel calumpnia nostri vel heredum nostrorum inperpetuum . Nos vero 7 heredes nostri defendemus adquietabimus 7 warantizabimus dictis canonicis totum dictum tenementum cum pertinenciis tanquam puram 7 perpetuam elemosinam liberam 7 quietam contra omnes homines inperpetuum . 7 ad hoc fideliter 7 sine dolo tenendum ./ tactis sancrosanctis ewangeliis iurauimus 7 insuper presens scriptum sigillis nostris confirmauimus . Hiis testibus Radulfo de Vher Hugone de Fulestowe Henrico sacrista Linc' Ricardo de Altari capellanis Ricardo de Stretton clerico commune Johanne filio Willelmi Elÿa filio Thoraldi Roberto [2] Johanne filio Walteri Radulfo filio Willelmi de Welton 7 aliis.

Text : MS—R1644.

Var. R. : [1] *sic : the name should probably be* Edith *as the next charter seems to refer to the same land.* [2] *blank in* MS.

ADD. CHART.

1577. Grant by Edith daughter of William son of Lelle of Welton [le Wold], in her widowhood, to the chapter of Lincoln, of a toft in Welton [le Wold]. (Query circa 1240–1250.)

Omnibus sancte matris ecclesie filiis ad quos presens scriptum peruenerit Editha filia Willelmi filii Lelle de Welton salutem . Noueritis me in viduitate mea concessisse 7 dedisse 7 hac presenti carta mea confirmasse deo 7 beate Marie 7 capitulo Linc' ecclesie vnum toftum in villa de Welton iacentem inter toftum Alani filii Alexandri[1] cum crofto pertinente ad eundem toftum pro salute anime mee 7 omnium antecessorum meorum in liberam puram 7 perpetuam elemosinam 7 quietam ab omni seculari seruicio 7 exactione . Et ego Editha 7 heredes mei warantizabimus 7 adquietabimus 7 defendemus predictum toftum cum crofto plenarie predicto capitulo inperpetuum contra omnes homines . Hiis testibus

Henrico capellano Johanne filio Thome Radulpho clerico Johanne filio Osberti (Johanne filio Alexandri (Willelmo filio Aldiet (Johanne filio eius Gilberto filio Willelmi (Galfrido filio Ernisii.

Text: MS—R1645.
Var. R.: [1] *sic: presumably* et terram Johannis filii Ernisii *has been omitted.*
Note: The charter is evidently some years later than the preceding one.

WITHCALL

438

1578. Grant by Rannulf son of Constantine of Withcall, with the assent of his wife and his heirs, to the chapter of Lincoln, of a toft and sixteen acres of land, eight on each side of the village of Withcall. (Late Henry II.)

Carta Ranulfi filii Constantini de xvi acris terre in Wikale. (A rubric.)

Vniuersis sancte matris ecclesie filiis presentibus ⁊ futuris . Rannulfus filius Costentini de Withcale salutem . Noscat uniuersitas uestra me dedisse ⁊ concessisse ⁊ hac presenti carta confirmasse consensu ⁊ assensu vxoris mee ⁊ heredum meorum . deo ⁊ sancte Marie ⁊ capitulo Lincolnie . quoddam toftum in Withcale quod [1]tenuit[1] Gwarinus iuxta toftum Normanni . ⁊ viii acras terre ex una parte uille . videlicet ad caput de Micledic . inter Lambertum de Scotenie[2] ⁊ campum de Raitheb'[3] . ⁊ ad Flaxland . ⁊ ad Scineburgstig[4] . ⁊ Bracerandale . ⁊ viii acras ex alia parte uille . Scilicet ad Laichedale medelclif dimidiam culturam cum dna (*sic*) . ⁊ ad Mathcacrae[5] . ⁊ ad Laichedale bodme . ⁊ ad Micledale[6] ex sut[7] parte uie . ⁊ pratum meum quod iacet in duabus partibus ad Sic daile . in puram [8]⁊[8] liberam ⁊ perpetuam elemosinam pro salute anime méé ⁊ vxoris méé ⁊ heredum meorum . ⁊ pro animabus patrum ⁊ matrum nostrarum ⁊ omnium antecessorum nostrorum . His[9] testibus . Roberto de Coudrai . Folcone filio Roberti . Cunano filio Johannis . [Willelmo de Luda[10]] . Hamone Boterel . Osberto de Gainesburc . aliis quam pluribus.

Endorsed: Contra Rannulfum filium Costentini de Withcale (early 13 cent.).
Slit for seal tag. Size: 8 x $3\frac{3}{8}$ inches.
Marginalia in A: (1) Wykale xvi acre (Q2). Also two faded notes (1) ? H; (2) ? noscat.
Texts: MS—Orig. Dij/88/3/29. A. R1623.
Note: Rannulf son of Coste had given land in Withcall to the Templars before 1185 (*Records of the Templars*, p. 107).
Var. R.: [1–1] R *omits.* [2] Scoteneye R. [3] Raythby R. [4] Stineburstig R. [5] Mathacrae A. [6] Michedale R. [7] suth A *and* R. [8–8] A *omits.* [9] Hiis A *and* R. [10] *Written in a different but possibly contemporary hand below the line in lighter ink. The name is given in this place in* A *but is entirely omitted in* R.

439

1579. Notification by Rannulf of Withcall that he has granted, at the wish and with the consent of Margaret his wife and his heirs, in the presence of the said Margaret, to the church of Lincoln and the Common, Osbert son of Ilbert, with Agnes his wife and their sons and daughters, together with a toft and a bovate in Withcall, which Ilbert had previously held. (1184–1192.)

Carta Rannulfi de Witkale de .i. tofto . ⁊ .i. bovata in Wikale. (A rubric.)

Omn[ibus sancte matris ecclesie filiis[1]] Rannulfus de Wickal[e[1] and[2]] salutem . Ad omnium noticiam peruenire desidero me de a[ssensu ⁊ de voluntate[1]] Margarete vxoris mee ⁊ heredum meorum presente predicta Margareta dedi[sse ⁊ concessisse in pu]ram ⁊ perpetuam elemosinam . deo ⁊ sancte Marie Linc' . ⁊ commun[e canonicorum . ibidem deo[1]] famulantium . Osbertum filium[2] Illeberti . ⁊ Agnetem vxorem suam ⁊ fili[os ⁊ filias eorum cum[1]] tofto ⁊ una bouata terre in Wikale[3] cum omnibus pertinentiis . absque aliquo [retenemento[1]] quem toftum ⁊ bouatam terre tenuit Illebertus . pater predicti Osberti in Wickale[3] . Hanc uero elemosinam solutam ⁊ quietam ab omni seculari seruitio ⁊ exactione . adquietabimus ⁊ warantizabimus contra omnes homines . His testibus . Lamberto de Scotenni[4] . Hugone de Scotenni[4] . Petro Can . de Hach . Winemero subdecano . Luca . Ricardo de Kÿma . Galfrido de Wickal'[3] . Rollando . Radulfo ⁊ multis aliis.

Endorsed : (1) Rannulfi de Wickale (early 13 cent.). (2) Withcal' (by Q).
Tag for seal. Size : 6¼ x 4⅜ inches.
Marginalia in A. : Wykale .j. tofto ⁊ .j. bovata (by Q2).
Texts : MS—Orig. Dij/88/3/27. A. R1624.
Var. R. : [1] *The words in square brackets are supplied from* A ; *the charter is damaged.* [2] A *repeats* filium. [3] Witkale A. Withcale R. [4] Scoteni A. Scoteny R.
Note : Winemer was subdean in 1184 (*Facsimiles of Charters in the British Museum*, p. 66). He became archdeacon of Northampton *circa* 1192 (Le Neve *Fasti Ecclesiae Anglicanae* ii, p. 55).

440

1580. Grant by Rannulf of Withcall, at the wish and with the consent of Margaret his wife and his heirs, in the presence of the said Margaret, to the church of Lincoln and the Common, of William son of Godric, Eda his wife and their sons and daughters, together with a toft and a bovate in Withcall which Godric formerly held. (1184–1192.)

Carta eiusdem Ranulfi . de alia terra . in eadem villa. (A rubric.)

Omnibus sancte matris ecclesie filiis Rannulfus de Witkale[1] salutem . Ad omnium noticiam peruenire desidero me de assensu 7 [2]de[2] uoluntate Margarete uxoris mee 7 heredum meorum presente predicta Margareta dedisse 7 concessisse in puram 7 perpetuam elemosinam deo 7 sancte Marie Linc' . 7 commune canonicorum ibidem deo famulantium * Willelmum filium Godrici 7 Edam uxorem suam 7 filios 7 filias eorum cum tofto . 7 una bouata terre in Witkale[1] cum omnibus pertinenciis absque aliquo retinemento . quem toftum 7 bouatam terre tenuit Godricus pater predicti Willelmi in Witkale[1] . Hanc uero elemosinam solutam 7 quietam ab omni seculari seruitio 7 exactione adquietabimus 7 warantizabimus contra omnes homines . Hiis testibus . Lamberto de Scotenni[3] . Hugo[4] de Scotenni[5] . Waltero Escrop . Radulfo de Cotingham[6] . Adam Rat . Henrico Franceis[7] . Radulfo . Rollando . magistro Galfrido . Gilleberto[8] capellano . Waltero filio Galfridi . Winemero subdecano . Johanne sacrista . Ricardo de Kym . Sansone[9] . 7 multis aliis.

Marginalia in A : Wykale (by Q2).
Texts : MS—A. R1625.
Var. R. : [1] Withcale R. [2–2] R *omits*. [3] Scoteny R. [4] *sic* : Hugone R. [5] Scoten' R. [6] Cotyngham R. [7] Fraunceys R. [8] Gilberto R. [9] Saus' R.

**Folio 84d.*

441

1581. Confirmation by William son of Rannulf of Withcall, of his father's gift mentioned in the preceding charter, to which he adds another toft in Withcall. (Circa 1200–1205.)

Carta Willelmi filii Ranulfi . de Wikale . ad confirmandum donum Ranulfi patris sui. (A rubric.)

Omnibus sancte matris ecclesie filiis Willelmus filius Ranullfi[1] de Witkale[1] salutem . Ad omnium noticiam peruenire desidero me concessisse 7 presenti carta mea confirmasse quicquid pater meus Rannullf*us*' de Wikale[2] dedit in puram 7 perpetuam elemosinam deo 7 ecclesie sancte Marie Linc' . 7 commune canonicorum ibidem deo famulantium . Scilicet Willelmum filium Godrici . 7 Edam uxorem suam [3]7[3] filios 7 filias eorum cum tofto 7 una bouata terre in Wikale[1] cum omnibus pertinenciis absque aliquo retinemento . quem toftum 7 bouatam terre tenuit Godricus pater predicti Willelmi in Witkale[2] . 7 ex donatione mea unum toftum quem Radulfus filius Askel tenuit . Hanc uero elemosinam solutam 7 quietam ab omni seculari seruitio 7 exactione ego 7 heredes mei adquietabimus 7 warantizabimus contra omnes homines . Hiis . testibus . magistro .W. cancellario .

domino .R. de Kym' . thesaurario . magistro .W. Blundo . domino .R. Scoto . Henrico de Derebi[4] . canonicis . Henrico filio Ranullfi . Rollando palmario . ⁊ multis aliis.

Texts: MS—A. R1627.
Var. R.: [1] *sic.* [2] Withcale R. [3–3] R *omits.* [4] Derby R.
Note: Le Neve gives Richard of Kyme as Treasurer in 1203 with a successor in 1206 (*Fasti* ii, p. 87).

442

1582. Agreement between R[oger] the dean and the chapter of Lincoln, and Margaret widow of Rannulf of Withcall. Margaret has released to them a toft in Withcall which she had claimed in virtue of dower. For this the dean and chapter have assigned to her two shillings yearly to be paid by William son of Godric, the tenant of the toft, and have also given her half a mark of silver. and she has sworn not to initiate any suit concerning the toft against the dean and chapter. (Early thirteenth century.)

Carta conuencionis inter capitulum Linc' . ⁊ Margaretam . relictam Ranulfi de Wikale. (A rubric.)

Indented

CYROGRAPHVM

Hec est conuentio facta inter .R. decanum . ⁊ capitulum Linc' ecclesie ⁊ Margaretam viduam Ranulfi de Withkale[1] . scilicet quod eadem Margareta quietum clamauit de se ⁊ de omnibus suis inperpetuum dicto capitulo quoddam toftum in Witkale[2] quod Radulfus filius Askell' tenuit . Quod eadem Margareta clamauit se contingere nomine dotis . Scilicet toftum illud quod Willelmus filius eiusdem Margarete contulit iamdicto capitulo in puram ⁊ perpetuam elemosinam . per cartam suam . Et pro ista quieta clamatione .· dicti .R. decanus ⁊ capitulum concesserunt dicte Margarete tota uita eius duos solidos annuatim in festo sancti Martini percipiendos per manum Willelmi filii Godrici qui toftum predictum tenet .· uel heredum suorum . Et preterea pro bono pacis dederunt eidem .M. in principio huius conuentionis dimidiam . marcam . argenti . Ipsa uero . Margareta coram eodem capitulo tactis sacrosanctis ewangeliis jurauit .· quod decetero per se uel [3]per[3] interpositam personam .· nullam molestiam aut controuersiam mouebit dicto capitulo aut suo tenenti de eodem tofto . Hiis testibus . Eudone capellano . Ada capellano . Willelmo de Beningwrth'[4] . Henrico filio Rannulfi de Withkale.[1]

Endorsed: xxxi (13 cent.).
Tag for seal. Size: 6½ x 3½ inches.
Marginalia in A: dotis.

Texts: MS—Orig. Dij/88/3/26. A. R1626.

Var. R.: [1] Witkale A. Withcale R. [2] Withcale R. [3–3] R *omits*. [4] Benyngworth' R.

Note: The date of Rannulf of Withcall's death is uncertain, but was probably late in the twelfth century. Roger became dean in 1195.

443

1583. Grant by Walter son of master Geoffrey of Withcall, to the church of Lincoln and the Common, of a toft and his *culturae* of Doddeswelle and Nethesti and other parcels of land in Withcall, including one of six acres lying in various places: if it shall be found that these six acres are not complete they shall be made up from Walter's demesne; if on the other hand there are more than six acres the surplus shall be merged again with his land. (Late twelfth century.)

Carta donacionis Walteri filii magistri .G. de Withale de terra in eadem. (A rubric.)

Omnibus sancte matris ecclesie filiis ad quos presens scriptum peruenerit ⸵ Walterus filius magistri Galfridi de Withcale[1] salutem . Nouerit vniuersitas uestra me assensu Galfridi * fratris mei dedisse ⁊ concessisse . ⁊ hac presenti carta mea confirmasse deo ⁊ beate Marie ⁊ commune canonicorum Lincol' ecclesie unum toftum in Withcale[1] quod fuit Thoraldi[2] bercarii . ⁊ in territorio eiusdem uille uersus orientem ⸵ culturam meam de Doddeswelle[3] . ⁊ culturam meam de Nethesti . ⁊ terram que iacet inter terras maioris ecclesie ⁊ Willelmi Beket proximas iuxta Nethesti ⸵ uersus orientem . ⁊ terram meam in Marthelundesbusc . ⁊ pratum meum in Dudemanholm . Preterea sex acras [4]terre[4] uersus occidentem . videlicet terras meas in Shewelles utrimque proximas terre Gileberti presbiteri . ⁊ terram meam que iacet inter terras Coste filii Godricii ⁊ Ricardi Boche[5] ⸵ in Ringesdale . ⁊ omnes terras meas in Stretefurlanges . ⁊ si iam dicte sex acre nondum plene ⁊ integre fuerint ⸵ illas de dominio meo proximo eidem terre in Stretefurlanges ⸵ adimplebo . Siquid uero residuum fuerit ⸵ ad terram meam redigatur . Hanc autem terram cum omni libertate quam ego ⁊ antecessores mei umquam in eadem terra habuimus[6] ⸵ dedi iam dictis canonicis in puram ⁊ liberam ⁊ perpetuam elemosinam pro animabus patris mei ⁊ matris mee ⁊ omnium antecessorum meorum . necnon ⁊ pro salute mea . ⁊ heredum meorum . Eandem etiam terram ego ⁊ heredes mei warantizabimus eis[7] in perpetuum contra omnes homines . Et ut ista donacio firma permaneat ⸵ hanc cartam sigilli mei appensione ⸵ corroboraui . Hiis testibus . Roberto Scauerib .

Gileberto filio Gode . Willelmo filio Gip .˙ presbiteris .˙ domino Radulfo . 7 Willelmo . 7 Henrico . 7 Simone filiis eius . Simone de Halintun'[8] . Roberto . filio Engeram . Willelmo filio Suein[9] . 7 multis aliis.

Endorsed : (1) Carta Walteri filii magistri Galfridi de Withcale (early 13 cent.). (2) xxxiii (late 13 cent.). (3) Withcale (by Q.)

Two tags for seals. Size : $8\frac{1}{4}$ x $4\frac{3}{8}$ inches.

Texts : MS—Orig. Dij/88/3/28. A. R1628.

Var. R. : [1] Withkale A. [2] Toraldi A. [3] Dodeswelle A. Dodeswell' R. [4]–[4] R *omits.* [5] Bochi R. [6] *the scribe apparently wrote* habuerunt *here and had to make an alteration.* habuerimus A. [7] *interpolated partly at the end, partly at the beginning of the line.* [8] Halington' R. [9] Swein A. Sweyn R.

**Folio* 85.

Hdl. . 8 : 5 .

444

1584. Grant by Walter son of Geoffrey of Withcall, to the church of Lincoln and the Common, of a croft and four acres of land in Withcall. (Circa 1200–1205.)

Carta eiusdem Walteri de .j. crofto . 7 .iiijor. acris terre in Wicchale. (A rubric.)

Vniuersis sancte matris ecclesie filiis ad quos presens scriptum peruenerit .˙ Walterus filius Galfridi de Withkale[1] salutem . Nouerit uniuersitas uestra me dedisse 7 concessisse 7 hac presenti carta mea confirmasse deo 7 beate Marie 7 commune canonicorum eiusdem ecclesie pro salute anime mee 7 omnium antecessorum meorum unum croftum in Withkale[1] quod uocatur Grescroft . 7 quod iacet ante ostium[2] Leuerici inter fontem 7 toftum quod fuit Ingeram . 7 quatuor acras terre arabilis in territorio eiusdem uille . scilicet duas acras terre arabilis[3] . ex occidentali parte uille in Hippeldale . 7 duas acras terre ex orientali parte eiusdem uille . in Fifueacre[4] [5]Dalselant scilicet ex australi parte illius culture . in puram . liberam . 7 perpetuam elemosinam . 7 quietam[5] ab omni seculari seruitio 7 exaccione . Et ego 7 heredes mei warantizabimus predicte ecclesie 7 commune canonicorum predictam donacionem contra omnes homines imperpetuum . Et ut hec mea donatio rata sit 7 stabilis .˙ illam sigilli mei munimine corroboraui . Hiis testibus . Waltero Blundo . Eudone tunc preposito . Willelmo de Sancto Petro . Radulfo filio Ernisii . Henrico filio Rannulfi . Roulando . Willelmo filio Rannulfi . Waltero clerico . Roberto stabulario.[6]

Marginalia in A : +.

Texts : MS—A. R1632.

Var. R. : [1] Withcale R. [2] hostium R. [3] *this word has been cancelled.* [4] Fisueacre R. [5]–[5] R *omits.* [6] staburario R.

Note : For Eudo the provost see vol. iv, p. 283. Walter Blund often witnesses with him. William son of Rannulf levied a fine in 1210 (*Final Concords* i, p. 103). Henry son of Rannulf made a grant to Bullington priory late in the twelfth century (*Danelaw Charters*, p. 74).

445

1585. Confirmation by William son of Rannulf of Withcall, of the preceding grant. (Circa 1200–1210.)

Carta Willelmi filii Ranulfi . ad confirmandum donum predicti Walteri. (A rubric.)

Omnibus Christi fidelibus ad quos presens scriptum peruenerit .˙ Willelmus filius Ranulfi de Withkale[1] salutem. Nouerit uniuersitas uestra me ratam ⁊ gratam habere . ⁊ hac presenti carta confirmasse donationem . concessionem . ⁊ confirmationem quas Walterus filius Galfridi de Withkale[1] fecit deo ⁊ beate Marie ⁊ commune * canonicorum Linc' ecclesie de uno crofto in Withcal[1] quod uocatur Grescroft . ⁊ de quatuor acris terre arabilis in territorio eiusdem uille cum omnibus pertinenciis in puram ⁊ perpetuam elemosinam sicut carta eiusdem Walteri quam predicti canonici exinde habent testatur . Vt autem hec mea confirmatio perpetuam optineat firmitatem .˙ eam presenti scripto ⁊ sigilli mei appositione corroboraui . Hiis testibus . Symone[2] Malcuuenant[3]. Thoma fratre eius Willelmo de Eboraco clerico . Petro de Cheuermund clerico . Malgero de Nethelham[4] Hugone filio Ade capellani.

Marginalia in A: (1) +. (2) quas. (3) +.
Texts: MS—A. R1633.
Var. R.: [1] Withcale R. [2] Simone R. [3] Malcuuenaunt R. [4] Netelham R.
Note: This charter is later than the preceding one. Thomas Malcovenant occurs in 1206 (L.R.S. xxii, no. 1367).

**Folio 85d.*

446

1586. Grant by Walter son of Geoffrey of Withcall, to the church of Lincoln and the Common, of two tofts, two acres and two perches of land in Withcall. (Late twelfth century.)

Carta Walteri filii Galfridi . de .ij^bus . toftis . ⁊ .ij. perticatis terre in Wicchale. (A rubric.)

Notum sit tam presentibus quam futuris quod ego Walterus filius Galfridi de Withcale dedi ⁊ concessi ⁊ hac presenti carta mea confirmaui deo ⁊ beate Marie ⁊ commune canonicorum Linc' ecclesie in territorio de Withcale unum toftum quod fuit Gille filii Adelsi . Et unum toftum quod fuit Adelsi . ⁊ duas acras terre que fuerunt predicti Gille . vnam scilicet proximo iacentem iuxta Noutestigate[1] uersus occidentem . ⁊ alium[2] iuxta Noutestigate uersus orientem . ⁊ terram meam in Brentedale usque ad plenitudinem duarum acrarum . ⁊ unam percatam terre in Dikedale . ⁊ aliam percatam iuxta Doddes Wellesti uersus orientem . in puram . liberam ⁊

perpetuam elemosinam pro animabus patris mei 7 matris mee 7 omnium antecessorum meorum . necnon 7 pro salute mea 7 heredum meorum . Hanc autem predictam terram ego 7 heredes mei warantizabimus predictis canonicis imperpetuum contra omnes homines . Et ut ista donatio firma 7 stabilis permaneat ⁏ hanc cartam sigilli mei appositione corroboraui . Hiis testibus . domino Rannulfo de Withcale . Roberto filio Willelmi . magistro Roberto de Gaitun'[3] . Alano presbitero . 7 Willelmo diacono fratre eius . Gileberto[4] capellano . Alano de Malbethorp[5] . Rolando de Withcale . Waltero clerico . 7 multis aliis.

Texts: MS—A. R1631.
Var. R.: [1] Notestigate R. [2] *sic*: aliam R. [3] Gartun R. [4] Gilberto R. [5] Malberthorp' R.
Note: Master Robert of Gayton le Wold witnesses late twelfth century (L.R.S. xviii, p. 51). Alan of Mablethorpe witnesses in 1182 (*ibid.*, pp. 102–3) and late twelfth century (*ibid.*, p. 107).

447

1587. Grant by Walter son of master Geoffrey of Withcall, to the chapter of Lincoln, of several parcels of land in Withcall. (Late twelfth century.)

Carta eiusdem Walteri de alia terra in Withkale. (A rubric.)

Vniuersis sancte matris ecclesie filiis ad quos presens scriptum peruenerit ⁏ Walterus filius magistri Galfridi de Withkale[1] salutem . Nouerit uniuersitas uestra me dedisse 7 concessisse 7 hac presenti carta mea confirmasse deo 7 beate Marie 7 capitulo Linc' dimidiam bouatam terre in territorio de Withkale[1] excepta una acra que iacet in mea cultura de Welleberh[2] . quam scilicet bouatam Kille[3] carpentarius tenuit de patre meo . Preterea dedi eis unam acram iuxta culturam de Karledale . 7 totam terram meam in Ketelberne Welle . 7 Crofteshoudland . 7 tres acras iuxta Retthibisti . 7 dimidiam acram in Hinghelbaldhou . quam Iggeramus[4] homo meus tenuit . Hanc autem donationem feci eis pro salute mea 7 meorum tam uiuorum quam defunctorum in puram 7 perpetuam elemosinam liberam 7 quietam ab omni seculari seruitio 7 exactione . Et ego 7 heredes mei warantizabimus predictum tenementum predicto capitulo Linc' contra omnes homines . Hiis testibus . Rannulfo de Widcale[5] . Henrico filio suo . Rolando . Alano de Malberthorp . Johanne persona de Nortun . Ricardo Boreas . Waltero capellano . Rogero de Lissewis . Roberto capellano . Waltero clerico.

Texts: MS—A. R1629.
Var. R.: [1] Withcale R. [2] Wellebergh' R. [3] *sic*: *but compare with* Gille carpentarius *in no.* 1590 *below*. [4] Ingelrammus R. [5] Withale R.

448

1588. Grant by Walter son of Geoffrey, to the church of Lincoln and the Common, of a toft and eighteen acres in Withcall, of which nine lie on the east and nine on the west of the village. Whatever is lacking in the nine acres on the east Walter will make good from his large *cultura* which lies south of the road to Maltby and whatever is lacking in the nine acres in the west, in Scotgate. (Late twelfth century.)

Carta eiusdem Walteri de xviii. acris terre in Wicekale. (A rubric.)

Sciant presentes ⁊ futuri quod ego Walterus filius Galfridi dedi ⁊ concessi ⁊ hac presenti * carta mea confirmaui deo ⁊ beate Marie ⁊ commune Linc' ecclesie in puram ⁊ perpetuam elemosinam unum tofthum[1] quod fuit Ingeram ⁊ decem ⁊ octo acras in territorio de Widthale[2] scilicet nouem acras ex parte orientali . ⁊ nouem ex parte occidentali . In orientali parte terram meam in Holegate que iacet iuxta uiam de Maltheby̌[3] ⁊ terram meam que iacet ex alia parte uie iuxta terram Rodlandi[4] . unam acram ⁊ dimidiam ad Standar . ⁊ dimidiam acram iuxta Inggelbaldhou ⁊ terram que iacet iuxta terminum terre de Thadewelle ⁊ dimidiam acram in pendulo montis que porrigitur usque ad predictum terminum . ⁊ unam acram quam Ingeram[5] tenuit . ⁊ dimidiam acram in Rauenesacres ⁊ unam percatam iuxta uiam de Karledale . Et quod deficit de istis nouem acris ego adimplebo de mangna[6] mea cultura que iacet iuxta uiam de Maltheby[7] uersus austrum . In occidentali parte totam terram meam in Scippendale . ⁊ terram meam in Scalebereu ⁊ terram meam ad Brincheldaleouedlan . ⁊ terram meam iuxta terram Galfridi Pidecok[8] . ⁊ terram meam in Ringedale[9] in superiori parte iuxta terram Costi filii Godrici . Et quod deficit de nouem acris ego adimplebo ad Scotgate[10] . Hanc donationem warantizabo eis contra omnes homines . Preterea innotescat omnibus quod prius dederam eis alias terras quas carta mea eis confirmaui . Hiis testibus . Alano de Malbertorp[11] . Willelmo filio Randulfi . Henrico fratre eius . Rodlando . Radulfo filio . Ernis . Et hec donacio ut illibata permaneat ⁖ sigilli mei appositione eam roboraui.

Endorsed : xxxv (late 13 cent.).
Tag for seal. Size : $6\frac{3}{4}$ x $5\frac{1}{2}$ inches.
Texts : MS—Orig. Dij/88/3/25. A. R1630.
Var. R. : [1] toftum A *and* R. [2] Withcale A *and* R. [3] Malteby A *and* R. [4] Rollandi A *and* R. [5] Inggeram A. [6] *sic* : magna A *and* R. [7] Malthebi A. Malteby R. [8] Pidekok A. [9] Bingedale A. [10] Stocgate R. [11] Malberthorp A *and* R.

**Folio* 86.

Hdl. . 8 . 6 .

449

1589. Confirmation by Rannulf of Withcall, of the gift of Walter son of Geoffrey of Withcall, to the chapter of Lincoln, from his fee. To this he adds half an acre of meadow in Withcall. (Late twelfth century.)

Carta Ranulfi de Wictkale . ad confirmandum donum dicti Walteri filii Galfridi. (A rubric.)

Sciant tam presentes quam futuri quod ego Rannulfus de Withkale[1] concessi 7 hoc presenti scripto confirmaui deo 7 beate Marie 7 commune canonicorum Linc' terram de feudo meo quam Walterus filius Galfridi de Withkale' predicte commune contulit in elemosinam . 7 quam Willelmus filius Godrici tenuit de predictis canonicis . inperpetuum .' pacifice possidendam . Preterea dedi 7 presenti carta confirmaui prefate commune unam dimidiam acram prati in North prato de Withkale[1] iuxta pratum Linc' ecclesie uersus Nord part[2] quod fuit Asceri de Sacsedale in puram liberam 7 perpetuam elemosinam pro animabus patris mei 7 matris mee 7 omnium antecessorum meorum . necnon 7 pro salute mea 7 heredum meorum . Et eisdem canonicis [3]ego[3] 7 heredes mei warantizabimus predictum pratum imperpetuum contra omnes homines . Et ut ista confirmatio 7 donatio firme permaneant . 7 irreuocabiles .' hanc cartam sigilli mei appensione corroboraui . Hiis testibus . Gilleberto[4] capellano . Alano de Malberthorp . Roberto filio Willelmi . magistro Roberto de Gaitun[5] . Alano presbitero . 7 Willelmo[6] diacono fratre eius . Gileberto[4] Templario . 7 multis.

Texts: MS—A. R1634.
Var. R.: [1] Withcale R. [2] Northpart R. [3–3] R *omits*. [4] Gilberto R. [5] Gartun' R. [6] Waltero R.

450

1590. Confirmation by Ralf son of Ernis and Basilia his wife, of Withcall, of various gifts made to the Common by Walter son of Geoffrey of Withcall. (Circa 1210–1220.)

Carta Radulfi filii Ernisii 7 Basillie . uxoris eius ad confirmandum donum predicti Walteri filii Galfridi. (A rubric.)

Vniuersis Christi fidelibus ad quos presens scriptum peruenerit .' Radulfus filius Ernisii 7 Basillia uxor eius de Withkal'[1] salutem . Nouerit vniuersitas uestra nos concessisse 7 presenti carta nostra confirmasse deo 7 beate Marie 7 commune canonicorum Lincoln' ecclesie omnes terras quas Walterus filius Galfridi eisdem canonicis dedit in villa de Withkal[2] 7 in territorio eiusdem ville . Scilicet vnum toftum quod fuit Gille filii Adelsi . 7 aliud * toftum quod fuit Adelsi

⁊ duas acras terre que fuerunt prefati Gille . ⁊ duas acras in Brentedale . ⁊ vnam perticatam in Dikedale . ⁊ aliam perticatam iuxta Doddeswell' Stig[3] . Item dimidiam bouatam excepta una acra . quam . scilicet . dimidiam bouatam Gille carpentarius aliquando tenuit . ⁊ unam acram iuxta culturam de Carledale . ⁊ totam terram suam in Ketelbernwell' ⁊ Crofteshoudland' . ⁊ tres acras iuxta Reithesb' Stigh' . ⁊ dimidiam acram in Hingelbaldhou . quam Ingelramus tenuit . Item vnum croftum quod uocatur Gressecroft[4] . ⁊ quatuor acras terre arabilis in territorio predicte ville . Scilicet duas acras in Hipeldale . ⁊ duas acras in Fifacredaleselant[5] . ⁊ vnum toftum quod fuit Thoraldi bercarii . ⁊ culturam suam [6]de Doddeswell' . ⁊ culturam suam[6] de Netestigh'[7] . ⁊ terram suam inter terras predicte ecclesie Linc' ⁊ terram Willelmi Beket . iuxta Netestigh'[7] . ⁊ terram suam in Martholundesbusc . ⁊ pratum suum in Dudemanholm'[8] . ⁊ sex acras terre ex occidentali parte ville . Item unum toftum quod fuit Ingelrami . ⁊ decem ⁊ octo acras terre arabilis . videlicet nouem ex una parte uille . ⁊ nouem ex alia . Has autem predictas terras cum pertinentiis ⁊ omnibus libertatibus ⁊ aisiamentis infra uillam ⁊ extra ad predictas terras pertinentibus ./ concedimus ⁊ confirmamus in puram ⁊ perpetuam elemosinam perpetuo possidendas . Et nos ⁊ heredes nostri eisdem canonicis prenominatas terras cum omnibus pertinentiis warantizabimus defendemus ⁊ adquietabimus erga[9] omnes homines . In huius autem rei robur ⁊ testimonium . presens scriptum sigillorum nostrorum apposicione corroborauimus . Hiis testibus . Conano . Rumfaro ⁊ Waltero capellanis . magistro Hugone de Mareseia . Willelmo filio Rannulfi de Withkal' Henrico fratre eius . Petro de Bekering' . Willelmo ⁊ Symone filiis eius . Petro de Bekering de Linc' . Petro de Cheuermund' clerico . Willelmo filio Ernisii de Beningworth'[10] . Philippo Hors . Johanne capellano . Alexandro ⁊ Benedicto ⁊ aliis.

Endorsed : (1) Confirmatio Withcal' Luthesk' (by Q). (2) xl.

Two tags for seals on the second of which is a broken seal : probably round with diameter 1¼ inches, green ; device—a bird.

IGILL' BĀSILIE FIL

Size : 6¼ x 8¼ inches.

Texts : MS—Orig. Dij/88/3/30. A. R1635.

Var. R. [1] Withcale R. [2] Withkale A. Withcale R. [3] Dodeswellestig R. [4] Grescroft A *and* R. [5] Fifacredalesland R. [6–6] R *omits*. [7] Nethestigh R. [8] Dudemansholm' A. [9] ergas (*sic*) A. [10] Beningword' A.

Note : Ralf son of Ernis and Basilia his wife were plaintiffs in levying a fine with William son of Rannulf about thirty-six acres of land in Withcall 14th Dec., 1210. They then granted the land to William de Cantilupe who became the sworn man of William son of Rannulf (*Final Concords* i, p. 103). Conan, Walter and Rumfar are frequent witnesses circa 1210–1220 (see vol. iv above, pp. 166, 195, 199 etc.).

**Folio 86d.*

ADD. CHART.

1591. Grant by Ralf le Franceis of Withcall, to the church of Lincoln and the Common, of half a toft and four selions of arable land in Withcall. (Circa 1230–1240.)

Omnibus Christi fidelibus ad quos presens scriptum peruenerit ∴ Radulfus le Franceis[2] de Witkal'[3] salutem in domino . Nouerit uniuersitas [uestra me dedisse 7 concessisse 7 hac pre[1]]senti carta mea confirmasse pro salute anime mee 7 antecessorum 7 successorum meorum deo 7 beate Marie 7 commune canonicorum [Linc' ecclesi[1]]e in puram . liberam 7 perpetuam elemosinam ∴ medietatem tofti mei in Witkal'[3] uersus orientem capiendam in longitudine 7 latitudine a uia regia uersus North . in longitudine usque ad aquam [4]currentem[4] uersus Sudh[5] cum edificiis in illa parte sitis . Et quatuor [seliones terre arabilis in territorio[1]] eiusdem uille duos seliones silicet[6] ex orientali parte uille . videlicet totum unum selionem ex North parte de Grenehau[7] inter terram [quam Siwatus quondam te[1]]nuit ∴ 7 terram quam Ricardus Lauedeman quondam tenuit . Et totum unum selionem apud Rauthelandes inter terram quam Gerardus Hoghel [quondam tenuit 7 terram que[1]] fuit quondam Radulfi filii Ernisii . Et ex West parte uille duos seliones videlicet totum unum selionem abuttantem super uiam regiam de [Buschau ex North parte uie inter terram quam[1]] Siwatus quondam tenuit . [7 terram quam[1]] Wilelmus filius Hawisie quondam tenuit . Et totum unum selionem qui abuttat super [uiam regiam de Buschau ex[1]] eadem parte uie ex West parte de Dike qui iacet [inter[1]] terram quam Astinus quondam tenuit ∴ 7 terram quam Arnaldus filius Gosse quondam tenuit [cum omnibus pertinenciis liberta[1]]tibus 7 eisiamentis infra uillam 7 extra in [omnibus locis[1]] Habend*am* 7 tenend*am* prefatis canonicis in puram . liberam 7 perpetuam elemosinam . [liberam 7 quietam ab omni seruicio 7 exaccione seculari[1]] 7 demanda Et ego Radulfus 7 heredes mei guarantizabimus . adquietabimus 7 defendemus ∴ totam predictam medietatem [tofti predicti cum edificiis cum[1]] terra arabili pre[scripta[1]] cum omnibus pertinentiis suis ∴ predictis canonicis contra omnes homines in perpetuum tanquam puram . liberam 7 perpetuam [elemosinam Et in huius rei[1]] testimonium ∴ presens scriptum fide pro me 7 heredibus meis interposita ∴ sigillo meo confirmaui . Hiis testibus . Johanne tunc persona de [Withcale Willelmo tunc capellano de[1]] eadem uilla Waltero filio Willelmi Henrico filio Ranulfi Henrico filio suo Roberto Beket' Lamberto clerico . Ricardo carpentario Waltero filio suo [Willelmo clerico 7 multis aliis[1]].

Endorsed: Carta Radulfi Le Franceis de With . . . . (13 cent.).
Tag for seal. Size: 8¾ x 3¾ inches.
Texts: MS—Orig. Dij/88/3/31. R1638.
Var. R.: [1] *the words in square brackets are supplied from* R, *the charter having been injured by damp.* [2] Frаunceys R. [3] Withcale R. [4]–[4] R *omits.* [5] Suth R. [6] *sic*: scilicet R. [7] Greneham R.
Note: John was instituted parson of Withcall by Hugh of Wells before the end of 1218 (L.R.S. iii, p. 67). The date of his successor's institution is not known.

ADD. CHART.

1592. Grant by Walter son of William son of Godric of Withcall, to the church of Lincoln and the Common, of a toft with its buildings and the arable land pertaining thereto in Withcall. (Circa 1230–1240.)

Omnibus Christi fidelibus ad quos presens scriptum peruenerit . Walterus filius Willelmi filii Godrici de Wÿthal[1] . salutem in domino . Nouerit vniuersitas uestra me dedisse concessisse . 7 hac presenti carta mea confirmasse pro salute anime mee 7 antecessorum 7 successorum meorum deo 7 beate Marie 7 commune canonicorum Linc' ecclesie in liberam puram 7 perpetuam elemosinam . vnum toftum cum edificiis in Wÿthcal'[1] quod fuit quondam Radulfi filii Hernisii[2] quod [abuttat ex au[3]]strali parte contra curiam aule domini Willelmi . de Kantilupo[4] 7 vnam partem terre arrabilis predicto tofto pertinentis que abutat versus [occidentem super tof[3]]tum aule ex parte occidentali uille 7 uersus orientem contra terram Willelmi clerici cum libero introitu 7 exitu infra uillam 7 extra . Tenend' [7 habend' prefatis[3]] canonicis in puram liberam 7 perpetuam elemosinam . liberam . 7 quietam . ab omni seruicio 7 exaccione seculari 7 demanda . Et ego Walterus [7 heredes[3]] mei predictum toftum cum predicta terra 7 omnibus pertinenciis suis prefatis canonicis contra omnes homines tanquam puram 7 perpetuam elemosinam [warantizabimus[3]] deffendemus 7 adquietabimus inperpetuum . Et in huius rei testimonium ./ presens scriptum fide pro me 7 heredibus meis interposita ./ sigillo meo confirmaui . T[estibus domino Hen[3]]rico filio Willelmi filii Ranulfi . Henrico filio Ranulfi . Roberto Beket . Petro stabulario Lamberto clerico . Willelmo clerico Arnaldo Templario [Henrico[3]] filio Henrici.

Endorsed: (1) xliiij. (2) Carta Walteri filii Willelmi filii Godrici de Withale . de vno tofto cum edificiis in eadem villa (13 cent.).
Tag for seal. Size: 9¾ x 3¼ inches.
Texts: MS—Orig. Dij/88/3/32. R1639
Var. R.: [1] Withcale R. [2] Ernisii R. [3] *supplied from* R: *the charter has been injured by damp.* [4] Cantilupo R.
Note: William son of Godric, father of this grantor, was given as a *nativus* to the Chapter in no. 1580 above. Walter married Matilda daughter of Ralf son of Ernis (see the two following charters). Henry son of William son of Rannulf was holding land in Withcall in 1242 (*Book of Fees* ii, p. 1055).

ADD. CHART.

1593. Grant by Ralf son of Ernis of Withcall, with the consent of Basilia his wife, to Walter son of William son of Godric, in frank marriage with Ralf's daughter Matilda, of six acres of land in Withcall. (Circa 1214–1220.)

Sciant presentes 7 futuri quod ego Radulfus filius Ernisii de Withkal'[1] de assensu 7 consensu Basillie uxoris mee dedi 7 concessi 7 presenti carta mea confirma[vi[2]] Waltero filio Willelmi filii Godrici sex acras terre arabilis in territorio de Withkal'[1] in liberum maritagium cum Matilda filia mea quam idem Walterus duxit in uxorem . Scilicet duas acras apud Wolfhou . 7 tres perticatas apud Scatgate . 7 quinque perticatas apud Osbernhou . 7 . unam acram apud Skilgates[3] . 7 unam acram apud Hemminghill' . Habendas 7 tenendas cum omnibus pertinentiis suis eisdem Waltero 7 Matilda 7 heredibus ex eis prouenientibus . libere quiete 7 hereditarie . Et ego Radulfus 7 heredes mei predictis Waltero 7 Matilde 7 heredibus ex eis procreandis prenominatas sex acras cum pertinentiis libertatibus 7 aisiamentis ; warentizabimus . defendemus 7 adquietabimus erga omnes homines inperpetuum . In huius autem rei robur 7 testimonium . presens scriptum sigilli mei apposicione corroboraui . Hiis testibus . Conano sacrista ecclesie Linc' magistro Hugone de Mares' . Willelmo persona de Tuxford' . Petro de Bekering' . Willelmo 7 Symone filiis eius . Willelmo filio Rannulfi de Withkal'[2] . Henrico fratre eius . Petro de Cheuermund' . Willelmo filio Ernisii[4] de Beningworth' . Petro de Bekering' de Linc' . P[hil[2]]ippo Hors 7 aliis.

Endorsed: Withkhall': vi acr' (13 cent.).
Tag for seal. Size: 6½ x 4½ inches.
Texts: MS—Orig. Dij/88/3/33. R1637.
Var. R.: [1] Withcale R. [2] *supplied from* R: *a hole in the document.* [3] Stilgates R. [4] Hernisii R.
Note: For the dates of Conan as sacrist see vol. iv, p. 281 above.

ADD. CHART.

1594. Notification by William son of Godric of Withcall that, with the assent of his lords Roger, the dean and the chapter of Lincoln, he has granted to Walter his son and his wife Matilda in frank marriage, all the lands which he holds of the canons in Withcall. These lands the canons had of the gift of Walter son of Geoffrey of Withcall and by the confirmation of Ralf and Basilia. William saves to himself possession during his life as a layman and to his wife reasonable dower should she survive him. Meanwhile he will maintain Walter and Matilda in his own house to the best of his ability. (Circa 1214–1220.)

Notum sit[1] omnibus[1] tam presentibus quam futuris quod ego Willelmus filius Godrici de Withkal'[2] de assensu 7 uoluntate dominorum meorum Rogeri decani 7 canonicorum Lincoln' ecclesie . dedisse 7 concessisse 7 presenti carta mea confirmasse Waltero filio meo 7 Matilde sponse sue filie Radulfi filii Ernisii 7 Basillie uxoris sue in liberum maritagium ∴ omnes terras quas tenui de eisdem canonicis in villa de Withkal'[2] 7 in territorio eiusdem ville . illas scilicet terras quas ipsi canonici habent ex donatione Walteri filii Galfridi de Withkal'[2] . 7 confirmatione predictorum Radulfi 7 Basillie . Habendas 7 tenendas cum omnibus pertinentiis eisdem Waltero 7 Matilde 7 heredibus ex eis procreandis libere . quiete 7 hereditarie . Salua mihi possessione mea quamdiu uixero in seculari habitu . Salua etiam Ede uxori mee exinde rationabili dote sua si ipsa me superuixerit . Et sciendum quod ego Willelmus . exhibebo dictos Walterum 7 Matildem uxorem suam . 7 pro posse meo ministrabo eis necessaria in domo[3] mea omnibus diebus mee uite ∴ iuxta facultates meas . In huius autem rei robur 7 testimonium . presens scriptum sigilli mei appositione corroboraui . Hiis testibus . Conano sacrista ecclesie Lincoln' . magistro Hugone de Mares' . Willelmo persona de Tuxford' . Petro de Bekering . Willelmo 7 Sýmone filiis eius . Willelmo filio Rannulfi de Withkal'[2] . Henrico fratre eius . Petro de Cheuermund' . Willelmo filio Ernis[ii[4]] de Beningworth' . Petro de Bekering de Lincoln' . Philippo Hors . Johanne Alexandro 7 Benedicto 7 aliis.

Endorsed : Wikal' (late 13 cent. : ? by Q).
Tag for seal. Size : 9¼ x 3¾ inches.
Texts : MS—Orig. Dij/88/3/34. R1636.
Var. R. : [1] R *omits*. [2] Withcale R. [3] doma (*sic*) R. [4] *a hole in the charter.*

GRIMOLDBY

451

1595. Grant by Robert son of Edric Bugge of Grimoldby, to the church of Lincoln and the Common, of two selions of land in Grimoldby. (Before 25th Sept., 1205.)

Carta Roberti filii Edrici Bugge de .ij. selionibus in Grimolby. (A rubric.)

Omnibus sancte matris ecclesie filiis ad quos presens scriptum peruenerit . Robertus filius Edrici Bugge[1] de Grimolbi[2] salutem . Nouerit uniuersitas uestra me dedisse 7 concessisse 7 hac presenti mea carta[3] confirmasse deo 7 beate 7[4] Marie 7 commune canonicorum Linc' ecclesie duas seliones [5]terre[5] in uilla[6] de Grimolbi[2] que iacent iuxta toftum quod fuit Radulfi filii Asger uersus meridiem in puram 7 perpetuam elemosinam liberam 7 solutam ab omni seruicio seculari 7 exactione tacita uel manifesta . 7 Ego Robertus 7 heredes mei warantizabimus commune dictorum canonicorum supradictas duas seliones contra omnes homines . Hiis testibus .W. subdecano . magistro .R. de Holm . Henrico de Derebi[7] canonicis Linc' . Ada. filio Ranulfi . Ricardo[8] filio Aze . Roberto filio Ode[9] . Waltero filio Ade . Alano filio Aceri . W. filio Hernis[10] . Roberto filio Hernis[10] 7 multis aliis.

Endorsed: (1) Jordebur (by Q). (2) cxiij. (3) Grimolby (late 13 or early 14 cent.). (4) Grimesbi .ij. seliones . [*struck through*] (13 cent.).

Seal on tag: Oval, 1¾ x 1¼ inches, cream, a variety of fleur-de-lys.

SIGILL' ROBERTI BUG'

Size: 6⅝ x 2⅛ inches.

Texts: MS—Orig. Dij/71/2/35. A. R1641.

Var. R.: [1] Brigge R. [2] Grimoldby R. [3] R *has* carta mea. [4] *sic*: A *and* R *omit.* [5]–[5] R *omits.* [6] A *has* via. [7] Derby R. [8] A *has* Roberto. [9] Odonis R. [10] Ernisii R.

Note: William de Bramfeld the subdean was murdered in the cathedral 25th Sept., 1205. The date at which he entered upon the office is uncertain, but Richard Kentensis held it 1197–8 (H. E. Salter (ed.) *Cartulary of the Abbey of Eynsham.* Oxford Record Society, vol. i, p. 47). It is he not William of Blois who witnesses (see no. 1680 which is after 1196 and has the first four witnesses to this charter).

452

1596. Grant by Ralf son of Robert of Saltfleetby, to the church of Lincoln and the Common, of a toft and half a bovate of land in Grimoldby and an acre and a perch of meadow in Saltfleetby (Before 25th Sept., 1205.)

Carta Radulfi filii Roberti de Saltfleby . de .i. dimidia bovata terre . 7 . i tofto in Grimolby. (A rubric.)

Omnibus sancte matris ecclesie filiis ad quos [1]presens[1] scriptum peruenerit . Radulfus filius Roberti de Saltfletebi[2] salutem . Nouerit uniuersitas uestra me dedisse 7 concessisse 7 hac presenti mea carta[3] confirmasse deo 7 beate Marie 7 commune canonicorum Linc' ecclesie toftum quod fuit Radulfi filii Asger in uilla de Grimolbi[4] 7 unam dimidiam bouatam[5]* terre in campis eiusdem uille cum omnibus pertinenciis suis 7 aisiamentis 7 libertatibus que pertinent ad uillam de Grimolby 7 unam acram 7 unam percatam prati in campis de Saltfletibi[2] in Rooluesdale . in puram 7 perpetuam elemosinam solutam 7 liberam ab omni seculari seruicio 7 exactione tacita uel manifesta pro salute animarum parentum meorum 7 omnium antecessorum meorum . 7 Ego Radulfus 7 heredes mei warantizabimus predictam donacionem concessionem 7 confirmacionem commune dictorum canonicorum contra omnes homines . Hiis testibus .W. subdecano . magistro Roberto de Holm Henrico de Derebi[6] canonicis Linc'.

Ricardo filio Aze . Gileberto[7] filio Rogeri de Manneb' .W. de Mannebi . Roberto filio Odonis de Mannebi . Radulfo clerico . Roberto filio Matildis 7 multi alii.[8]

Endorsed: (1) Grimolby (by Q). (2) Grimolb' dimidia bovata (13 cent.). (3) cxiiij (13 cent.).

Seal on tag: round, 1¼ inches diameter, cream, a conventional device.

+ **SIGILL' RADVLFI FILII ROB'**

Size: 6½ x 2¼ inches.

Texts: MS—Orig. Dij/71/2/34. A. R1640.

Var. R.: [1–1] A *omits.* [2] Saltfleteby R. [3] R *has* carta mea. [4] Grimoldby R. [5] R *has a blank where* bovatam *should come.* [6] Derby R. [7] Gilberto R. [8] *sic:* aliis multis A, multis aliis R.

**Folio* 87.

Hdl. . 8 . 7 .

ALVINGHAM

453

1597. Grant by Hamelin son of Thorald of Alvingham, to the church of Lincoln and the Common, of ten acres of land, five on each side of the village, together with a toft in Alvingham. (Circa 1200.)

Carta Hamelini filii Thoraldi . de .x. acris . 7 .i. tofto in Aluingham. (A rubric.)

Sciant presentes 7 futuri quod ego Hamelinus filius Toraldi de Alwinham[1] dedi 7 concessi 7 hac presenti carta mea confirmaui deo 7 beate Marie 7 commune canonicorum Linc' ecclesie decem acras terre arabilis in teritorio de Alwinham[1] . scilicet quinque acras ex una parte uille 7 totidem ex alia parte [2]uille[2] . 7 unum toftum in eadem [uil]la . scilicet illud toftum quod iacet inter toftum Pigot[3] 7 toftum Ricardi filii sacerdotis in puram 7 perpetuam elemosinam pro salute anime [2]mee[2] 7 omnium antecessorum meorum . Et ego 7 heredes mei warantizabimus predictam terram prenominato capitulo 7 prefatum toftum contra omnes homines inperpetuum . Et ut hec mea donacio firma permaneat ∴ sigilli mei munimine eam corroboraui . Hiis testibus Eudone preposito . Waltero Blundo iuniore[4] . Wiardo[5] . Ricardo filio Ace[6]. Ace[6] Norman . Roberto filio Godefridi[7] . Hereberto[8] filio Johannis.

Endorsed: (1) Carta Hamelini filii Toraldi de Haluingham (13 cent.). (2) Aluingham (13 cent.).

Slit for seal tag. Size: 5¾ x 3 inches.

Marginalia in A: (1) ?. (2) -b.

Texts: MS—Orig. Dij/66/1/2. A. R.1488.

Var. R.: [1] Aluinham A. Aluingham R. [2–2] R *omits.* [3] Pygot R. [4] R *has* Ivone *for* iuniore. [5] Wyardo R. [6] Aze A. [7] Godefrai A *and* R. [8] Herberto R.

Note: For the dates of Eudo the provost, see vol. iv, p. 283 above.

454

1598. Grant by Roger Carbonel, to the church of Lincoln and the Common, of a toft and half a bovate of land in Alvingham. (Late twelfth century.)

Carta Rogeri de Carbonel . de .i. tofto . ⁊ dimidia . bouata terre in Aluingham. (A rubric.)

Omnibus Christi fidelibus ad quos presens scriptum peruenerit . Rogerus[1] Carbonel salutem Nouerit vniuersitas vestra me dedisse ⁊ concessisse . ⁊ hac presenti carta mea confirmasse deo . ⁊ beate Marie . ⁊ commune canonicorum Linc' ecclesie pro salute anime mee . ⁊ omnium antecessorum meorum . in puram ⁊ perpetuam elemosinam . liberam ⁊ qvietam ab omni seculari seruicio ⁊ exactione .: vnum toftum in villa de Aluingham . qvi est inter toftum Ricardi Winde[2] . ⁊ toftum Toraldi filii . Vlfkel . ⁊ dimidiam bouatam terre in territorio eiusdem ville ad eundem toftum pertinentem . cvm omnibus pertinentiis in villa . ⁊ extra villam in pratis . in campis . Qvem toftum . ⁊ qvam scilicet . dimidiam bouatam terre .: tenuit Alardus filius . Leuiue . Hanc autem donationem ego ⁊ heredes mei . prefate ecclesie . ⁊ commune canonicorum eiusdem ecclesie contra omnes homines warantizabimus . Hiis testibus . magistro .W. Blundo canonico . magistro Roberto . de Gatton'[3] . Ricardo filio Ace[4] . Willelmo filio Alfsi . Waltero de Sais . Hamelino de Couingham[5] decano.[6]

Endorsed: (1) Luthhesk' (by Q). (2) Aluingham (by Q). (3) iij (13 cent.).
Seal on tag—round, cream, about 1¼ inches diameter, fleur de lys.
. . . . ARBVNEL

Size: 6 x 3 inches.
Texts: MS—Orig. Dij/66/1/1. A. R1489.
Var. R.: [1] A *adds* de. [2] Wynde R. [3] Gaiton' A. [4] Aze A. [5] Cotyngham R. [6] R *adds* ⁊ aliis.
Note: Master Robert of Gayton le Wold and Hamelin dean of Covenham both witness late in the twelfth century (L.R.S. xviii, pp. 51, 107).

455

1599. Grant by Tenggi son of Osbert, to the church of Lincoln and the Common, of a toft and a half bovate of land, five acres on each side of the village of Alvingham. (Late twelfth century.)

Carta Tengi filii Osberti . de .i. tofto ⁊ dimidia . bouata terre in Aluingham. (A rubric.)

Vniuersis sancte matris ecclesie filiis ad quos presens scriptum peruenerit .: Tenggi filius Osberti salutem . Nouerit uniuersitas uestra me dedisse ⁊ concessisse ⁊ hac presenti carta mea confirmasse deo ⁊ beate Marie ⁊ commune canonicorum Linc' ecclesie . in puram ⁊ perpetuam elemosinam pro salute anime mee 7 antecessorum meorum . vnum toftum * in Aluingham . quod iacet inter croftum monacorum[1] de Parco Lude . 7 viam . 7 abutat super toftum Hugonis filii Burgard ex occidentali parte . 7 super uiam ecclesie ex orientali parte . 7 dimidiam bouatam terre in territorio eiusdem uille . scilicet . quinque acras terre ex orientali parte uille . 7 quinque acras terre ex occidentali parte uille . cum libero exitu 7 introitu . 7 cum omnibus aliis eisiamentis infra uillam . 7 extra uillam . Hanc autem donacionem 7 concessionem deo 7 predicte ecclesie caritatiue collatam ∴ Ego 7 heredes mei warantizabimus eis contra omnes homines . Et ut hec donacio 7 concessio rata 7 stabilis in perpetuum perseueret ∴ presentis scripti seriem sigilli mei attestacione communiui . Hiis . testibus . Ricardo capellano de Aluingham[2] . Odone Galle . Willelmo persona de Salfleteb'[3] . Hugone le Neucumen . Ricardo filio Ace . Willelmo filio Roberti . de Cokeringt' . Cost' de Aluingham.

Endorsed : (1) Tengi de Aluingham (13 cent.). (2) iiij (13 cent.). (3) Carta Tenggi . de uno tofto . . . . terre . in Aluingham . Johannes tenens reddit annuatim .xij. denarios . ad festum . Sancti Johannis baptiste (13 cent.).

Slit for seal tag. Size : 6¼ x 4 inches.

Texts : MS—Orig. Dij/66/1/3. A. R1490.

Var. R. : [1] monachorum A *and* R. [2] Aluinham A. [3] Saltfleteb' A. Saltfleteby R.

Note : Odo Galle, William parson of Saltfleetby, Hugh Newcomen and Richard son of Azo all occur as grantors and witnesses at this date (*Danelaw Charters*, pp. 392, 394, 396–7).

**Folio 87d.*

ADD. CHART.

1600. Grant by Henry, the dean, and the chapter of Lincoln, to John of Cockerington for so long as he shall remain a layman, of their tenement in Alvingham, which has escheated through the felony of John son of Hugh. John shall pay a yearly render of half a mark of silver and if he shall be fifteen days late in payment the dean and chapter may re-enter on the land. He shall maintain the buildings in good condition and remove nothing without the chapter's consent. He shall not let the land or any part of it to the prejudice of the chapter nor alienate it without their consent. The dean and chapter reserve the right of coercion in the agreement and after John's death the land shall freely revert to them. (Circa 1245–1250.)

Indented

CYROGRAPHUM

Vniuersis Christi fidelibus presens scriptum visuris uel audituris ∴ H. decanus 7 capitulum Linc' salutem in domino sempiternam . Noueritis nos concessisse 7 dimisisse Johanni de Cokerinton' quamdiu vixerit in habitu seculari terram illam cum pertinenciis que est eschaeta nostra per feloniam Johannis filii Hugonis quondam tenentis nostri in villa de Aluingham reddendo inde annuatim nobis dimidiam marcam argenti . ad duos terminos scilicet . quadraginta denarios ad Pascha . 7 quadraginta denarios ad festum Sancti Michaelis . Ita quod si dictam firmam vltra quindecim dies a termino computandos nobis non soluerit .' cadet a dicte terre cum pertinenciis possessione . ita quod licebit nobis dictam terram ingredi . 7 de eadem prout uoluerimus absque alicuius contradiccione disponere Idem uero Johannes edificia in dicta terra existencia in bonu statu sustentabit . nec inde aliquid ammouebit nisi ob ipsorum melioracionem . sine consensu nostro nec dictam terram uel aliquam ipsius partem alicui aliquo vnquam tempore ad firmam dimittet ad detrimentum nostrum uel juris nostri elongacionem . vel aliquo alienacionis genere a nobis alienabit . sine consensu nostro . Cohercione super premissis nobis in perpetuum reseruata . Post decessum uero dicti Johannis de Cokerinton' . memorata terra cum omnibus pertinenciis suis absque omni reclamacione uel contradiccione heredum dicti Johannis uel alicuius ex parte ipsius libera 7 soluta ad nos reuertetur . Hec omnia fideliter obseruanda idem Johannes de Cokerinton' . super sacrosancta .' corporale prestitit juramentum . Testibus dominis .N. cancellario . 7 R. thesaurario . magistris .R. de Grauel' . Ricardo Cornub' . 7 R. de Pereton' . dominis .R. de Bollesouers . 7 Thoma de Askeby canonicis Linc' . Ricardo . . . . Rogero de Thurvill' . tunc clerico Commune Linc' ecclesie.

Endorsed : Contra Johannem de Cokerinton' de terra nostra in Aluingham . (13 cent.).

There is no hole for a seal tag, but the charter has been torn where one should have been.

Size : 7¾ x 5¾ inches.

Text : MS—Orig. Dij/66/1/4.

Note : Henry de Lexington was dean 1245–1253. The first, third, fourth, fifth and sixth witnesses to this charter are also witnesses to one issued between 1239 and 1245 (vol. iv, no. 1320 above), and Nicholas the chancellor, Robert of Bolsover and Roger of Turville witness together 10th April, 1247 (*ibid.*, no. 1321). John of Cockerington was a juror in 1242 (*Book of Fees*, ii, p. 1052).

ADD. CHART.

1601. Grant by Richard the dean, and the chapter of Lincoln, to John of Alvingham, clerk, and his heirs, of a toft and buildings which John son of Hugh Cost formerly held of them in Alvingham. For this John shall pay a yearly render of half a mark. (1257.)

Omnibus Christi fidelibus presentem cartam inspecturis vel audituris Ricardus decanus 7 capitulum Linc' ecclesie salutem in domino . Nouerit vniuersitas vestra nos concessisse 7 hac presenti carta nostra confirmasse magistro Johanni de

Aluingham clerico 7 heredibus suis vel suis assignatis exceptis viris religiosis 7 Judeis vnum toftum cum edificiis 7 totam terram cum omnibus pertinenciis suis 7 redditibus que aliquando tenuit de nobis Johannes filius Hugonis Cost in villa de Aluingham . Tenend' 7 habend' predicto Johanni 7 heredibus suis vel suis assignatis sicut predictum est inperpetuum libere quiete pacifice 7 hereditarie Reddendo inde annuatim nobis dimidiam marcam argenti ad duos anni terminos videlicet ad Pascha quadraginta denarios 7 ad festum sancti Michaelis quadraginta denarios pro omnibus secularibus seruiciis consuetudinibus exaccionibus 7 demandis . In cuius rei testimonium presentem cartam sigilli nostri munimine duximus roborandam Testibus domino Johanne de Kokerington tunc vicecomite Lincoln' domino Willelmo de Mannebẏ magistro Johanne de Perton Ricardo de Trẏnn Ricardo filio Johannis de Aluingham Wẏgotto de eadem Thoma fili Willelmi de eadem 7 aliis.

Text : MS—R1491.

Note : The dean is Richard Gravesend 1254–8. John of Cockerington was sheriff in 1257.

GRAINTHORPE

456

1602. Grant by Robert of Legbourne, to the church of Lincoln and the Common, of a toft and other land, formerly of Wlsi, in Grainthorpe. (1196–1203.)

Carta Roberti de Lekeburne de terra in Germundtorp. (A rubric.)

Sciant presentes 7 futuri quod ego Robertus de Lekeburne concessi 7 dedi 7 hac presenti carta mea confirmaui deo 7 beate Marie 7 commune canonicorum Linc' ecclesie totum illud toftum quod fuit Wlsi in Germundtorp[1] ex[2] North parte de Swine[3] . 7 totam terram que fuit eiusdem Wlsi a uia de Swinesbrigge[4] apud orientem usque ad mare . habentem latitudinis septem percatas 7 dimidiam . in puram 7 perpetuam elemosinam pro salute anime méé 7 omnium antecessorum meorum . Et ego 7 heredes mei warantizabimus totum prenominatum toftum 7 terram prenominatam prenominato capitulo contra omnes homines . Et ut hec mea donatio imperpetuum rata permaneat ·/ sigilli mei munimine corroboraui . Hiis testibus . magistro .W. precentore Linc' ecclesie . magistro Willelmo cancellario . Ricardo de Kyma . magistro Waltero Blundo . Eudone de Sancto Botulfo . Waltero Blundo capellano . Willelmo de Lekeburne . Ricardo de Sumercotes . Roberto de Millei . 7 multis aliis.

Texts: MS—A. R1516.
Var. R.: [1] Germethorp' R. [2] in *in* R. [3] Swyne R. [4] Swynesbrigge R.
Note: William of Blois was precentor 1196–1203. For the family of Legbourne see H. and K.F., vol. ii, pp. 106–9.

457

1603. Grant by John son of Gikel of Yarborough, knight, to the church of Lincoln and the Common, of various parcels of land and meadow with pasture, in the salt marsh of Grainthorpe, which Robert Mancelot had formerly held of him. (Circa 1210–1220.)

Carta Johannis filii Gikel de Gerdeburg de terra in Germuntorp. (A rubric.)

Omnibus Christi fidelibus ad quos presens scriptum peruenerit Johannes filius Gikel de Yerdheburc'[1] miles salutem . Noueritis me diuine pietatis intuitu 7 pro salute anime mee dedisse 7 concessisse 7 presenti carta mea confirmasse deo 7 beate Marie 7 commune canonicorum Linc' ecclesie totam terram illam quam Robertus Mancelot[2] tenuit de me in territorio de Germunthorp[3] . [4]Scilicet medietatem unius Saltcoteholm'[4] que continet in latitudine septem percatas 7 dimidiam . que iacet inter terram Toraldi[5] Mancelot[2] 7 terram Roberti palmarii . Item quatuor acras terre in Estcroft[6] uersus occidentem cum uia adiacente que ducit uersus aquilonem . Item tres percatas terre in Littelcroft que iacent inter terram dicti Toraldi[5] 7 infantium Radulfi filii Costi . Item tres acras 7 dimidiam in Northcroft[7] que iacent inter terram predicti Toraldi[5] 7 inter Annegate . Item unam acram 7 dimidiam scilicet medietatem unius selionis qui iacet iuxta terram infantium predictorum predicti Radulfi ex parte australi qui se extendit in longitudine a terra Johannis filii Ouc usque ad finem eiusdem campi . Item duas acras prati que iacent in Haghedailes inter pratum prefati Toraldi[5] 7 pratum de Elkington'[8] . Item unam acram prati in Estdailes inter pratum sepedicti Toraldi[5] 7 pratum de Elkinton'[9] . cum medietate pasture quam quondam Ricardus Mancelot[2] habuit in marisco salso de Germentorp[3] . Habenda 7 tenenda cum omnibus pertinenciis libertatibus 7 aisiamentis infra villam 7 extra . in puram 7 perpetuam elemosinam liberam . solu*tam . quietam ab omni seruitio seculari 7 exactione . Et ego Johannes 7 heredes mei warantizabimus eisdem canonicis totas prefatas terras cum omnibus pertinenciis suis defendemus 7 adquietabimus erga omnes homines imperpetuum . In huius autem rei robur 7 testimonium presenti scripto sigillum meum apposui . Testibus . Thoma de Norton' . Conano . Henrico de Torpell' . Rogero de Neuport capellanis .

[4]Osberto de Neuport[4] . Ricardo de Neuport . Roberto Scoto . Widone de Keles' . Mauricio de Neuport . Thoma de Waltham . Rogero de Neuport . ⁊ multis aliis.

Texts : MS—A. R1510.

Var. R. : [1] Jerdeburg R. [2] Mauncelot R. [3] Germethorp R. [4–4] R *omits*. [5] Thoraldi R. [6] Escroft R. [7] North'croft R. [8] Elkinton R. [9] Elkington' R.

Note : John son of Gikel of Yarborough was steward of the soke of Gayton circa 1200 (*Danelaw Charters*, p. 352). He occurs at various intervals in the records all through the early part of the thirteenth century and was adjudged guilty of novel disseisin in 1218 (Selden Society, vol. liii, no. 180). The witnesses occur about 1210–1220 (see nos. 1132, 1135, 1147 and others in vol. iv, above).

**Folio* 88.

Hdl. . 8 . 8 .

458

1604. Grant by Thorald son of Richard Mancelot, to the church of Lincoln and the Common, of four acres of arable land in Grainthorpe. (Circa 1210–1215.)

Carta Thoraldi de .iiijor. acris in Germunthorp . de feofacione. (A rubric.)

Omnibus Christi fidelibus ad quos presens scriptum peruenerit ∴ Thoraldus filius Ricardi Mancelot[1] salutem . Nouerit uniuersitas uestra me diuine pietatis intuitu [2]me[2] dedisse ⁊ concessisse ⁊ presenti carta mea confirmasse deo ⁊ beate Marie ⁊ commune canonicorium Linc' ecclesie quatuor acras terre arabilis in territorio de Germuntorp[3] . Scilicet duas acras proximas terre monialium de Aluingham uersus septentrionem . ⁊ in Litelcroft[4] unam acram inter terram Hamelini decani ⁊ terram Radulfi filii Coste et unam acram ibidem inter terram Hugonis aucupis ⁊ Annegate . Habendas ⁊ tenendas in puram ⁊ perpetuam elemosinam cum omnibus pertinenciis [2]suis[2] liberas solutas ⁊ quietas ab omni seruitio seculari ⁊ exactione . Et ego ⁊ heredes mei warentizabimus dictis canonicis prenominatas quatuor acras cum pertinenciis contra omnes homines imperpetuum . In huius autem rei robur ⁊ testimonium presens scriptum sigilli mei appositione corroboraui . Hiis testibus . Conano ⁊ Waltero capellanis . Vmfrido Syre[5] de Suthbroc[6] . Roberto de Stowe . Thoma de Norton' . Petro de Cheuermund . Elya[7] de Braiton' . ⁊ aliis.

Texts : MS—A. R1500.

Var. R. : [1] Mauncelot R. [2–2] R *omits*. [3] Germethorp R. [4] Litelcroft R. [5] Sire R. [6] Suthbrok R. [7] Elia R.

Note : For the witnesses compare nos. 1305 and 1372 in vol. iv, above.

459

1605. Confirmation of the preceding grant by John son of Gikel of Yarborough. (Circa 1210–1215.)

Carta Johannis Gikel ad confirmandum illas .iiij^{or}. acras. (A rubric.)

Notum sit omnibus tam presentibus quam futuris quod ego Johannes [1]filius[1] Gikel de Jerburc[2] concessi ⁊ presenti carta mea confirmaui deo ⁊ beate Marie ⁊ commune canonicorum Linc' ecclesie donationem quam Thoraldus Mancelot[3] dedit eisdem canonicis . videlicet quatuor acras terre in territorio de Germentorp[4] . Scilicet duas acras inter toftum eiusdem Thoraldi ⁊ terram monialium de Aluingham . ⁊ unam acram in Litel Croft[5] propinquiorem terre Hamelini uersus austrum . ⁊ unam acram inter Anegate[6] . ⁊ terram Hugonis aucupis propinquiorem terre eiusdem Hugonis uersus aquilonem . Habendas ⁊ tenendas cum omnibus pertinenciis suis in puram ⁊ perpetuam elemosinam . liberas solutas ⁊ quietas ab omni [1]seculari[1] seruitio ⁊ exactione . vt autem hec mea confirmatio rata ⁊ stabilis permaneat .' eam presenti scripto ⁊ sigilli mei appositione corroboraui . Hiis testibus . Johanne persona de Tedletorp[7] . Waltero de Hambi[8] . Ricardo filio Vmfridi . Roberto filio Ricardi . [1]Ricardo[1] de Humberstain[9] . Willelmo de Midley . Petro de Cheuermund [1]clerico[1] . Willelmo filio Ernisii . Hugone Knotting[10] . ⁊ aliis.

Texts: MS—A. R1512.
Var. R.: [1–1] R *omits*. [2] Jordeburg R. [3] Mauncelot R. [4] Germethorp R. [5] Littelcroft R. [6] Annegate R. [7] Thedelthorp' R. [8] Hamby R. [9] Humberstayn R. [10] Knottyng' R.

460

1606. Notification by John of Grainthorpe, son of Auke, that by his advice Hugh of Holderness, the falconer, and Lewara his wife have given to the chapter of Lincoln three acres of land in Grainthorpe. (Circa 1200.)

Carta de dono Hugonis de Holdernesse per consilium Johannis de Germuntorp. (A rubric.)

Omnibus sancte matris ecclesie filiis ad quos presens scriptum peruenerit Johannes de Germuntorp[1] filius Hauke salutem . Notum sit uniuersitati uestre Hugonem de Holdernesse aucupem ⁊ Lewaram sponsam eius consilio ⁊ assensu meo dedisse deo ⁊ beate Marie ⁊ capitulo Linc' * ecclesie de terra quam tenuerunt in Germuntorp[1] tres acras terre arabilis [2]⁊ dimidiam[2] . ⁊ dimidiam percatam in Suthcroft .

7 dimidiam acram prati in Cudailles . tenendas in puram 7 perpetuam elemosinam . 7 ego Johannes 7 heredes mei warantizabimus predicto capitulo hanc predictam terram contra omnes homines . [Hiis testibus[3]] Jordano filio Thoraldi . Thoraldo filio Mirield[4] . Roberto filio Ederici[5] . Ricardo Mancelot[6] Arnald West . Ricardo filio Baldrici . Ada filio Jordani . Alano filio Aliz[7] vidue . Osberto filio Ricardi . Rumfaro 7 Roberto 7 Waltero filiis Roberti . Willelmo 7 Cost 7 Johanne 7 Radulfo filiis Siward . Roberto 7 Thoraldo filiis Ricardi.

Texts : MS—A. R1508.

Var. R. : [1] Germethorp' R. [2–2] R *omits.* [3] *supplied from* R : A *has omitted this.* [4] Mirild' R. [5] Edrici R. [6] Mauncelot R. [7] Alicie R.

Note : Compare the witnesses of this charter with those who are mentioned in and who witness nos. 1610 and 1611, below.

**Folio 88d.*

461

1607. Grant by Hugh of Holderness, the falconer, with the advice and assent of Lewara his wife, sister and heir of Alan son of Seldwar', to the church of Lincoln and the Common, of land and meadow in Grainthorpe. (Circa 1200.)

Carta Hugonis de Holdernesse de terra 7 prato in Germuntorp. (A rubric.)

Omnibus sancte matris ecclesie filiis ad quos presens scriptum peruenerit Hugo de Holdernesse auceps salutem . Nouerit uniuersitas uestra me consilio 7 assensu Leware vxoris méé 7 sororis Alani filii Seldwar' 7 heredis[1] dedisse 7 concessisse 7 hac presenti carta mea confirmasse deo 7 beate Marie 7 commune Linc' ecclesie in puram 7 perpetuam elemosinam de terra quam teneo in Germuntorp[2] tres acras terre arabilis 7 dimidiam . 7 dimidiam percatam in Suthcroft . 7 dimidiam[3] prati in Cudailles . Hanc uero donationem ego Hugo 7 Lewara uxor mea 7 heredes nostri[4] warantizabimus contra omnes homines . Hiis testibus . Roberto 7 Siward filiis Edrici . Jordano filio Thoraldi . Thoraldo filio Miriild'[5] . Ricardo Mancelot . Arnaldo West . Osberto filio Ricardi . Rumfaro 7 Roberto filiis Roberti . Willelmo 7 Cost 7 Thoraldo[6] filiis Siward . Ricardo filio Balderici[7] . Stephano de Holdernesse . Alano filio Alicie vidue . Roberto filio Thoraldi.

Texts : MS—A. R1514.

Var. R. : [1] R *adds* me. [2] Germethorp R. [3] *sic* : R *adds* acram. [4] mei R. [5] Mirild' R. [6] Theobaldo R. [7] Baldrici R.

462

1608. Confirmation by John son of Gikel of Yarborough of the preceding grant. (Circa 1200.)

Carta Johannis filii Gikelli ad confirmandum dictam terram . 7 aliam in Germunthorp. (A rubric.)

Sciant omnes tam presentes quam futuri quod ego Johannes filius[1] Gikelli de Jerburc[2] pro salute anime méé 7 antecessorum meorum concessi 7 confirmaui deo 7 ecclesie sancte Marie Linc' . 7 capitulo eiusdem loci quatuor acras terre . 7 dimidiam percatam in [3]Germunthorp[4] 7[5] tres acras terre arabilis 7 dimidiam . 7 dimidiam perticatam in[3] illo loco qui dicitur Suthcroft . 7 dimidiam[6] prati in Cudailles . quas predictum capitulum Lincolnie habet ex dono Hugonis aucupis de Holdernesse . tenendas 7 habendas in perpetuam elemosinam libere 7 quiete ab omni seculari seruitio . Hiis testibus . Hamelino decano de Couenham . Roberto palmario de Germuntorp[4] . Osberto filio Ricardi . Gilberto filio Gikel . Jordano filio Thoraldi . Thoraldo filio Miriild'[6] . Ricardo Mancelot.[7]

Marginalia in A: x acras.
Texts: MS—A. R1513.
Var. R.: [1] R *repeats* filius. [2] Jerdeburg' R. [3–3] *added in the margin by* Con. [4] Germethorp' R. [5] scilicet R. [6] R *adds* acram. [6] Mirild' R. [5] Mauncelot R.

463

1609. Grant by John son of Gikel of Yarborough, to the church of Lincoln and the Common, of the land in Grainthorpe which Walter Moysent had formerly held. (1196–1203.)

Carta feofamenti eiusdem Johannis de quadam alia terra in Germundthorp. (A rubric.)

Vniuersis sancte matris ecclesie filiis ad quod presens scriptum peruenerit . Johannes filius Gikel de Yerdburch[1] salutem . Nouerit uniuersitas uestra me dedisse 7 concessisse . 7 hac presenti carta mea confirmasse deo 7 beate Marie 7 commune Linc' ecclesie terram illam in Germundtorp[2] . scilicet . illam quam Walterus Moysent tenuit in villa de Germundtorp[2] ex boreali parte de Swine . habentem quatuor perticatas latitudinis . que . scilicet . terra incipit a uia de Swinesbrigge . 7 finit super Couenham Landemare[3] . in puram 7 perpetuam elemosinam pro salute anime méé 7 patris mei 7 matris méé 7 omnium antecessorum meorum . Et ego 7 heredes mei warantizabimus terram prenominatam prenominato capitulo contra omnes homines . Et ut hec mea donatio inperpetuum rata permaneat ∴ sigilli mei munimine corroboraui . Hiis testibus * . magistro Willelmo precentore

Linc' ecclesie . Ricardo de Kyma . magistro Waltero Blundo . Eudone de Sancto Botulpho . Gileberto Pilate[4] . Ricardo de Hardres capellano . Waltero Blundo capellano.

Texts: MS—A. R1511.
Var. R.: [1] Jerdeburg R. [2] Germethorp' R. [3] Landmare R. [4] Pẏlat' R.
Note: William of Blois was precentor 1196–1203.

**Folio* 89.
Hdl. . 8 . 9 .

464

1610. Grant by Ralf son of Brian of Welton, to the church of Lincoln and the Common, of the land which Thorald son of Mirild held of him in Grainthorpe, including the fishing rights attached to one of the parcels. (Circa 1200.)

Carta feofamenti Radulfi filii Briani de quadam terra in Germunthorp. (A rubric.)

Sciant presentes 7 futuri quod ego Radulfus filius Briani de Welleton[1] concessi 7 dedi 7 hac presenti carta mea confirmaui deo 7 beate Marie 7 commune canonicorum Linc' ecclesie pro salute anime méé 7 omnium antecessorum meorum in puram 7 perpetuam elemosinam totam terram quam Thoraldus filius Miriilde[2] de Germuntorp[3] tenuit de me . excepto prato in Germuntorp[3] quod est inter pratum Willelmi de Waghena[4] 7 fossatum uersus orientem . Huius terre prenominate héé sunt partes . scilicet toftum cum omnibus pertinentiis suis in quo idem Thoraldus manet . 7 croftum unum inter terram Jordani 7 viam . 7 croftum unum inter Hauedic 7 terram Ricardi filii Baldrici . 7 croftum unum quod iacet inter terras Roberti filii Edrici . Et tres selliones ex occidentali parte de Grescroft . 7 tres selliones ad Harestikes . 7 quatuor acre prati in Suthfurlanges . 7 unus sellio iuxta terram meam . 7 terram Roberti filii Edrici . 7 toftum unum ad Houtoftes . Et octo selliones in Litlecroft[5] . 7 una daila a diuisa[6] de Couenham usque ad mare . que habet in latitudine sex percatas . simul cum piscatura in mare . 7 Striholm cum pastura pertinente . Hanc terram prenominatam warantizabo ego Radulfus 7 heredes mei prenominato capitulo contra omnes homines . Et ut hec mea donatio imperpetuum rata 7 illibata permaneat ∴ sigilli mei appositione corroboraui . Hiis testibus . Willelmo decano ciuitatis Linc' . Rogero de Cukewald decano . Eudone de Sancto Botulfo capellano . Hamelino de Couenham decano . Willelmo de Karleton' . Widone de Hacham[7] . Ricardo filio Ace . Roberto de Germuntorp[3] . Jordano de Germuntorp[3] . Adam filio suo.

Texts: MS—A. R1506.

Var. R.: [1] Welton R. [2] Mirild R. [3] Germethorp'. [4] Wagthena R. [5] Littelcroft. [6] devisa R. [7] Hagham R.

Note: Ralf son of Brian of Welton is found frequently in the late twelfth and early thirteenth century. William dean of the city of Lincoln probably held office about 1200–1210. There is no trace of him in the rolls of Hugh of Wells, in the first ten years of whose pontificate Gilbert de Innocentibus was in office (L.R.S., iii, p. 55. See also no. 1300 in vol. iv, above). Roger de Cuxwold attests as dean 1186–1200 (*Danelaw Charters*, p. 188) and 1196–1203 (no. 1456 in vol. iv, above). William of Wawne occurs in 1202 (L.R.S., xxii, no. 879). Robert son of Edric was impleaded by Simon son of Baldric in 1203 (C.R.R. ii, p. 184).

465

1611. Grant by Richard son of Baldric of Grainthorpe, to the chapter of Lincoln, of a yearly rent of sixpence which Rumfar of Grainthorpe son of Robert the palmer and Ralf son of Siward paid him for the land and a salt pan with its meadow which Baldric had had in Grainthorpe. (Circa 1200.)

Carta feofamenti . Ricardi de Germunthorp de redditu sex denariorum annuorum in eadem. (A rubric.)

Sciant omnes tam presentes quam futuri quod ego Ricardus de Germuntorp[1] filius Baldrici pro salute anime méé 7 antecessorum meorum concessi 7 dedi 7 hac presenti carta mea confirmaui in puram 7 perpetuam elemosinam deo 7 ecclesie beate Marie Linc' 7 eiusdem loci capitulo redditum sex denariorum per annum in Germuntorp[1] . Quem uidelicet redditum Rumfarus de Germuntorp[1] filius Roberti palmeri 7 Radulfus de eadem uilla filius Siward soluerunt michi per annum de tota terra illa quam habuit Baldricus pater meųs infra toftum Arnegrim[2] patrui sui 7 de tota terra quam idem Baldricus habuit infra toftum iacentem ex occidentali parte predicti tofti Arnegrim[2] . 7 de tota terra quam idem Baldricus [3]habuit[3] infra Calue Croft . 7 de ipsa salina que fuit Arnegrim[2] cum holmo suo . 7 cum omnibus pertinenciis suis . Et ego Ricardus 7 heredes mei warantizabimus predictam concessionem 7 donationem predicti redditus sex denariorum per annum in Gurmuntorp[1] deo 7 predicte ecclesie Linc' 7 eiusdem loci capitulo contra omnes uiros 7 mulieres . Hiis testibus . Hamelino de Couenham decano . Radulfo capellano . Ricardo de Luthene* . clerico . Radulfo de Jerburc[4] filio Willelmi . Osberto 7 Willelmo filiis Ricardi . Waltero clerico . Thorraldo filio Miriild' . Roberto Mancelot[5] . Adam filio Jordani . Alano filio Alicie vidue.

Texts: MS—A. R1499.
Var. R.: [1] Germethorp'. [2] *sic.* [3]–[3] R *omits.* [4] Jerdeburg R. [5] Mauncelot R.

**Folio 89d.*

Hdl. Communa Luesk'

466

1612. Grant by Richard son of Baldric of Grainthorpe, to the church of Lincoln and the Common, of several parcels of land in Grainthorpe, specifying in the case of the first that the place of entry shall be eight feet wide. (Circa 1215–1220.)

Carta Ricardi Baldrici de terra in Germundethorp. (A rubric.)

Sciant presentes ⁊ futuri quod ego Ricardus filius Baldrici de Germuntorp[1] dedi ⁊ concessi ⁊ presenti carta mea confirmaui deo ⁊ beate Marie ⁊ commune canonicorum Lincoln' ecclesie duas acras terre in Germuntorp[1] inter terram Ligholf ⁊ terram Radulfi filii Roberti palmarii cum libero introitu ⁊ exitu . octo pedum in latitudine uersus uiam ecclesie de Germuntorp[1] . ⁊ in magno croft ·/ unam acram . ⁊ in Kalue Croft unam acram . ⁊ duas acras inter terram fratrum Hospitalis ⁊ terram Thoraldi[2] filii Seward[2] . iuxta curiam Radulfi palmarii uersus orientem . ⁊ tres acras ex aquilonali parte de Swine inter terram Willelmi Burre ⁊ terram Rumfari . Habendas ⁊ tenendas cum omnibus pertinenciis . libertatibus . ⁊ aisiamentis infra uillam ⁊ extra . in puram ⁊ perpetuam elemosinam . liberas . solutas . ⁊ quietas ab omni seculari seruitio ⁊ exactione . Et ego Ricardus ⁊ heredes mei warantizabimus eisdem canonicis terras prenominatas cum pertinenciis defendemus ⁊ adquietabimus erga omnes homines imperpetuum . In huius autem rei robur ⁊ testimonium presenti scripto sigillum meum apposui . Hiis testibus . Thoma de Norton' . Henrico de Torpell' . Willlemo de Tuxford . Symone de Cancia . Willelmo de Mannecestr' . Symone de Torp[3] . Wynemero[4] . Ricardo de Neuport . Willelmo de Milley . Petro de Cheuermund . Willelmo filio Ernisii . ⁊ aliis.

Marginalia in A: x. x. There has been another note which is now illegible.
Texts: MS—A. R1498.
Var. R.: [1] Germethorp' R. [2] R. *omits*. [3] Thorp' R. [4] R *adds* Waleranno *before* Wynemero.
Note: For these witnesses see the Glentham, Hackthorn and Searby charters in vol. iv, above.

467

1613. Grant by Ralf son of Coste, with the assent of Alice his wife, and his heirs, to the church of Lincoln and the Common, of four acres of land in Grainthorpe. (Circa 1210.)

Carta Radulfi filii Coste de terra in Germundthorp. (A rubric.)

Omnibus Christi fidelibus ad quos presens scriptum peruenerit ·/ Radulfus filius Coste salutem . Noueritis me de assensu 7 consensu Alicie uxoris mee 7 heredum meorum dedisse 7 concessisse 7 presenti carta mea confirmasse deo 7 beate Marie 7 commune canonicorum Linc' ecclesie quatuor acras terre arabilis in territorio de Germuntorp[1] . Scilicet duas acras 7 dimidiam ex parte australi ecclesie eiusdem uille que [2]iacent inter terram Thoraldi Mancelot 7 terram Willelmi Baius . 7 vnam acram 7 dimidiam que[2] abutissant super Sandwath . que iacent inter terram Osberti nepotis Hamelini decani . 7 terram Willelmi fratris eiusdem Osberti . Habendas 7 tenendas cum omnibus pertinenciis suis in puram 7 perpetuam elemosinam . liberas . solutas . 7 quietas ab omni seculari seruitio 7 exactione . Et ego 7 heredes mei warantizabimus eisdem canonicis prenominatas quatuor acras cum pertinenciis contra omnes homines inperpetuum . In huius autem rei robur 7 testimonium ⁏ presens scriptum tam sigilli mei quam sigilli predicte Alicie uxoris mee appositione est corroboratum . Hiis testibus . Conano 7 Waltero capellanis . Andrea de Sumercotes[3] . Roberto Mancelot[4] . Hugone Knotting[5] . Willelmo de Midley[6] . Petro de Cheuermund . Roberto de Stowe . Elya de Braiton'[7] . Willelmo Painell'[8] . Philippo Hors . 7 aliis.

Texts: MS—A. R1502.

Var. R.: [1] Germethorp' R. [2–2] R *omits.* [3] Somercotes R. [4] Mauncelot R. [5] Knottyng R. [6] Milley R. [7] Branton' R. [8] Paynell' R.

Note: This charter must be earlier than 1603 above, in which the children of Ralf son of Coste are referred to as if their father were dead, but the witnesses suggest a date not much before 1215.

468

1614. Grant by Alice daughter of Hamelin of Yarborough, formerly [rural] dean, in her widowhood, to the church of Lincoln, of a croft in Grainthorpe. (After 1202, probably not later than circa 1210.)

Carta Alicie filie Hamelini de terra data Linc' ecclesie . in viduitate sua. (A rubric.)

Sciant tam presentes quam futuri quod ego Aliz filia Hamelini de Jerdeburg quondam decani in viduitate mea existens dedi 7 concessi 7 hac presenti carta * mea confirmaui pro salute anime méé 7 antecessorum meorum deo 7 ecclesie beate Marie Linc' in puram 7 perpetuam elemosinam quoddam croftum[1] in Germuntorp[2] quod Wlned[3] aliquando tenuit . 7 ego Aliz 7 heredes mei warantizabimus 7 defendemus predicte ecclesie Linc' prenominatum croftum[1] in Germuntorp[2] contra omnes homines . Et ut hec mea donatio stabilis 7 illibata permaneat ⁏ presentem cartam sigilli mei appositione corroboraui . Hiis . testibus . Johanne abbate de Fontibus . Warino abbate de Parco . Hamelino decano de Couenham . Willelmo Jordani[4]. Jordane[4] de Bracheneberg[5] . Willelmo de Alkentun[6] . Osberto filio Ricardi . Lamberto clerico de Neubald'.

Marginalia in A: Germethorp (by Q2).
Texts: MS—A. R1507.
Var. R.: [1] toftum R. [2] Germethorp' R. [3] Wolned R. [4] *sic*: filio *presumably omitted*. [5] *sic*. [6] Brakenberg' R. [7] Alkenton' R.
Note: This charter cannot be earlier than 1202 when John occurs as abbot of Louth Park (V.C.H. Lincs. ii, p. 140). Warin occurs in 1207 (*ibid.*) and there were two other abbots before the election of Richard in 1227 (*ibid.*). At Fountains three Johns followed in succession during this period. Alice was the daughter of Hamelin dean of Yarborough and parson of Alvingham, not of Hamelin dean of Covenham. For this family see L.R.S. xviii, p. xvi. Hamelin the dean of Covenham may have been alive in 1203. Pipe Roll, 5 John, P.R.S., N.S. xvi, p. 109, but is not mentioned in the rolls of Hugh of Wells. Rannulf of Cawkwell was dean in the first nine years of Hugh of Wells' pontificate.

**Folio* 90.

Hdl. Luesk' . 9 . 0 . Communa

469

1615. Confirmation by Brian of Yarborough, son of Hamelin, of the croft given by the preceding charter. (After 1202: probably not later than circa 1210.)

Carta de quodam crofto in Germethorp'. (A rubric.)

Sciant tam presentes quam futuri quod ego Briennus de Jerburc[1] filius Hamelini concessi ⁊ hac presenti carta mea confirmaui pro salute anime mee ⁊ antecessorum meorum deo ⁊ ecclesie beate Marie Linc' in puram ⁊ perpetuam elemosinam quoddam croftum in Germuntorp[2] . quod Wolnech[3] tenuit aliquando . Et ego Briennus ⁊ heredes mei warantizabimus ⁊ defendemus predicte ecclesie Linc' predictum croftum in Germuntorp[2] contra omnes homines . Et ut hec confirmatio in posterum rata ⁊ illibata permaneat ∴ presens scriptum sigilli mei appositione corroboraui . Hiis testibus . [4]abbate de Fontibus . Warino abbate de Parco . Hamelino de Couenham decano . Willelmo Jordani . Jordano de Bracheneberg[5] . Willelmo de Alkingtun . Osberto filio Ricardi . Rumfaro . ⁊ Waltero . ⁊ Radulfo filiis Roberti de Germuntorp[2].

Marginalia in A: Germethorp (by Q2).
Texts: MS—A. R1504.
Var. R.: [1] Jerdburc R. [2] Germethorp R. [3] Wolueth R. [4] R *adds* Johanne *before* abbate. [5] Bracumberche R.

470

1616. Grant by Jordan son of Thorald of Grainthorpe, to the church of Lincoln and the Common, of a toft and various parcels of land and meadow in Grainthorpe. (Circa 1200.)

Carta de .ij. acris 7 dimidia in Toftes de Germethorp'. (A rubric.)

Sciant presentes 7 futuri quod ego Jordanus filius Thoraldi de Germundtorp[1] concessi 7 dedi . 7 hac presenti carta mea confirmaui deo 7 beate Marie 7 commune canonicorum Linc' ecclesie pro salute anime mee 7 omnium antecessorum meorum [in][2] puram 7 perpetuam elemosinam [3]duas[3] acras 7 dimidiam in Toftes . que iacent iuxta terram meam . et toftum unum quod abutissat super uiam 7 super terram Alani filii Alicie . et [4]tres[4] acras prati in Mikeldeile que iacent inter terram meam 7 terram Alani . et unam acram terre que iacet inter terram meam 7 terram Alani . et unam acram prati que iacet inter terram meam 7 terram Asgeri in Cudeiles . Et unum sellionem in Litelcroft[5] . et terciam partem unius percate terre a Couenham Landemare usque ad Hauedich . et unam percatam terre a Hauedich usque ad mare . et sextam partem unius acre terre a uia usque ad Wel[6] . et ego Jordanus 7 heredes mei warantizabimus terram prenominatam prenominato capitulo contra omnes homines . Et ut hec mea donatio inperpetuum rata permaneat .' sigilli mei munimine corroboraui . Hiis testibus . Willelmo decano ciuitatis Linc' . Rogero de Cukewald decano . Eudone de Sancto Botulfo capellano . Willelmo clerico filio Johannis de Sumercotes . Radulfo filio Briani . Adam filio Jordani de Germuntorp'. Alano filio Alicie.

Marginalia in A: Germethorp' (by Q2).
Texts: MS—A. R1501.
Var. R.: [1] Germethorp' R. [2] *supplied from* R: *there is a stain in* A. [3–3] *blank in* R. [4] R *omits*. [5] Litelcroft' R. [6] Welle R.
Note: For the date see note to 1610 above, to which both William the dean and Roger of Cuxwold were witnesses.

ADD. CHART.

1617. Grant by Roger the dean and the chapter of Lincoln, to Walter son of Ralf of Grainthorpe, of four acres of land in Grainthorpe, which they had of the gift of Ralf son of Coste and Alice his wife. For this Walter shall pay a yearly render of twelvepence for all service. (Before 1224.)

Vniuersis sancte matris ecclesie filiis ad quos presens scriptum peruenerit Rogerus decanus 7 capitulum Linc' ecclesie salutem eternam in domino . Nouerit vniuersitas vestra nos concessisse 7 presenti carta nostra confirmasse Waltero filio Radulfi de Germethorp quatuor acras terre arrabilis in territorio de Germethorp quas habemus ex dono Radulfi filii Coste de assensu 7 consensu Alicie vxoris sue 7 heredum suorum scilicet duas acras 7 dimidiam ex parte australi ecclesie eiusdem ville que iacent inter terram Thoraldi

Mauncelot ⁊ terram Willelmi Baÿus et vnam acram ⁊ dimidiam que abuttissant super Sandwath que iacent inter terram Osberti nepotis Hamelini decani ⁊ terram Willelmi fratris eiusdem Osberti Habendas ⁊ tenendas de nobis cum pertinenciis eidem Waltero ⁊ heredibus suis in feodo ⁊ hereditate libere ⁊ quiete Reddendo inde nobis duodecim denarios pro omni seruicio ⁊ exaccione scilicet sex denarios ad Pascha ⁊ sex denarios ad festum sancti Michaelis . In huius autem rei robur ⁊ testimonium presens scriptum sigilli nostri apposicione corroborauimus.

Text: MS—R1503.

Note: The dean is probably Roger de Rolveston. The grant must be later than 1617 above, which is probably about 1210–1215.

Add. Chart.

1618. Grant by Roger the dean, and the chapter of Lincoln, to William of Bayeux, of a croft in Grainthorpe which they had of the gift of Alice daughter of Hamelin of Yarborough. For this William shall pay a yearly render of twelvepence. (Before 1224.)

Vniuersis Christi fidelibus ad quos presens scriptum peruenerit Rogerus decanus ⁊ capitulum Lincoln' salutem eternam in domino . Nouerit vniuersitas vestra nos concessisse Willelmo de Baÿus croftum in Germethorp quod habemus de dono Alicie filie Hamelini de Jerdeburg quondam decani quod Wlned aliquando tenuit Tenendum de nobis in feudo ⁊ hereditate illi ⁊ heredibus suis . Reddendo inde nobis annuatim duodecim denarios scilicet sex denarios ad festum sancti Michaelis ⁊ sex denarios ad Pascha . Et vt hec nostra concessio rata ⁊ illibata perseueret inposterum .' eam presenti scripto ⁊ sigilli nostri patrocinio communimus . Valete.

Text: MS—R1505.

Add. Chart.

1619. Release and quitclaim by John son of Auke of Grainthorpe, with the assent of Leviva his sister, and of his friends, to Hugh the falconer, of Holderness, of an acre and half a perch of land in Grainthorpe. In exchange for this Lewara wife of Hugh, with the counsel and consent of her friends, has given John a selion called Long Selion in Grainthorpe. (Circa 1200.)

Sciant omnes tam presentes quam futuri quod ego Johannes filius Auke de Germethorp consilio et assensu Leuiue sororis mee ⁊ amicorum meorum dedi ⁊ concessi ⁊ hac presenti carta mea confirmaui ⁊ quietas clamaui inperpetuum de me ⁊

heredibus meis Hugoni aucupi de Holdernesse 7 heredibus suis vnam acram terre 7 dimidiam parcatam in Germethorp in illo loco qui dicitur Suthcroft que iacet proximo[1] loco ex australi parte terre predicti Hugonis quam idem Hugo habuit ex dono Alani filii Seldwar quarum caput orientale extendit se super illud antrum quod dicitur Grist 7 quarum capud occidentale extendit se super terram Willelmi de Wathne . Et ego Johannes 7 heredes mei warantizabimus predicto Hugoni 7 heredibus suis hanc predictam acram terre 7 dimidiam percatam in Germethorp contra omnes viros 7 mulieres . Et pro hac donacione 7 concessione 7 quietaclamacione Lewara sponsa predicti Hugonis consilio 7 assensu amicorum ipsius Leware dedit mihi vnum selionem in Germethorp que dicitur Longa Selio que iacet proximo[1] loco iuxta meas seliones ex septemtrionali parte cuius capud occidentale extendit se super antrum Toftes 7 cuius capud orientale extendit se super terram Jordani filii Thoraldi . Hiis testibus Willelmo de Lekeburn' Roberto filio eius Ricardo filio Roberti de Somercotes Herberto de Lekeburn Jordano de Brakenberg Roberto de Manneby Warino de Hallaẏ Hamelino decano de Couenham Waltero de Lascelles Roberto 7 Siwardo filiis Edrici Jordano filio Thoraldi Thoraldo filio Mirild Willelmo Cost 7 Johanne 7 Thoraldo 7 Radulfo filiis Jordani Alano 7 Thoraldo filiis Alicie vidue Roberto 7 Thorald 7 Radulpho filiis Ricardi Mauncelot.

Text: MS—R1509.
Var R.: [1] *sic.*

ADD. CHART.

1620. Grant by Hugh son of Arnold of Grainthorpe, to the church of Lincoln and the Common, of a croft containing three acres of land in Grainthorpe. (Circa 1223–1230.)

Sciant presentes 7 futuri quod ego Hugo filius Arnaldi de Germethorp dedi concessi 7 hac presenti carta mea confirmaui deo 7 beate Marie 7 commune canonicorum Lincoln' ecclesie vnum croftum continens tres acras terre arabilis in territorio de Swerdeburg quod vocatur Alualdecroft quod iacet inter terram Johannis filii Briani versus austrum 7 terram Basilie filie Alicie versus aquilonem Tenendum 7 habendum cum omnibus pertinenciis libertatibus 7 aisiamentis infra villam 7 extra 7 cum libero introitu 7 exitu in puram 7 perpetuam elemosinam liberam solutam 7 quietam ab omni seculari seruicio 7 exaccione 7 demanda . Et ego 7 heredes mei predictum croftum cum pertinenciis prenominatis canonicis warantizabimus defendemus 7 adquietabimus contra omnes homines 7 feminas inperpetuum . Et in huius rei robur

⁊ testimonium presenti scripto sigillum meum apposui . Hiis testibus Elẏa succentore Linc' Henrico de Torpell' Philippo de Tumba beati Hugonis Roberto de Balderton vicario Linc' ecclesie Petro Galle Waltero de Oxcumbe Roberto de Gunnebẏ Willelmo filio Ernisii Ernisio fratre suo Hugone Knottẏng ⁊ aliis.

Text: MS—R1515.

Note: Elias was succentor in 1223–4 (see above, vol. iv, p. 280), but Henry de Torpell' is not usually found after 1230.

CAWTHORPE IN COVENHAM ST. BARTHOLOMEW.

471

1621. Grant by Alexander son of Roger of Covenham, to the church of Lincoln, of half a toft, six acres of arable land, four acres of meadow less half a perch, and eight selions of land in Cawthorpe [in Covenham St. Bartholomew parish]. (Late twelfth century.)

Carta de medietate unius tofti . sex acris terre . arabilis ⁊ .iiijor. acris prati in Cailthorn'. (A rubric.)

Vniuersis sancte matris ecclesie filiis ad quos presens scriptum peruenerit :· Alexander filius Rogeri de Couenham salutem . Nouerit uniuersitas uestra me assensu ⁊ consensu uxoris mee ⁊ heredum meorum concessisse ⁊ dedisse ⁊ hac presenti carta mea confirmasse deo ⁊ beate Marie Linc' . ⁊ canonicis ibidem deo seruientibus medietatem unius tofti in uilla de Ca*letorp[1] quod uocatur Walbodecroft[2] [3]scilicet[3] . ex occidentali parte prenominati crofti . ⁊ sex acras terre arabilis in territorio de Couenham . ⁊ quatuor acras prati in Adestanefen dimidia percata minus . In longa reia quinque selliones de terra arabili . ⁊ duas[4] selliones in Goutemare[5] . ⁊ unam[6] sellionem iuxta Thoruoithesich ex orientali parte . Et pratum prenominatum iacet inter pratum prioris de Couenham ⁊ pratum quod fuit Normanni . Et ego ⁊ heredes mei warantizabimus prenominatam terram deo ⁊ beate Marie Linc' . ⁊ canonicis ibidem deo seruientibus contra omnes homines . istam terram prenominatam dedi eis pro salute anime mee ⁊ patris mei ⁊ matris mee . ⁊ omnium antecessorum meorum in puram ⁊ perpetuam elemosinam . Et ut hec mea donatio inperpetuum rata ⁊ illibata permaneat :· sigilli mei munimine corroboraui . Hiis testibus . Reginaldo priore[8] de Couenham . Hamelino decano de Couenham . Warino de Haule . Eudone capellano de Sancto Botulfo . Gileberto[9] Pilate[10] . Ricardo de Hardres . Johanne de Wikeford' [3]capellano[3] . Alexandro [3]del[3] Bicht[11] . ⁊ multis aliis.

Marginalia in A: Kaylthorp' (by Q2).
Texts: MS—A. R1492.
Var. R.: [1] Calthorp' R. [2] Walbodecroft' R. [3] R *omits*. [4] duos R. [5] Boutemare R. [6] unum R. [7] Thornorthesich R. [8] rectore R. [9] Gilberto R. [10] Pilat' R. [11] Byth' R.
Note: Reginald prior of Covenham and Hamelin the dean witness together mid Henry II (L.R.S. xviii, p. 107), but this charter is probably late twelfth century. Warin de Haulee occurs late twelfth century and circa 1200 (*ibid.*, pp. 52, 46) and was holding land in Covenham in 1212 (*Book of Fees*, i, p. 154). Hamelin the dean witnesses with Gilbert Pilate and Eudo the chaplain (almost certainly identical with Eudo of Boston) 1196–1202 (see no. 1375 in vol. iv, above).

**Folio 90d.*

Hdl. Luesk'

YARBOROUGH

472

1622. Grant by Wimarc daughter of Ralf of Yarborough, to the church of Lincoln and the Common, of a toft and twenty acres of land, ten on each side of the village, in Yarborough. (Circa 1200.)

Omnibus sancte matris ecclesie filiis ad quos presens scriptum peruenerit .' Wimarc[1] filia Radulfi de Jerburg'[2] salutem . Nouerit uniuersitas uestra me dedisse ⁊ hac presenti carta mea confirmasse deo ⁊ ecclesie beate Marie Linc' toftum quendam in villa de Jereburg'[2] qui iacet iuxta terram Willelmi de Lincoln' uersus occidentem cum pertinentiis suis . videlicet cum viginti acris terre . decem ex una parte eiusdem uille .' ⁊ decem ex alia . in puram ⁊ perpetuam elemosinam . pro salute anime mee ⁊ omnium parentum meorum . Hanc autem terram warantizabimus ego ⁊ heredes mei predicte ecclesie contra omnes homines tenendam de nobis[3] libere ⁊ quiete ab omni seruitio ⁊ exactione . Hiis testibus . Ricardo de Hardres . Helya[4] uicario . Eudone preposito . Willelmo de Linc' . Willelmo de Saltfleteb'[5] . Willelmo de Sumerecotes[6] . Hamelino filio Gileberti.[7]

Marginalia in A: (1) Jerneburg' (by Q2). (2) Willelmus filius Ace . . . de Jerdburg' (much faded).
Texts: MS—A. R1494.
Var. R.: [1] Wẏmarc R. [2] Jerdeburg' R. [3] *sic*. [4] Elya R. [5] Willelmo de Saltfletebẏ R. [6] Somercotes R. [7] Gilberti R.
Note: For the dates of Eudo the provost see vol. iv, p. 383, above.

473

1623. Confirmation by Azo son of Ralf of Yarborough of the preceding grant. (Circa 1200.)

Omnibus sancte matris ecclesie filiis ad quos presens

scriptum peruenerit Aze filius Radulfi de Jerhburg[1] salutem . Nouerit uniuersitas uestra me concessisse 7 hac presenti carta mea confirmasse deo 7 ecclesie beate Marie Linc' donum Wimarc[2] filie Radulfi de Jerhburc[3] . scilicet quendam[4] toftum in villa de Jerburg'[3] . qui iacet iuxta terram Willelmi de Linc' . uersus occidentem cum pertinenciis suis . scilicet cum viginti acris terre . decem uero ex una parte eiusdem uille . 7 decem ex alia in puram 7 perpetuam elemosinam pro salute anime mee 7 omnium parentum meorum . hanc autem terram warantizabimus ego 7 heredes mei predicte ecclesie contra omnes homines . Hiis testibus . Ricardo de Hardres . Helya[5] uicario . Eudone preposito . Willelmo de Linc' . Willelmo de Saltfletebi[6] . Willelmo de Sumercotes[7] . Hamelino filio Gileberti.[8]

Marginalia in A : Confirmacio (by Q2).
Texts : MS—A. R1493.
Var. R. : [1] Jerdeburgh R. [2] Wymarc R. [3] Jordeburg' R. [4] quoddam R. [5] Elya R. [6] Salfleteby R. [7] Somercotes R. [8] Gilberti R.
Note : It seems possible that Azo son of Ralf may be identical with Azo *nepos* of Hamelin the clerk of Yarborough (*Danelaw Charters*, p. 114).

Add. Chart.

1624. Grant by Richard son of Azo, to the church of Lincoln and the Common, of a toft, twenty-four acres of land, twelve on each side of the village and four acres of meadow in Yarborough. (Circa 1240.)

Omnibus Christi fidelibus presentibus 7 futuris Ricardus filius Ace salutem . Noueritis me dedisse concessisse 7 hac presenti carta mea confirmasse deo 7 beate Marie 7 commune canonicorum Linc' ecclesie vnum toftum in Ierdeburg' quod iacet inter toftum Radulfi filii Martini 7 quoddam toftum quod vocatur Dunẏngtoft cum viginti quatuor acris terre quarum duodecim iacent ex vna parte ville 7 duodecim ex altera cum quatuor acris prati . Tenend' 7 habend' dictis canonicis inperpetuum cum omnibus pertinenciis libertatibus 7 aisiamentis infra villam 7 extra in puram 7 perpetuam elemosinam libere 7 quiete ab omni seruicio 7 exaccione seculari . Et ego 7 heredes mei defendemus adquietabimus 7 warantizabimus dictis canonicis dictum tenementum[1] libertatibus 7 aisiamentis tanquam puram 7 perpetuam elemosinam liberam 7 quietam contra omnes homines inperpetuum . Vt ad hoc fideliter 7 sine dolo tenendum ego pro me 7 pro heredibus meis tactis sacrosanctis ewangeliis iuraui 7 insuper presens scriptum sigillo meo confirmaui . Hiis testibus Henrico sacrista Linc' ecclesie Ricardo capellano Hugone de Harington Eudone de Farlestorp Ricardo de Stretton clerico Petro Galle Waltero de Oxcumb' Radulfo de Somercotes

Willelmo filio Ace Herberto filio Roberti Ada 7 Acardo clericis 7 aliis.

Text : MS—R1495.
Var. R. : [1] *sic* : cum *presumably omitted.*
Note : This grantor is probably the son of the grantor of the previous charter. For the dates of Henry the sacrist see vol. iv, p. 281, above. Richard de Stretton witnesses frequently circa 1240–50 (*ibid.*, nos. 1406, 1413 and others, above). Hugh of Harrington was party to fines in 1245 and 1248 (L.R.S., xvii, pp. 18, 23, 44). Walter of Oxcumbe witnesses 1239–45 (see vol. iv, nos. 1407–1411, above).

ADD. CHART.

1625. Grant by Walter son of Alan of Welton [le Wold], to the church of Lincoln and the Common, of three and a half tofts, thirty-six acres of arable land, of which eighteen lie on each side of the village, and nine acres of meadow in Yarborough. (Circa 1245–1247.)

Omnibus Christi fidelibus Walterus filius Alani de Welton salutem . Noueritis me dedisse concessisse 7 hac presenti carta mea confirmasse deo 7 beate Marie 7 commune canonicorum Linc' ecclesie tria tofta 7 dimidium in Jerdeburg' scilicet illud toftum quod iacet inter toftum Ricardi filii Johannis 7 toftum monialium de Aluingham 7 illud toftum quod vocatur Emmethoft in quo mansit Robertus Bŷne illud dimidium toftum quod vocatur Merwentoft 7 dimidium toftum quod vocatur Basiltoft cum decem 7 octo acris terre arabilis ex vna parte eiusdem ville 7 decem 7 octo acras terre ex altera parte ville cum nouem acris prati cum omnibus pertinenciis libertatibus 7 aisiamentis infra villam 7 extra . Tenend' 7 habend' dictis canonicis in puram 7 perpetuam[1] liberam solutam 7 quietam ab omni seruicio 7 exaccione seculari . Et ego 7 heredes mei defendemus 7 warantizabimus totum dictum tenementum cum pertinenciis libertatibus 7 aisiamentis dictis canonicis tanquam puram 7 perpetuam elemosinam liberam 7 quietam contra omnes homines inperpetuum . Et in huius rei robur 7 testimonium presens scriptum iuramento interueniente sigillo meo confirmaui . Hiis testibus Roberto tunc abbate de Barling' Henrico sacrista .R. succentore Linc' Ricardo de Stretton clerico Petro Galle Waltero de Oxecumb Herberto de Saltfleteby Thoma de Welton Johanne Galle Simone fili Auŷne 7 aliis.

Text : MS—R1496.
Var. R. : [1] *sic* : elemosinam *presumably omitted.*
Note : For the dates of Henry the sacrist see vol. iv, p. 281, above. If the succentor's initial is correct he is probably Richard of Leicester, who occurs between 1247 and 1253 (*ibid.*, p. 280). Rollain occurs as sacrist between those dates so that this charter is probably not long after 1245 (*ibid.*, p. 281). Elias is found as succentor 1223 to 1245 (*ibid.*, p. 280). The date of the election of Robert as abbot of Barlings is not known. He must be the second of that name (V.C.H. Lincs., ii, p. 204).

Add. Chart.

1626. Grant by Richard son of John son of Gikel of Yarborough, to the church of Lincoln and the Common, of twenty acres of arable land, two acres of meadow, and a yearly render of twelvepence from the capital messuage of the successors of John son of Gikel in Yarborough. (Circa 1240.)

Omnibus Christi fidelibus ad quos presens scriptum peruenerit . Ricardus filius Johannis filii Gikel' de Jerdburg'[1] salatem[2] . in domino . Nouerit vniuersitas vestra me dedisse et concessisse et hac presenti carta mea confirmasse deo et beate Marie et matrice[3] ecclesie Linc' et canonicis ibidem deo et gloriose uirgini Marie seruientibus .' pro salute anime mee et antecessorum meorum . in liberam et puram[4] perpetuam elemosinam . vinginti[5] acras terre arabilis in teritorio de Jerdburg'[6] .' videlicet ex Est parte eiusdem uille nouem acras et tres perticatas terre arabilis . quorum[7] duos seliones ex West parte de Suht Fen[8] qui iacent proximo inter terram Ade le Vauasur et terram Roberti palmer et tres seliones qui iacent proximo inter terram que fuit Willelmi filii Ace et terram Roberti filii Mathelin et quinque seliones qui abuttant super forarium predictorum trium selionum . et sex seliones . ex West parte de Mickelmare qui iacent ex West parte terre . Marierie[9] de Linc' et unum selionem ex West parte de Mickelmare qui iacet[10] proximo inter terram Simonis de Hacham[11] et terram que fuit Willelmi le Curtaÿs . et tres seliones terre ex West parte Hou . qui iacent proximo inter terram predicti Simonis de Hacham . et terram predicti Ade le Vauasur . et unum selionem qui iacet ex Westparte de Morland' proximo inter terram que fuit predicti Willelmi filii Ace et terram Roberti Ruse . Et ex West parte eiusdem uille decem acras et unam perticatam terre quorum[7] quatuor seliones qui iacent apud Hosmundmare proximo inter terram Thome filii Roberti . et uiam et duos seliones apud Holmare qui iacent proximo inter terram predicti Gilberti[12] le Vauasur et terram Alani Hardewin . et unum selionem qui iacet apud Littelhou proximo inter terram Roberti palmer . et terram Alicie Lutte . et duos seliones qui iacent proximo inter terram Gilberti[13] Wauasur[14] et terram Radulfi le Curtays ex Est parte de Holmare . et tres seliones ex West parte de Holmare . qui iacent proximo inter terram Roberti filii Ricardi et terram Thome filii Roberti . et unum selionem qui iacet proximo inter terram predicti Thome filii Roberti et terram Thome filii Andree et duo seliones iacentes ex utraque parte terre predicte Marierie[15] de Linc' . et duo selones[16] apud Dickefurlanges qui iacent proximo inter terram Roberti pastoris . et terram predicte Marierie de Linc' et unus[2] selio ex Suht[17] parte le Duyt qui iacet proximo inter terram Roberti Ferant . et terram Hamelini[13] filii Cost' et unus selio ex West . parte de Thorpland qui iacet proximo inter terram prioris de Alwingham et terram Ade le Wauasur[14] et duo seliones qui iacent proximo inter terram predicti prioris et terram predicti Hamelini filii Cost' . Preteria[19] dedi predicte ecclesie duas acras prati in Suht Fen[8] que iacent proximo inter pratum Roberti palmer et pratum Roberti Ferant . et duodecim denarios de redditu . reddendos de capitali mesuagio [20]ex successoribus[20] Johannis [21]filii[21] Gikel' . de Jerdeburg' ad duos terminos anni . videlicet ad Pascha sex denarios[22] .˙ ad festum sancti Michaelis sex denarios . Habend' et tenend' in liberam et puram et perpetuam ellemosinam[23] . Et ego Ricardus et heredes mei gwarantizabimus defendemus et de omnibus seruiciis adquietabimus predictas vingintas[5] acras terre arabilis et predictas duas acras prati cum predicto redditu predicte matrice ecclesie et predictis canonicis ibidem deo et beate Marie seruientibus contra omnes homines imperpetuum . Hiis testibus domino Haraldo filio Humfridi domino Willelmo de Mannebi[24] . Ricardo filio Humfridi Philippo Galle . Willelmo ad Ecclesiam de Mannebi . Waltero de Oxecub'[25] . Roberto filio Ricardi de Jerdburg' Herberto de Saltfledby[26] Matheo Burel . Ricardo clerico ⁊ al[iis].

Endorsed : (1) Jordebur' .xx. acre et .ij. prati et .xij.d. redditus (13–14 cent.). (2) Luthesk (query by Q). (3) x (13 cent.).

Slit for seal tag. Size : 10¾ x 6 inches.

Texts : MS—Orig. Dij/88/3/54. R1497.

Var. R. : [1] Jerdeburg' R. [2] *sic.* [3] *sic* : matrici R. [4] et *omitted* : R *has* ⁊. [5] *sic* : R *has* viginti. [6] Jordeburg R. [7] *sic* : quarum R. [8] Suth ffen R. [9] Marie R. [10] iacent R. [11] Hagham R. [12] *sic.* [13] R *adds* le. [14] Vauasur R. [15] Margerie R. [16] *sic* : seliones R. [17] suth R. [18] Hemelini R. [19] *sic* : preterea R. [20–20] R *omits and has instead* quod fuit. [21–21] R *omits.* [22] R *adds* et. [23] *sic* : elemosinam R. [24] Mannebŷ R. [25] Oxcumbe R. [26] Saltfleteby R.

Note : Richard son of John held land in Yarborough and Grainthorpe in 1242 (*Book of Fees*, ii, p. 1053). Gilbert Vavasur was a juror in that year (*ibid.*, p. 1052) and levied fines in 1234 (*Final Concords*, i, p. 273) and in 1257 (L.R.S., xvii, p. 148). Harold son of Humphrey presented to Saltfleetby S. Peter church 1238–9 (L.R.S., xi, p. 117).

LEGBOURNE

474

1627. Printed at no. 398 in volume II, above, from a text in Cant.

It was copied into the lower margin of A by Q2.

Marginalia in A : xv libratae de Lekeburn.

Folio 91.

Hdl. . 9 . 1 .

475

1628. Printed at no. 402 in volume II, above, from MS. Orig. Dij/50/2/2.

The hand of the scribe of the copy in A is circa 1260.

476

1629. Printed at no. 400 in volume II, above, from a text in Cant.

It was copied into the lower margin of A by Q2.

Folio 91d.

This folio is blank.

Folio 92.

Hdl. Ludesch' . 9 . 2 .

SALTFLEETBY

477

1630. Grant by Ketel Dumping, to the church of Lincoln, of five acres of his free land, with his son Odo, on the altar of the cathedral. Odo shall hold the land of the cathedral for a yearly pension of twelve pence to be paid on the Tuesday of Pentecost. Whitsun week, 1176.

Omnibus sancte matris ecclesie filiis presentibus ⁊ futuris Ketellus Dumping[1] salutem . Nouerit uniuersitas uestra me dedisse deo ⁊ sancte Marie quinque acras terre de libera terra mea ⁊ eas cum filio meo Odone super altare sancte Marie obtulisse in puram ⁊ perpetuam elemosinam ⁊ idem predictus Odo tenebit de deo ⁊ sancta Maria predictas quinque acras iure hereditario reddendo canonicis sancte Marie sub annua pensione duodecim denarios in die Martis Pentecostes . ⁊ ne in posterum possit hec donatio in irritum reuocari ∴ hac presenti carta mea illam confirmaui ⁊ sigilli mei testimonio corroboraui . ⁊ facta est hec donatio anno ab incarnatione domini . M^{o}. C^{o}.L.X.X.VI^{to}. in septimana Pentecostes.

Endorsed : (1) Ketelli dumping de Saltfletbi v. acr : (? 12 cent.). (2) .j. (3) .j. (13 cent.).

Tag for seal. Size : 6¾ x 2¼ inches.

Marginalia in A : Saltfletbie v. acr' red' ecclesie Linc' 12d. die martis Pentecostes (16 cent.).

Texts : MS—Orig. Dij/86/2/25. A. R1594.

Var. R. : [1] Dumpẏng R.

Note : In these charters of Saltfleetby, Somercotes and Skidbrook much of the dating has been based on charters relating to the same villages in Professor Stenton's *Danelaw Charters* and *Free Peasantry of the Northern Danelaw*, Kungl. Humanistiska Vetenskapssamfundet i Lund 1926, pp. 73–185.

478

1631. Grant by Robert son of William, to the church of Lincoln and the Common, of an acre of land in Saltfleetby, half on the south and half on the north side of the village. (Late twelfth century.)

Omnibus sancte matris ecclesie filiis ad quos presens scriptum peruenerit Robertus filius Willelmi salutem in domino . Nouerit uniuersitas uestra me dedisse 7 presenti carta confirmasse deo 7 sancte Marie Linc' in puram 7 perpetuam elemosinam . unam acram terre in Saltflebi[1] inter toftum Walteri de Stiuet'[2] 7 Roberti filii Augrim . cuius una medietas iacet a parte australi . 7 alia a parte boreali . hanc donationem presenti sigillo[3] dignum duxi coroborare . His[4] testibus . Roberto filio Augrim . Hugone fratre eius . Hugone Neuchum . [5]Wigot[5] . Reginaldo . Alano . 7 multis aliis.

Endorsed : (1) Roberti filii Willelmi (early 13 cent.). (2) xxij (13 cent.).
Tag for seal. Size : 5 x $2\frac{1}{2}$ inches.
Marginalia in A : (1) Salfleteby . una acra (by Q2). (2) i acra (16 cent.).
Texts : MS—Orig. Dij/86/2/34. A. R1617.
Var. R. : [1] Saltfleby A. Salfleteby R. [2] Stiuetun A. Stiueton' R. [3] sigilli (*sic*) R. [4] *sic* : hiis A *and* R. [5–5] R *omits*.

479

1632. Grant by Reginald son of Asger of Saltfleetby, to the chapter of Lincoln, of six acres of land in Saltfleetby. (Late Henry II.)

Vniuersis sancte matris ecclesie filiis ad quos presens scriptum peruenerit .ᐟ Reginaldus filius Asgeri de Saltfletb'[1] salutem . Nouerit uniuersitas uestra me dedisse 7 concessisse 7 hac mea carta confirmasse deo 7 sancte Marie 7 capitulo Lincol' sex acras terre arabilis in territorio de Saltfletb'[1] que iacent ex aquilonali parte de Maredich inter terram Roberti filii Gamel . 7 terram Roberti Galle in puram 7 perpetuam elemosinam pro salute anime mee 7 antecessorum meorum habendas 7 tenendas libere 7 quiete 7 honorifice absque omni seruitio 7 exactione . Et ego Reginaldus 7 heredes mei warantizabimus deo 7 beate Marie 7 prius dicto capitulo Lincol' hanc predictam terram contra omnes homines . 7 omnes calumpnias . Hiis testibus . Symone[2] clerico . Gileberto[3] filio Stepi[4] . Waltero filio presbiteri . Willelmo fratre suo . Willelmo filio Roberti . Eustachio huius carte scriptore.

Marginalia in A : (1) Salfleteby sex acras (by Q2). (2) vi acr' (16 cent.).
Texts : MS—A. R1595.
Var. R. : [1] Salfleteby R. [2] Simone R. [3] Gilberto R. [4] Stepý R.

480

1633. Grant by Robert and Wigot sons of William of Saltfleetby, to the church of Lincoln, of two acres of land in Saltfleetby. (Late twelfth century.)

Omnibus sancte matris ecclesie filiis[1] ad quos presens scriptum peruenerit . Robertus 7 Wigot filii Willelmi de Salfletebi[2] . salutem . Nouerit uniuersitas uestra nos concessisse 7 dedisse 7 presenti carta confirmasse deo 7 sancte Marie Lincol' . pro animabus nostris 7 parentum nostrorum 7 antecessorum nostrorum in puram 7 perpetuam elemosinam duas acras terre in Saltfletebi[3] que iacent inter toftum Walteri de Stiuetun quod tenet de ecclesia Sancte Marie Linc' . 7 toftum Roberti filii Augrim . 7 has duas acras terre deo 7 sancte Marie Linc' nos 7 heredes nostri contra omnes warantizabimus . His[4] testibus . Roberto filio Mole . Hugone Neucum' . Reginaldo Seilbert . Roberto filio Augrim . Hugone fratre suo . Kungwine filio Siward . Ricardo filio Seleue . 7 multis aliis.

Endorsed : (1) Roberti 7 Wigoti filiorum Willelmi de Salfletebi (13 cent.). (2) xx (13 cent.). (3) xiiij (13 cent.).

Two tags, of which the first has lost its seal, the second retaining one : round, $1\frac{3}{8}$ inches, cream, conventional device.

+ **SIGILL' WIGOT · FILII WI[LL]ELMI**

Size : 5 x $3\frac{3}{8}$ inches.

Marginalia in A : (1) Salfletebẏ duas acras (by Q2). (2) 2 acr' (16 cent.).

Texts : MS—Orig. Dij/86/2/37. A. R1615.

Var. R. : [1] filius (*sic*) R. [2] Salfleteb' A. Salfleteby R. [3] Saltfleteby A. Salfleteby R. [4] *sic* : hiis A *and* R.

Note : Robert son of Mole and Hugh Newcomen both occur late twelfth century (*Danelaw Charters*, pp. 388, 390).

481

1634. Grant by Ralf son of Robert of Saltfleetby, with the consent of his wife and his heirs, to the church of Lincoln and the Common, of two and a half acres of land in Saltfleetby. (Late twelfth century.)

Omnibus sancte matris ecclesie filiis ad quos presens scriptum peruenerit ∴ Radulfus filius Roberti de Saltefleteb'[1] salutem in domino . Nouerit uniuersitas uestra me de consensu uxoris méé 7 heredum meorum dedisse 7 concessisse deo 7 beate Marie 7 commune Linc' ecclesie duas acras 7 dimidiam* . que terminantur ad Gript in puram 7 perpetuam elemosinam cum omnibus aisiamentis que ad illam terram pertinent in uilla predicta . Et ut hec donatio rata permaneat ∴ ego 7 uxor mea sigillorum nostrorum appensione roborauimus . Hiis testibus .W. persona . Adam de Grimmolbi[2] . Hugone

Neucumene[3] . Roberto filio Godefridi . Radulfo clerico Ghuingwine[4] . 7 magistro Johanne de Merston'.[5]

Texts: MS—A. R1614.
Var. R.: [1] Salfletebÿ R. [2] Grimoldeby R. [3] Neucome R. [4] Ghuimgwine R. [5] Merst' R.
Note: Adam of Grimoldby placed himself on the Grand Assize *temp.* Richard I (C.R.R., i, p. 11).

**Folio 92d.*

482

1635. Grant by Robert of Raithby, with the consent of Hilda his wife and Hugh his son and heir, to the church of Lincoln and the Common, of three and a half acres of the fee of the count of Brittany in Saltfleetby. (Late Henry II.)

Vniuerse[1] sancte matris ecclesie filiis presentibus 7 futuris Robertus de Reithebi[2] salutem . Nouerit uniuersitas uestra me dedisse 7 concessisse 7 hac mea carta confirmasse consensu Hÿlde[3] uxoris méé 7 Hugonis filii mei 7 heredis canonicis sancte Marie Linc' 7 commune eorum in puram 7 perpetuam elemosinam tres acras terre arabilis 7 dimidiam acram terre in gaira in Salfledebi[4] de feudo comitis Britannie . hanc terram obtuli ego super altare sancte Marie Linc' . Jurauimus etiam tactis sacrosanctis ewangeliis ego 7 Hugo filius meus 7 heres quod warantizabimus hanc terram canonicis Linc' contra omnes homines . huius donationis sunt testes . Willelmus de Amundeuilla . magister Walterus de Braitoft'[5] . Willelmus Plantecardus . Robertus de Sancto Lucio . Girardus sacerdos . [6]Robertus sacerdos[6] . Ricardus uicarius de Subroc . Walterus de Leggesbi[7] diaconus . Jordanus de Swalwe[8] . 7 multi alii.

Endorsed: (1) Roberti de Raithebi . in Salfletebi (13 cent.). (2) viij (13 cent.).
Seal on tag—round, 1⅜ inches, cream, a quadruped, query a horse.

SIGILLVM . RO . . . . REI

Size: 7¾ x 2½ inches.
Marginalia in A: (1) Saltfletby iii. acras dimidiam terre arabilis (? by Q2). (2) + .
Texts: MS—Orig. Dij/86/2/24. A. R1596.
Var. R.: [1] *sic*: universis R. [2] Reÿtheby R. [3] Hilde R. [4] Salfleteby R. [5] Braytoft' R. [6–6] R *omits.* [7] Legesby R. [8] Swalewe A.
Note: Robert of Raithby witnesses late twelfth century (*Danelaw Charters*, p. 395). William de Amundeville made a grant in Friesthorpe about that time (see no. 1234 in vol. iv, above) and witnessed about the same time (*Danelaw Charters*, pp. 48, 245). Hugh son of Robert of Raithby occurs in 1202 (L.R.S., xxii, no. 1033). Master Walter of Bratoft occurs before 1183 (see no. 1374 in vol. iv, above).

483

1636. Grant by John son of Stepi of Saltfleetby, with the advice and assent of Matilda his wife, and of his heirs and friends, to the church of Lincoln and the Common, of six acres of land in Saltfleetby, namely the half of a toft which was of Stepi his father. Should the half toft be less than six acres the deficiency is to be made good in the capital croft on the south of the other croft. (Circa 1200.)

Sciant presentes 7 futuri quod ego Johannes filius Stepi[1] de Salfletebi[2] consilio 7 assensu Matildis uxoris mee 7 heredum meorum 7 amicorum concessi 7 dedi 7 hac presenti carta mea confirmaui deo 7 beate Marie 7 commune canonicorum Linc' ecclesie sex acras terre arabilis in territorio de Salfletebi[3] . scilicet dimidiam partem tofti quod fuit patris mei Stepi ad Ecclesiam Omnium Sanctorum in Salfletebi[4] . scilicet partem orientalem . Et si aliquid deficiat in crofto illo de sex acris terre ∴ capient in crofto capitali in parte orientali ex australi parte predicti crofti . ut plenarie habeant sex acras terre arabilis in predicto loco . in puram 7 perpetuam elemosinam pro salute anime mee 7 omnium antecessorum meorum . Et ego Johannes 7 heredes mei warantizabimus sex acras prenominatas prenominato capitulo contra omnes homines . Et ut hec mea donatio inperpetuum rata permaneat ∴ sigilli mei munimine corroboraui . Hiis testibus . Eudone de Sancto Botulfo capellano . Waltero Blundo capellano . Ricardo de Hardres capellano . Johanne de Wÿkefort[5] . Willelmo persona de Salfletebi[2] . Willelmo filio Johannis de Sumercotes[6] . Auko de Sumercotes[6] . Roberto filio Auke de Sumercotes[7] . Willelmo filio Godrici de Scitebroc.[8]

Endorsed: (1) Carta Johannis filii Stepi de Saltfletb' Rogerus Berker tenet . pro xij. denariis (13 cent.). (2) iiij (13 cent.). (3) xv (late 13 cent.). (4) Salfleteb' .vj. acr' (13 cent.). (5) Carta Johannis filii Stepi Rogerus Berker pro xij denariis . ad festum Sancti . Michaelis (13 cent.).

The endorsements are in different hands.

Seal on tag—round, 1½ inches, cream, fleur de lys.

+ **SIGILLVM . . . . . NIS FILII . ST'**

Size: 7¼ x 4¼ inches.

Marginalia in A: Saltfletby vi acras terre (? by Q2).

Texts: MS—Orig. Dij/86/2/27. A. R1597.

Var. R.: [1] Stepÿ R. [2] Salfleteby R. [3] Salfleteby A *and* R. [4] Saltefletebi A. Salfleteby R. [5] Wykeford R. [6] Summecotes A. Somercotes R. [7] Somercotes R. [8] Skitbrok R.

Note: Eudo of Boston (probably identical with Eudo the provost), Walter Blund and Richard de Hardres witness many charters with William of Blois as precentor 1196–1203 (e.g. see nos. 1140–1, 1358, 1456).

484

1637. Grant by Avina daughter of Athelstan, to the church of Lincoln and the Common, of all the land which was of her father in Saltfleetby. (Circa 1200.)

Notum sit tam presentibus quam futuris quod Auina filia Adelstan dedi [1]7[1] concessi 7 hac presenti carta mea confirmaui assensu heredum meorum deo ⁊ beate Marie ⁊ commune canonicorum Lincol' ecclesie totam terram que fuit patris mei in Saufletebi[2] uersus orientem juxta ecclesiam Omnium Sanctorum que jacet inter Neudic ⁊ pratum in puram ⁊ perpetuam elemosinam pro animabus patris mei ⁊ matris mee ⁊ omnium antecessorum meorum . necnon . ⁊ pro salute mea ⁊ omnium heredum meorum . Hanc autem terram ego * ⁊ heredes mei warantizabimus predictis canonicis imperpetuum contra omnes homines . Et ut ista donacio firma permaneat ∴ hanc cartam sigilli mei appensione corroboraui . Hiis testibus . Roberto clerico de Stokes . Willelmo ⁊ Johanne suo fratre de Saufletebi[3] . Gileberto[4] Pilato[5] . Ricardo seruiente eius . Helia[6] de Brunne . ⁊ multis aliis.

Endorsed: (1) vij (late 13 cent.). (2) . . . ne filie Adestan (13 cent.). (3) In Salfleteb' (13 cent.). (4) xij (13 cent.).

Seal on tag—pointed oval, 1½ x 1 inches, cream, a flower.

\+ SIGILLVM AVIИE

Size: 6½ x 3¾ inches.

Marginalia in A: Saltfletby (? by Q2).

Texts: MS—Orig. Dij/86/2/26. A. R1601.

Var. R.: [1–1] R *omits.* [2] Salfletebi A. Salfleteby R. [3] Salfleteby A *and* R. [4] Gilberto R. [5] *sic*: Pilate A. Pylato R. [6] Helya A. Elya R.

**Folio* 93.

Hdl. Salfletby . 9 . 3 .

485

1638. Confirmation by Richenilda daughter of Athelstan of the preceding grant. (Circa 1200.)

Sciant omnes tam presentes quam futuri quod ego Richenilda[1] filia Adestani assensu ⁊ consensu Walteri mariti mei ⁊ heredes[2] mei confirmauimus deo ⁊ capitulo sancte Marie Lincolniensis ecclesie . donacionem terre illius que iacet ex orientali parte cimiterii Omnium Sanctorum de Salfletebi[3] ∴ factam ab Auina sorore mea deo ⁊ predicto capitulo sancte Marie . Et ut hec donacio rata ⁊ inconcussa in posterum perseueret eam sigilli mei apposicione duxi roborandam[4] . His[5] testibus . Willelmo persona de Bransuelle[6] . Joanne[7] fratre eius . Jurdano[7] de Baiocis . Roberto de Dirintun[7] . Joanne[7] de Lue . Ricardo de Bloxam . Lamberto . de Couenam.[10]

Endorsed: (1) Confirmacio Richenilde filie Adestan de donatione terre quam Auina soror sua fecit (13 cent.). (2) Salfletebi (13 cent.). (3) viij (late 13 cent.). (4) xiij (13 cent.).

Seal on tag—pointed oval, 1⅜ x ⅞ inches, fleur de lys.

\+ SIGILLVM RICHENILDE

Size: 6¾ x 3⅛ inches.

Marginalia in A: Saltfletby (? by Q2).

Texts: MS—Orig. Dij/86/2/33. A. R1602.

Var. R.: [1] Richelinda A. Rechenilda R. [2] *sic*: heredis R. [3] Salfleteby A *and* R. [4] corroborandam R. [5] *sic*: hiis A *and* R. [6] Bransewelle R. [7] *sic.* [8] Jordano R. [9] Diritun' A. Dirington' R. [10] Couenham A *and* R.

486

1639. Grant by Humphrey son of Walter and Alice his wife, with the consent of their heirs, to the church of Lincoln, of a toft and various parcels of land in Saltfleetby. This land and the family of one of the tenants shall be held by Richard son of Humphrey and Alice, of the church of Lincoln, for a yearly rent of three shillings to be paid on the octave of the Nativity of the Virgin. This gift was made for their own souls and those of their relatives, especially for the soul of Robert their son and because Humphrey through weakness and old age is unable to fulfil a vow of pilgrimage. (Circa 1200.)

Omnibus Christi fidelibus ad quos presens scriptum peruenerit . Humfridus filius Walteri . 7 Aliz sponsa sua salutem 7 benedictionem in domino . Nouerit uniuersitas uestra quod[1] nos concessu[2] 7 consilio heredum nostrorum dedimus 7 hac presenti carta nostra confirmauimus deo 7 sancte Marie Lincoln' ecclesie in puram 7 perpetuam elemosinam unum toftum proximum cimiterii Sancti Petri in Saltfletebi[3] in Suth parte . 7 xiij. acras in proximo crofto in parte orientali cimiterii iuxta predictum croftum . 7 totam terram Ache filii Saxe 7 totam terram nostram in gaire . 7 iij. acras que iacent inter Johannem Trute 7 Angerum[4] nigrum 7 xiiij. acras que fuerunt Godrici Houeth[5] . 7 duas acras terre que sunt iuxta predictas .xiij.[6] acras . hanc terram predictam liberam 7 quietam tenebit Ricardus filius noster . 7 heredes sui cum omnibus infantibus Godrici Houeth de deo 7 sancta Maria Lincoln' ecclesie in feudo 7 hereditate . quam ego Humfridus 7 Aliz sponsa mea dedimus deo 7 ecclesie sancte Marie Lincoln' in puram 7 perpetuam elemosinam pro salute animarum nostrarum . 7 [1]pro animabus[1] patrum nostrorum 7 matrum nostratum[7] 7 omnium antecessorum nostrorum . 7 nominatim pro anima Roberti filii nostri 7 pro uiuis 7 defunctis 7 maxime pro peregrinatione quam ego Humfridus susceperam quam pro corporis mei[8] inbecillitate [1]7 senectute[1] non potui perficere . 7 pro omnibus uotis nostris 7 excessibus . Pro hac terra predicta reddet predictus Ricardus filius noster 7 heredes sui deo 7 ecclesie sancte Marie Lincoln' annuatim .iij. solidos pro salute animarum nostrarum . Hanc terram predictam tenebit prefatus Ricardus 7 heredes sui de deo 7 ecclesia sancte Marie Lincoln' libere 7 quiete . 7 solute ab omni terreno seruicio in omnibus pertinenciis 7 omnibus libertatibus . Et pro hac predicta terra adquietabit[9] nos 7 heredes nostros prefatus Ricardus 7 heredes sui de firma predicta aput deum 7 sanctam Mariam Lincolniensis ecclesie octaua die natiuitatis sancte Marie . Hiis testibus

Willelmo filio Roberti . Ricardo fratre eius . Waltero fratre eorum . Herberto filio Willelmi . Roberto filio Willelmi . [1]Rogero filio Durant[1] . Willelmo de Sais . Ricardo de Mautebi[10] . Johanne de Suthlei[11] . Ricardo de Ormeresbi.[12]

Endorsed: (1) Humfridi filii Walteri de Salfletebi (13 cent.). (2) xj (late 13 cent.). (3) ij (13 cent.). (4) .ij. (13 cent.).

Seal on tag—round, $1\frac{3}{4}$ inches, cream, a ? lion facing left.

+ SIGILLVM H FILII W . . . . . .

Size: $8\frac{3}{4}$ x 5 inches.

Marginalia in A: (1) Saltfletby (? by Q2). (2) iij solidi (16 cent.).

Texts: MS—Orig. Dij/86/2/38. A. R1605.

Var. R.: [1] R *omits*. [2] consensu R. [3] Salfleteby R. [4] Augerum R. [5] Houet R. [6] *sic*. [7] *sic*: nostrarum A *and* R. [8] me R. R *has* et . [9] acquietabit R. [10] Mauteby R. [11] Sutheley R. [12] Ormesby R.

Note: From this and the three subsequent charters it appears that Alice daughter of Robert son of Gilbert of Legbourne, also called La Conestable, was married to Humphrey son of Walter of Saltfleetby. Mr. Farrer in *Honours and Knights' Fees*, vol. ii, p. 108, thought she married Harold son of Humphrey who was in fact her son, and identified her incorrectly with Alice widow of Harold who impleaded the steward of the Earl of Chester in 1212 (C.R.R. vi, pp. 209–210). This Harold was Alice's brother and was father of a certain Gilbert and died before 1185 when William son of Robert of Legbourne offered ten marks to have the wardship of Gilbert son of Harold (*H. and K.F.* ii, p. 107). Humphrey was apparently dead by the Hilary term 1203 when Alice—through her son Harold—was suing the prior of Legbourne for the advowson of Saltfleetby St. Peter church (C.R.R. ii, p. 174) and she stated that Robert son of Gilbert had given her the advowson on her marriage which took place before the foundation of Legbourne Priory (L.R.S. xxii, no. 239). Robert son of William son of Robert son of Gilbert was vouched to warranty (C.R.R. ii, p. 305). The case was settled in Easter Term 1206 in favour of Alice (*ibid.*, vol. iv, p. 105) and the advowson descended to Harold son of Humphrey (L.R.S. ix, pp. 156, 181). The other sons of the marriage were Robert, who was dead when this charter was made, Richard and Walter, who occur frequently in the first half of the thirteenth century, and Thomas, who was dead before 1230 (*Final Concords* i, p. 225). This charter was probably made shortly before the death of Humphrey.

487

1640. Confirmation by Walter son of Humphrey, with the consent of his wife and his heirs, of the gift of his father to the church of Lincoln. (Early thirteenth century.)

Vniuersis sancte matris ecclesie filiis ad quos presens scriptum peruenerit ∴ Walterus filius Vmfridi[1] salutem * . Nouerit vniuersitas vestra me consensu vxoris mee 7 heredum meorum ∴ concessisse 7 hac presenti carta mea confirmasse . deo 7 ecclesie sancte Marie Linc' . 7 commune canonicorum ibidem deo seruiencium ∴ donum patris mei in uilla[2] Saltefletesbi[3] . cum omnibus libertatibus 7 asiamentis in uilla 7 extra uillam . sicut carta Ricardi fratris mei testatur . in puram 7 perpetuam elemosinam pro animabus patris 7 matris mee 7 omnium antecessorum meorum . 7 ego Walterus 7 heredes mei warantizabimus predictum donum predicte ecclesie contra omnes homines . Et vt concessio ista rata 7 illesa permaneat . illam presentis sigilli mei apposicione corroboraui . Hiis testibus . Ricardo . de Kima[4] . magistro

Waltero Blundo . Rogero Scotto[5] . Petro de Hungherẏ[6] . canonicis . Hernisio[7] del[8] marisco . Willelmo persona de Saltfletebi[9] . Johanne fratre eius . Simone[10] . clerico . Roberto filio Walteri . Waltero de Sais . ⁊ multis aliis.

Endorsed : (1) xij (late 13 cent.). (2) Confirmacio Walteri de Salfletebi de dono patris sui (13 cent.). (3) iij (13 cent.).
Seal on tag—round, 1¾ inches, cream, an heraldic beast facing right.

+ **SIGILL' WA** . . . .

Size : 6⅛ x 3⅞ inches.
Marginalia in A : Saltfletby (? by Q2).
Texts : MS—Orig. Dij/86/2/32. A. R1607.
Var. R. : [1] Humfridi R. [2] R *adds* de. [3] Saltfleteby A. Salfleteby R. [4] Kyma A *and* R. [5] Scoto A *and* R. [6] Hungery A. Hungri R. [7] Ernisio R. [8] de A *and* R. [9] Saltfleteby A. Salfleteby R. [10] Symone A.

**Folio 93d.*

488

1641. Grant by Alice daughter of Robert son of Gilbert of Legbourne, with the consent of her heirs, to the church of Lincoln and the Common, of various tenements in Saltfleetby together with their holders and their families. (Early thirteenth century.)

Sciant presentes ⁊ futuri quod ego Aliz filia Roberti filii Gilberti[1] de Lecheburn'[2] concessu heredum meorum dedi ⁊ concessi ⁊ hac presenti carta confirmaui deo ⁊ beate Marie ⁊ commune canonicorum Linc' in teritorio de Salfletheb'[3] terram que fuit Riginaldi[4] . ⁊ terram Johannis . ⁊ terram Yaelf ⁊ terram Sigwardi[5] ⁊ totam Hamelini dailam preter .xx^{ti} . acras uersus occidentem . ⁊ terram Rogeri Boune . ⁊ terram Walteri filii Roberti . ⁊ seruicium Roberti filii Mole ⁊ Luce Croft ⁊ forlandas apud mare ⁊ toftum proximum cimiterio Sancti Petri in australi parte . ⁊ .xv^{cim} . acras in proximo crofto in orientali parte . ⁊ totam terram Acche filii Sax ⁊ terram Godrici Houet . ⁊ totam gairam ex occidentali parte terre Acche Mudding . in puram ⁊ perpetuam elemosinam pro salute anime mee ⁊ Roberti [6]filii[6] mei ⁊ omnium antecessorum meorum . Et ego ⁊ heredes mei hanc terram predictam cum omnibus hominibus ⁊ cum infantibus eorum deo ⁊ beate Marie ⁊ commune canonicorum contra omnes homines warantizabimus in perpetuum . Hiis testibus . Roberto filio Willelmi . Eudone preposito . Waltero Albo . Ricardo filio Roberti . Adam Muter . Johanne de Sais.[7]

Endorsed : (1) xiiij (late 13 cent.). (2) Carta Alicie filie Roberti de Lekeburn' (13 cent.). (3) x (13 cent.).
Seal on tag—1⅝ inches, round, cream, conventional device.

+ **S' ALIZ FIL' ROBERTI FILII GELEBRTI DE TA . .**

Size : 6⅜ x 4⅛ inches.
Marginalia in A : Saltfletby (? by Q2).
Texts : MS—Orig. Dij/86/2/31. A. R1609.
Var. R. : [1] Gileberti A. [2] Lecheburn A. Lekeburn' R. [3] Saltfleteby A. Salfleteby R. [4] Reginaldi A *and* R. [5] Siwardi R. [6]–[6] *blank in* R. [7] Saẏs R.

489

1642. Confirmation by Walter son of Humphrey, with the consent of his heirs, of the preceding grant made by Alice his mother. (Early thirteenth century.)

Sciant presentes ⁊ futuri quod ego Walterus filius Vmfridi[1] concessu heredum meorum concessi ⁊ hac presenti carta mea confirmaui deo ⁊ beate Marie ⁊ commune canonicorum Linc' donum matris mee . in puram ⁊ perpetuam elemosinam pro salute anime mee ⁊ omnium antecessorum meorum . scilicet terram Riginaldi[2] . ⁊ terram Johannis . ⁊ terram Yaelf . ⁊ terram Sigwardi[3] . ⁊ totam Hamelini dailam preter .xx^{ti} acras uersus occidentem ⁊ terram Rogeri Boune . ⁊ terram Walteri filii Roberti ⁊ seruicium Roberti filii Mole ⁊ Luce croft . ⁊ forlandas uersus mare . ⁊ tofptum proximum cimiterio Sancti Petri in australi parte . ⁊ xv^{cim} . acras in proximo crofto in orientali parte . ⁊ terram Acche filii Sax ⁊ terram Godrici Houet ⁊ gairam in occidentali parte terre Acche[4] Mudding in territorio de Salfletheb'[5] . Et ego ⁊ heredes mei hanc terram predictam deo ⁊ beate Marie ⁊ commune canonicorum contra omnes homines warantizabimus inperpetuum . Hiis testibus . Roberto filio Willelmi . Eudone preposito . Waltero Albo . Ricardo filio Roberti . Johanne de Sais[6] . Thoma filio Vmfridi . Adam Muter.

Endorsed: (1) Confirmatio Walteri filii Humfridi de dono Alicie (13 cent.). (2) xiij (late 13 cent.). (3) xj (13 cent.).
Tag for seal. Size: 7⅜ x 3 inches.
Marginalia in A: (1) Saltfletby (? by Q2). (2) + cum.
Texts: MS—Orig. Dij/86/2/30. A. R1608.
Var. R.: [1] Humfridi R. [2] Reginaldi R. [3] Siwardi R. [4] Acchee R. [5] Salfleteby A *and* R. [6] Says R.

490

1643. Confirmation by Robert son of William of Legbourne of the gift made to the church of Lincoln by Alice daughter of Robert son of Gilbert. (Early thirteenth century.)

Sciant presentes ⁊ futuri quod ego Robertus filius Willelmi de Lecheburn concessi ⁊ hac presenti carta mea confirmaui deo ⁊ beate Marie ⁊ commune canonicorum Linc' in puram ⁊ perpe*tuam elemosinam pro salute anime mee ⁊ omnium antecessorum meorum totam terram quam Aliz filia Roberti filii Gilberti[1] dedit deo ⁊ beate Marie ⁊ commune canonicorum de feudo meo in teritorio de Salfletheb'[2] . Et ego Robertus ⁊ heredes mei hanc terram predictam deo ⁊ beate Marie ⁊ commune canonicorum Linc' sicut carta prefate Aliz testatur ∴ contra omnes [3]homines[3] warantibimus[4] in perpetuum . Hiis testibus . Eudone preposito . Waltero Albo . Ricardo filio Roberti . Adam Muter[5] . Johanne de Sais[6] Thoma de Wiern'.[7]

Endorsed : (1) Confirmatio Roberti filii Willelmi de Lekeburn (13 cent.). (2) xv (late 13 cent.). (3) xvj (13 cent.).

Seal on tag—round, $1\frac{1}{2}$ inches, cream, a quadruped, query a horse, facing left. + **SIGILL** . . . .

Size : 6 x $3\frac{1}{4}$ inches.

Marginalia in A : Saltfletby (? by Q2).

Texts : MS—Orig. Dij/86/2/29. A. R1610.

Var. R. : [1] Gileberti A. [2] Salfletby A. Salfleteby R. [3–3] R *omits.* [4] *sic* : warantizabimus A *and* R. [5] Mouter R. [6] Saẏs R. [7] Wẏern R.

**Folio* 94.

Hdl. . 9 . 4 .

491

1644. Grant by Ingeram of Saltfleetby, with the consent of his wife and his heirs, to the church of Lincoln, of five acres of land in a plot twenty-one perches in width in Saltfleetby. (Circa 1190.)

Notum sit omnibus sancte matris eclesie[1] filiis quod ego Hingeram[2] de Salfetibi[3] consilio ⁊ asensu vxoris mee ⁊ heredum meorum dedi ⁊ concessi ⁊ hac carta mea confirmaui deo ⁊ sancte matri eclesie beate Marie Lincolniensi[4] pro salute anime mee ⁊ antecessorum meorum quinque acras[5] terre mee in aquilonali parte de Hegedic videlicet in latitudine viginti ⁊ unius percarum ⁊ in longitudine donec fiant plene .v. acre de predicta latitudine . Hanc predictam terram dedi in puram ⁊ perpetuam elemosinam liberam ⁊ quietam ab omni seculari seruicio . ⁊ ego ⁊ heredes mei warantizabimus illam predictam terram contra omnes homines . His[6] testibus . Willelmo persona . Johanne fratre eius . ⁊ Waltero fratre eorum . Johanne de Cunigesholm[7] . Roberto filio suo . Reginaldo fratre suo . Gocelino de Strubbi .[8] Radulfo filio suo . Roberto fratre eius . Gilberto fratre eorum ⁊ Jacobo eorum fratre . Petro filio Alnet . Roberto filio Gamel . Reginaldo filio Roberti ⁊ fratribus suis ⁊ pluribus aliis.

Endorsed : (1) Ingerami de Salfletebi (13 cent.). (2) v acr' (13 cent.). (3) .iiij. (13 cent.).

The charter is torn where the seal tag should have been.

Size : $8\frac{3}{4}$ x $5\frac{7}{8}$ inches.

Marginalia in A : v acr' (16 cent.).

Texts : MS—Orig. Dij/86/2/1. A. R1603.

Var. R. : [1] *sic* : ecclesie A *and* R. [2] Ingeram R. [3] Salfletb' A. Salfleteby R. [4] *sic.* [5] R *omits* acras *which has been inserted over the line by the same sixteenth century hand as the Marginalia in A.* [6] *sic* : hiis A *and* R. [7] Connyngessholm R. [8] Strubby R.

Note : Ingeram of Saltfleetby was dead before 12th April, 1209, when his widow Tola levied a fine touching dower with Philip Galle (*Final Concords* i, p. 85). The chapter granted five acres of land in Saltfleetby to Alice daughter of Ingeram before 1195 (see no. 1649 below), but as it is said to lie North of Newedic not of Hegedic as in this deed the two cannot be identified with certainty. This charter is primitive in form.

492

1645. Grant by Osbert son of Godiva, with the consent of his wife and his heirs, to the church of Lincoln and the Common, of land in Saltfleetby, six and a half perches wide and in length stretching from Mar Dike to the land of Hugh son of Decche. (Circa 1200.)

Sciant omnes tam presentes quam futuri quod ego Osbertus filius Godiue[1] consensu ⁊ consilio uxoris méé ⁊ omnium heredum meorum dedi ⁊ concessi ⁊ hac presenti carta mea confirmaui in puram ⁊ perpetuam elemosinam deo ⁊ capitulo sancte Marie Lincolnie .vj. perticatas terre ⁊ dimidiam . in latitudine . ⁊ in longitudine .˙/ a Mardic usque ad terram Hugonis filii Decche . Hec predicta terra iacet inter terram Roberti filii Wigoti que est ex orientali parte . ⁊ terram Willelmi ad Clotam que est ex occidentali . Hanc predictam terram ego Osbertus ⁊ heredes mei warantizabimus liberam ⁊ quietam ab omni seculari seruicio deo ⁊ capitulo sancte Marie Lincolnie . Hiis testibus . Johanne clerico . Simone clerico . Rogero clerico . Roberto capellano . Roberto filio Leppe . Aschello de cimiterio . Petro filio Alnethi.

Endorsed : (1) Carta Osberti filii Godiue de Saltfletbi (13 cent.). (2) ix. (13 cent.). (3) v (late 13 cent.).

Seal on tag—oval, $1\frac{1}{2}$ x $1\frac{3}{8}$ inches, conventional device.

+ **SIGILLVM OSBERTI**

Size : $5\frac{1}{8}$ x $2\frac{1}{4}$ inches.

Marginalia in A : (1) Saltfletby (? by Q2). (2) vi pertica' terre et dimid' (16 cent.).

Texts : MS—Orig. Dij/86/2/28*a*. A. R1598.

Var. R. : [1] A *adds* de Seufletebi *above the line in a slightly later hand.*

Note : Osbert son of Godiva made a grant to Odo Galle circa 1200 (*Free Peasantry*, p. 127).

493

1646. Confirmation by Osbert son of Godiva of Saltfleetby, to the chapter of Lincoln, of land in the toft and croft lying between Mar Dike and the land of Hugh son of Decche in Saltfleetby. (Circa 1200.)

Omnibus sancte matris ecclesie filiis ad quos presens scriptum peruenerit Osbertus filius Godiue de Salfletebi[1] salutem . Nouerit uniuersitas uestra me concessisse ⁊ hac mea presenti carta confirmasse deo ⁊ capitulo sancte Marie Linc' . ecclesie in puram ⁊ perpetuam elemosinam vj. perticatas terre ⁊ dimidiam . ⁊ iiij^{or}. pedes ⁊ dimidium in latitudine in tofto ⁊ crofto que iacent inter[2] Mardic[3] ⁊ terram Hugonis filii Decche in parte orientali iuxta uiam liberas ⁊ quietas ab omni seruicio seculari . Ego uero ⁊ heredes mei warantizabimus predictum tenamentum[4] predicto capitulo sancte

Marie contra omnes homines . His[5] testibus . Willelmo persona de Salfletebi[1] . Johanne fratre suo . Odone Galle . Roberto filio Mole . Waltero filio Willelmi . Roberto fratre eius . Odone Dumpinc[6] . Roberto filio Alware.

Endorsed : (1) Osberti filii Godiue de Salfletebi (13 cent.). (2) .xvj (late 13 cent.). (3) vij. (13 cent.).

Fragment of seal on tag ; cream, probably similar to that on the preceding charter.

+ S . . . .

Size : 5⅛ x 2⅛ inches.

Marginalia in A : Saltfletby (? by Q2).

Texts : MS—Orig. Dij/86/2/28b. A. R1611.

Var. R. : [1] Salfletb' A. Salfleteby R. [2] in R. [3] Maredic R. [4] *sic* : tenementum A *and* R. [5] *sic* : hiis A *and* R. [6] Dumping' R.

494

1647. Confirmation by William *nepos* of Osbert son of Godiva of the preceding grant. (Circa 1200.)

Omnibus sancte matris ecclesie filiis ad quos presens scriptum peruenerit ∴ Willelmus nepos Osberti filii * Godiue salutem . Nouerit uniuersitas uestra me concessisse 7 hac mea presenti carta confirmasse deo 7 capitulo sancte Marie Linc' ecclesie in puram 7 perpetuam elemosinam .vi. perticatas terre . 7 dimidiam . 7 .iiii^{or}. pedes 7 dimidium in latitudine in tofto 7 crofto que iacent inter Mardic 7 terram Hugonis filii Decche in parte orientali iuxta uiam liberas 7 quietas ab omni seruitio seculari . Et ut hec concessio rata 7 inconcussa inposterum perseueret ∴ eam sigilli mei munimine duxi roborandam . Hiis testibus . Willelmo persona de Saltfletb' . Johanne fratre suo . Odone Galle . Roberto filio Mole . Waltero filio Willelmi . Roberto fratre eius . Odone Dumpinc . Roberto filio Alware.

Text : MS—A.

**Folio 94d.*

495

1648. Grant by Hugh and Oggrim sons of Alverun, to the church of Lincoln and the Common, of two acres of their free land in Saltfleetby. Whitsun week 1176.

Vniuersis sancte matris ecclesie filiis presentibus 7 futuris Hugo 7 Oggrimus filii Aluerun salutem . Nouerit uniuersitas uestra nos dedisse deo 7 sancte Marie duas acras terre de libera terra nostra in Rastoluecroft in angulo de Suwest . 7 eas super altare sancte Marie cum presenti carta nostra optulisse in puram 7 perpetuam elemosinam . Et ne in posterum possit hec donatio in irritum reuocari ∴ hac presenti carta nostra illam confirmauimus . 7 sigillorum nostrorum testimonio corroborauimus . 7 facta est hec donatio anno ab incarnatione domini .Mo . Co . lxxvito . in septimana Pentecostes.

Text: MS—A.

Folio 95.

Hdl. . 9 . 5 .

This folio is blank.

ADD. CHART.

1649. Grant by Haimo, the dean, and the chapter of Lincoln, to Alice daughter of Ingeram, of five acres of land in Saltfleetby. For this she shall pay a yearly render of threepence and may make whomsoever she wishes her heir. (1189–1195.)

Hamo decanus 7 capitulum ecclesie Lincolniensis omnibus ad quos littere presentes peruenerit salutem . Noueritis nos dedisse 7 concessisse 7 presenti carta[1] confirmasse Alicie filie Inkelram v. acras terre in Salfletebi[2] ex aquilonali parte de Newedic proximas eidem Newedic[3] tenendas de nobis in feodum 7 hereditatem sibi 7 illi quem inde heredem constituere uoluerit . reddendo inde nobis in festo Sancti Michaelis iij. denarios . liberas ab omni alio seruicio 7 consuetudine.

Endorsed: Salfletebi .v. acr' (13–14 cent.).
Fragment of seal on tag, cream: the second seal of the Chapter (see vol. ii, frontispiece and pp. 340–1). There is no counterseal.
Size: 4¼ x 2¼ inches.
Marginalia in R: Nota v. acras concessas red' iij*d* (in the same 16 cent. hand which has annotated the Saltfleetby charters in A).
Texts: MS—Orig. Dij/86/2/8. R1604.
Var. R.: [1] R *adds* nostra. [2] Salfleteby R. [3] Newdic R.
Note: The dates given are those of Haimo the dean.

ADD. CHART.

1650. Grant by Alice daughter of Ingeram of Saltfleetby, to Henry her son and his heirs, of five acres of land in Saltfleetby, to be held of the church of Lincoln for a yearly render of twelve pence. (Circa 1223–1230.)

Sciant presentes 7 futuri quod ego Alicia filia Ingeram [1]de Salfletebi[2] dedi 7 concessi 7 hac mea presenti carta confirmaui Henrico filio meo 7 heredibus suis .v. acras terre in Salfletebi[2] ex aquiloni[3] parte de Neudich proximas eiusdem[4] Neudich' . quas tenui de ecclesia Lincoln' . Tenendas sibi 7 heredibus suis de predicta ecclesia liberas & quietas pro xij denariis annuatim pro omni seculari seruicio 7 exaccione . sicut carta testatur quam habeo de decano ecclesie Linc' 7 eiusdem ecclesie capitulo . Hiis testibus . Rogero vicario . de

Sckitebroc[5] . Willelmo le Muer . Radulfo filio Ernisii . Johanne filio Wimarc[6] . Willelmo filio Willelmi . Roberto . Bla . Simone Chnotting.[7]

Endorsed : xxj (late 13 cent.).
Tag for seal. Size : 5½ x 2 inches.
Texts : MS—Orig. Dij/86/2/20. R1616.
Var. R. : [1] Mergeram (*sic*) R : *the original is not clear and the scribe of* R *seems to have been confused.* [2] Salfleteby R. [3] *sic* : aquilonali R. [4] *sic.* [5] Skitbrok' R. [6] Wẏmark' R. [7] Knottẏng' R.
Note : Roger of Skidbrook was instituted vicar of Skidbrook 1223–4 (L.R.S. ix, p. 131). The date of the appointment of his successor is not known, but Roger was apparently still in office in the time of Grosseteste (A.A.S.R., vol. xxxix, pt. 2, p. 187). As Alice had received the grant of the land at least thirty years earlier, it is possible that this grant was made not long after Roger's institution.

Add. Chart.

1651. Quitclaim by Eva widow of Thomas son of Thomas of Louth, to the church of Lincoln, of a toft and a croft and two selions of land in Saltfleetby. (Circa 1230–1240.)

Omnibus sancte matris ecclesie filiis ad quos presens scriptum peruenerit Eua[1] condam[2] vxor Thome filii Thome de Luda salutem in domino . Noueritis me pro salute anime mee et Thome condam[2] viri mei et omnium antecessorum meorum in pura viduitate mea et libera potestate mea dedisse . et hac presenti carta mea confirmasse . et omnino quietumclammasse[3] deo et ecclesie beate Marie Linc' et decano et canonicis ibidem deo et beate Marie seruientibus toftum . et croftum in Salflettebi[4] quos Robertus Bondeman aliquando tenuit cum omnibus pertinenciis suis . et duos seliones terre arabilis jacentes in Salflettebi[4] juxta terram Ricardi filii Humfridi[5] juxta Sighwarthdaẏle[6] cum pertinenciis suis . et terram que fuit Roberti Froste cum omnibus pertinenciis suis sine aliquo retenemento . Tenend' . et habend' deo ⁊ dicte ecclesie beate Marie et decano et canonicis ibidem deo et beate Marie seruientibus in liberam . et puram et perpetuam elemosinam solutam et quitam[7] ab omni terreno seruicio . Et ego Eua[1] et heredes mei dictas terras cum omnibus pertinenciis suis deo et dicte ecclesie beate Marie et dicto decano et canonicis ibidem [8]deo[8] seruientibus sicuti[9] nostram liberam et puram elemosinam contra omnes homines inperpetuum warantizabimus . adquietabimus . et defendemus . Hiis testibus . domino Haraldo fillio[10] Humfridi . Stephano capellano de Salflettebi[4] . Waltero persona de Raẏthebi[11] . Gikello persona de Salflettebi[4] . Waltero de Oxecumbe[12] . Willelmo le Muer[13] . Willelmo [8]filio[8] Roberti . Johanne fratre eius . Ricardo fillio[10] Johannis . Simone de Hacham[14] ⁊ aliis.

Endorsed : (1) xviij (late 13 cent.). (2) Eua de Luda (13 cent.). (3) Salfleteb' (13 cent.).
Tag for seal : this tag is a strip cut from a charter written by the same scribe

and seems to be a version of the same possibly discarded because it was not sufficiently precise : it omits the fact that Robert Bondeman was the former tenant of the croft granted.

Size : 7 x 3⅝ inches.

Texts : MS—Orig. Dij/86/2/19. R1613.

Var. R. : [1] Ena R. [2] quondam R. [3] quietamclamasse R. [4] Salfleteby R. [5] Vmfridi R. [6] Sigwarthdaile. [7] quietam R. [8–8] R *omits*. [9] sicut R. [10] *sic* : filio R. [11] Raÿtheby R. [12] Oxcumbe R. [13] Mouter R. [14] Hagham R.

Note : Walter of Conisholme was instituted to Raithby 1225–6 (L.R.S., ix, p. 145). He died in 1273 (L.R.S. xi, p. 53). It is uncertain which of the three Saltfleetby churches Gikel held, but it was probably All Saints, to which there are no recorded institutions until Margery widow of Alan of Moulton presented in 1252–3; unfortunately the name of the clerk is missing from the roll (L.R.S. xi, p. 131). Philip of Saltfleet was presented by Odo Galle to St. Clement 1224–5 (*ibid.*, p. 137), and the succession at St. Peter where Harold son of Humphrey was the patron is continuous for this period. Eva widow of Thomas son of Thomas levied a fine touching dower on 8th July, 1236 (*Final Concords* i, p. 294).

Add. Chart.

1652. Grant by Philip de Midley, son of Rannulf de Midley, to W[illiam] the dean, and the chapter of Lincoln, of a toft, a croft and fifteen acres of land in Saltfleetby. (1223–1239.)

Omnibus Christi fidelibus ad quos presens scriptum pervenerit ∴ Philippus de Midley filius Rannulfi de Midley . salutem . Noverit universitas vestra me . intuitu dei ⁊ pro salute anime mee ⁊ antecessorum ⁊ successorum meorum dedisse ⁊ concessissee ⁊ hac presenti carta mea confirmasse ∴ deo ⁊ beate Marie ⁊ .W. decano ⁊ capitulo ecclesie Lincolniensis . ⁊ eorum successoribus unum toftum cum uno crofto in villa de Salfleteby . scilicet quod iacet inter toftum Hugonis filii Godrici ⁊ quoddam fossatum quod vocatur Maredik[1] . Et decem acras terre in territorio eiusdem ville . videlicet illas decem acras terre que iacent in Mikledeile[2] inter terram abbatis de Parco versus orientem . ⁊ terram Odonis Galle que est versus occidentem . ⁊ inter terram Andree de Midley versus meridiem . ⁊ abbutissant super Maredikgate versus aquilonem . Et tres acras in Northacras . que iacent inter terram Ricardi filii Humfridi ⁊ terram Roberti filii Godefridi . Et unam acram in Northheinges[3] . que inter terras Ricardi filii Humfridi iacet . Et unam acram in Thirnholm . que abbutissat super Maredik . que iacet inter terram Andree de Midley ⁊ terram ecclesie beati Petri . Habenda ⁊ tenenda cum omnibus pertinentiis . libertatibus . ⁊ hesiamentis[4] infra villam ⁊ extra . libere quiete ⁊ pacifice in liberam puram ⁊ perpetuam elemosinam . libera soluta ⁊ quieta ab omni seculari servitio exactione ⁊ demanda . Et ego Philippus ⁊ heredes mei predictas terras cum pertinenciis . memoratis decano ⁊ canonicis ecclesie [5]Lincoliensis[5] ⁊ eorum successoribus warantizabimus defendemus ⁊ aquietabimus de omnibus . erga omnes homines imperpetuum . In huius rei robur ⁊ testimonium . presenti scripto sigillum meum apposui . Hiis testibus Haraldo filio Humfridi . Ricardo fratre eius . Salomone clerico . Willelmo capellano . Willelmo filio Ernisii de Scitebrok[6] . Iuone Rauen . Waltero de Oxecumb'[7] . Oseberto[8] filio Roberti . Salomone filio Roberti . Waltero fratre eius . Durant seruiente . Gilberto filio Salomonis . ⁊ multis aliis.

Endorsed: (1) Salfletebi .j. toft' cum crofto (13 cent.). (2) *On the fold on the obverse of the charter* Willelmus filius Gilberti Aky de Salfleteb' .iii. solidos (13 cent.).

Seal on tag, round, 1 inch diameter, green, fleur de lys.

SIGILL' PHILIPPI DE MILLAI

Texts: MS—Orig. Dij/86/2/21. R1599.

Var. R.: [1] Maredyk R. [2] Mikeledeyle R. [3] Northhenges R. [4] *sic*: aisiamentis R. [5]–[5] R *omits.* [6] Skitbrok R. [7] Oxcumbe R. [8] Osberto R.

Add. Chart.

1653. Confirmation and quitclaim by Peter son of Robert of Legbourne, to the chapter of Lincoln, of all the land which William son of Gilbert son of Aki had of the gift of Philip de Midley in Saltfleetby. (Circa 1225–1240.)

Omnibus sancte matris ecclesie filiis presentibus ⁊ futuris ad quos presens scriptum peruenerit ∴ Petrus de Lekeburn' filius Roberti salutem in domino . Nouerit uniuersitas uestra me quieteclamasse de me ⁊ [1]de[1] heredibus meis in perpetuum . ⁊ hac presenti carta mea confirmasse ∴ deo ⁊ capitulo beate Marie Linc' ∴ totam terram quam Willelmus filius Gilberti filii Aki[2] habuit de donacione Philippi de Milley in Salfledeb'[3] . uidelicet unum toftum ⁊ croftum inter terram Roberti filii Hugonis . ⁊ Maredicgate[4] . Et quatuor acras terre arabilis in Northunderth[5] inter terram Ricardi filii Humfridi ex una parte ∴ ⁊ terras[6] Willelmi [filii[7]] Roberti [1]⁊ Roberti[1] filii Godefridi ex altera [1]parte[1] . Et unum selionem in Thirnholm inter terram ecclesie sancti Petri ∴ ⁊ terram Andree de Millay[8] . Et undecim acras prati in capite boreali de Mickeldayle[9] inter pratum abbatis ⁊ conuentus de Parco Lude ⁊ pratum [1]Willelmi filii Roberti ex una parte ∴ ⁊ pratum[1] Andree Galle ex altera [1]parte[1] . Et unam acram prati in North[pratis[7]] inter prata Ricardi filii Humfridi ad utramque partem . plenarie . ⁊ integre . absque ullo retinemento . Habend' ⁊ tenend' in liberam [1]⁊[1] puram ⁊ perpetuam elem[osinam[7]] pro salute anime mee ⁊ antecessorum ⁊ successorum meorum[10] ∴ Quod nec ego Petrus nec heredes mei quicquam iuris aliquo modo de cetero inde uendicare poterimus . Et ego Petrus ⁊ heredes mei gwarantizabimus deo ⁊ capitulo beate Marie Linc' hanc predictam elemosinam prout [carta Phillipi[7]] de Milley[11] quam [idem[7]] capitulum inde habet testatur ∴ contra omnes homines in perpetuum . Hiis testibus . Andrea

Galle . Willelmo filio Roberti . [Waltero de Oxcumbe Petro Galle[7]] . [G[7]]eruasio de Thorp . Andrea de Mille[ẏ . Johanne filio[7]] Ranulfi de Luda . Thoma clerico . ⁊ [aliis[7]].

No ancient endorsement visible.
Slit for seal tag. Size : 8⅜ x 3½ inches.
Texts : MS—Orig. Dij/86/2/9. R1600.
Var. R. : [1–1] R *omits*. [2] Akẏ R. [3] Salfleteby R. [4] Maredikgate R. [5] North' Hunderth' R. [6] terram R. [7] *supplied from* R : *the charter is injured*. [8] Millai R. [9] Mikeldail R. [10] nostrorum R. [11] Millay R.
Note : Peter of Legbourne had succeeded his father before 1225 when he presented to Raithby church (L.R.S. ix, 99). He was holding land in 1242–3 (*Book of Fees*, ii, p. 1059). Walter of Oxcumbe claimed land in Saltfleetby in 1228 (C.P.R. 1225–32, p. 209). He and Gervase of Thorp were jurors in 1242 (*Book of Fees*, ii, p. 1053).

Add. Chart.

1654. Grant by Roger the dean, and the chapter of Lincoln, to Richard son of Humphrey, of all the land in Saltfleetby which they had of the gift of Humphrey son of Walter and Alice his wife, as well as the land there which they had of the gift of Eva widow of Thomas son of Thomas of Louth. For this Richard shall pay a yearly render of five shillings, half within the octave of Easter and the other half within the octave of Michaelmas. (1239–1245.)

Omnibus Christi fidelibus ad quos presens scriptum peruenerit Rogerus decanus ⁊ capitulum Linc' ecclesie salutem in domino . Nouerit vniuersitas vestra nos concessisse ⁊ hac presenti carta nostra confirmasse . Ricardo filio Vmfridi filii Walteri ⁊ heredibus suis vel assignatis suis quibuscumque preterquam viris religiosis ⁊ Judeis terram nostram in territorio de Salfletebẏ totam scilicet terram que fuit Reginaldi ⁊ totam terram que fuit Johannis Trute ⁊ totam terram que fuit Ẏalf ⁊ totam terram que fuit Sigward' ⁊ totam Hamelẏndaile preter viginti acras versus occidentem et totam terram Rogeri Boune ⁊ totam terram que fuit Walteri filii Roberti ⁊ seruicium filii Roberti Mole[1] ⁊ Lucecroft' ⁊ fforlandes apud mare ⁊ totum toftum proximo cimiterio Sancti Petri in australi parte ⁊ quindecim acras in proximo crofto in orientali parte) et totam terram que fuit Acke filii Saxe) et totam terram que fuit Godrici Houeth' et totam gaẏram ex occidentali parte terre Acke Mudding') que omnia habuimus scilicet ex dono predicti Vmfridi filii Walteri ⁊ Alicie vxoris eius) concessimus eciam eidem Ricardo filio Vmfridi toftum ⁊ croftum nostrum cum omnibus pertinenciis suis in Salfletebẏ que Robertus Bondeman tenuit aliquando ⁊ duos selliones terre arabilis cum omnibus pertinenciis suis iacentes in territorio de Salfletebẏ iuxta terram eiusdem

Ricardi vel Vmfridi iuxta Sigwardaẏle ⁊ terram que fuit Roberti Frost' cum omnibus pertinenciis suis que quidem habuimus de dono Eue quondam vxoris Thome filii Thome de Luda . Habend' ⁊ tenend' dicto Ricardo vel[2] Vmfrido ⁊ heredibus suis vel cuicumque vel quandocumque ea dare legare vel assignare voluerint preterquam viris religiosis et Judeis libere) integre) ⁊ pacifice inperpetuum . Reddendo inde singulis annis nobis ⁊ commune ecclesie nostre quinque solidos) medietatem . scilicet . infra octabis Pasche ⁊ aliam medietatem infra octabis Sancti Michaelis pro omni seruicio exaccione ⁊ demanda seculari . Et in huius rei testimonium presens scriptum sigilli nostri munimine duximus roborandum . Testibus .N. cancellario .W. subdecano . magistris Serlone ⁊ Ricardo Cornubie dominis .R. de Boll' ⁊ Thoma de Askeb' canonicis Linc') Elẏa succentore) Henrico sacrista Ricardo de Strettona Johanne filio Fulconis ⁊ aliis.

Text: MS—R1606.

Var. R.: [1] *sic*: *cf. no.* 1641 *above, where the service granted is that of Robert son of Mole.* [2] *sic*: *query* filio omitted.

Note: The dates given are those of Roger de Weseham as dean. The attestations of Nicholas the chancellor and William of Benniworth the subdean show that it is he and not Roger de Rolveston.

Add. Chart.

1655. Grant by Roger the dean, and the chapter of Lincoln, to John the clerk of Saltfleetby, son of Osbert the chaplain, of two acres in Saltfleetby, for a yearly render of sixpence. (Query 1195–1224.)

Omnibus sancte matris ecclesie filiis ad quos presens scriptum peruenerit Rogerus decanus ⁊ capitulum ecclesie Linc' salutem eternam in domino . Nouerit vniuersitas vestra nos concessisse ⁊ presenti carta nostra confirmasse Johanni clerico de Salfletebẏ filio Osberti capellani duas acras terre cum domibus inedificatis in villa de Salfletebẏ in parochia sancti Petri quas Alexander capellanus ⁊ Gilbertus frater euis aliquando de nobis tenuerunt Habendas ⁊ tenendas eidem Johanni ⁊ cuicumque assignare voluerit exceptis viris religiosis ⁊ Judeis in feodo ⁊ hereditate libere ⁊ quiete . Reddendo inde nobis per annum sex denarios ad festum sancti Johannis Baptiste pro omni seruicio ⁊ exaccione . In huius autem rei robur ⁊ testimonium presens scriptum sigilli nostri apposicione corroborauimus.

Text: MS—R1612.

Note: It is uncertain which dean Roger this is, but it may be noted that Roger de Rolveston frequently issued such grants with no witnesses.

Folio 95d.
Hdl.

Sumercotts

SOMERCOTES

496

1656. Grant by Andrew son of Robert of Somercotes, to the church of Lincoln and the Common, of ten acres of land in Somercotes and three in Skidbrook. (Circa 1190–1200.)

Sciant tam presentes quam futuri quod ego Andreas filius Roberti de Sumercotes[1] dedi ⁊ concessi ⁊ [2]hac[2] presenti carta mea confirmaui deo ⁊ beate Marie ⁊ commune canonicorum Linc' [2]ecclesie[2] tredecim[3] acras terre . decem videlicet in territorio de Sumercotes[1] . Scilicet unum toftum quod iacet inter domos Johannis filii Alani . [2]⁊ Alani[2] filii Radulfi . ⁊ dimidiam acram terre inter domos Willelmi filii Alnad ⁊ Hacke filii Lelle . ⁊ tres seliones super Grene ante portam Alani filii Hemming[4] inter terras ecclesie sancte Marie de Sumercotes[1] ⁊ Gileberti[5] filii Ascer . ⁊ vnam selionem inter terram Reginaldi filii Croc ⁊ Hadic in Sumeret . Et tres acras in territorio de Scitebroc[6] . iuxta Meles inter Aldehauene[7] ⁊ Huche toftes[8] . in liberam puram ⁊ perpetuam elemosinam pro animabus patris ⁊ matris méé ⁊ omnium antecessorum meorum . Necnon ⁊ pro salute mea ⁊ omnium heredum meorum . Hanc uero terram ego ⁊ heredes mei warantizabimus predictis canonicis imperpetuum contra omnes homines . Et ut ista donatio irreuocabilis permaneat ∴ hanc cartam sigilli mei appensione corroboraui . Hiis testibus . Willelmo ⁊ Jordano decanis . magistro Hugone Blundo . Roberto de Mareis[9] . Hernisio filio Gille . Wigot[10] filio Leppe . Alano filio Hemming[4] . Hugone filio Iuonis . Alano filio Radulfi . ⁊ multis aliis.

Marginalia in A: Sumercotes xiii acras terre (? by Q2).
Texts: MS—A. R1541.
Var. R.: [1] Somercotes R. [2–2] R *omits*. [3] tresdecim R. [4] Hemmyng' R. [5] Gilberti R. [6] Skitbroc R. [7] Haldehauene R. [8] Hucketoftes R. [9] Mareys R. [10] Wygoto R.
Note: John son of Alan witnesses *circa* 1200–1205 (no. 1671 below). William and Jordan witness 1183–89 (no. 1201 in vol. iv above) and early thirteenth century (no. 910 in vol. iii above). It is uncertain whether William is to be identified with William son of Martel, dean of the city of Lincoln *circa* 1200, or with William the dean, son of Ulf, who witnesses a charter of William son of Martel late in the twelfth century (Dij/80/3/32). I am indebted to Mr. J. W. F. Hill for drawing my attention to the latter charter. Robert son of Jordan the dean witnesses late twelfth century (*Danelaw Charters*, p. 53). Master Hugh Blund witnesses *circa* 1200 (see no. 1361 in vol. iv. above).

497

1657. Grant by Richard son of Robert of Somercotes, to the church of Lincoln and the Common, of seven acres of arable land in Somercotes and six acres of meadow in Saltfleetby. (Late twelfth century.)

Sciant presentes 7 futuri quod ego Ricardus filius Roberti de Sumerecotes[1] dedi 7 concessi 7 hac presenti carta mea confirmaui deo 7 beate Marie 7 commune [2]canonicorum[2] Linc'[3] .vii. acras terre in territorio de Sumerecotes[1] que iacent in quodam clauso quod est inter toftum Petri filii Ailsi 7 toftum Ricardi Stalwardiman[4] 7 sex acras prati que iacent in crofto quod fuit Godrici filii Swani . in puram 7 perpetuam elemosinam pro salute anime méé 7 antecessorum meorum . Et ego 7 heredes mei warantizabimus predictam terram 7 [2]prefatum[2] pratum prefato capitulo contra omnes homines imperpetuum . Et ut hec mea donatio rata permaneat .' eam sigilli mei munimine corroboraui . Hiis testibus . Waltero Blundo iuniore . Ricardo de Hardres . [2]Thoma de Hardres[2] . Jordane[5] de Brakenbere[6] . Roberto de Manneby . Johanne filio Gikel.

Marginalia in A: Sumercotes vij acras terre (? by Q2).
Texts: MS—A. R1524.
Var. R.: [1] Somercotes R. [2–2] R *omits.* [3] R *adds* ecclesie. [4] Stalwardman R. [5] *sic.* [6] Brakenberg' R.
Note: Richard son of Robert of Somercotes was the son of Robert son of Gilbert of Legbourne (*Danelaw Charters*, p. 350). He married Hawis daughter of Philip of Kyme, who granted him land in Hallington (*ibid.*, p. 351). John son of Gikel of Yarborough was steward of Gayton soke late in the twelfth century (*ibid.*, p. 352).

498

1658. Confirmation by Robert son of William of Legbourne of the preceding grant made to them by Richard son of Robert his uncle. (Late twelfth century.)

Omnibus hoc scriptum uisuris uel audituris Robertus filius Willelmi de Lekeburne salutem . Sciatis me concessisse 7 hac presenti carta mea confirmasse in puram 7 perpetuam elemosinam deo 7 beate Marie 7 commune canonicorum Linc' illam donationem quam Ricardus filius Roberti auunculus meus fecit eis scilicet septem acras terre in territorio de Sumerecotes[1] in quodam clauso quod iacet inter toftum Petri filii Ailsi 7 toftum Ricardi Stalwordiman[2] . 7 sex acras prati que iacent in crofto quod fuit Godrici filii Swani . Et ego 7 heredes mei warantizabimus predictam donationem prenominato capitulo contra omnes homines imperpetuum . Et ut ista mea concessio rata permaneat .' eam sigilli mei munimine roboraui . Hiis testibus . Waltero Blundo iuniore . [3]Ricardo de Hardres[3] . Jordano de Brakenberg' . Roberto de Manneby . Johanne filio Jukel.[4]

Marginalia in A: Sumercotes vij acras terre (? by Q2).
Texts: MS—A. R1527.
Var. R.: [1] Somercotes R. [2] Stalwordman R. [3–3] R *omits.* [4] Gikel R.

Folio 96.

Hdl. Ludhesk' . 9 . 6 .

499

1659. Grant by Arnold son of Ache of Somercotes, with the consent of his wife, to the church of Lincoln, of an acre of land in Somercotes. (Circa 1200.)

Notum sit omnibus ad quos presens scriptum peruenerit quod ego Arnaldus filius Ache de Sumercotes dedi in puram 7 perpetuam elemosinam assensu uxoris méé pro animabus antecessorum meorum deo 7[1] sancte Marie Linc' unam acram terre in tofto meo a parte occidentali que incipit a capite australi [2]protractam[2] uersus boream secundum medietatem latitudinis eiusdem tofti . 7 ne hec donatio possit irritari ∴ eam testimonio sigilli mei roboraui . Hiis testibus . Willelmo clerico . Roberto filio Willelmi . Alano filio Hemr'[3] . Reginaldo fratre suo . Godrico filio Hederic . 7 multis aliis.

Marginalia in A : Sumercotes j. acram terre (? by Q2).
Texts : MS—A. R1538.
Var. R. : [1] R *adds* ecclesie. [2–2] *blank in* R. [3] *sic* : Hemmyng' R.

500

1660. Grant by William son of Ivo of Somercotes, to the chapter of Lincoln, of various parcels of arable land in Somercotes. (Circa 1200.)

Omnibus sancte matris ecclesie filiis Willelmus filius Iuonis de Sumercotes[1] . salutem . Noueritis me dedisse 7 concessisse 7 presenti carta confirmasse pro animabus antecessorum meorum 7 salute mea 7 meorum deo 7 beate Marie 7 capitulo Linc' unum croftum .v. acrarum in Sumercotes[1] quod est inter croftum[2] meum 7 croftum Rogeri prepositi . 7 duas acras 7 dimidiam terre arabilis in loco qui dicitur Sumerhette . proximas terre Gilberti filii Leuiue ex parte australi . 7 vnam[3] terre arabilis super Grene iuxta terram que fuit Gunewar[4] ex parte occidentali habendas 7 possidendas in liberam [5]7[5] puram 7 perpetuam elemosinam quietas ab omni terreno seruitio . Ego enim 7 heredes mei eas eis warantizabimus contra omnes homines . 7 ab omni seruitio adquietabimus.

Marginalia in A : Sumercotes .j. croftum v acrarum (? by Q2).
Texts : MS—A. R1543.
Var. R. : [1] Somercotes R. [2] toftum R. [3] *sic* : R *adds* acram. [4] Gunewat R. [5–5] R *omits*.

501

1661. Grant by Richard son of Robert of Somercotes, to the church of Lincoln and the Common, of a toft in Somercotes—

namely five and a half acres of arable land and five and a half acres of meadow. (Circa 1200.)

Vniuersis sancte matris ecclesie filiis Ricardus filius Roberti de Sumercotes[1] salutem . Nouerit uniuersitas uestra me dedisse ⁊ concessisse ⁊ hac mea presenti carta confirmasse deo ⁊ beate Marie ⁊ commune canonicorum Linc' ecclesie pro salute anime méé ⁊ omnium antecessorum meorum in puram ⁊ perpetuam elemosinam unum toftum in Sumercotes[1] iacentem inter terram Willelmi de[2] Wra ⁊ terram Willelmi Lewestren[3] iuxta Hengdic[4] . Scilicet quinque acras terre ⁊ dimidiam . ⁊ quinque acras prati ⁊ dimidiam in capite crofti Willelmi del[5] Wra inter terram Willelmi filii Alfsi . ⁊ terram Willelmi filii Godrici . Hanc autem donationem ego Ricardus ⁊ heredes mei warantizabimus predictis canonicis contra omnes homines ⁊ adquietabimus . Hiis testibus . Andrea fratre magistri Willelmi de Sumercotes[1] . Malgero de Nethelham[6] . Willelmo filio Godrici . Hugone filio Lelle . Roberto le Vauassur[7] . Waltero filio Auine[8] . Roberto de Hambi[9] . Ricardo de Federstan.

Marginalia in A: Somercotes unum toftum (? by Q2).
Texts: MS—A. R1525.
Var. R.: [1] Somercotes R. [2] del R. [3] Le Westren R. [4] Hendic R. [5] de R. [6] Netelham R. [7] Vauasur R. [8] Anne R. [9] Hamby R.
Note: Richard son of Robert of Somercotes, Robert Vavasur and William son of Godric all occur in the late twelfth century (see no. 1602 above and *Danelaw Charters*, pp. 397–399). William son of Godric was the son-in-law of William son of Robert of Legbourne. He was therefore the nephew by marriage of Richard, son of Robert. The latter occurs in 1201 (C.R.R. i, p. 374) and in 1202 (L.R.S. xxii, no. 1023).

502

1662. Confirmation of the preceding grant by Robert son of William of Legbourne. (Circa 1200.)

Vniuersis sancte matris ecclesie filiis Robertus filius Willelmi de Lekeburne salutem . Nouerit uniuersitas uestra me concessisse ⁊ hac mea presenti carta confirmasse deo ⁊ sancte Marie ⁊ commune canonicorum Linc' ecclesie pro salute anime méé ⁊ omnium antecessorum in puram ⁊ perpetuam elemosinam donationem Ricardi filii Roberti de Sumercotes[1] . scilicet unum toftum in Sumercotes[1] iacentem inter terram Willelmi del Wra . ⁊ terram Willelmi le Westren iuxta Hendig[2] . ⁊ quinque acras terre [3]⁊ dimidiam[3] . ⁊ quinque acras prati ⁊ dimidiam . in capite crofti Willelmi del Wra . inter terram Willelmi filii Alfsi . ⁊ terram Willelmi filii Godrici . Hiis testibus . Andrea fratre magistri Willelmi de Sumercotes[1] . Malgero de Netelham * . Willelmo filio Godrici . Hugone filio Lelle . Roberto le Vauassur[4] . Waltero filio Auine . Roberto de Hambia . Ricardo de Federstan.

Marginalia in A : (1) Somercotes (? by Q2). (2) unum toftum (16 cent.).
Texts : MS—A. R1526.
Var. R. : [1] Somercotes R. [2] Hendic R. [3–3] R *omits.* [4] Vauasur R.

******Folio 96d.*

505

1663. Grant by Peter son of Ailsi, to the church of Lincoln and the Common, of two acres and a perch of land in Somercotes. (Circa 1200.)

Vniuersis sancte matris ecclesie filiis ad quos presens scriptum peruenerit Petrus filius Aeilsi[1] salutem . Nouerit uniuersitas uestra me dedisse 7 concessisse 7 hac presenti carta mea confirmasse deo 7 beate Marie 7 commune Linc' ecclesie in territorio de Sumerecote[2] duas acras 7 perticatam terre arabilis que iacent inter terram Gileberti[3] clerici 7 terram Roberti filii Edrici in puram 7 perpetuam elemosinam . 7 hanc donationem warantizabimus ego 7 heredes mei deo 7 predicte commune contra omnes homines . Hiis testibus . magistro Ricardo de Hardres . magistro Johanne de Merstun[4] . Ricardo filio Roberti . Alano filio Emming[5] . Arngrim filio Godrici . Roberto filio Ediue . Gunni[6] filio Mille . Willelmo filio Acche . Petro fratre eius . Willelmo filio Roberti . Andrea filio Roberti.

Marginalia in A : Sumercotes ii acras 7 perticatam (? by Q2).
Texts : MS—A. R1533.
Var. R. : [1] Aelsi R. [2] Somercotes R. [3] Gilberti. [4] Merston' R. [5] Emmyng R. [6] Guni R.
Note : See *Free Peasantry,* p. 135.

506

1664. Grant by Basing son of Osgot, to the church of Lincoln and the Common, of two and a half acres of land in Somercotes. (Circa 1200.)

Sciant presentes 7 futuri quod ego Basind filius Hosgoti[1] de Sumercotes dedi 7 concessi 7 hac presenti carta mea confirmaui deo 7 beate Marie 7 commune canonicorum Linc' in puram 7 perpetuam elemosinam pro salute anime méé 7 omnium antecessorum meorum duas acras terre 7 dimidiam in territorio de Sumercotes[2] que iacent inter terram ecclesie sancte Marie eius[3] eiusdem uille . 7 terram .W. filii Ailsi . Et ego 7 heredes mei warantizabimus predicte commune prefatam terram contra omnes homines imperpetuum . Et ut hec mea donatio rata permaneat 7 inconcussa ; eam sigilli mei appositione corroboraui . Hiis testibus . Waltero Blundo iuniore . Ricardo de Hardres . Sampsone capellano . Andrea filio Roberti .W. filio Ailsi . Alano filio Radulfi.

Marginalia in A: Sumercotes ij acr' ⁊ dimid' (? by Q2).
Texts: MS—A. R1542.
Var. R.: [1] Osgoti R. [2] Somercotes R. [3] *sic*: R *omits* eius.

505

1665. Grant by Basing son of Osgot, to the church of Lincoln and the Common, of eight and a half acres of land in Somercotes from the Great Eau to the road on the South (Circa 1200.)

Omnibus sancte matris ecclesie filiis ad quos presens scriptum peruenerit ;' Basing filius Osgoti de Sumercotes[1] salutem . Nouerit uniuersitas uestra me pro salute anime méé ⁊ omnium antecessorum meorum concessisse ⁊ dedisse ⁊ hac presenti carta mea confirmasse deo ⁊ beate Marie ⁊ commune canonicorum Linc' ecclesie in puram ⁊ perpetuam elemosinam octo acras terre arabilis ⁊ dimidiam in territorio de Sumercotes[1] . scilicet á A.[2] (usque ad uiam uersus austrum . scilicet illas que iacent inter terram Alani filii Asceri . ⁊ terram Gileberti[3] filii Asceri . Et ego Basing ⁊ heredes mei warantizabimus terram prenominatam prenominato capitulo contra omnes homines . Et ut hec mea donatio imperpetuum rata permaneat sigilli mei munimine[4] corroboraui . Hiis testibus . Eudone de Sancto Botulfo capellano . Ricardo de Hardres capellano . Johanne de Wikeford[5] capellano . Waltero Blundo capellano . Radulfo filio Briani de Welleton'[6] . Willelmo filio Johannis de Sumerecotes[1] . Johanne filio Alani . Andrea filio Roberti . Lamberto filio Reginaldi . Petro filio Ernisii.

Marginalia in A: Sumercotes viij acr' ⁊ dimid' (? by Q2).
Texts: MS—A. R1530.
Var. R.: [1] Somercotes R. [2] *sic.* [3] Gilberti R. [4] munime (*sic*) R. [5] Wicford' R. [6] Welton' R.
Note: The " A " of this charter is the dyke known at the present time as the Great Eau (*Free Peasantry*, p. 136).

506

1666. Grant by Lambert son of Reginald and Ernis son of Gunni, to the church of Lincoln and the Common, of four acres of land in Somercotes. (Circa 1200.)

Omnibus sancte matris ecclesie filiis ad quos presens scriptum peruenerit ;' Lambertus filius Reginaldi . ⁊ Ernisius filius Gune de Sumerecotes[1] salutem . Nouerit uniuersitas uestra nos pro salute anime nostre ⁊ omnium antecessorum nostrorum concessisse ⁊ dedisse . ⁊ hac presenti carta nostra confirmasse deo ⁊ beate Marie ⁊ commune canonicorum Linc' ecclesie in puram ⁊ perpe*tuam elemosinam quatuor acras terre arabilis in territorio de Sumerecotes[1] . scilicet a Sour usque ad uiam . Scilicet illas que iacent inter terram Magnus[2] ⁊ terram Roberti filii Ediue . Et ego Lambertus ⁊ Ernisius warantizabimus terram prenominatam prenominato capitulo contra omnes homines . Et ut hec nostra donatio imperpetuum rata permaneat : sigillorum nostrorum appositione corroborauimus . Hiis testibus . Eudone de Sancto Botulfo capellano . Ricardo de Hardres capellano[3] . Radulfo filio Briani de Welleton[4] . Willelmo filio Johannis de Sumercotes[1] . Johanne filio Alani . Andrea filio Roberti . Basing filio Osgoti.

Marginalia in A: Sumercotes iiij acr' (? by Q2).
Texts: MS—A. R1529.
Var. R.: [1] Somercotes R. [2] *sic*: Mangeri (*sic*) R. [3] R *adds* Johanne de Wicford' capellano Waltero Blundo capellano. [4] Welton' R.
Note: See the succeeding grant which is 1196–8 and in which Lambert son of Reginald is grantor and Ernis son of Gune a witness. William son of John of Somercotes was party to a fine levied in 1202 (*Final Concords*, i, p. 38).

**Folio* 97.

Hdl. . 9 . 7 .

507

1667. Grant by Lambert son of Reginald of Somercotes, to the church of Lincoln, of two acres of land with a toft in Somercotes. (1196–1198.)

Vniuersis Christi fidelibus ad quos presens scriptum peruenerit : Lambertus filius Reginaldi de Sumercotes[1] salutem . Nouerit uniuersitas uestra me concessisse ⁊ dedisse ⁊ hac presenti carta mea confirmasse deo ⁊ beate Marie Linc' . ⁊ canonicis ibidem deo seruientibus duas acras terre arabilis in territorio de Sumercotes[1] cum tofto quod iacet inter terram Roberti capellani ⁊ terram Willelmi filii Godrici Hachet pro salute anime méé ⁊ patris mei ⁊ matris méé ⁊ omnium antecessorum meorum in puram ⁊ perpetuam elemosinam . Et ego ⁊ heredes mei warantizabimus terram prenominatam prenominato capitulo contra omnes homines . Et ut hec mea donatio imperpetuum rata permaneat : sigilli mei munimine corroboraui . Hiis testibus . magistro Willelmo precentore[2] . magistro Ricardo subdecano . Ricardo de Kyma . magistro Waltero[3] Blundo . Eudone capellano . [4]Gileberto Pilate . Roberto capellano de Sumercotes[1] . magistro Roberto[4] de Gaitune[5] . Willelmo clerico de Sumercotes[1] . Ernisio filio Guue.[6]

Marginalia in A: Sumercotes ij acr' terre (? by Q2).
Texts: MS—A. R1528.
Var. R.: [1] Somercotes R. [2] R *adds* magistro Willelmo cancellario. [3] Willelmo R. [4]–[4] R *omits*. [5] Gayton' R. [6] *sic*: Gune R.
Note: William of Blois was precentor 1196–1203. Richard Kentensis occurs as sub-dean 1197–8 (*Cartulary of the Abbey of Eynsham*, edited by H. E. Salter, Oxford Historical Society, vol. i, p. 47). In 1198 he became archdeacon of Northampton (*ibid.*, footnote).

508

1668. Grant by Wigot of Somercotes, **with the counsel and consent of his heirs,** to the church of Lincoln, of ten acres of land, a toft and three other parcels of land in Somercotes. (Late twelfth century.)

Sciant tam presentes quam futuri quod ego Wigot[1] de Sumercotes[2] consilio 7 consensu heredum meorum dedi deo 7 sancte Marie Linc' pro anima mea 7 pro animabus patris mei 7 matris méé 7 omnium parentum meorum decem acras terre in territorio de Sumercotes[3] in puram 7 perpetuam elemosinam . scilicet proximum croftum quod iacet ex occidentali parte domus Gileberti[4] filii Leiuiue[5] . Et toftum proximum ex Norpart[6] domus prenominati Gileberti[4] . 7 duos selliones iacentes ex Nortpart[6] predicti tofti . 7 .iiijor. seliones super Grene iacentes ex Nortpart[7] domus Willelmi filii Ailsi . Scilicet inter terram Ricardi filii Roberti . 7 Godrici filii Ranulfi . Et tres selliones iacentes inter terram Roberti filii Godricii[7] 7 predictum croftum . Hiis testibus . Alano filio Hemming . Reginaldo fratre suo . Hugone filio Iuonis[8] . Willelmo filio Ailsi . Alano filio Radulfi . Willelmo fratre suo . Andrea filio Roberti . Willelmo filio Iuonis[8] . Roberto filio Aceri[9] . Willelmo fratre suo . 7 multis aliis.

Marginalia in A: Sumercotes x acr' terre (? by Q2).
Texts: MS—A. R1552.
Var. R.: [1] Wygotus R. [2] Somercot' R. [3] Somercotes R. [4] Gilberti R. [5] Leiuue R. [6] Northpart R. [7] Godrici R. [8] Ẏuonis R. [9] Asceri R.

509

1669. Grant by Gilbert the clerk of Somercotes, to the church of Lincoln and the Common, of two and a half acres and one perch of arable land as well as a piece of land ten perches long and one broad, in Somercotes. (Circa 1200.)

Vniuersis sancte matris ecclesie filiis ad quos presens scriptum peruenerit ∴ Gilebertus[1] clericus de Sumercote[2] salutem . Nouerit uniuersitas uestra me dedisse [3]7 concessisse[3] 7 hac presenti carta mea confirmasse deo 7 beate Marie 7 commune Linc' ecclesie in territorio de Sumercote[2] duas acras ⁊ dimidiam terre arabilis . ⁊ unam perticatam . ⁊ unam portionem terre habentem decem perticatas in longum . ⁊ unam in latum . Que terra tota iacet inter terram Willelmi filii Eilsi . ⁊ terram Petri filii Eilsi in puram ⁊ perpetuam elemosinam . Hanc autem donationem warantizabimus ego ⁊ heredes mei predicte commune contra omnes homines . Hiis testibus . magistro Ricardo de Hardres preposito . magistro Johanne de Merstun . Ricardo filio Roberti * de Sumercote[2] . Alano filio Hemming[4] . Hugone filio Yuonis[5] . Willelmo filio Eilsi[6] . Radulfo filio Asgeri . Willelmo filio Roberti . Roberto filio Asceri.

Marginalia in A: Sumercotes ij acras ⁊ dimidiam (? by Q2).
Texts: MS—A. R1549.
Var. R.: [1] Gilbertus R. [2] Somercotes R. [3–3] R *omits.* [4] Hemmyng R. [5] Ivonis R. [6] Eẏlsẏ R.

**Folio 97d.*

Hdl. Communa

510

1670. Grant by Alan son of Ralf of Somercotes, to the church of Lincoln and the Common, of half an acre of land in Somercotes. (Circa 1200.)

De .i. dimidia acra terre in Somercotes. (A rubric.)

Omnibus sancte matris ecclesie filiis ad quos presens scriptum peruenerit : Alanus filius Radulfi de Sumercotes[1] . salutem . Nouerit uniuersitas uestra me dedisse ⁊ concessisse ⁊ presenti carta confirmasse deo ⁊ ecclesie sancte Marie Linc' . ⁊ commune canonicorum ibidem deo seruientium unam dimidiam acram terre in Sumercotes[1] in puram ⁊ perpetuam elemosinam cum omnibus libertatibus ⁊ aisiamentis [2]in uilla[2] ⁊ extra uillam . ⁊ cum omnibus pertinenciis . scilicet illam dimidiam acram que est inter terram Willelmi filii Ailsi[3] ⁊ Willelmi filii Acke . Et ego warantizabo predictam terram predictis canonicis contra omnes homines . Et ut ista donatio firma ⁊ inconcussa permaneat : illam sigilli mei impressura corroboraui . Hiis testibus . Gilleberto . Pilate[4] . Jone tunc temporis Linc' ecclesie preposito . magistro Nicholao . Willelmo filio Aelsi[5] . Willelmo filio Roberti Hugone filio Yuonis[6] . ⁊ multis aliis.

Marginalia in A: Sumercot' dimidiam acram (? by Q2).
Texts: MS—A. R1548.
Var. R.: [1] Somercotes R. [2–2] R *has* infra villam. [3] Aelsi R. [4] Pylat' R. [5] Aelsy R. [6] Ivonis R.
Note: For Ion the provost see vol. iv, p. 283, above.

511

1671. Grant by Walter son of Ingeram, to the church of Lincoln and the Common, of twenty-one acres of land in Somercotes. (Before 1198.)

Carta Ingerami . de Somercotes. (A rubric.)

Sciant presentes 7 futuri quod ego Walterus filius Ingeram dedi 7 concessi 7 hac presenti carta mea confirmaui deo 7 Sancte Marie 7 commune capituli[1] ecclesie Linc' in puram 7 perpetuam elemosinam uiginti unam acram[2] terre . uidelicet toftum 7 croftum que iacent inter domum Radulfi filii Ernisii 7 uiam que est ab oriente . 7 tres acras extremas uersus occidentem in Encroft . 7 quatuor acras prati ab aquilone del Encroft iuxta terram Willelmi Norwegie . 7 unam acram prati in Brictiue daile . 7 tres acras in parrochia de Sumercotes[3] inter terram Andréé 7 uiam cum omnibus aisiamentis ad illas pertinentibus . Et ut hec donatio mea illibata permaneat ∴ sigilli mei appositione eam roboraui . Testibus . Thoma capellano . Waltero Blundo juniore . Willelmo clerico de Sumercotes[3] . Gileberto[4] filio Godrici . Randulfo filio Basing[5] . Gileberto[4] fratre eius Askel filio Basing'[5] . Johanne filio Alani de Sumercotes[3] . Gileberto[4] filio Randulfi . Martino fratre eius.

Marginalia in A: (1) acram x (faded). (2) Sumercotes xxi acras (? by Q2).
Texts: MS—A. R1553.
Var. R.: [1] canonicorum R. [2] *sic*: acram *is added in the margin.* [3] Somercotes R. [4] Gilberto R. [5] Basyng' R.
Note: The land granted in this charter was quitclaimed by the donor's mother 1196–1198 (see no. 1673 below). Walter son of Ingeram and Muriel his wife were mentioned as tenants of land in Somercotes in 1202 (L.R.S. xxii, no. 124).

512

1672. Confirmation of the preceding grant by Richard of the Park, knight. (1198–1205.)

Confirmatio de eadem terra. (A rubric.)

Omnibus sancte matris ecclesie filiis ad quos pr[esens scriptum peruenerit R[1]]icardus de Parco miles salutem . Nouerit uniuersitas uestra me concessisse 7 hac presenti mea carta[2] confirmasse deo 7 beate Marie 7 commune canonicorum Linc' ecclesie totam donacionem quam dedit eis Walterus filius Ingeram uidelicet uiginti 7 unam acram[3] terre cum omnibus pertinenciis suis sicuti continetur in carta quam habet ecclesia Linc' de eodem Waltero . 7 ego Ricardus 7 heredes mei warantizabimus memorate ecclesie donationem supradicti Walteri pro salute animarum parentum 7 omnium antecessorum meorum[4] ∴ contra omnes homines . Hiis testibus .W. cancellario .W. subdecano . magistro . Roberto de Holm . Henrico de Derebi[5] . canonicis . Willelmo de[6] Petro 7 Johanne de Wikefort[7] capellanis . Willelmo clerico de Sumercotes[8] . Gileberto[9] filio Godrici . Randulfo[10] filio Basing' . Gileberto[9] fratre eius 7 multis aliis.

Endorsed: (1) Ric' de . . . . . de Skitebroc (13 cent.). (2) xxxix.

Tag for seal. Size: 5½ x 1¾ inches.

Marginalia in A: (1) Sumercot' (? by Q2). (2) Confirmacio de eadem terra (16 cent.).

Texts: MS—Orig. Dij/87/1/1. A. R1556.

Var. R.: [1] *supplied from* A: *the charter is injured.* [2] R *has* carta mea. [3] *sic.* [4] nostrorum R. [5] Derbỳ R. [6] R *adds* Sancto. [7] Wikeford A. Wycford R. [8] Somercotes R. [9] Gilberto R. [10] Radulfo R.

Note: This charter has apparently been wrongly endorsed and classed with the Skidbrook charters since the thirteenth century. It is entered with those of Skidbrook in R.

William de Bramfeld the subdean held office before the death of bishop Hugh I but not before 1198. He was murdered in the cathedral 25th September, 1205.

513

1673. Quitclaim by Muriilda wife of Ingeram of Mablethorpe of all her right and claim in the twenty-one acres of land which Walter her son gave to the church of Lincoln and the Common. (1196–1198.)

Quieta clamatio de eadem. (A rubric.)

Vniuersis Christi fidelibus ad quos presens scriptum peruenerit ./ Muriilda[1] uxor Ingeram de Malbertorp[2] salutem . Nouerit uniuersitas uestra me quietumclamasse totum ius 7 clamium * quod habebam in viginti acris terre 7 una acra[3] quas Walterus filius meus dedit deo 7 beate Marie 7 commune canonicorum Linc' ecclesie . Et pro ista quietaclamatione dedit mihi Robertus filius Basing de Scitebroc[4] coram capitulo Linc' duas marcas 7 dimidiam . Et ego Miriilda tactis sacrosanctis euaungeliis[5] coram capitulo Linc' iuraui 7 affidaui quod nunquam per me uel per alium super terra prenominata questionem uel calumpniam mouebo . Et ad hanc quietam clamationem corroborandam ./ sigillum meum in testimonium presenti scripto apposui . Hiis testibus . magistro Willelmo precentore Linc' ecclesie . magistro .R. subdecano . Ricardo de Kyma . Rogero Scoto . magistro Waltero Blundo . Eudone de Sancto Botulfo . Willelmo filio Walteri . Eudone de Fugelestorp . Jordano de Barkenberge[6] . Johanne de Sumerecotes[7] . Gileberto[8] de Karleton[9] . Gileberto[8] Fluri[10] . Radulfo filio Ernisii de Scitebroc[11] . Hugone Cnotting[12] . Willelmo filio Johannis . Andrea de Sumerecotes.[7]

Marginalia in A: Sumercotes (? by Q2).

Texts: MS—A. R1554.

Var. R.: [1] Miriilda R. [2] Malberthorp R. [3] R *adds* prati. [4] Scitbrok' R. [5] ewangeliis R. [6] Brakenberg' R. [7] Somercotes R. [8] Gilberto R. [9] Karletune R. [10] Flury R. [11] Skitbrok R. [12] Knottyng' R.
Note: William of Blois became precentor in 1196. For Richard Kentensis see no. 1667 above.

**Folio* 98.

Hdl. Luesk' . 9 . 8 . Communa

514

1674. Grant by William son of Ailsi of Somercotes, to the church of Lincoln and the Common, of a piece of land in Somercotes. (Circa 1200.)

Vniuersis sancte matris ecclesie filiis ad quos presens scriptum peruenerit ∴ Willelmus filius Aelsi de Sumercotes[1] salutem . Nouerit uniuersitas uestra me dedisse 7 concessisse 7 presenti carta confirmasse deo 7 ecclesie sancte Marie Linc' 7 commune canonicorum ibidem deo seruientium . totam terram meam scilicet que est inter terram Alani filii Radulfi 7 Willelmi filii Asgher in puram 7 perpetuam elemosinam cum omnibus pertinenciis . 7 aesiamentis [2]in uilla[2] 7 extra uillam . Et ego warantizabo predictam terram que est in Sumercotes[1] ∴ predictis canonicis contra omnes homines . Et ut donatio ista rata 7 firma permaneat ∴ illam[3] sigilli mei appositione corroboraui . Hiis testibus . magistro Nicholao . Eudone[4] preposito . Gilleberto[5] Pilate[6] . Willelmo filio Aelsi[7] . Roberto filio Hugonis . 7 multis aliis.

Marginalia in A: Sumercotes (? by Q2).
Texts: MS—A. R1544.
Var. R.: [1] Somercotes R. [2–2] infra villam R. [3] eam R. [4] Edone (*sic*) R. [5] Gilberto R. [6] Pylat' R. [7] Aelsy R.
Note: For Eudo the provost see vol. iv, p. 283, above.

515

1675. Grant by Auke of Somercotes, with the consent of his heirs, to the church of Lincoln and the Common, of twenty-three and a half acres of land in Somercotes. (Circa 1200.)

Sciant presentes 7 futuri quod ego Auke de Sumerecotes[1] assensu heredum meorum concessi 7 dedi 7 hac presenti carta mea confirmaui deo 7 beate Marie 7 commune canonicorum Linc' ecclesie in puram 7 perpetuam elemosinam pro salute anime méé 7 omnium antecessorum meorum viginti tres acras terre 7 dimidiam in territorio de Sumercotes[1] . scilicet tredecim[2] acras 7 dimidiam in uno tofto propinquiori tofto meo ex aquilonali parte . 7 duas acras super Westlanges[3] . 7 unam acram in Adelmanneholm . 7 septem acras prati in

Folmethecroft . iuxta pratum sanctimonialium de Lekeburne ex parte aquilonali . Et ego Auke 7 heredes mei warantizabimus viginti tres acras [4]terre[4] prenominatas 7 dimidiam prenominato capitulo contra omnes homines . Et ut hec mea donatio imperpetuum rata permaneat ; sigilli mei appositione corroboraui . Hiis testibus . Eudone de Sancto Botulfo capellano . Waltero Blundo capellano . Ricardo de Hardres capellano . Johanne de Wikeford[5] . Willelmo persona de Salfletb'[6] . Willelmo filio Johannis de Sumercotes[1] . Rogero mercatore de Malbertorp[7] . Johanne filio Stepi[8] de Saltefleteb'[6] . Willelmo filio Godrici de Scitebroc.[9]

Marginalia in A : Sumercotes (? by Q2). (2) xxxiii acras et dimidiam (16 cent.).
Texts : MS—A. R1534.
Var. R. : [1] Somercotes R. [2] tresdecim R. [3] Westlandes R. [4–4] R *omits*. [5] Wicford R. [6] Salfleteby R. [7] Malberthorp R. [8] Stepy̆ R. [9] Scitbrok R.
Note : The first three witnesses occur frequently between 1196 and 1203 (e.g. nos. 1140–1, 1257, 1298 in vol. iv, above). William rector of Saltfleetby occurs frequently about this date (*Danelaw Charters*, pp. 392, 394, 399).

Folio 98d.

515a

1676. Grant by William son of Asger, to the church of Lincoln and the Common, of two acres and a perch of land in Somercotes. (Circa 1200.)

Vniuersis sancte matris ecclesie filiis ad quos presens scriptum peruenerit ; Willelmus filius Asgheri salutem . Nouerit uniuersitas uestra me dedisse 7 concessisse 7 hac carta mea confirmasse deo 7 beate Marie 7 commune Linc' ecclesie in territorio de Sumerecote[1] duas acras 7 perticatam terre que iacent inter terram Basing filii Osgoti . 7 terram que fuit Petri clerici in puram 7 perpetuam elemosinam . Hanc autem donationem warantizabimus ego 7 heredes mei deo 7 predicte commune contra omnes homines . Hiis testibus . magistro Ricardo . de Hardres . magistro Johanne de Merst' . Ricardo filio Roberti . Alano filio Emming[2] . Arngrim filio Godrici . Roberto filio Ediue . Gunni[3] filio Mille . Willelmo filio Acche . Petro fratre eius . Willelmo filio Roberti . Andrea.[4]

Marginalia in A : Sumercotes ij acras et perticatam (? by Q2).
Texts : MS—A. R1532.
Var. R. : [1] Somercotes R. [2] Emmy̆g R. [3] Guny R. [4] R *adds* filio Roberti.

516

1677. Grant by Robert son of William of Somercotes, to the church of Lincoln and the Common, of a toft containing four acres, three acres of land, and twenty acres of meadow in the marsh, in Somercotes. (Circa 1200.)

Omnibus sancte matris ecclesie filiis ad quos presens scriptum peruenerit Robertus filius Willelmi de Sumercotes[1] salutem in domino . Nouerit uniuersitas uestra me dedisse 7 presenti carta[2] confirmasse deo 7 sancte Marie Linc' . 7 commune canonicorum ibidem deo seruientium pro salute anime méé 7 antecessorum meorum toftum unum quatuor acrarum in Sumercotes[1] quod fuit Reginaldi filii Hedereci[3] inter masuagia[4] Hugonis filii Yuonis . 7 Petri filii Swain[5] iuxta pontem . 7 tres acras terre arabilis ex altera parte uie ex opposito prefati tofti . [6]7 .xx^{ti}. acras prati in marisco de Sumercotes[1] proximas prato Hucce[7] filii Hederici[8] uersus orientem[6] . [9]7[9] hec eis in puram 7 perpetuam elemosinam concessi . vt hec donatio stabilis 7 firma permaneat . eam sigilli mei testimonio confirmaui . Hiis testibus . Wig'[10] preposito . Willelmo filio Wigot . Roberto filio Godrici . Willelmo filio Johannis . Willelmo filio Ailsi . Alano filio Heming[11] . Hugone filio Yuonis . 7 multis aliis.

Marginalia in A : (1) *X* Rob (*much faded*). (2) Sumercotes .j. toftum 7 iiij acras (? by Q2). (3) *X*. 7 .xx. acras prati in marisco de Sumercotes proximas prato Hucche filii Hederici versus orientem (*much faded*). *These words were omitted by the original scribe in the charter but added in the right hand margin beside it. The scribe who wrote the first marginale copied the words into the lower margin.*

Texts : MS—A. R1551.

Var. R. : [1] Somercotes R. [2] R *adds* mea. [3] Hederici R. [4] *sic :* mesuagia R. [5] Swayn R. [6–6] *omitted in the charter but added* (*probably by* O) *in the margin.* [7] Bucche R. [8] Hederec' R. [9–9] R *omits.* [10] Wigot' R. [11] Hemmyng' R.

517

1678. Grant by Basing and William, sons of Acke of Somercotes, to the church of Lincoln and the Common, of an acre and a half of arable land in Somercotes. (Circa 1200.)

Vniuersis sancte matris ecclesie filiis ad quos presens scriptum peruenerit ∴ Basing 7 Willelmus filii[1] Ache[2] de Sumercotes[3] salutem . Nouerit uestra uniuersitas[4] nos dedisse 7 concessisse 7 presenti carta nostra confirmasse [5]deo[5] 7 ecclesie sancte Marie Linc' . 7 commune canonicorum ibidem deo seruientium in puram 7 perpetuam elemosinam vnam acram terre arabilem[6] 7 dimidiam in campis de Sumercotes[3] cum omnibus pertinenciis . 7 aisiamentis [7]in uilla[7] 7 extra uillam . uicinas scilicet terre Willelmi filii Asgher . 7 sellioni predicti Willelmi . Et ut ista concessio firma 7 inconcussa permaneat ∴ illam sigilli nostri impositione corroborauimus . Hiis testibus . domino Waltero Albo canonico . Linc' ecclesie . Yone[8] preposito . Johanne capellano de Wikeford[9] . Gilleberto[10] Pilato . Alano filio Emyg[11] . Roberto filio Azeri . Willelmo filio Aelsi . Roberto [5]filio[5] Basing . 7 multis aliis.

Marginalia in A ; Sumercotes .j. acram 7 dimidiam (? by Q2).

Texts : MS—A. R1531.
Var. R. : [1] filius (*sic*) R. [2] Acke R. [3] Somercotes R. [4] R *has* uniuersitas vestra. [5]–[5] R *omits*. [6] *sic* : arabilis R. [7]–[7] R *has* infra villam. [8] Ẏuone R. [9] Wykeford R. [10] Gilberto R. [11] *sic*.
Note : Walter Blund was a canon between 1198 and 1203 (see vol. iii, no. 674, above). For Ion the provost see vol. iv, p. 283, above.

518

1679. Grant by Godric son of Alfneth, to the church of Lincoln, of four acres of arable land in Somercotes. (1196–1198.)

Vniuersis sancte matris[1] [2]ecclesie[2] filiis ad quos presens scriptum peruenerit ∴ Godricus filius Alfneth salutem . Nouerit uniuersitas uestra me concessisse 7 dedisse 7 hac presenti carta mea confirmasse deo 7 beate Marie Linc' . 7 canonicis ibidem deo seruientibus quatuor acras terre arabilis in territorio de Sumercotes[3] que iacent inter terram Roberti capellani . 7 terram Walteri filii Roberti . scilicet tres acras in Aldecroft . 7 unam acram iuxta terram Willelmi filii Godrici Haket uersus orientem . pro salute anime méé 7 patris mei 7 matris méé 7 omnium antecessorum meorum . Et ego 7 heredes mei warantizabimus terram prenominatam prenominato capitulo contra omnes homines . Et ut hec mea donatio imperpetuum rata permaneat ∴ sigilli mei munimine corroboraui . Hiis testibus * . magistro Willelmo precentore Linc' ecclesie . magistro Willelmo cancellario . magistro Ricardo subdecano . Ricardo de Kyma . magistro Waltero Blundo . Eudone capellano . Gileberto[4] Pilate[5] . Roberto capellano de Sumercotes[3] . magistro Roberto de Gaitune[6] . Willelmo clerico de Sumercotes[3] . Ernsio[7] filio Guue.[8]

Marginalia in A : Sumercotes iiij acras terre (? by Q2).
Texts : MS—A. R1547.
Var. R. : [1] Marie (*sic*) R. [2]–[2] R *omits*. [3] Somercotes R. [4] Gilberto R. [5] Pẏlat' R. [6] Gaytun R. [7] *sic* : Ernisio R. [8] *sic* : Gune R.
Note : For the date see the note to no. 1673 above. This grantor is probably son to Alneth son of Hemming in no. 1683 below, and nephew to Godric son of Hemming and his wife Hawis.

**Folio* 99.

Hdl. . 9 . 9 .

519

1680. Confirmation by Richard of the Park, knight, to the church of Lincoln and the Common, of two acres of land in Somercotes, which they had of the gift of Godric son of Alfneth. (1198–1205.)

Omnibus sancte matris ecclesie filiis ad quos presens scriptum peruenerit ∴ Ricardus de Parco miles salutem . Nouerit uniuersitas uestra me concessisse 7 hac presenti carta mea confirmasse deo ⁊ beate Marie ⁊ commune canonicorum Linc' ecclesie pro salute animarum parentum ⁊ omnium antecessorum meorum donationem quam dedit ecclesie Linc' Godricus uidelicet duas acras terre sicuti continetur in carta quam habet ecclesia Linc' de eodem Godrico filio Alfueneth . Et ego Ricardus ⁊ heredes mei warantizabimus donationem predicti Godrici memorate ecclesie contra omnes homines . Hiis testibus .W. cancellario .W. subdecano . magistro Roberto de Holm . Henrico de Dereby[1] canonicis .W. de Sancto Petro . Johanne de Wikeford[2] capellanis . Gileberto[3] clerico . Wigote[4] filio Osberti . Roberto filio Gunnild . Willelmo filio Ailsi . ⁊ multis aliis.

Marginalia in A: Sumercotes (? by Q2).
Texts: MS—A. R1557.
Var. R.: [1] Derbý R. [2] Wykeford R. [3] Gilberto R. [4] Wygoto R.
Note: This charter is placed with the Skidbrook charters in R. The original is now lost, but may have been placed with the Skidbrook charters in the thirteenth century like no. 1672, above.

520

1681. Grant by Gilbert son of Magnus of Somercotes, to the church of Lincoln and the Common, of four acres of land in Somercotes. (Henry II.)

Notum sit [1]tam[1] presentibus quam futuris quod ego Gilebertus[2] filius Magni de Sumercotes[3] dedi ⁊ concessi quatuor acras terre in campo de Sumercotes[3] iuxta uiam que dicitur Hunderfure[4] a parte boreali deo ⁊ sancte Marie Linc' in puram ⁊ perpetuam elemosinam pro animabus antecessorum meorum liberas ⁊ quietas ab omni seculari seruitio . ⁊ hanc donationem testimonio sigilli mei confirmaui . Hiis testibus . Sampsone de Newerch[5] . Ricardo de Let[6] . ⁊ Roberto de Scamelesbi[7] . ⁊ multis aliis.

Marginalia in A: Sumercotes iiij acras terre (? by Q2).
Texts: MS—A. R1546.
Var. R.: [1–1] R *omits*. [2] Gilbertus R. [3] Somercotes R. [4] Hunderfore R. [5] Newerk' R. [6] Delet R. [7] Scamlesbý R.
Note: The form of this charter with no warranty clause is early. If Samson of Newark may be identified with the canon of that name, as seems probable, he is found as a witness in 1165 (above, no. 915, in vol. iv) and 1189–95 (vol. ii, no. 338 (vi), vol. iii, no. 689). On the other hand, Gilbert son of Magnus of Somercotes made a grant late in the twelfth century (*Danelaw Charters*, pp. 399–400) and a Robert son of Odo of Scamblesby is found in 1202 (L.R.S. xxii, no. 1026).

521

1682. Grant by Godric son of Hemming of Somercotes, with the assent of Hawis his wife and his heirs, to the chapter of Lincoln, of eight and a half acres of land in Somercotes. (Circa 1195.)

Sciant tam presentes quam futuri quod ego Godricus filius Hemmig[1] de Sumercot'[2] assensu vxoris méé Hawis 7 heredum meorum dedi 7 concessi 7 hac presenti carta mea confirmaui deo 7 beate Marie 7 capitulo Linc' in puram 7 liberam 7 perpetuam elemosinam 7 solutam ab omni seruitio seculari pro animabus patris mei 7 matris méé 7 omnium parentum meorum octo acras terre 7 dimidiam in territorio de Sumercot[2] cum omnibus pertinenciis suis . scilicet quatuor in Esecroft[3] duas 7 dimidiam in Wilbur croft . duas in Meeles[4] proximas terre Godricii[5] Hacat in parte occidentali . Predictam uero terram ego 7 heredes mei warantizabimus[6] imperpetuum contra omnes homines . Et ut ista donatio firma permaneat ∴ hanc cartam sigilli mei appensione corroboraui . Hiis testibus . Roberto filio Willelmi de Lekeburne . Willelmo de Fetherstan' . Willelmo filio Johannis de Sumercot[2] . Roberto filio eius . Roberto de Mareis[7] Waltero filio eius . Waltero filio Hugonis de Scitebroc[8] . Willelmo filio Dauidis . 7 Alano fratre suo.

Marginalia in A : Sumercotes viij acras 7 dimidiam (? by Q2).
Texts : MS—A. R1522.
Var. R. : [1] Hemming R. [2] Somercotes R. [3] Estcroft R. [4] Meles R. [5] Godrici R. *in* R warantizabimus *follows* homines. [7] Mareys R. [8] Skitbrok' R.
Note : Professor Stenton, *Free Peasantry*, points out that it is probable that this charter and the succeeding one refer to the same piece of land, in which case this is probably slightly earlier, as Hawis said she had been claiming it as dower. She was certainly a widow in 1202 (L.R.S. xxii, no. 108).

522

1683. Quitclaim by Hawis wife of Godric of Somercotes, to the chapter of Lincoln, of all her claim in virtue of dower, in the land which Alneth son of Hemming holds of the chapter. (1196–1200.)

Omnibus sancte matris ecclesie filiis ad quos presens scriptum peruenerit ∴ Hawis[1] uxor Godrici de Sumercotes[2] salutem . Nouerit uniuersitas uestra me totum ius quod clamaui in terra quam Alneth filius Hemmig tenet de capitulo Linc' quietum clamasse capitulo Linc' . scilicet de illo tenemento quod clamaui [3]in villa[3] de Sumercotes[2] tanquam dotem * meam pro anima mea 7 antecessorum meorum . [3]7[3] ne in posterum predicta quietantia mea in irritum possit correuocari ∴ illam iure iurando 7 sigilli mei appositione corroboraui . Hiis testibus . Willelmo precentore Linc' ecclesie . magistro Alexandro [3]archidiacono[3] . Ricardo de Kyma[4] . magistro Waltero[5] Blundo . magistro Willelmo de Frisebi[6] . canonicis . Sampsone capellano de Sumercotes . Roberto capellano de Sumercotes[2] . Willelmo clerico de Sumercotes[2] .

Marginalia in A: Sumercotes (? by Q2).
Texts: MS—A. R1523.
Var. R.: [1] Hawÿs R. [2] Somercotes R. [3]–[3] R *omits*. [4] Kyme R. [5] Willelmo R. [6] Freseby R.
Note: William of Blois was precentor 1196–1203. Alexander archdeacon of the West Riding of Lindsey (Stow) occurs late twelfth century (L.R.S. xviii, p. 84) as well as with some of the present witnesses 1196–1203 (see no. 1118 in vol. iv, above). William was archdeacon of the West Riding in 1201 (C.R.R. i, p. 442).

Folio 99d.

523

1684. Notification by William the clerk of Somercotes that he has given to the church of Lincoln a toft containing two acres and one perch of land and an acre of meadow in Somercotes. (Circa 1200.)

Omnibus sancte matris ecclesie filiis ad quos presens scriptum peruenerit Willelmus clericus de Sumercote[1] salutem . In uestram cupio uenire noticiam quod ego dedi 7 concessi in puram 7 perpetuam elemosinam deo 7 sancte Marie Linc' pro animabus parentum 7 antecessorum meorum toftum unum in Sumercote[1] a parte orientali tofti Hederici in quo continentur due acre terre 7 pertica una . 7 unam acram prati in Scuppeholm . iuxta Aslacheow[2] . Et ne ista donatio possit duci in irritum eam appensione sigilli mei roboraui . Hiis testibus . Sampsone sacerdote . Godrico filio Hedrici . Arnaldo filio Hacke . Ricardo Sampsonis[3] . 7 multis aliis.

Marginalia in A: Sumercotes .j. toftum (? by Q2).
Texts: MS—A. R1539.
Var. R.: [1] Somercotes R. [2] Haslachehou R. [3] *sic*: filio *presumably omitted*.
Note: William the clerk of Somercotes witnesses two charters nos. 1671, 1672, above, circa 1200.

524

1685. Grant by John of Carlton, to the church of Lincoln, of a messuage and two acres of meadow in [? South] Somercotes and three acres of arable land in North Somercotes. He also records the grant made with his consent by his brother Alan, of eight perches of arable land in Somercotes. (Early Henry II.)

Johannes de Karletona omnibus sancte matris ecclesie filiis presentibus 7 futuris Francis 7 Anglis salutem . Nouerit uniuersitas uestra me dedisse 7 concessisse 7 presenti carta mea confirmasse in puram 7 perpetuam elemosinam deo 7 beate Marie 7 canonicis Linc' ecclesie mansuram que fuit Roberti de Hardena . 7 duas acras prati . 7 in parrochia beate Marie tres acras terre arabilis . 7 Alanus frater predicti Johannis concessu ipsius Johannis donat prenominatis canonicis similiter in puram . 7 imperpetuam elemosinam octo perticatas terre arabilis partim in Aldecroft . 7 partim iuxta . 7 ego Johannes 7 Alanus frater meus 7 heredes nostri prenominatas terras adquietabimus de omni seculari seruitio erga omnes homines . Hanc autem donationem fecimus beate Marie 7 predictis canonicis habendam 7 possidendam cum omni libertate in introitibus 7 exitibus 7 pasturis fide nostra interposita . Valete . Testibus .H. decano . 7 Ailf*redo* de Point' . 7 H. de Alei . 7 Eustachio de Catebi . 7 Hosberto sacerdote de Salfletabi . 7 multis aliis.

Marginalia in A : (1) +. (2) Sumercotes (? by Q2).
Text : MS—A.
Note : Eustace of Cadeby witnesses circa 1155 and early Henry II (L.R.S. xviii, pp. 58, 105) and 1157–1163 (*Free Peasantry*, p. 109). He was the son of Swan of Cadeby (*ibid.*). H. the dean may be either Hamelin of Yarborough or his brother Hamelin of Covenham. Osbert the priest of Saltfleetby witnesses a Kirkstead charter in 1180 (*B. M. Cottonian MS., Vespasian E xvii*, f. 160).

525

1686. Confirmation of the preceding grant by William son of John of Carlton. **(Early Henry II.)**

Vniuersis sancte matris ecclesie filiis Willelmus filius Johannis de Karletun salutem . Nouerit uniuersitas uestra me concessisse 7 hac presenti carta mea confirmasse in puram 7 perpetuam elemosinam deo 7 beate Marie 7 canonicis Linc' ecclesie omnem terram quam Johannes pater meus prenominate ecclesie donauit . 7 carta sua confirmauit . scilicet . mansuram que fuit Roberti de Harden 7 duas acras prati . 7 in parrochia beate Marie tres acras terre arabilis . Noueritis etiam me confirmasse donationem Alani auunculi quam dedit prescripte ecclesie in puram 7 perpetuam elemosinam consensu Johannis patris mei scilicet . octo perticatas terre arabilis partim in Aldecroft . 7 partim iuxta . Has uero prenominatas terras Johannes pater meus 7 Alanus auunculus meus adquietauerunt ab omni seruicio seculari . 7 ego ex parte mea adquietabo erga omnes homines . hanc autem donationem fecimus deo 7 beate Marie 7 predictis canonicis habendam 7 possidendam cum omni libertate * in introitibus 7 exitibus 7 pasturis fide nostra interposita . Valete . Huius confirmationis testes sunt . Willelmus decanus de Bradele . Hamelinus decanus . Jordanus sacerdos de Luda . Willelmus de Hall' . Johannes de Cuninhesholm . Walterus de Richebroc . Petrus clericus magistri Petri . Willelmus filius Galfridi.

Marginalia in A : Sumercotes (? by Q2).
Text : MS—A.
Note : William of Carlton occurs frequently from the reign of Henry II until the early thirteenth century (*Danelaw Charters*, pp. 80, 113, 125, 146 etc., and L.R.S. xxviii, no. 139, 145, 148). William dean of Bradley witnesses 1175–1181 and late Henry II (*Danelaw Charters*, pp. 5, 201). Hamelin the dean witnesses frequently. Jordan the priest of Louth witnesses no. 1688, below, and may be identical with Jordan the clerk of Louth in 1155 (*Danelaw Charters*, p. 214).

**Folio* 100.

526

1687. Confirmation of the two preceding grants by Robert son of Julian of Horbling. (Early Henry II.)

Vniuersis sancte matris ecclesie filiis Robertus filius Juliani de Horbelinche salutem . Nouerit uniuersitas uestra me confirmasse in puram 7 perpetuam elemosinam deo 7 sancte Marie 7 canonicis Linc' ecclesie donationem terre quam Johannes de Karletun . 7 Alanus frater eius 7 Willelmus filius Johannis dederunt predicte ecclesie sicut carta Johannis 7 Willelmi filii eius confirmatum est . Hanc donationem confirmaui predicte ecclesie liberam ab omni seruitio seculari : sicut patronus terre prenominate . huius confirmationis testes sunt . Willelmus decanus de Braidele . Hamelinus decanus . Jordanus sacerdos . de Luda . Willelmus de Hall' . Johannes de Cuninchesholm' . Walterus de Richebroc . Petrus clericus magistri Petri . Willelmus filius Galfridi.

Marginalia in A: Sumercot' (? by Q2).
Text: MS—A.
Note: Roger Mustel pledged his faith to warrant certain lands to Sixle in the hand of Robert son of Julian of Horbling (L.R.S. xviii, p. 17). The charter of Roger is almost certainly before 1184 about which time Roger died. For the Mustel family see *Early Yorkshire Charters*, vol vi, *The Paynel Fee*, edited by C. T. Clay, pp. 252–4.

527

1688. Confirmation by Basilia, to the church of Lincoln, of all the land of her dower in Somercotes which they had of the gift of John her husband and William her son. (Early Henry II.)

Notum sit omnibus hominibus tam presentis etatis quam futuri posteritatis quod ego Basilia concessi 7 hac presenti carta [1]mea[1] confirmaui canonicis ecclesie sancte[2] Marie Linc' totam terram de dote mea in Sumerecotes[3] in puram 7 perpetuam elemosinam quam dominus meus Johannes eis dedit 7 carta sua confirmauit . 7 Willelmus filius meus hoc ipsum eisdem concessit . 7 carta sua confirmauit . Teste Capitulo Lude : cum aliis personis subscriptis . Gilleberto[4] scilicet priore de Burewell'[5] . Jordano[6] presbitero de Lude . Adam alumpnus[7] eius . Rumfaro presbitero . magistro Roberto de Gait'[8] . Benedicto . Muriilda[9] de Luda . Paueia[10] . Tonn' . Aliz . Muriilda[9] . Jeua[11] . Aliz . Duchti . Annais[12] . Iuetta.

Marginalia in A: Sumercotes (? by Q2).
Texts: MS—A. R.1545.
Var. R.: [1] R *omits*. [2] beate R. [3] Somercotes R. [4] Gilberto R. [5] Burwelle R. [6] Jurdano R. [7] *sic*. [8] Gaẏt R. [9] Mirild' R. [10] Paueẏe R. [11] Lena R. [12] Annays R.
Note: Gilbert prior of Burwell occurs before 1150 (V.C.H. Lincs., ii, p. 239). Bernard prior occurs late Henry II (*Danelaw Charters*, p. 304). Jordan clerk of

Louth occurs circa 1155 (*ibid.*, p. 314). Master Robert of Gayton le Wold witnesses late in the twelfth century (L.R.S. xviii, p. 51).

The rest of the folio is blank.

Folio 100d, blank.

ADD. CHART.

1689. Grant by Godric son of Osbert of Somercotes, to the church of Lincoln and the Common, of a croft containing an acre with the buildings thereon and three acres of land in Somercotes. (Circa 1240.)

Omnibus Christi fidelibus Godricus filius Osberti de Somercotes salutem . Noueritis me dedisse concessisse ⁊ hac presenti carta mea confirmasse deo ⁊ beate Marie ⁊ commune canonicorum Linc' vnum croftum in villa de Somercotes quod continet vnam acram cum suis edificiis ⁊ pertinenciis ⁊ iacet inter terram Andree ⁊ terram Fulconis ⁊ abuttat super regiam stratam ⁊ tres acras terre in territorio eiusdem ville quarum vna iacet inter terram Walteri filii Ricardi ⁊ terram Willelmi filii Andree) vna acra iacet in occidentali latere crofti Roberti filii Ediue) vna acra abuttat super Fendẏk' versus occidentem ⁊ super terram Radulfi filii Willelmi versus orientem . Tenend' ⁊ habend' prefatis canonicis cum pertinenciis asiamentis libertatibus suis infra villam ⁊ extra in puram ⁊ perpetuam elemosinam) liberam ⁊ quietam ab omni seruicio ⁊ exactione seculari . Et ego ⁊ heredes mei adquietabimus defendemus ⁊ warantizabimus prefatum tenementum cum pertinenciis prefatis canonicis contra omnes homines inperpetuum . Et in huius rei robur ⁊ testimonium presens scriptum mediante iuramento sigillo meo confirmaui Hiis testibus Elẏa succentore) Henrico sacrista Lincoln' Ricardo de Stretton' clerico Rogero vicario de Skitbrok' . Waltero de Oxcumbe Roberto le Noreẏs Simone Knottẏng' et aliis.

Text: MS—R1518.

Note: For Elias the succentor and Henry the sacrist see vol. iv, pp. 280–1, above. Roger was instituted as vicar of Skidbrook 1223–4 (L.R.S. ix, p. 121). No other institution is recorded until 1265–6, when the name of the new vicar's predecessor is not given (L.R.S. xx, p. 21).

ADD. CHART.

1690. Confirmation by William son of Osbert of Somercotes of the preceding charter. (Circa 1240.)

Omnibus Christi fidelibus Willelmus filius Osberti de Somercotes salutem . Noueritis me ratam ⁊ gratam habere donacionem ⁊ confirmacionem quam Godricus frater meus fecit deo ⁊ beate Marie ⁊ commune canonicorum Linc' ecclesie de vno crofto cum pertinenciis in villa de Somercotes) et iacet inter terram Fulconis molendinarii) 7 regiam stratam 7 de tribus acris terre in territorio eiusdem ville quarum vna iacet inter terram Walteri filii Ricardi 7 terram Willelmi filii Andree) vna acra iacet in occidentali latere crofti Roberti filii Ediue) vna acra abuttat super Fendik' versus occidentem) 7 super terram Radulfi filii Willelmi versus orientem . Et ego 7 heredes mei defendemus 7 warantizabimus prefatis canonicis totum prefatum tenementum cum pertinenciis 7 libertatibus suis infra villam 7 extra vt puram liberam 7 perpetuam elemosinam contra omnes homines inperpetuum . Et ne ego vel heredes mei contra ratihabitacionem 7 confirmacionem meam venire possimus presens scriptum iuramento mediante sigillo meo confirmaui . Hiis testibus Elẏa succentore) Henrico sacrista Linc' Ricardo de Strettona clerico Rogero vicario de Skitbrok' Waltero de Oxcumbe Ricardo le Noreẏs Simone Knottẏng' 7 aliis.

Text : MS—R1519.

ADD. CHART.

1691. Grant by Ralf son of Osbert of Somercotes, to the church of Lincoln and the Common, of a croft containing two acres, and of three selions of land in Somercotes. (Circa 1240.)

Omnibus Christi fidelibus Radulphus filius Osberti de Somercotes salutem . Noueritis me dedisse) concessisse 7 hac presenti carta mea confirmasse deo 7 beate Marie 7 commune canonicorum Linc' ecclesie vnum croftum in Somercotes) quod continet duas acras 7 iacet inter terram Willelmi filii Andree 7 terram Radulphi de Boueṙya 7 abuttat super aquam versus aquilonem 7 super regiam stratam versus austrum 7 vnum selionem super Hutgrene inter terram Willelmi filii Aylsi 7 terram Radulphi de Boueria) vnum selionem in Estacres inter terram prefati Radulphi) 7 terram Rogeri filii Boniue 7 vnum selionem in Westacres inter terram Ricardi filii Stepẏ 7 terram Petri filii Basing' Tenend' 7 habend' prefatis canonicis cum omnibus pertinenciis 7 libertatibus suis infra villam 7 extra in puram 7 perpetuam elemosinam liberam 7 quietam ab omni seruicio 7 exactione seculari Et ego 7 heredes mei adquietabimus defendemus) 7 warantizabimus prefatis canonicis prefatum tenementum cum pertinenciis 7 libertatibus suis contra omnes homines inperpetuum . Et in huius rei robur 7 testimonium presens scriptum) iuramento interueniente sigillo meo confirmaui . Hiis testibus Elẏa succentore Henrico sacrista Linc' Willelmo de Maiori Altari capellano) Waltero de Oxcumb' Simone Knottẏng' 7 aliis.

Text : MS—R1520.

ADD. CHART.

1692. Grant by William *nepos* of Ostercus (*sic* : *recte* **Osbert**) son of Godiva, to the chapter of Lincoln, of six and a half perches of land in Saltfleetby. (Circa 1200.)

Omnibus sancte matris ecclesie filiis ad quos presens scriptum peruenerit Willelmus nepos Osterci[1] filii Godiue salutem . Nouerit vniuersitas vestra me concessisse 7 hac mea presenti carta confirmasse deo 7 capitulo sancte Marie Linc' ecclesie in puram 7 perpetuam elemosinam sex perticatas terre 7 dimidiam 7 .iiij^or^. pedes 7 dimidium in latitudine in tofto 7 crofto que iacent inter Mardic 7 terram Hugonis filii Decche in parte orientali iuxta viam) liberas 7 quietas ab omni seruicio seculari . Et vt hec concessio rata 7 inconcussa inposterum perseueret :' eam sigilli mei munimine duxi corroborandam) Hiis testibus) Willelmo persona de Salfletebẏ Johanne fratre suo Odone Galle Roberto filio Mole) Waltero filio Willelmi) Roberto fratre eius Odone Dumpic[2] Roberto filio Alware.

Text : MS—R1521.
Var. R. : [1] *sic :* recte Osbertus ; cf. no. 1647 above. [2] *sic.*
Note : This charter is a transcript of 1647 above, but was not identified with it in time to print the two together. It relates to Saltfleetby, but in R is placed in Somercotes.

ADD. CHART.

1693. Grant by Rumfar son of Auke of Somercotes, to the church of Lincoln and the Common, of four acres of land in Somercotes. (Circa 1230–1240.)

Omnibus Christi fidelibus Rumpharus filius Auke de Somercotes salutem . Noueritis me dedisse concessisse 7 hac presenti carta mea confirmasse deo 7 beate Marie 7 commune canonicorum Linc' ecclesie quatuor acras terre in villa de Somercotes) quarum due iacent inter terram Willelmi filii Roberti filii Auke versus aquilonem) 7 terram Willelmi filii Roberti filii Arngrim versus austrum 7 abuttant versus orientem super terram Radulfi de Scampton' 7 super terram Willelmi filii Roberti versus occidentem) Relique due acre iacent inter terram Willelmi le Muter que est versus occidentem 7 regiam stratam que est versus orientem 7 abuttant super eandem stratam versus aquilonem 7 terram Willelmi filii Roberti versus austrum Tenend' 7 habend' prefatis canonicis cum omnibus pertinenciis suis libertatibus 7 aisiamentis infra villam 7 extra in puram 7 perpetuam elemosinam) liberam 7 quietam ab omni seruicio 7 accione[1] seculari . Et ego 7 heredes mei defendemus) adquietabimus 7 warantizabimus prefatam terram cum pertinenciis) libertatibus prefatis canonicis contra omnes homines inperpetuum . Et in huius rei ⁊[1] testimonium presens scriptum iuramento interueniente sigillo meo confirmaui . Hiis testibus Elẏa succentore) Henrico sacrista Linc' Ricardo de Stretton' Simone Knottẏng' Roberto Lenorum) Willelmo ad Montem Willelmo filio Roberti filii Auke Willelmo filio Osberti ⁊ aliis.

Text : MS—R1535.
Var. R. : [1] *sic*.
Note : For Elias the succentor and Henry the sacrist see vol. iv, pp. 280–1.

ADD. CHART.

1694. Confirmation by William son of Auke of the preceding grant made by Rumfar his brother. (Circa 1230–1240.)

Omnibus Christi fidelibus Willelmus filius Auke salutem . Noueritis me ratam ⁊ gratam habere donacionem ⁊ concessionem quam fecit Rumpharus frater meus decano ⁊ capitulo Lincoln' ecclesie de quatuor acris terre in villa de Somercotes) quarum due iacent inter terram Willelmi filii Roberti filii Auke versus aquilonem ⁊ terram Willelmi filii Roberti filii Argrim versus austrum) et abuttant versus orientem super terram Rumphari de Scampton' ⁊ super terram Willelmi filii Roberti versus occidentem) Relique due acre iacent inter terram Willelmi le Mouter que est versus occidentem ⁊ regiam stratam que est versus orientem ⁊ abuttant super eandem stratam versus aquilonem ⁊ terram Willelmi filii Roberti versus austrum Tenend' ⁊ habend' prefatis canonicis cum omnibus pertinenciis suis) libertatibus ⁊ aisiamentis infra villam ⁊ extra in puram ⁊ perpetuam elemosinam liberam ⁊ quietam ab omni seruicio ⁊ exactione seculari . Et ego ⁊ heredes mei defendemus) adquietabimus ⁊ warantizabimus prefatam donacionem ⁊ concessionem cum pertinenciis libertatibus prefatis canonicis contra omnes homines imperpetuum . Et in huius rei robur ⁊ testimonium presens scriptum iuramento interueniente sigillo meo confirmaui . Hiis testibus Elẏa succentore Henrico sacrista Linc' Ricardo de Stretton' clerico Simone Knottẏng') Roberto le Norne Willelmo ad Montem) Willelmo filio Roberti filii Auke) Willelmo filio Osberti ⁊ aliis.

Text : MS—R1536.

ADD. CHART.

1695. Acknowledgement by William son of Auke that he is bound to pay the dean and chapter of Lincoln a yearly render of eighteenpence for four acres of land in Somercotes. He may not sell, give or pledge the land without the consent of the dean and chapter, who, however, will not warrant it to him or his heirs. (Circa 1230–1240.)

Omnibus Christi fidelibus Willelmus filius Auke salutem . Noueritis me teneri decano 7 capitulo Lincoln' ecclesie in annuo redditu decem 7 octo denariorum) reddendo ad duos anni terminos scilicet ad festum sancti Michaelis in nouem denariis) 7 ad Pascha in nouem denariis pro quatuor acris terre cum pertinenciis quas teneo de eodem capitulo in villa de Somercotes) Quam quidem terram non licebit michi vel heredibus siue assignatis meis vendere) dare) vel inuadiare vel aliquo modo alienare sine licencia decani 7 capituli Lincoln' ecclesie) Preterea sciendum quod prefatus decanus 7 capitulum non tenebuntur defendere adquietare vel warantizare predictam terram michi vel heredibus vel assignatis meis contra aliquos homines . Et in huius rei robur 7 testimonium presens scriptum iuramento interueniente sigillo meo confirmaui . Hiis testibus Elӯa succentore) Henrico sacrista Lincolnie Ricardo de Stretton' clerico) Simone Knottӯng') Roberto le Norne) Willelmo ad Montem) Willelmo filio Roberti filii Auke Willelmo filio Osberti 7 aliis.

Text : MS—R1537.

ADD. CHART.

1696. Grant by William son of William of Somercotes, to the church of Lincoln and the Common, of a toft and four acres of land in Somercotes. (Circa 1230–1240.)

Omnibus Christi fidelibus Willelmus filius Willelmi de Somercotes salutem . Noueritis me dedisse concessisse 7 hac presenti carta mea confirmasse deo 7 beate Marie 7 commune canonicorum Linc' ecclesie . vnum toftum in villa de Somercotes quod iacet inter toftum quod fuit Radulfi filii Gunnilde 7 hostium[1] in quo manet Matilda Buck' 7 quatuor acras terre in territorio eiusdem ville) quarum tres seliones iacent in Nordakres 7 duo in Sudakres Tenend' 7 habend' dictis canonicis cum omnibus pertinenciis suis) libertatibus 7 aisiamentis infra villam 7 extra in puram 7 perpetuam elemosinam liberam 7 quietam ab omni seruicio 7 exaccione seculari . Et ego 7 heredes mei adquietabimus defendemus 7 warantizabimus dictis canonicis prefatum tenementum cum pertinenciis 7 libertatibus suis contra omnes homines inperpetuum . Et in huius rei robur 7 testimonium presens scriptum iuramento mediante sigillo meo confirmaui . Hiis testibus Elӯa succentore Willelmo 7 Rogero capellanis Ricardo de Stretton' clerico Waltero de Oxcumb' Johanne de Kokerington' Andrea de Somercotes Johanne filio Alani Petro de Scuppeholm' Ricardo filio Radulfi Radulfo filio Willelmi Andrea Frend ⁊ aliis.

Text: MS—R1540.
Var. R.: [1] *sic: possibly a word has been omitted.*

ADD. CHART.

1697. Grant by William son of Robert of Somercotes, to William son of Henry of Somercotes, of all the land which he holds of the dean and chapter of Lincoln. William son of Henry shall hold of the dean and chapter in chief and pay a yearly render of eighteenpence. (Circa 1220–1230.)

Sciant presentes ⁊ futuri quod ego Willelmus filius Roberti de Somercot' dedi) concessi ⁊ presenti carta mea confirmaui Willelmo filio Henrici de Somercot' ⁊ heredibus suis totam terram quam habui in Aldecroft' de feuodo[1] capituli Linc' ecclesie que iacet inter terram Asgeri ⁊ terram Osberti de Hospitali ⁊ abuttat super Wÿburgcroft' versus austrum ⁊ versus aquilonem super communem pasturam ⁊ vnam acram terre arrabilis de eodem feuodo[1]) que iacet inter terram Wydonis ⁊ Osberti de Hospitali ⁊ abuttat super Sÿht ex vna parte ⁊ super communem pasturam ex alia parte) Habendam ⁊ tenendam in capite de dominis meis decano ⁊ capitulo Linc' ecclesie in puram ⁊ perpetuam elemosinam sibi ⁊ heredibus suis in feuodo[1] ⁊ hereditate) libere ⁊ quiete ⁊ honorifice cum omnibus pertinenciis libertatibus ⁊ liberis consuetudinibus) Reddendo inde annuatim dictis decano ⁊ capitulo decem ⁊ octo denarios) scilicet ad Pascha .ix. denarios) ⁊ ad festum Sancti Michaelis .ix. denarios . pro omni seruicio ⁊ exactione seculari . Et ego ⁊ heredes mei warantizabimus dictam terram cum omnibus pertinenciis libertatibus ⁊ aliis aisiamentis dicto Willelmo ⁊ heredibus suis contra omnes homines inperpetuum . Et in huius rei robur ⁊ testimonium huic scripto sigillum meum apposui . Hiis testibus Thoma sacrista Petro de Keuermund' ⁊ Rogero de Bohun canonicis Linc') Roberto capellano de Somercotes Roberto ⁊ Ricardo filiis Radulphi) Willelmo filio Asgeri Roberto filio Arngrim) Willelmo ⁊ Petro filiis Ernisii) Willelmo ⁊ Ernisio filiis Godrici Willelmo filio Hugonis) Willelmo filio Godrici ⁊ aliis.

Text: MS—R1550.
Var. R.: [1] *sic.*
Note: For the dates of Thomas the sacrist see vol. iv, p. 281, above.

Folio 101.

Hdl. Ludesch' ·|· ϕ ·|·

SKIDBROOK AND SOMERCOTES

528

1698. Grant by William son of Geva of Somercotes, to the church of Lincoln and the Common, of five acres of arable land in Skidbrook and an acre of meadow in Somercotes. (Circa 1200.)

Sciant presentes 7 futuri quod ego Willelmus filius Geue de Sumercotes[1] concessi 7 dedi 7 hac presenti carta mea confirmaui deo 7 beate Marie 7 commune canonicorum Linc' ecclesie quinque acras terre arabilis in territorio de Scitebroc[2] . 7 unam acram prati in prato de Sumercotes[1] . scilicet dimidiam acram inter pratum Willelmi Mutere[3] 7 Rochelundedeile . 7 dimidiam acram inter pratum sacerdotis de Lekeburne quod uocatur Lekeburnedeile[4] 7 pratum Hugonis filii Asgeri in puram 7 perpetuam elemosinam pro salute anime méé 7 omnium antecessorum meorum . Huius autem terre prenominate héé sunt partes . scilicet due acre inter terram Roberti filii Gunnilde . 7 terram que fuit Gileberti[5] filii Ailrici . 7 tres acre inter Aiecroft[6] 7 terram Roberti filii Gunnilde . Hanc autem terram prenominatam 7 pratum prenominatum warantizabo ego Willelmus 7 heredes mei prenominato capitulo contra omnes homines . Et ut hec mea donatio imperpetuum rata 7 inconcussa permaneat ; sigilli mei appositione corroboraui . Hiis testibus . Eudone de Sancto Botulfo . capellano . Waltero Blundo capellano . Johanne de Wikeford[7] capellano Alexandro del[8] Bycht[9] . Willelmo persona de Scitebroc[2] . Alano fratre eius . Roberto filio Gunnilde de Scitebroc[2] . Rogero filio Yadiue[10] . Andrea de Sumercotes[1] . Alano filio Hemming.

Marginalia in A: (1) Sumercotes ·j· acr' prati 7 v acr' terre. (2) Skytebrok' (by Q2).

Texts: MS—A. R1590.

Var. R.: [1] Somercotes R. [2] Skitbrok' R. [3] Muter R. [4] Lekeburnedeyle R. [5] Gilberti R. [6] Aicroft R. [7] Wycford R. [8] de R. [9] Bicht R. [10] Eadiue R.

Note: This charter was confirmed before 25th September, 1205 (see next deed.) The witnesses occur frequently about 1200.

529

1699. Confirmation by Richard of the Park, knight, of the preceding grant with the addition of three acres of his own land in Skidbrook. (1198–1205.)

Omnibus sancte matris ecclesie filiis ad quos presens scriptum peruenerit ; Ricardus de Parco miles salutem .

Nouerit uniuersitas uestra me concessisse ⁊ hac presenti mea carta[1] confirmasse deo ⁊ beate Marie ⁊ commune canonicorum Linc' ecclesie donationem quam dedit eis Willelmus filius Geue de Sumercotes[2] cum carta sua donationem illam continente ⁊ confirmante . ⁊ me ipsum de proprio tenemento meo dedisse [3]⁊ concessisse[3] ⁊ hac eadem etiam carta confirmasse eidem loco tres acras terre in Scitebroc[4] que iacent inter terras Roberti filii Gunnild ⁊ terras que fuerunt Gileberti[5] filii Eilric . uidelicet due acre in Est croft[6] ⁊ una dimidia acra in Mechedaile[7] . ⁊ una dimidia acra in tofto Hugonis filii Edric in puram ⁊ perpetuam elemosinam liberam ⁊ solutam ab omni seculari seruitio ⁊ exactione pro salute parentum ⁊ omnium antecessorum meorum . Et ego predictus Ricardus ⁊ heredes mei warantizabimus memorate commune iam dictorum canonicorum tam donationem meam quam donationis Willelmi filii Geue concessionem ⁊ confirmationem contra omnes homines . Hiis testibus .W. cancellario .W. subdecano . magistro Roberto de Holm[8] . ⁊ Henrico de Derebi[9] canonicis .W. de Sancto Petro . Waltero Blundo . Johanne de Wikeford' . capellanis . Willelmo filio Johannis de Sumercotes[2] . Radulfo filio Ernis[10] de Scitebroc[4] . ⁊ multis aliis.

Marginalia in A: (1) Sumercotes. (2) Confirmatio (by Q2).
Texts: MS—A. R1555.
Note: For the date see note to 1680 above.
Var. R.: [1] carta mea R. [2] Somercotes R. [3]–[3] R *omits*. [4] Skitbrok' R. [5] Gilberti R. [6] Escroft R. [7] Metheldaile R. [8] Holm' R. [9] Dereby R. [10] Ernisii R.

SKIDBROOK

530-696

1700. Grant by Boniva daughter of Basing de Fleichemare [*recte* Bleichemare], to the chapter of Lincoln, of an acre and a half of land in Wulfhou and Lefsicroft [in Skidbrook]. (Late twelfth century.)

Universis sancte matris ecclesie filiis ad quos presens scriptum peruenerit Boniua filia Blasing[1] de Fleichemare[2] salutem . Nouerit uniuersitas uestra me dedisse ⁊ concessisse ⁊ hac presenti carta mea confirmasse deo ⁊ beate Marie ⁊ capitulo Linc' ecclesie vnam acram terre ⁊ dimidiam . illam . scilicet . acram que . jacet in Wlfhou[3] . ⁊ dimidiam scilicet acram ∴ que jacet in Lefsicrof[4] versus West in puram ⁊ perpetuam elemosinam . liberas ⁊ quietas ab omni seculari[5] exactione . ⁊ ego Boniua ⁊ heredes mei warantizabimus predictum tenementum predicto capitulo Linc'[6] contra omnes homines . Hiis testibus . Willelmo[7] clerico de Sancto Botolfo .

Antonio filio Luck[8] de Leche[9] . Bricio filio Henrici . Radulfo filio[10] de Affordebi . Rannulfo filio Baldrici de Lec[9] . Odone[11] filio Heming.[12]

Endorsed : (1) fleichemar' .i. acram. (2) xii. (3) ex[tt]. de .i. acra 7 dimidia. (4) Hoiland'. (5) Framton. (6) Fraumptona. (7) Subbetofts Gosberchirch'.
Tag for seal. Size : 6½ x 3½ inches.
Texts : MS—Orig. Dij/87/1/22*a*. A530 and 696. R1899.
Var. R. : [1] Blasig A696 and R. [2] Fleychemare A696. Bleichemare R. [3] Wlhou R. [4] Lefsicroft A530 and R. [5] A696 *adds* servicio 7. [6] Lincolnie A530. [7] W. in A696. [8] Luce A530. Luock A696. Luok R. [9] Leke A696. Lek' R. [10] *sic* : a blank has been left in R after filio. [11] Ode R. [12] Hemig' R.
Note : The endorsement of this charter is apparently erroneous, although at first sight the attestations of William the clerk of Boston and Antony son of Luck of Leake suggest its origin in Holland. The original scribe of A placed it with the Skidbrook charters, but Q2 entered it again in Holland. Its provenance from Skidbrook seems to be proved by the charter of Boniva daughter of Basing de Blaikemare of Skidbrook printed by Professor Stenton (*Danelaw Charters*, p. 399). Fleichemare seems to be an error for Bleichemare which is given in R and in the dean and chapter's grant of the land (no. 1735 below), which is entered by the scribe of R with the Skidbrook charters. Wulfhou is mentioned in nos. 1710, 1713 and 1731 below. Boniva had a nephew Gilbert son of Brun of Theddlethorpe, who quitclaimed the land which she had given to Odo Galle in Skidbrook after a suit begun by writ of mort d'ancestor 1222–1226. (*Free Peasantry*, p. 130).

Folio 101d.

531

1701. Grant by Robert son of Sigward of Saltfleetby, to the church of Lincoln and the Common, of six acres of land in Skidbrook. (Circa 1210.)

Sciant presentes 7 futuri quod ego Robertus filius Sigward[1] de Saltfleteby[2] dedi 7 concessi 7 presenti carta mea confirmaui deo 7 beate Marie 7 commune canonicorum Linc' ecclesie sex acras terre in territorio de Skitebroc[3] que iacent inter terram Gilberti Blundi . 7 terram Gode filie Aluiue[4] . Habendas 7 tenendas cum omnibus pertinenciis suis in puram 7 perpetuam elemosinam . liberas . solutas 7 quietas ab omni seruitio seculari 7 exactione . Et ego Robertus 7 heredes mei prefatis canonicis warentizabimus prenominatas sex acras cum omnibus pertinenciis suis contra omnes homines imperpetuum . vt autem hec mea donatio firma 7 stabilis permaneat ∴ eam presenti scripto 7 sigilli mei appositione corroboraui . Hiis testibus . Conano . Waltero . 7 Willelmo de Tingehurst capellanis . Willelmo persona de Salfleteby[2] . Odone Galle . Willelmo de Midlei[5] . Andrea filio Roberti de Sumercotes[6] . Petro de Cheuermund . Rogero Malherbe . Willelmo filio Ernisii . Hugone Knotting[7] . Phillippo Pullan' . Alexandro . 7 Benedicto . 7 aliis.

Marginalia in A : Skitebrok vi acr' terre (? by Q2).
Texts : MS—A. R1586.
Var. R. : [1] Sigwarth' R. [2] Salfleteby R. [3] Skitbrok' R. [4] Alviue R. [5] Midley R. [6] Somercotes R. [7] Knottÿng R.

532

1702. Grant by Roger Knotting of Skidbrook, to the church of Lincoln and the Common, of a close containing six acres, and two acres of land in Skidbrook. (Early thirteenth century.)

Sciant presentes 7 futuri quod ego Rogerus Knotting[1] de Skitebroc[2] dedi 7 concessi 7 presenti carta mea confirmaui deo 7 beate Marie 7 commune canonicorum Linc' ecclesie unum clausum in quo continentur sex acre terre in territorio de Skitebroc[3] inter uiam que ducit ad ecclesiam ex una parte 7 Waterlade ex alia . 7 preterea duas acras in Brothercroft proximas terre Willelmi persone uersus occidentem . habenda 7 tenenda in puram 7 perpetuam elemosinam liberam solutam 7 quietam ab omni seculari seruitio 7 exactione . pro salute anime méé 7 omnium antecessorum [4]7 successorum[4] meorum . Et ego 7 heredes mei warentizabimus predicte commune prefatas terras cum pertinenciis contra omnes [4]homines[4] imperpetuum[5] . vt [4]autem[4] hec mea donatio firma 7 inconcussa permaneat ∴ eam presenti scripto 7 sigilli mei appositione corroboraui . Hiis testibus . Alano de Marton' . Roberto filio Galfridi . Willelmo filio Aluredi de Teford . Roberto filio Gileberti[6] . Roberto filio Alani de Marton' . Waltero capellano . Thoma de Ardres . Roberto Scotto . Henrico de Orskinct' . Petro de Cheuermund clerico . 7 aliis.

Marginalia in A: Skitebrok vi acr' terre (? by Q2).
Texts: MS—A. R1563.
Var. R.: [1] Knottẏng R. [2] Skitbroc R. [3] Skitbrok' R. [4]–[4] R *omits.* [5] R *adds* et. [6] Gilberti R.
Note: The grantor was the brother of Hugh Knotting (see no. 1722 below) and is identical with Roger son of Wigot son of Asger, the grantor in 1719 below and with Roger son of Wigot of Skidbrook in 1721, below. William the parson held office jointly with Walter (see no. 1710, below). In 1223–4 Roger was instituted to a vicarage of three parts of the church, while Richard was parson of the fourth part. This suggests that William held office early in the century. (See note to no. 1725, below.)

533

1703. Grant by Richard son of Jocelin of Skidbrook, to the church of Lincoln and the Common, of seven acres of arable land in Skidbrook. (Circa 1210–1220.)

Sciant presentes 7 futuri quod ego Ricardus filius Jocelini de Skitebroc[1] dedi 7 concessi 7 presenti carta mea confirmaui deo 7 beate Marie 7 commune canonicorum Linc' ecclesie septem acras terre arabilis in territorio de Skitebroc[1] in Oxencroft inter terram Gode filie Aluiue 7 terram Dauid filii Leues . Habendas 7 tenendas cum omnibus pertinenciis suis in puram 7 perpetuam elemosinam . liberas . solutas . 7 quietas ab omni seruitio seculari 7 exactione . Et ego 7 heredes mei prefatas septem acras cum pertinenciis predictis[2] canonicis warentizabimus defendemus 7 adquietabimus erga omnes homines imperpetuum . In huius autem donationis robur 7 testimonium presens scriptum sigilli mei appositione corroboraui . Hiis testibus . Conano sacrista . Waltero 7 Rumfaro capellanis . [3]Odone Galle[3] . Andrea filio Roberti de Sumercotes[4] . Willelmo de Midlei[5] . Ricardo de Humberstan[6] . Petro de Cheuermund' . Philippo Hors . Johanne presbitero . Alexandro . 7 aliis.

Marginalia in A: (1) Thomas filius Ricardi de Skitebroc. (2) Skytebrok vii acr' terre (? by Q2).
Texts: MS—A. R 1592.
Var. R.: [1] Skitbrok' R. [2] prefatis R. [3–3] R *omits*. [4] Somercotes R. [5] Midley R. [6] Humberstayn R.
Note: For the date of Conan as sacrist see vol. iv, p. 281, above.

Folio 102.
Hdl. . | . ϕ . 2 .

534

1704. Grant by Ralf son of Ernis of Skidbrook, to the church of Lincoln and the Common, of seven acres of arable land in Skidbrook. (Circa 1210–1220.)

Sciant presentes 7 futuri quod[1] Radulfus filius Ernisii de Skitebroc[2] dedi 7 concessi 7 presenti carta mea confirmaui deo 7 beate Marie 7 commune canonicorum Lincoln' ecclesie . septem acras terre arabilis in territorio de Skitebroc[2] que jacent inter Askel Land ex una parte 7 Vt gang ex alia . Habendas 7 tenendas cum omnibus pertinentiis in puram 7 perpetuam elemosinam . liberas solutas 7 quietas ab omni seruitio 7 exaccione seculari . Et ego 7 heredes mei prefatas septem acras cum pertinentiis predictis canonicis warentizabimus . defendemus 7 adquietabimus erga omnes homines inperpetuum . Vt autem hec mea donatio firma 7 stabilis permaneat ∴ eam presenti scripto 7 sigilli mei appositione corroboraui . Hiis testibus . Conano sacrista . Waltero 7 Rumfaro capellanis . Odone[3] Galle . Andrea filio Roberti de Sumercotes[4] . Willelmo de Midlei[5] . Petro de Cheuermund' . Ricardo de Humberstain[6] . Philippo Hors . Johanne presbitero . Alexandro . Benedicto . 7 aliis.

Endorsed: (1) xlij (late 13 cent.). (2) Luthesce (late 13 cent.).
Written on the fold: Hugo filius Ricardi (13 cent.).
Tag for seal. Size: 8 x 4 inches.
Marginalia in A: (1) Skytebrok vii acr' terre (? by Q2). (2) Hugo filius Ricardi de Skitebroc (13 cent.). (3) de Scitebroc *has been written in the top margin near the headline, but is nearly illegible.*
Texts: MS—Orig. Dij/87/1/18. A. R.
Var. R.: [1] R *adds* ego. [2] Skitbrok R. [3] Eudone R. [4] Somercotes R. [5] Midley R. [6] Humberstayn R.

535

1705. Grant by Ernis son of Ernis of Skidbrook, to the church of Lincoln and the Common, of various parcels of land in Skidbrook. (Circa 1210–1220.)

Omnibus Christi fidelibus ad quos presens scriptum peruenerit ./ Ernisius filius Ernisii de Skitebroc[1] salutem . Nouerit vniuersitas uestra me diuine pietatis intuitu dedisse 7 concessisse 7 presenti carta mea confirmasse deo 7 beate Marie 7 commune canonicorum Lincoln' ecclesie ./ duas acras 7 dimidiam ex parte septentrionali ecclesie de Skitebroc[1] . que iacent inter uiam ex una parte 7 Waterlade ex alia . 7 quatuor acras iuxta croftum Osberti filii Willelmi ex parte australi que abutissant super duas vias . 7 vnam acram 7 dimidiam iuxta terram Ricardi fratris mei apud Meles iuxta mansionem Angeri . 7 unam acram 7 dimidiam in Grene . inter terram Auicie 7 viam ecclesie . Item dimidiam acram inter terram Andree de Sumercotes[2] 7 terram Willelmi filii Vmfridi ex parte occidentali domus eiusdem Willelmi 7 duas acras 7 dimidiam in Tole Toftes[3] iuxta terram Ricardi fratris mei . 7 duas acras 7 dimidiam in Rauenescroft inter terram Willelmi Norensis[4] 7 terram Line . Habendas 7 tenendas in puram 7 perpetuam elemosinam . liberas solutas 7 quietas ab omni seculari seruitio 7 exaccione . Et ego 7 heredes mei warentizabimus eisdem canonicis prenominatas terras cum omnibus pertinentiis suis contra omnes [5]homines[5] inperpetuum . In huius [5]autem[5] rei robur 7 testimonium ./ presens scriptum sigilli mei appositione corroboraui . Hiis testibus . Conano 7 Waltero capellanis . Willelmo de Tuxford' . Andrea de Sumercotes[2] . Waltero clerico . Petro de Cheuermund' . [5]clerico[5] . Hugone Knotting'[6] . Roberto de Stowe . Willelmo Painell'[7] . Philippo 7 aliis.

Endorsed: (1) xlv (late 13 cent.). (2) Skitebrok (late 13 cent.).
Slit for seal tag. Size: 8¼ x 4 inches.
Marginalia in A: Skytebrok ii acr' et dim' (? by Q2).
Texts: MS—Orig. Dij/87/1/2. A. R1562.
Var. R.: [1] Skitbrok'. [2] Somercotes R. [3] Tole Croftes A. Toletoftes R. [4] Noreis R. [5]–[5] R *omits*. [6] Knottẏng R. [7] A *omits*: Paẏnel R.

536

1706. Grant by Adam son of Osbert of Somercotes, to the church of Lincoln and the Common, of an acre and a half of land in Skidbrook. He undertakes to make in perpetuity as much of the sea-dike as is proper to that land. (Late twelfth century.)

Notum sit tam presentibus quam futuris quod ego Adam filius Osberti de Sumercotes[1] dedi 7 concessi 7 hac presenti carta mea confirmaui deo 7 beate Marie 7 commune canonicorum Linc' ecclesie in territorio de Schitebroc[2] unam acram terre 7 dimidiam in Aicroft del este[3] . [4]iuxta fossam que fuit Wigoti[5] filii Aasgeri[6] cum pertinenciis omnibus . 7 aisiamentis eiusdem uille in omnibus locis in puram liberam 7 perpetuam elemosinam pro animabus patris mei 7 matris méé 7 omnium antecessorum meorum necnon 7 pro salute mea 7 heredum meorum . Hanc autem terram ego 7 heredes * mei warantizabimus predictis canonicis imperpetuum contra omnes homines . Et sedic in quantum prefate terre competit imperpetuum faciemus . Et ut ista donatio firma permaneat . hanc cartam sigilli mei appensione corroboraui . Hiis testibus . Willelmo de Karletun[7] . magistro Willelmo de Sumercot'[1] . Andrea 7 Radulfo fratribus eius . Gileberto[8] clerico de Sumercot'[1] . Johanne filio Alani . Alano filio Radulfi . Alano filio Hemming[9] . Willelmo filio Dauid . 7 multis.[10]

Marginalia in A : (1) Skytebrok i acr' 7 dim' (? by Q2). (2) x (faded. (3) *in lower margin* x partem versus West.

Texts : MS—A. R1585.

Var. R. : [1] Somercotes R. [2] Skitbrok' R. [3] est R. [4] A *has apparently omitted* partem versus West, *which has been noted in the lower margin on folio* 102. R, *however, has* versus West partem. [5] Wẏgoti R. [6] Asgeri R. [7] Carleton R. [8] Gilberto R. [9] Hemmyng R. [10] *sic*.

Note : William of Carlton occurs at various dates between 1180 and 1200 (*Danelaw Charters*, pp. 113, 125, 394, etc.) and above no. 1686. He may be identical with the steward of Norman de la Charité in 1200 (no. 1504 above). The witnesses of this charter are identical with those of 1718, below.

**Folio 102d.*

537

1707. Grant by Richard son of Asger, to the church of Lincoln and the Common, of seven and a half acres of land lying in two places in Skidbrook. (Circa 1180.)

Omnibus sancte matris eclesie filiis ad quos presens scriptum[1] peruenerit Ricardus filius Asghari salutem . Sciatis me concessisse 7 dedisse 7 hac carta mea confirmasse deo 7 beate Marie Lincolniensis eclesie 7 commune canonicorum ibidem deo seruientium in puram 7 perpetuam elemosinam iiij. acras terre 7 dimidiam in Fencropt[2] iuxta terram Alani filii Dauid 7 alias iij. acras in Schitebrroch[3] scilicet . tophtum[4] 7 crophtum[5] ubi sedit Ascerus filius Ovgrimi[6] . His[7] testibus . magistro Johanne . Alano filio Ricardi . Radulfo filio Ernulphi[8] .W. filio Wigoti[9] 7 multis aliis.

Endorsed : (1) lvj (13 cent.). (2) Ricardi filii Asgari . de Skiteb' (13 cent.)

Tag for seal. Size : $5\frac{1}{2}$ x $1\frac{3}{4}$ inches.

Marginalia in A : Skydebrok iiij acr' 7 dim' (? by Q2).

Texts : MS—Orig. Dij/87/1/19. A. R1574.

Var. R. : [1] scriptum *is interlineated.* [2] Fencroft R. [3] Schitebroch A. Skitbrok R. [4] *sic* : toftum A and R. [5] *sic* : croftum A *and* R. [6] Ougimi R. [7] *sic* : hiis A *and* R. [8] Arnulphi R. [9] Wẏgoti R.

Note : The date is that suggested by Professor Stenton in *Free Peasantry*, p. 128.

538

1708. Grant by Ivo son of Simon, to the church of Lincoln and the Common, of twelve acres of land and meadow in Skidbrook. (Circa 1210–1215.)

Sciant presentes 7 futuri quod ego Iuo[1] filius Sẏmonis[2] dedi 7 concessi 7 presenti carta mea confirmaui deo 7 beate Marie 7 commune canonicorum Lincoln' ecclesie duodecim acras terre in territorio de Skitebroc[3] . videlicet in tofto cum crofto sex acras inter terram Hugonis filii Humfridi[4] . 7 puplicam[5] stratam . in Hallecroft . duas acras inter terram Ricardi filii Leues 7 terram Ernisii . 7 super dailam quatuor acras prati .ʼ inter pratum Radulfi filii Ernisii .ʼ 7 pratum Andree de Sumercotes[6] . Habendas 7 tenendas cum omnibus pertinentiis suis in puram 7 perpetuam elemosinam . liberas solutas 7 quietas ab omni seculari seruitio 7 exaccione . Et ego 7 heredes mei warentizabimus eisdem canonicis prenominatas duodecim acras cum pertinenciis contra omnes homines imperpetuum . vt autem hec mea donatio rata 7 inconcussa permaneat .ʼ eam presenti scripto 7 sigilli mei appositione corroboraui . Hiis testibus . Conano . Waltero . 7 Rumfaro capellanis . Andrea de Sumercotes[6] . Alano de Normanb'[7] . Willelmo filio Willelmi filii Eilsi . Petro de Cheuermund clerico . Willelmo de Midlei[8] . Ricardo de Humberstain[9] . Mauritio de Neuport clerico . Willelmo filio Willelmi filii Eilsi . Henrico filio Roberti . Philippo Pullano . Johanne sacerdote . Alexandro 7 Benedicto 7 aliis.

Endorsed: (1) lvij (13 cent.). (2) Ex dono Ẏuonis filii Symonis .xij. ac' in Skitebroc . quas Andreas de Sumercotes confirmat (13 cent.).

Tag for seal. Size: 6¾ x 4¼ inches.

Marginalia in A: Skidebrok xii acr' terre (? by Q2).

Texts: MS.—Orig. Dij/87/1/20. A. R1575.

Var. R.: [1] Yuo R. [2] Syimonis A. Simonis R. [3] Skitbrok' R. [4] Vmfridi R. [5] publicam A. pupplicam R. [6] Somercotes R. [7] Normanby A *and* R. [8] Millaẏ R. [9] Humberstayn R.

539

1709. Confirmation by Andrew son of Robert of Somercotes of the preceding grant. (Circa 1210–1215.)

Sciant presentes 7 futuri quod ego Andreas filius Roberti de Sumercotes[1] concessi 7 presenti carta mea confirmaui donationem quam Yuo filius Symonis[2] fecit deo 7 beate Marie 7 commune canonicorum Linc' ecclesie de duodecim acris terre in territorio de Skitebroc[3] . Cuius quidem terre héé sunt partes . videlicet in tofto cum crofto predicti Symonis[2] sunt sex acre inter terram Hugonis filii Vmfridi 7 publicam stratam . In Allecroft[4] due acre inter terram Ricardi filii

Leues 7 terram Ernisii . 7 super dailam[5] quatuor acras prati . inter pratum Radulfi filii Ernisii 7 pratum meum . Has autem predictas duodecim acras cum omnibus pertinenciis [6]suis[6] ego Andreas prefatis * canonicis confirmaui in puram 7 perpetuam elemosinam perpetuo possidendas . liberas solutas 7 quietas ab omni seculari seruitio 7 exactione . Et ego 7 heredes mei warentizabimus predictis canonicis prenominatas duodecim acras cum omnibus pertinenciis suis contra omnes homines imperpetuum . In huius autem rei robur 7 testimonium ∴ presens scriptum sigilli mei appositione corroboraui . Hiis testibus . Conano . Waltero . Rumfaro . 7 Hardio capellanis . Ricardo de Humberstain[7] . 7 Johanne de Bict diaconis . Petro de Cheuermund' . Willelmo de Midlei[8] . Mauritio de Neuport clerico . Willelmo filio Willelmi filii Eilsi . Philippo Pullano . Alexandro . 7 Benedicto . 7 aliis.

Marginalia in A: Skydebrok xii acr' (? by Q2).
Texts: MS—A. R1576.
Var. R.: [1] Somercotes R. [2] Simonis R. [3] Skitbrok' R. [4] Hallecroft R. [5] dayÿlam R. [6–6] R *omits.* [7] Humberstayn R. [8] Midleÿ R.

* *Folio* 103.

Hdl. Ludhesk'.

. i . ɸ . 3 .

540

1710. Grant by Osbert son of William of Skidbrook, to the church of Lincoln and the Common, of forty acres of land and meadow in Skidbrook. (Early thirteenth century.)

[Notum sit tam presentibus quam futuris quod ego Hosbertus[2] filius Willelmi de Schitebroc[3] dedi 7 concessi 7 hac presenti carta mea confirmaui deo 7 beate Marie[1]] 7 commune cano[nicorum Linc' [4]ecclesie[4] quadraginta acras terre 7 prati in territorio[1]] de Schitebroc[3] . videlic[et quinque acras terre[1]] in Magnhus croft . Et tres acras terre prox[imas eisdem quinque acris uersus Westpart[1] .] 7 quinque acras terre in Suhth[all[1]]ecroft[5] . inter terras Simonis[6] 7 Andree de Sumercot'[7] . Et vndecim acras terre in [Cucroft[8] proximas[1]] vltimo dictis quinque acris versus Norhtpart[9] . Et duas acras terre 7 dimidiam in Alfwine deile . 7 unam acram terre [7 dimidiam[1]] in Wulfhou[10] . Et quatuor acras prati inter terras Willelmi filii Roberti de Lekeburne . 7 Edmundi de Saltfletebi[11] . [Et dimidiam[1]] partem de Aicroft[12] . in puram liberam 7 perpetuam elemosinam pro animabus patris mei 7 matris mee 7 omni[um antecessorum[1]] meorum . necnon 7 pro salute mea 7 heredum meorum . Hanc uero predictam terram ego 7 heredes mei waranti[zabimus prefatis[1]] canonicis imperpetuum contra omnes homines . Et vt ista donacio firma 7 stabilis p[ermaneat[1]] .: hanc [cartam[1]] sigilli mei appensione corroboraui . His[13] testibus . magistro Willelmo de Sumercot' . [Andrea 7 Radulf[1]]o fratribus eius . Waltero 7 Willelmo personis de Scitebroc[3] . Radulfo filio Hernisii[14] . Willelmo No[rreis[15] . Alano[1]] filio Ricardi . Roberto de Mareis[16] . Rannulfo filio Aschil . Roberto[17] Bas[ing . Martino filio Ad[1]]elidis . Waltero filio Hace . 7 multis aliis.

Endorsed: Osberti filii Willelmi de Scitebroc (13 cent.).
Tag for seal. Size: 7 x 5 (circa) inches.
Marginalia in A: Skidebrok xl acr' terre 7 prati (? by Q2).
Texts: MS—Orig. Dij/87/1/5. A. R 1573.
Var. R.: [1] *The words in square brackets have been supplied from* A *as the charter is mutilated.* [2] Osbert R. [3] Skitbrok' R. [4–4] R *omits.* [5] Suthallecroft A. Suthhallecroft' R. [6] Symonis A. [7] Somercotes R. [8] Chucroft R. [9] Nortpart A. Northpart R. [10] Wlfhou A *and* R. [11] Salfletbi A. Salfleteby R. [12] Haycroft' R. [13] *sic*: hiis A *and* R. [14] Ernisii R. [15] Noreÿs R. [16] Mareÿs R. [17] A *and* R *add* filio.
Note: For the succession of parsons in Skidbrook see notes to charters 1702, above, and 1725, below.

541

1711. Grant by Osbert son of William, to the church of Lincoln and the Common, of five acres of land with common pasture in Skidbrook. (Circa 1190–1200.)

Sciant tam presentes quam futuri quod ego Hosbertus[1] filius Willelmi dedi 7 concessi 7 hac presenti carta mea confirmaui deo 7 beate Marie 7 commune canonicorum Lincol' ecclesie quinque acras terre in territorio de Scitebroc[2] .: cum communi pastura eiusdem ville que jacent juxta Meles . quatuor videlicet que proximo jacent juxta domum Rogeri filii Eadþive[3] in Norhtpart[4] . 7 vnam acram proximo jacentem juxta eandem domum in Sud[part[5] . in[6]] liberam puram 7 perpetuam elemosinam pro animabus patris mei 7 [matris méé[6]] . 7 omnium antecessorum meorum . necnon 7 pro salute mea 7 omnium heredum meorum . Hanc autem terram ego 7 heredes [7]mei[7] warantizabimus prenominatis canonicis imperpetuum contra omnes homines[8] . Et ut ista donacio rata 7 irreuocabilis permaneat .: hanc cartam sigilli [7]mei[7] appensione corroboraui . Hiis testibus . Willelmo 7 Jordano decanis . magistro Hugone Blundo . Andrea filio Roberti . Willelmo filio Dauid . Hugone genero Dauid . Alano filio Gille[9] . 7 Radulfo filio eius . Roberto de Mares[10] . Hernisio[11] filio Rannulfi . Roberto filio Hosberti[12] . Waltero filio Hugonis . 7 multis aliis.

Endorsed: (1) Osberti filii Willelmi . de Skiteb' (13 cent.). (2) liiij (late 13 cent.).
Tag for seal. Size: 4⅞ x 4⅝ inches.

Marginalia in A: Skidebrok v. acr' terre (? by Q2).
Texts: MS—Orig. Dij/87/1/4. A. R1572.
Var. R.: [1] Osbert R. [2] Skitbrok' R. [3] Ead [blank] R. [4] Northpart A *and* R. [5] Suthpart R. [6] *supplied from* A: *there is a hole in the charter.* [7]–[7] R *omits.* [8] R *adds* inperpetuum (*sic*). [9] Galle R. [10] Mareis A *and* R. [11] Ernisio R. [12] Osberti R.
Note: For the date see note to no. 1656, above.

Folio 103d.

541a

1712. Grant by Askel son of Basing, with the consent of Alice his wife and his heirs, to the church of Lincoln and the Common, of a toft and half of four selions of land in Skidbrook. (Late twelfth century.)

Vniuersis sancte matris ecclesie filiis ad quos presens scriptum peruenerit ∴ Askel filius Basing de Skitebroc[1] salutem . Nouerit uniuersitas uestra me dedisse 7 concessisse 7 hac presenti carta mea confirmasse deo 7 beate Marie 7 commune[2] Linc' ecclesie in territorio de Skytebroc[1] toftum unum qui iacet a meridie iuxta Tytebregge[3] . 7 medietatem . iiij^{or} sellionum terre arabilis qui porriguntur in eundem toftum de consensu Alicie uxoris méé 7 heredum meorum in puram 7 perpetuam elemosinam . Hanc autem donationem ego 7 heredes mei warantizabimus predicte commune contra omnes homines . Testibus . Thoma sacerdote de Skytebroc[1] . Willelmo persona de Skitebroc[1] . Alano fratre eius . Roberto de Marisco . Willelmo Norno . [4]Dauid[4] filio Leue . Waltero filio Hugonis sacerdotis de Skitebroc[1] . Rogero filio Eadiue . Martino.

Marginalia in A: Skidebrok' i. toft. 7 terr' (? by Q2).
Texts: MS—A. R1589.
Var. R.: [1] Skitbrok' R. [2] R *adds* canonicorum. [3] Titebregge R. [4] R *omits.*

542

1713. Grant by Alan son of David, to the church of Lincoln and the Common, of five acres of land in Skidbrook. (Early thirteenth century.)

Omnibus Christi fidelibus ad quos presens scriptum peruenerit ∴ Alanus filius Dauid de Schitebroc[1] salutem . Noueritis me dedisse 7 concessisse 7 presenti carta mea confirmasse deo 7 beate Marie 7 commune canonicorum Lincoln' ecclesie ∴ quinque acras terre in territorio de Schẏtebroc[1] ∴ scilicet tres acras 7 dimidiam in Wlfhou . 7 unam acram 7 dimidiam in Haẏcoluecroft ∴ in puram 7 liberam 7 perpetuam elemosinam . liberas . solutas 7 quietas ab omni seculari seruitio 7 exactione . Et ego 7 heredes mei warentizabimus predictis canonicis prenominatas quinque acras cum pertinenciis .' contra omnes homines imperpetuum . In huius itaque rei robur 7 testimonium .' presenti scripto sigillum meum apposui . Hiis testibus . magistro Gilberto[2] de Malbertorp'[3] . Waltero de Malbertorp'[3] . Willelmo de Midlei[4] . Ricardo filio Ace . Johanne filio Johannis [5]de Aluingham[5] . Coste de Aluingham' . Petro clerico clerico[6] 7 aliis.

Endorsed : (1) Skitebrok (13–14 cent.). (2) lij (late 13 cent.).
Tag for seal. Size : 6½ x 2¾ inches.
Marginalia in A : Skydebrok v. acr' terre (? by Q2).
Texts : MS—Orig. Dij/87/1/13. A. R1569.
Var. R. : [1] Skitbrok'. [2] Gileberto A. [3] Malberthorp' R. [4] Midley R. [5–5] R *omits.* [6] *sic* : A *and* R *omit the second* clerico.
Note : The grantor was appealed of infraction of the King's Peace by Randulf Bla in 1202 (L.R.S. xxii, no. 646). A John of Alvingham, who may be the fifth witness, occurs in 1206 (*ibid.* no. 1523). Gilbert of Mablethorpe witnesses as a canon 1203–1206 (no. 350 in vol. iv., above).

543

1714. Grant by Hugh son of Humphrey, to the church of Lincoln and the Common, of a toft and a croft in Skidbrook. (Late Henry II.)

Omnibus sancte matris ecclesie filiis ad quos presens scriptum peruenerit .' Hugo filius Vmfridi salutem . Sciatis me dedisse 7 concessisse 7 hac carta mea confirmasse deo 7 beate Marie Linc' ecclesie 7 commune canonicorum ibidem deo seruientium in puram 7 perpetuam elemosinam unum toftum 7 croftum in Scitebroc[1] que tenuit de me 7 [2]de[2] patre meo in eadem uilla Gilebertus[3] filius Godrici . Hiis testibus . Johanne de Merston' . Henrico de Meleford . Andrea filio Roberti . Johanne filio Alani . Hugone filio Yuonis . 7 multis aliis.

Marginalia in A : Skidebrok j. toftum 7 croftum (? by Q2).
Texts : MS—A. R1587.
Var. R. : [1] Skitbrok' R. [2–2] R *omits.* [3] Gilbertus R.
Note : The absence of a warranty clause suggests that this charter is of a date before 1200, probably several years before 1200.

544

1715. Grant by Hugh Knotting, to the church of Lincoln and the Common, of half an acre of land in Skidbrook. (Circa 1210–1215.)

Sciant presentes 7 futuri quod ego Hugo Knotting[1] diuine pietatis intuitu dedi 7 [con[2]]cessi 7 presenti carta mea confirmaui deo 7 beate Marie 7 commune canonicorum Lincoln' ecclesie .' dimidiam acram terre in territorio de Skŷtebroc[3] . que iacet iuxta Meles [4]inter terram Willelmi Norensis[5] [4] ex una parte . 7 terram Clementis fratris eius ex alia . Habendam 7 tenendam cum omnibus pertinentiis [4]suis[4] in puram 7 perpetuam elemosinam liberam solutam 7 quietam ab omni seculari seruitio 7 exaccione . Et ego 7 heredes mei prenominatis canonicis predictam terram cum pertinentiis warentizabimus 7 adquietabimus erga omnes homines imperpetuum . vt autem hec mea donatio firma 7 stabilis permaneat .' eam presenti scripto 7 sigilli mei appositione corroboraui . Hiis testibus . Conano 7 Waltero capellanis . Philippo de Tymberlund' . * Ricardo de Humberstain[6] . Petro de Cheuermund . Alexandro de Bict clerico . Alexandro Costard . Waltero filio Brianni[7] . Petro filio Ade . Philippo 7 Benedicto . 7 aliis.

Endorsed : Skitebrok (13 cent.).
Fragment of seal on tag—green, probably round with conventional device—
. . M.H. . . . NIS · FI . . . .
Marginalia in A : Skidebrok' dim' acre terre (? by Q2).
Texts : MS—Orig. Dij/87/1/22. A. R1564.
Var. R. : [1] Knottŷng R. [2] *supplied from* A : *the charter is torn.* [3] Sckitebroc A. Skitbrok' R. [4–4] R *omits.* [5] Norrensis A. [6] Humberstayn R. [7] Briani A *and* R.
Note : This grantor is identical with Hugh son of Wigot son of Asger the grantor in 1720, below, and with Hugh son of Wigot Knotting in 1722, below.

* *Folio* 104.

Hdl. . I . ϕ . 4

545

1716. Grant by Ernis son of Haac Knotting of Skidbrook, to the chapter of Lincoln, of three acres and a perch in Skidbrook. (Circa 1200.)

Omnibus sancte matris ecclesie filiis ad quos presens scriptum peruenerit . Hernisius filius Haac Cnocting[1] de Schitebroc[2] salutem . Nouerit uniuersitas uestra me assensu heredum meorum dedisse 7 concessisse 7 hac presenti carta mea confirmasse deo 7 beate Marie 7 capitulo Lincol' ecclesie tres acras terre in teritorio de Schitebroc[2] 7 unam parcatam . scilicet duas acras terre in Esthaldecrof[3] proximas terre Basing[4] orientali parte 7 unam acram terre 7 unam parcatam in Westhaldecrof[5] proximas terre Basing in occidentali .' parte in puram 7 perpetuam elemosinam pro salute anime mee 7 pro animabus omnium antecessorum meorum . Ego uero 7 heredes mei predictum tenementum uuarentizabimus[6] predicto capitulo contra omnes homines . Et ut ista concessio 7 donacio rata permaneat sigilli mei aposicione[7] corroboraui .

His[8] testibus . Basing . Hugone Cnocting[9] . Rogero fratre eius. Radulfo filio Hernisii . Willelmo fratre eius . Roberto del Marais[10] . Dauid homine sancte Marie . [11]Rogero homine sancte Marie[11] . Willelmo Norne . Roberto fratre eius . 7 multis aliis.

Endorsed : (1) Ernisii filii Acche Cnotting . de Skiteb' (13 cent.). (2) xli (late 13 cent.).

Tag for seal. Size : 5⅜ x 3⅜ inches.

Marginalia in A : Skidebrok' iij. acr' terre (? by Q2).

Texts : MS—Orig. Dij/87/1/12. A. R1558.

Var. R. : [1] Knotting A. Knotting' R. [2] Skitbrok' R. [2] Esthaldecroft A. Esthaldecroft' R. [4] *sic* : R *adds* in. [5] Westhaldecrof' R. [6] *sic* : warentizabimus A. warantizabimus R. [7] *sic* : appositione A. apposicione R. [8] *sic* : hiis A *and* R. [9] Cnoting A. Knotting' R. [10] Marays R. [11–11] A *omits*.

546

1717. Grant by Geoffrey son of Alan the clerk of Skidbrook, to the church of Lincoln and the Common, of two and a half acres of arable land in Skidbrook. (Circa 1210–1215.)

Omnibus Christi fidelibus ad quos presens scriptum peruenerit ∴ Galfridus filius Alani clerici de Skitebroc[1] salutem eternam in domino . Nouerit uniuersitas uestra me diuine pietatis intuitu dedisse 7 concessisse 7 presenti carta mea confirmasse deo 7 beate Marie 7 commune canonicorum Linc' [2]ecclesie[2] duas acras 7 dimidiam terre arabilis in territorio de Skitebroc[1] que iacent inter terras que fuerunt Roberti de Marisco ex parte occidentali mansionis eiusdem Roberti . habendas 7 tenendas cum omnibus pertinenciis suis in puram 7 perpetuam elemosinam liberam solutam 7 quietam ab omni seculari seruitio 7 exactione . Et ego 7 heredes mei warentizabimus predictas duas acras 7 dimidiam cum pertinenciis memoratis canonicis contra omnes homines imperpetuum . vt igitur hec mea donatio [2]perpetuam[2] obtineat firmitatem ∴ eam presenti scripto 7 sigilli mei appositione corroboraui . Hiis testibus . Johanne de Wikeford[3] . Conano . 7 Waltero capellanis . Petro de Cheuermund . 7 Waleranno clericis . Pagano carpentario . Roberto filio Theobaldi . Willelmo filio Eilsi[4] . Hugone Knotting[5] . 7 aliis.

Marginalia in A : (1) Skidebrok ij. acr' 7 dim' terre (? by Q2). (2) terras + (*much faded*).

Texts : MS—A. R1571.

Var. R. : [1] Skitbrok' R. [2–2] R *omits*. [3] Wycford' R. [4] Eylsi R. [5] Knottyng R.

547

1718. Grant by Robert son of Godric, to the church of Lincoln and the Common, of various parcels of land in Skidbrook. (Late twelfth century.)

Sciant tam presentes quam futuri quod ego Robertus filius Godrici dedi 7 concessi 7 hac presenti carta mea confirmaui deo 7 beate Marie 7 commune canonicorum Linc' ecclesie duas acras terre in Schitebroc[1] que iacent inter domum meam 7 domum que fuit Aace clerici 7 tres percatas que[2] inter domos Willelmi filii Aschel . 7 Alani filii Asgeri . 7 acram 7 dimidiam inter terras predicti Alani 7 Roberti filii Rogeri in Meddeldele[3] cum omnibus aisiamentis eiusdem uille in omnibus locis in puram liberam 7 perpetuam elemosinam pro animabus patris mei 7 matris méé . 7 omnium antecessorum meorum . necnon 7 pro salute mea 7 omnium heredum meorum . Hanc uero terram ego 7 heredes mei warantizabimus imperpetuum contra omnes homines . * Et ut ista donatio firma permaneat ∴ hanc cartam sigilli mei appensione confirmaui . Hiis testibus . Willelmo de Karlet'. magistro Willelmo de Sumercot'[4] . Andrea 7 Radulfo fratribus eius . Gileberto[5] clerico de Sumercot'[4] . Johanne filio Alani . Alano filio Radulfi . Alano filio Hemming[6] . Willelmo filio Dauid . Alano fratre eius . Galfrido [7]filio[7] Alani . Symone[8] fratre eius.

Marginalia in A : Skidebrok ij. acr' terre (? by Q2).
Texts : MS—A. R1578.
Var. R. : [1] Skitbrok' R. [2] *sic* : R *adds* iacent. [3] Middeldele R. [4] Somercotes R. [5] Gileberto R. [6] Hemmyng R. [7–7] R *omits*. [8] Simone R.
Note : William of Carlton occurs at various dates between 1180 and 1200 (*Danelaw Charters*, pp. 113, 125, 394 etc.). He may be identical with the steward of Norman de la Charité in 1200 (no. 1504 above). The witnesses of this charter are identical with that of 1706, above.

* *Folio 104d.*

548

1719. Grant by Roger son of Wigot son of Asger of Skidbrook, to the church of Lincoln, of nine acres of land, less one perch, in Skidbrook and half his salt meadow with the sandy tract pertaining to it. (Circa 1200.)

Vniuersis sancte matris ecclesie filiis ad quos presens scriptum peruenerit ∴ Rogerus filius Wigoti[1] filii Asgeri de Scitebroc[2] salutem . Nouerit uniuersitas uestra me concessisse 7 dedisse 7 hac presenti carta mea confirmasse deo 7 beate Marie Linc' . 7 canonicis ibidem deo seruientibus nouem acras terre arabilis una perticata minus in territorio de Scitebroc[2] que iacent in Aicroft[3] uersus partem aquilonalem iuxta sedic . 7 dimidium holmi de salino . 7 totum sablunarium ad idem holmium[4] pertinens cum omnibus aisiamentis eiusdem uille in omnibus locis . Istam terram prenominatam dedi eis pro salute anime méé 7 patris mei 7 matris méé 7 antecessorum meorum in puram 7 perpetuam elemosinam . Et ut hec mea donatio in posterum rata 7 illibata permaneat ∴ sigilli mei munimine corrobaraui . Hiis testibus . Eudone capellano . Gileberto[5] Pilate[6] . Ricardo de Hardres . Alexandro del Bicht[7] . Adam Coldric . Johanne filio Yleberti . Willelmo de Karletun[8] . magistro Willelmo de Sumercot'[9] . Johanne filio Alani . Andrea filio Roberti . Radulfo filio Roberti . Hugone Cnotting[10] . Willelmo filio Dauid . Alano de[11] Hemming.[12]

Marginalia in A: Skidebrok ix acr' 7 j. pertic' (? by Q2).
Texts: MS—A. R1580.
Var. R.: [1] Wẏgoti R. [2] Skitbrok' R. [3] Haycroft R. [4] holmum R. [5] Gilberto R. [6] Pẏlat R. [7] Bict' R. [8] Karleton' R. [9] Somercotes R. [10] Knotting' R. [11] *sic*: filio R. [12] Hemmẏng R.
Note: For Eudo see vol. iv, p. 383 above. The next three witnesses all occur with William of Blois as precentor 1196–1203 (nos. 1357–8 in vol. iv, above). For William of Carlton see note to the preceding charter. The exact meaning of *sablunarium* in l. 8 and of *sablunatorium* (no. 1721, l. 7) is not clear. It may be sand in which case there is a parallel grant of a saltpan with sand in L.R.S., xviii, p. 106.

549

1720. Grant by Hugh son of Wigot son of Asger, to the church of Lincoln, of an acre and a perch in Skidbrook. (Circa 1200.)

Vniuersis sancte matris ecclesie filiis ad quos presens scriptum peruenerit . Hugo filius Wigoti[1] filii Asgeri de Scitebroc[2] salutem . Nouerit uniuersitas uestra me concessisse 7 dedisse 7 hac presenti carta mea confirmasse deo 7 beate Marie [3]Linc'[3] . 7 canonicis ibidem deo seruientibus unam acram terre arabilis 7 unam perticatam[4] in territorio de Scitebroc[5] que iacet in Aicroft uersus partem aquilonalem iuxta terram illam quam Rogerus frater meus dedit deo 7 beate Marie Linc' 7 canonicis ibidem deo seruientibus . Istam terram prenominatam dedi eis pro salute anime méé 7 patris mei 7 matris méé 7 omnium antecessorum meorum in puram 7 perpetuam elemosinam . Et ut hec mea donatio in posterum rata 7 illibata permaneat ∴ sigilli mei munimine corroboraui . Hiis testibus . Eudone capellano . Gileberto[6] Pilate[7] . Ricardo de Hardres . Adam Coldric . Roberto nepote Ade . Roberto de Mixebiri[8] . magistro Willelmo de Sumercotes[9] . Willelmo de Karlet*ona* . Johanne filio Alani . Andrea[10] filio Roberti.

Marginalia in A: Skidebrok j. acr' 7 .j. pertic' (? by Q2).
Texts: MS—A. R1581.
Var. R.: [1] Wẏgoti R. [2] Skitbroc R. [3–3] R *omits*. [4] percatam R. [5] Skitbrok' R. [6] Gilberto R. [7] Pẏlat R. [8] Mixebẏr' R. [9] Somercotes R. [10] Anr' R: d *has probably been accidentally omitted.*
Note: For the witnesses see the note to the preceding charter.

550

1721. Grant by Roger son of Wigot of Skidbrook, to the church of Lincoln and the Common, of seven and a half acres of land and half of a salt meadow with half of the sandy tract pertaining to that meadow. The canons may extend the meadow both to the east and the west. They shall be responsible for making the sea-dike. (Circa 1200.)

Notum sit tam presentibus quam futuris quod ego Rogerus filius Wigotis[1] de Schitebroc[2] dedi ⁊ concessi ⁊ hac presenti carta mea confirmaui deo ⁊ beate Marie ⁊ commune canonicorum Linc' ecclesie quandam terram in territorio de Schitebroc[2] videlicet .vii. acras [3]terre[3] ⁊ dimidiam in Aicroft[4] uersus aquilonem iuxta sedic . ⁊ dimidietatem[5] vnius holmi de salino . ⁊ dimidietatem sablunatorii ad idem holmum pertinentis quod fuit Wigotis[1] filii Askeri de Schitebroc[6] cum omnibus aisiamentis eiusdem ville in omnibus locis . ⁊ quantum predicti canonici poterunt dilatare predictum holmum * uersus orientem uel uersus occidentem ad utilitatem eorum facient ipsi sedic ;' prout competit predicto holmo . Hanc autem donationem feci eis in puram ⁊ perpetuam elemosinam pro animabus patris mei ⁊ matris méé ⁊ omnium antecessorum meorum necnon pro salute mea ⁊ heredum meorum . Et ego ⁊ heredes mei warantizabimus predictam terram predictis canonicis[7] contra omnes homines . Et ut ista donatio firma permaneat ;' hanc cartam sigilli mei appositione corroboraui . Hiis testibus . Willelmo de Karlet' . magistro Willelmo de Sumercotes[8] . Andrea fratre suo . Gileberto[9] clerico de Sumercotes[8] . Radulfo clerico . Alano filio Radulfi . Alano filio Hemming[10] . Willelmo filio Dauid . Alano fratre suo . Galfrido . Alano filio[11] Dauid.

Marginalia in A: Skydebrok' vij acr' ⁊ dim' (? by Q2).
Texts: MS—A. R1579.
Var. R.: [1] *sic*: Wẏgoti R. [2] Skitbrok' R. [3–3] R *omits*. [4] Haycroft R. [5] *sic*: medietatem R. [6] Skitbroc R. [7] R *adds* imperpetuum. [8] Somercotes R. [9] Gilberto R. [10] Hemmyng R. [11] filiis R.

* *Folio* 105.

Hdl. Ludhesk

. 1 . ϕ . 5 .

551

1722. Confirmation by Hugh son of Wigot Knotting of the preceding grant to which he adds the other half of the salt meadow. (Circa 1200.)

Sciant tam presentes quam futuri quod ego Hugo filius Wigoti[1] Chonoting[2] de Schitebroc[3] concessi ⁊ hoc scripto meo[4] confirmaui deo ⁊ beate Marie ⁊ commune canonicorum Linc' terram quam Rogerus frater meus predictis canonicis contulit in elemosinam . videlicet sex acras terre in Aicroft iuxta sedic . ⁊ dimidietatem unius salini . Et preterea dedi prefate commune aliam medietatem eiusdem salini in puram liberam ⁊ perpetuam elemosinam pro animabus antecessorum meorum . Et ut ista confirmatio ⁊ donatio rate imperpetuum[5] permaneant : hoc scriptum sigilli mei appositione[6] confirmaui . Hiis testibus . Hamelino decano . Brian filio Hamelini . Gileberto[7] clerico de Sumercot'[8] . Roberto filio Godrici . Gerardo filio Aldan . Radulfo filio Hernisii[9] . Gileberto[1] filio Johannis.

Marginalia in A: Skidebrok vj acr' terre (? by Q2).
Texts: MS—A. R1582.
Var. R: [1] Wygoti R. [2] Knottẏng' R. [3] Skitbrok' R. [4] meo scripto R. [5] in-posterum R. [6] appensione R. [7] Gilberto R. [8] Somercotes R. [9] Ernisii R.
Note: Hamelin the dean of Covenham witnesses frequently from the reign of Henry II to early thirteenth century. Brian son of Hamelin was the son of Hamelin the dean of Yarborough brother of the first witness (L.R.S. xviii, p. xvi).

552

1723. Quitclaim by Beatrice widow of Wigot Knotting, to the church of Lincoln and the Common, of six acres of land and a saltpan in Skidbrook, given to them by her sons. Roger her son has given her other land in exchange for this. (Circa 1200.)

Notum sit tam presentibus quam futuris quod ego Beatricia que fui vxor Wigoti[1] Chnotting[2] quietamclamaui deo ⁊ beate Marie ⁊ commune canonicorum Linc' ecclesie terram quam Rogerus filius meus ⁊ Hugo filius meus predictis canonicis contulerunt in elemosinam . videlicet sex acras terre in territorio de Scitebroc[3] . scilicet in Aicroft[4] iuxta sedic ⁊ unam sedem salini pro escambio quod predictus Rogerus michi fecit in eodem Aicroft[4] [5]proximo uersus Suthpart[5] . Et ut ista quietaclamatio imperpetuum permaneat : hoc scriptum sigillo meo confirmaui . Hiis testibus . Hamelino decano . Brian[6] filio Hamelini . Gileberto[7] clerico de Sumercot'[8] . Roberto filio Godrici . Gerardo filio Aldan . Radulfo filio Hernisii[9] . Gileberto[1] filio Johannis.

Marginalia in A: Skidebrok vi acr' terre (? by Q2).
Texts: MS—A. R1583.
Var. R.: [1] Wẏgoti R. [2] Knottẏng' R. [3] Skitbrok' R. [4] Qicroft' R. [5]–[5] R *omits*. [6] Briano. [7] Gilberto. [8] Somercotes R. [9] Ernisii R.

553

1724. Grant by Godric son of Alnad, to the church of Lincoln and the Common, of three acres of land in Skidbrook. (Circa 1200.)

Notum sit tam presentibus quam futuris quod ego Godricus

filius Alnad dedi [1]⁊[1] concessi ⁊ hac presenti carta mea confirmaui deo ⁊ beate Marie ⁊ commune canonicorum Linc' ecclesie tres acras terre in territorio de Scitebroc[2] que iacent inter terras ecclesie Linc' quas Dauid filius Osberti tenuit in puram liberam ⁊ perpetuam elemosinam pro animabus patris mei ⁊ matris méé ⁊ omnium antecessorum meorum necnon ⁊ pro salute mea ⁊ heredum meorum . Hanc autem terram ego ⁊ heredes mei[3] warantizabimus imperpetuum contra omnes homines . Et ut ista donatio firma ⁊ stabilis permaneat ∴ hanc cartam sigillo meo confirmaui . Hiis testibus . Gileberto[4] clerico . Wigote[5] filio Hosberti[6] . Roberto filio Gunnilde . Willelmo filio Ailsi . Galfrido Sureis . Andrea fratre magistri Willelmi de Sumercot'[7] . Galfrido filio Margarete.

Marginalia in A: Skidebrok iij acr' terre (? by Q2).
Texts: MS—A. R1577.
Var. R.: [1]–[1] R *omits.* [2] Skitbrok' R. [3] R *adds* eis. [4] Gilberto R. [5] Wẏgoto R. [6] Osberti R. [7] Somercotes R.

Folio 105d.

Hdl. Communa

This folio is blank except for the following note in the centre by Q.

Wapentach de Jordeburg'
Barton super Humbriam
Omnibus

ADD. CHART.

1725. Grant by Richard parson of Skidbrook, to the church of Lincoln and the Common, of a toft and a croft in Skidbrook. (Circa 1220–1230.)

Omnibus Christi fidelibus . Ricardus persona ecclesie de Scẏtebroc[1] salutem . Noueritis me dedisse concessisse . ⁊ hac presenti carta mea confirmasse . deo ⁊ beate Marie ⁊ commune canonicorum Lincoln' ecclesie . vnum thoftum[2] ⁊ croftum in villa de Scytebroc[1] . que jacent apud Dunes inter terram . Roberti le Norraẏs[3] . ⁊ terram . Roberti filii Clementis . [4]⁊[4] ex occidentali parte jacent inter terram prefati Roberti . ⁊ terram Thome Burre . Tenendum ⁊ habendum prefatis canonicis cum omnibus pertinenciis ⁊ libertatibus suis infra villam ⁊ extra in puram ⁊ perpetuam elemosinam liberam ⁊ quietam ab omni seruicio ⁊ exaccione seculari . Et ego ⁊ heredes mei adquietabimus defendemus ⁊ warantizabimus prefatis canonicis prefatum tenementum cum pertinenciis ⁊ libertatibus suis contra omnes homines inperpetuum . Et in huius rei robur ⁊ testimonium presens scriptum iuramento interueniente sigillo meo confirmaui . Hiis testibus . Waltero de Oxcumb' . Sẏmone[5] Knoting[6] . Ade[7] filio Galfridi . Roberto le Norraẏs[8] . Raẏngoto[9] . ⁊ aliis.

Endorsed : (1) Luthesce (13 cent.). (2) l.
Written on the fold—Hugo filius Galfridi (13 cent.).
Fragment of seal on tag ; green wax, probably round.
Size : $7\frac{3}{4}$ x $3\frac{1}{2}$ inches.
Texts : MS—Orig. Dij/87/1/3. R1567.
Var. R. : [1] Skitbrok' R. [2] toftum R. [3] Noreys R. [4]–[4] R *omits*. [5] Simone R. [6] Knotting R. [7] *sic* : Alano R. [8] Noreys R. [9] Reẏngoto R.
Note : William son of Robert quitclaimed to the Abbot of Torr (Devon) the fourth part of the advowson of Skidbrook 2nd June 1223 (*Final Concords* i, p. 164). When Roger of Skidbrook was instituted on the Abbot's presentation to the vicarage of Skidbrook 1223–4 (L.R.S. ix, p. 131) the rights of Richard the rector, who held a fourth part of the church, were expressly safeguarded during his lifetime (*ibid.*, p. 132). Robert le Noreys and Simon Knotting both occur in the next charter.

ADD. CHART.

1726. Grant by Thomas son of William of Skidbrook, to the church of Lincoln and the Common, of a toft and a croft containing four acres lying within the croft which was formerly of Hugh at the Hall. (Circa 1230–1240.)

Omnibus Christi fidelibus Thomas filius Willelmi de Schẏtebroc[1] salutem . Noueritis me dedisse concessisse ⁊ hac presenti carta mea confirmasse ∴ deo ⁊ beate Marie ⁊ commune canonicorum Lincoln[2] vnum toftum cum vno crofto in villa de Schẏtebroc[1] quod continet infra se quatuor acras terre ⁊ iacet infra croftum quod fuit Hugonis ad aulam uersus orientem ⁊ abutat super Utgange uersus austrum . ⁊ terram que fuit Radulfi filii Ernisii ∴ uersus aquilonem tenendum ⁊ habendum prefatis canonicis cum omnibus pertinenciis suis . libertatibus . ⁊ aisiamentis infra uillam ⁊ extra in puram ⁊ perpetuam elemosinam liberam ⁊ quietam ab omni seruicio ⁊ exaccione seculari . Et ego ⁊ heredes mei defendemus ⁊ warantizabimus prefatis canonicis . totum prefatum tenementum cum omnibus pertinenciis suis . libertatibus ⁊ aisiamentis ∴ contra omnes homines inperpetuum . Et in huius rei testimonium ∴ presens scriptum iuramento mediante ∴ sigillo meo confirmaui . Hiis testibus . Henrico sacrista . Roberto Scoto . Ricardo de Strettona . Adam de Altari . Roberto le Noraẏs[3] . Sẏmone Knothing'[4] . Thoma ad pontem . ⁊ aliis.

Endorsed : (1) Luthesce (13 cent.). (2) lj.
Fragment of seal on tag—round, $1\frac{3}{8}$ inches, green, eight petalled flower.
+ SIGILL' THOM . . . .
Size : $7\frac{1}{10}$ x $4\frac{4}{10}$ inches.
Texts : MS—Orig. Dij/87/1/6. R1568.
Var. R. : [1] Skitbrok' R. [2] R *adds* ecclesie. [3] Noreys R. [4] Knottẏng R.
Note : For Henry the sacrist see vol. iv, p. 281 above.

ADD. CHART.

1727. Grant by Robert le Norreis of Skidbrook, to the church of Lincoln and the Common, of land lying in Meles in Skidbrook. (Circa 1230–1240.)

Omnibus Christi fidelibus Robertus le Norraÿs[1] de Scÿtebroc[2] salutem . Noueritis me dedisse . concessisse 7 hac presenti carta mea confirmasse deo 7 beate Marie 7 commune canonicorum Linc' ecclesie quandam terram quam habui in territorio de Scÿtebroc[3] 7 jacet in loco qui dicitur Meles 7 extendit in longitudine a mari usque[4] Hanedÿk[5] inter terram Willelmi [6]Muther 7 terram Willelmi[6] ad ecclesiam tenendam 7 habendam dictis canonicis cum pertinenciis libertatibus . 7 aisiamentis suis infra villam 7 extra in puram 7 perpetuam elemosinam liberam 7 quietam ab omni seruicio 7 exactione seculari . 7 ego 7 heredes mei defendemus 7 warantizabimus prefatam terram cum pertinenciis libertatibus 7 aisiamentis ut puram 7 perpetuam elemosinam prefatis canonicis contra omnes homines inperpetuum 7 in huius rei testimonium .' presens scriptum juramento mediante .' sigillo meo confirmaui . Hiis testibus . Waltero de Oxcum'[7] . Roberto ad Dÿk' . Roberto filio Hugonis . Reÿngot[8] . [9]Ernisio Gelle[9] . Roberto Blah' . Simone Konthing[10] 7 aliis.

Endorsed : (1) xlix (13 cent.). (2) Skitebrok (13 cent.).
Seal on tag—round, $1\frac{1}{4}$ inches, green, fleur de lys.

+ S' RO . . . TI LE NORREIS

Size : $7\frac{3}{8}$ x $4\frac{1}{4}$ inches.
Texts : MS—Orig. Dij/87/1/16. R1566.
Var. R. : [1] Noreÿs R. [2] Skitbrok' R. [3] Skitbroc R. [4] R *adds* ad. [5] Hanedik' R. [6]–[6] R *omits*. [7] Oxcumbe R. [8] Reÿngoto R. [9]–[9] Ermÿgelle (*sic*) R. [10] Knottÿng R.

ADD. CHART.

1728. Grant by Ernis son of Ernis of Skidbrook, to the church of Lincoln and the Common, of a croft in Skidbrook. (Circa 1220–1230.)

Sciant presentes 7 futuri quod ego Ernisius filius Ernisii de Skitebroc'[1] diuine pietatis intuitu 7 pro salute anime mee 7 omnium antecessorum [2]7 successorum[2] meorum dedi 7 concessi 7 presenti carta mea confirmaui deo 7 beate Marie 7 commune canonicorum Linc' ecclesie .' vnum croftum in villa de Skitebroc'[1] . quod abutissat super regalem uiam ex una parte . 7 terram Willelmi fratris mei ex alia . 7 jacet inter terram prefati Willelmi 7 communem uiam eiusdem ville . Habendum 7 tenendum cum omnibus pertinenciis libertatibus 7 aisiamentis infra uillam 7 extra . in puram 7 perpetuam elemosinam . liberam . solutam . quietam ab omni [3]seculari seruicio[3] 7 exaccione . Et ego Ernisius 7 heredes mei warantizabimus prefatis canonicis croftum predictum cum pertinenciis defendemus 7 adquietabimus in omnibus contra omnes homines inperpetuum . In huius autem rei robur 7 testimonium presenti scripto sigillum meum apposui . Testibus . Odone Galle . [2]Petro Galle[2] . Radulfo filio Ernisii . [2]Ricardo filio Ernisii[2] . Willelmo Muterio . Alano filio Radulfi . Roberto fratre eius . Hugone Knotting'[4] . Roberto Norensi . Galfrido filio Margarete . 7 aliis.

Endorsed : (1) xliiij (13 cent.). (2) Skitebrok (13 cent.).
Written on the fold—Will' fil Ernisii de Skitebroc (13 cent.).
Seal on tag—round, 1⅝ inches, green, a sexfoil.
. . . ERN . . . .
Size : 6½ x 4½ inches.
Texts : MS—Orig. Dij/87/1/17. R1561.
Var. R. : [1] Skitbrok' R. [2–2] R *omits*. [3–3] servicio seculari R. [4] Knottẏng R.

ADD. CHART.

1729. Grant by Richard son of Ernis of Skidbrook, to the church of Lincoln and the Common, of a toft containing three acres, with his *Moldfang* and the seadike adjacent to it extending from the public road on the west of the seadike to the great creek on the North part of Saltcoteholm and an acre and a half of meadow. (Circa 1220–1230.)

Omnibus Christi fidelibus ad quos presens scriptum peruenerit .˙. Ricardus filius Ernisii de Scẏtebroc[1] salutem Noueritis me dedisse . concessisse 7 hac presenti carta mea confirmasse deo 7 commune canonicorum beate Marie Linc' vnum toftum in quo continentur tres acre terre in territorio de Scẏtebroc[1] . 7 jacet inter toftum quod fuit Osberti filii Willelmi 7 toftum Ernisii fratris mei cum meo moldfang' quod est inter moldfang' Radulfi fratris mei 7 moldfang' predicti Willelmi . cum Sedẏc[2] ei[3] adiacente quod extendit se in longitudine a publica via ex occidentali parte dicti Sedẏc[2] quod est uersus orientem usque ad magnum kryc ex aquilonali parte de Saltcoteholm' predicti Radulfi . 7 vnam acram prati ad[4] Cotestedes inter pratum quod fuit Andree 7 pratum Willelmi filii Ernisii 7 dimidiam acram prati super Daẏle inter pratum Roberti Bla 7 pratum Willelmi filii Ernisii 7 dimidiam acram[5] in Brictiuedaẏle[6] inter pratum quod fuit Willelmi filii Ernisii 7 Radulfi patris sui Tenend' 7 habend' dictis canonicis cum omnibus pertinenciis in liberam puram 7 perpetuam elemosinam liberam 7 quietam ab omni seruicio 7 exactione seculari . Et ego 7 heredes mei warantizabimus . defendemus . 7 adquietabimus dictum toftum cum prato 7 aliis supradictis cum pertinenciis dictis canonicis tamquam liberam puram 7 perpetuam elemosinam erga omnes homines in perpetuum . 7 in huius rei robur 7 testimonium . huic scripto sigillum meum apposui . Hiis testibus . Elẏ[7] succentore . magistro Willelmo de Hornecastr'[8] . Abraham . Philippo de Tumba capellanis . Ricardo de Laẏcestr'[9] . Roberto Scoto . Warino vicario . Odone Galle . Petro Galle . Waltero de Oxcume[10] . Roberto deldẏc[11] . Roberto filio Hawẏs' . Andrea fratre suo . 7 aliis.

Endorsed: (1) xliij (13 cent.). (2) Luthesce (13 cent.). (3) Skitebrok (13 cent.).

Tag for seal. Size: 8 x 4 inches.

Texts: MS—Orig. Dij/87/1/21—A. R1560.

Var. R.: [1] Skitbrok R. [2] Sedic R. [3] eidem R. [4] in R. [5] R *adds* prati. [6] Brictiuedale R. [7] *sic*: Elẏa R. [8] Horncastr' R. [9] Leyc' R. [10] Oxcumbe R. [11] del Dẏc R.

Note: For Elias the succentor see vol. iv, p. 280, above. The next five witnesses are found witnessing at various dates between 1220 and 1240 (nos. 1172–3, 1175, 1281–2, etc., in vol. iv, above). It is not easy to assign a definite date. Odo Galle occurs at various dates from late Henry II until the third decade of the thirteenth century. He levied a fine in 1226 (*Final Concords* i, p. 205). Peter Galle levied a fine in 1209 (*ibid.*, p. 85). He was in mercy " for a very great transgression " in 1219 (Selden Society, vol. viii, no. 793).

A *moldfang* is apparently an alternative word for sandpit or place where sand could be taken, *molde* being glossed as *sabulam* in the Anglo-Saxon period. (See Bosworth—Toller A.S. dictionary.) I am indebted to Professor Stenton for this interpretation.

ADD. CHART.

1730. Notification by Robert Norreis of Skidbrook that, with the consent of his heirs, he has given to Andrew son of Robert of Somercotes the land in Saltcoteholm in Skidbrook with a sandy tract which he bought from William son of Humphrey, and a yearly rent of sixteen pence in exchange for the land which Andrew had in the reed-bed on the south side of the house of Clement, Robert's brother, and for half an acre of land in Saltcroft. (Circa 1230–1240.)

Sciant presentes 7 futuri quod ego Robertus Noreẏs de Skitbroc consensu 7 consilio heredum meorum dedi in excambium Andree filio Roberti de Somercotes 7 heredibus suis vel cui assignare voluerit terram quam habui in Saltcoteholm quam acquisiui de Willelmo filio Vmfridi cum salunario ad eam pertinente iacentem inter terras ipsius Andree 7 sexdecim denarios singulis annis reddendos ad quatuor terminos videlicet ad Natale domini quatuor denarios ad Pascha quatuor denarios ad festum Sancti Bothulfi quatuor denarios ad festum Sancti Michaelis quatuor denarios pro terra quam idem Andreas habuit in junctario ex suth' parte domus Clementis fratris mei que iacet inter terram filiorum Ernisii filii Gille 7 terram filiorum Dauidis clerici ⁊ et pro dimidia acra in Saltecroft' iacente in capite terre mee versus North' . Et ego Robertus 7 heredes mei warantizabimus predictam terram datam in excambium predicto Andree (⁊ predictos sexdecim denarios ei annuatim reddendos pro terra prenominata quam michi dedit inperpetuum contra omnes homines . Hiis testibus . Radulfo filio Ernisii Willelmo Ricardo fratribus suis (Willelmo Noreẏs (Clemente fratre suo (Hugone Knottẏng' (Willelmo filio Willelmi de Somercotes (Andrea filio Johannis.

Text: MS—R1565.
Note: Robert Norreys occurs 1230–45 (see no. 1733, below). Ralf son of Ernis and his brothers occur frequently 1210–1240.

ADD. CHART.

1731. Grant by Roger, the dean, and the chapter of Lincoln to Hugh Knotting of Skidbrook of all the land which they had of the gift of Roger son of Wigot and of Alan son of David in Skidbrook. For this Hugh shall pay a yearly render of eighteenpence. (Before 1224: probably early thirteenth century.)

Omnibus Christi fidelibus ad quos presens scriptum peruenerit Rogerus decanus ⁊ capitulum Linc' ecclesie eternam in domino salutem . Nouerit vniuersitas vestra nos concessisse ⁊ presenti carta nostra confirmasse Hugoni Knottẏng' de Skitbrok'[1] quas habemus ex dono Rogeri filii Wẏgoti de eadem villa scilicet vnum clausum in quo continentur sex acre inter viam que ducit ad ecclesiam ex vna parte ⁊ Waterlade ex alia ⁊ duas acras in Brothercroft' propinquiores terre Willelmi persone versus occidentem . Et preterea quinque acras quas habemus ex dono Alani filii Dauid in territorio eiusdem ville (videlicet tres acras ⁊ dimidiam in Wlfhou ⁊ acram ⁊ dimidiam in Haicoluecroft' . Habend' ⁊ tenend' de nobis sibi ⁊ heredibus suis in feodo ⁊ hereditate libere ⁊ quiete . Reddendo inde nobis annuatim decem ⁊ octo denarios pro omni seruicio ⁊ exactione scilicet nouem denarios ad Pascha ⁊ nouem denarios ad festum Sancti Michaelis . Vt autem hec nostra concessio perpetuam obtineat firmitatem .' eam presenti scripto et sigilli nostri apposicione corroborauimus.

Text: MS—R1570.
Var. R.: [1] terras *seems to have been omitted here.*
Note: It seems probable that the dean is Roger de Rolveston as he mentions William the parson. In 1223–4 Richard was parson (see note to 1725, above), while William occurs as joint parson with Walter circa 1200 (see nos. 1702, 1710, above). For the gift of Roger son of Wigot see no. 1702 above and for the gift of Alan son of David see no. 1713 above.

ADD. CHART.

1732. Grant by Hugh son of Gilbert of Skidbrook, to the church of Lincoln and the Common, of three acres of land in Skidbrook. (Circa 1230–1245.)

Omnibus Christi fidelibus Hugo filius Gilberti de Skitbrok' salutem . Noueritis me dedisse ʻ concessisse ⁊ hac presenti carta mea confirmasse deo ⁊ beate Marie ⁊ commune canonicorum Linc' tres acras terre arabilis in territorio de Skitbrok' ʻ quarum due acre iacent inter terram Simonis Knottẏng' ⁊ terram que fuit Walteri Eudonis[1] ʻ ⁊ abuttant super regiam stratam versus occidentem ʻ tercia autem acra iacet infra Tolecostis[2] inter terram que fuit Radulfi filii Ernisii ⁊ terram Willelmi fratris sui Tenend*as* ⁊ habend*as* prefatis canonicis cum omnibus pertinenciis suis libertatibus ⁊ aisiamentis infra villam ⁊ extra in puram ⁊ perpetuam elemosinam liberam ⁊ quietam ab omni seruicio ⁊ exactione seculari . Et ego ⁊ heredes mei defendemus ⁊ warantizabimus predictis canonicis prefatum tenementum cum pertinenciis suis libertatibus ⁊ aisiamentis contra omnes homines inperpetuum . Et in huius rei robur ⁊ testimonium presens scriptum scriptum[2] iuramento interueniente sigillo meo confirmaui . Hiis testibus Elẏa succentore Henrico sacrista Linc' Willelmo capellano custode maioris altaris Roberto le Noreẏs :' Simone Knottẏng' Akardo clerico ⁊ aliis.

Text: MS—R1584.
Var. R.: [1] *sic*: filio *presumably omitted.* [2] *sic.*
Note: For the dates of Elias as succentor and Henry as sacrist see vol. iv, pp. 280–1, above.

ADD. CHART.

1733. Acknowledgment by William son of Hugh at the Hall, that he is bound to pay to the dean and chapter of Lincoln twelvepence a year for a toft and a croft containing four acres which he holds of them in Skidbrook. He may not sell or in any way alienate them without the consent of the dean and chapter. (Circa 1230–1240.)

Omnibus Christi fidelibus Willelmus filius Hugonis ad aulam salutem . Noueritis me teneri decano ⁊ capitulo Linc' ecclesie per annum in duodecim denariis ʻ scilicet sex denariis ad Pascha ⁊ sex denariis ad festum Sancti Michaelis pro quodam tofto ⁊ crofto quod teneo de illis in villa de Skitbrok' que continent in se quatuor acras terre ⁊ iacent infra croftum quod fuit Hugonis ad aulam versus orientem ʻ Et sciendum quod non licebit michi vel heredibus meis dare vel assignare vendere vel aliquo modo alienare dictum tenementum sine licencia decani ⁊ capituli . Et in huius rei testimonium presens scriptum ʻ iuramento mediante sigillo meo confirmaui . Hiis testibus ʻ Henrico sacrista Ricardo de Strettona clerico Roberto le Noreẏs ⁊ aliis.

Text: MS—R1588.
Note: For Henry the sacrist see vol. iv, p. 281, above.

ADD. CHART.

1734. Grant by R[oger] the dean and the chapter of Lincoln, to Hugh son of Edric of Skidbrook, of nine acres of land and meadow in Skidbrook and Somercotes for a yearly render of twelvepence. (Before 1224: probably early thirteenth century.)

Omnibus sancte matris ecclesie filiis ad quos presens scriptum pervenerit .R. decanus ⁊ capitulum Linc' ecclesie salutem . Noverit universitas vestra nos concessisse ⁊ hac presenti carta nostra confirmasse Hugoni filio Edric de Skitbrok ⁊ heredibus suis .ix. acras terre quarum .v. acras habemus in Skitbrok duas scilicet inter terram Roberti filii Gunnild ⁊ terram que fuit Gilberti filii Ailrici ⁊ tres acras inter Ailcroft ⁊ terram Roberti filii Gunnild ⁊ unam acram prati in prato de Somercotes scilicet dimidiam acram inter pratum Willelmi Muter ⁊ Rokelundaile ⁊ dimidiam acram inter pratum sacerdotis de Lekeburne quod vocatur Lekeburnedaile ⁊ pratum Hugonis filii Askeri quas habemus ex dono Willelmi filii Geve de Somercotes ⁊ tres acras terre in Skitbrook' que iacent inter terras Roberti filii Gunnild ⁊ terras que fuerunt Gilberti filii Eilric videlicet due acre in Escroft ⁊ una dimidia acra in Metheldailes ⁊ una dimidia acra in tofto ipsius Hugonis quas habemus de dono Ricardi de Parco militis . Tenend' de nobis in feudo ⁊ hereditate libere ⁊ quiete reddendo inde nobis annuatim .xii. denarios ad festum sancti Michaelis pro omni servicio ad terram pertinente . Et ut hec nostra concessio rata ⁊ illibata permaneat eam sigilli nostri apposicione corroboravimus.

Text: MS—R1591.

Note: The grantor is probably Roger de Rolveston, who died in 1223. William son of Geva and Richard of the Park made grants before 1205 (see nos. 1698 and 1699, above).

ADD. CHART.

1735. Grant by the chapter of Lincoln, to Gilbert son of Hemming, of the land [in Skidbrook] which they had of the gift of Boniva daughter of Basing of Bleichmare, for a yearly render of twelve pence. (Late twelfth century.)

Vniuersis sancte matris ecclesie filiis ad quos presens scriptum peruenerit capitulum Lincoln' ecclesie salutem . Nouerit vniuersitas vestra nos dedisse ⁊ concessisse ⁊ presenti carta nostra confirmasse Gilberto filio Hemmÿng' vnam acram terre ⁊ dimidiam illas scilicet quas Boniua filia Basing' de Bleichemer' nobis dedit vnam scilicet acram terre que iacet in Wlfhou ⁊ dimidiam acram terre que iacet in Lefsicroft' versus West illi 7 heredibus suis Tenend' de nobis libere 7 quiete . Reddendo inde annuatim ad Pentecosten duodecim denarios pro omni seruicio.

Text: MS—R1593.
Note: For the date and other comments see no. 1700, above.

ELKINGTON AND DUNSTHORPE IN ELKINGTON

ADD. CHART.

1736. Grant by William son of Philip of Kyme, to the church of Lincoln, of a toft with its buildings and a croft in Dunsthorpe and a bovate of land in Elkington free of all secular service and suit of court. (1248–1258.)

Omnibus Christi fidelibus ad quos presens scriptum peruenerit . Willelmus filius Philippi de Kÿma salutem eternam in domino Nouerit vniuersitas vestra me dedisse . concessisse 7 hac presenti carta mea confirmasse pro salute anime mee 7 antecessorum meorum deo 7 beate Marie 7 ecclesie Lincolniensi 7 canonicis ibidem [1]deo[1] seruientibus in liberam puram 7 perpetuam elemosinam vnum toftum cum edificiis 7 vnum croftum cum pertinenciis in Dunstorp iacencia inter viam ex west parte 7 terram quam Henricus del Grene ex est parte quamdam[2] tenuit cum tota longitudine 7 latitudine latitudine[3] sua 7 vnam bouatam terre arabilis interritorio de Aukingtona cum omnibus pertinenciis . aisiamentis . 7 libertatibus suis infra villam 7 extra . sicut aliqua terra liberius 7 securius in puram 7 perpetuam[4] dari potest 7 concedi . videlicet illud toftum 7 croftum 7 illam bouatam terre cum omnibus pertinentiis suis que Ketel[5] Wÿther quondam tenuit . Tenendum 7 habendum deo 7 beate Marie 7 ecclesie Lincolniensi 7 prefatis canonicis . libere . quiete . 7 pacifice . in liberam . puram 7 perpetuam elemosinam quietam 7 solutam ab omni seculari seruicio . consuetudine et demanda 7 ab omnimodis curiarum sectis . Et ego predictus Willelmus de Kÿma[6] 7 heredes . mei deo 7 beate Marie 7 ecclesie Lincolniensi 7 prefatis canonicis predictum toftum [1]cum edificiis[1] 7 croftum 7 prefatam terram cum pertinenciis contra omnes homines . warantizabimus . defendemus . 7 adquietabimus in perpetuum . Et in huius rei testimonium 7 securitatem huic scripto, sigillum meum apposui . Hiis testibus . domino Ada del Yle . domino Roberto de Aukÿngton' . domino Ricardo de Alazun militibus . Willelmo de Ottebÿ[7] . Henrico de Witkale[8] . Waltero de Wÿckale[8] . Waltero Says de Luda . Petro filio Osberti de Wÿtkale[8] . Willelmo filio Abraham de Aukÿngton' . Henrico vicario de Appeleÿ[9] 7 aliis.

Endorsed: (1) Dunstorp (14 cent.). (2) Horncaster (13 cent.).
Seal on tag—broken, cream, pointed shield charged with a chevron.
Size: 8 x 6½ inches.
Texts: MS—Orig. Dij/69/2/41. R1647.
Var. R.: [1]–[1] R *omits*. [2] *sic*: quondam R. [3] *sic*: R *omits the repetition*. [4] *sic*: R *adds* elemosinam. [5] Kotel R. [6] Kima R. [7] Cateby R. [8] Withcale R. [9] Appelby R.

Note: For the Kyme family see *H. and K.F.* ii, pp. 118–127. In 1242 Simon of Kyme held a seventh part of a knight's fee of the old feoffment of Richard de Percy in Elkington (*Book of Fees* ii, p. 1054). William, Simon's brother, succeeded him in 1248 (*H. and K.F.* ii, p. 124). It is probable that the charter falls between this date and 1258, as Richard of Gravesend, who ceased to be dean in that year, granted William's gift on lease to Martin of Dunsthorpe. The dates of the institution and death or resignation of Henry vicar of Apley are not known.

Dunsthorpe was a hamlet in South Elkington, which has lost its separate status. It is almost certainly to be identified with Thorpe or Elkington Thorpe, a group of houses which lies to the east of the village of South Elkington (L.R.S. xix, p. lv).

ADD. CHART.

1737. Grant by Richard, the dean, and the chapter of Lincoln, to Martin of Dunsthorpe, of the toft with its buildings and the croft in Dunsthorpe, which they had of the gift of the lord William of Kyme. (1254–1258.)

Omnibus Christi fidelibus ad quos presens scriptum peruenerit Ricardus decanus 7 capitulum Linc' ecclesie salutem in domino . Nouerit vniuersitas vestra nos concessisse 7 hac presenti carta nostra confirmasse Martino de Dunstorp vnum toftum cum edificiis 7 vnum croftum cum pertinenciis in Donstorp' 7 vnam bouatam terre arabilis in territorio de Elkington cum pertinenciis videlicet illud toftum 7 croftum 7 illam bouatam terre que Ketel Wÿther quondam tenuit que etiam habemus de dono domini Willelmi de Kÿma in liberam puram 7 perpetuam elemosinam Tenendum 7 habendum dicto Martino 7 heredibus suis libere quiete 7 pacifice 7 hereditarie Reddendo inde nobis annuatim .xij. denarios ad duos terminos anni scilicet ad festum sancti Michaelis sex denarios 7 ad Pascha sex denarios pro omni seculari seruicio consuetudine exaccione 7 demanda . In cuius rei testimonium presenti scripto sigillum capituli nostri fecimus apponi.

Text: MS—R1648.
Note: The dates are those of Richard Gravesend as dean of Lincoln.

ADD. CHART.

1738. Grant by Philip, the dean, and the chapter of Lincoln, to William son of Walter of South Elkington, that he may hold of them the land which he had bought of William son of Thomas of Dunsthorpe their former tenant. He shall pay a yearly render of two pence and perform the other services due from the land. 21st September, 1289.

Nouerint vniuersi quod nos Philippus decanus 7 capitulum Linc' ecclesie concessimus Willelmo filio W[alteri[1]] de Suth Elkington[2] quod idem Willelmus 7 heredes sui libere possint tenere de nobis 7 successoribus nostris inperpetuum decem acras terre cum pertinenciis quas emit[3] de Willelmo filio Thome de Dunstorp quondam tenente nostro . sicut predictus Willelmus filius Thome eas de nobis tenuit . Reddendo nobis inde annuatim duos denarios ad duos anni terminos videlicet in festo Omnium Sanctorum vnum denarium 7 ad Pentecosten vnum denarium faciendo nichilominus omnia alia seruicia que predicta terra nobis 7 aliis quibuscumque debuit 7 facere consueuit . In cuius rei testimonium huic scripto cirographato[4] sigillum nostri capituli 7 sigillum predicti Willelmi mutuo sunt appensa Datum Linc' die sancti Mathei apostoli 7 ewangeliste anno domini . M° . CC° . Lxxx° . nono . Hiis testibus Alexandro Percẏ de North Elkington[5] Willelmo filio Johannis de eadem Johanne Abraham de Suth Elkington[2] Willelmo filio Radulphi de eadem Iuone dicto Chapelaẏn de eadem et aliis.

Endorsed: (1) ij (13 cent.). (2) Ludhesk (query by Q). (3) Transcriptum carte capituli in Suthelkington (query by Q).

Slit for seal tag. Size: 7 x 5¼ inches.

Texts: MS—Orig. Dij/69/3/20. R1649.

Var. R.: [1] *supplied from* R; *there is a stain on the charter.* [2] Suthelkington R. [3] tenuit R. [4] cirograffato R. [5] Northelkington R.

LOUTH

Add. Chart.

1739. Quitclaim by Geoffrey of Louth, clerk, to Robert Grosseteste bishop of Lincoln, of all his grove between the water-course of the spring of St. Helen and the water course of Asewell spring: excepting the ground which Adam son of Jordan holds for a silver halfpenny a year and the dower of Alice widow of Jordan the dyer during her lifetime. Geoffrey also quitclaims a piece of land four feet in width on the west part of the toft which was of Gilbert the dyer extending along the fullers road to the watercourse of Asewell to the south. For this quitclaim the bishop has given him a mark in *gersuma.* (1235–1253.)

Sciant presentes 7 futuri quod ego Galfridus de Lud*a* clericus dedi 7 concessi 7 quietum clamaui domino Roberto Grosseteste episcopo Linc' 7 ecclesie sue Linc' 7 successoribus suis ∴ totum lundum meum quod habui de donacione Walteri filii Roberti in uilla Lud' de feodo Ranulfi Schadiwaẏ inter cursum aque fontis sancte Elene .' ⁊ cursum aque fontis de Asewell' . preter chiminum monacorum de Parco . Excepta parte illa terre eiusdem lundi .' quam Adam filius Jordani tenet pro uno obulo argenti per annum ad Natale domini renddendo' predicto domino episcopo ⁊ successoribus suis . Et excepta dote Alicie quondam uxoris Jordani tinctoris tantum in uita sua . que post decessum illius predicto episcopo ⁊ successoribus suis in perpetuum remanebit . Concessi etiam ⁊ quietum clamaui predicto domino episcopo Linc' ⁊ successoribus suis mensuram quatuor pedum terre in latitudine ex West parte tofti quod fuit Gilberti tinctoris cum omnibus pertinenciis suis . ⁊ extendit se in longitudine a uia fullonum .' usque ad cursum aque de Asewell' uersus Sudh . Habend' ⁊ tenend' predicto domino episcopo ⁊ ecclesie sue Linc' ⁊ successoribus suis . libere . quiete . in feodo . ⁊ hereditate . Reddendo inde annuatim michi ⁊ heredibus meis unum obulum argenti ad Natale domini pro omnibus seruiciis ⁊ demandis . Et ego Galfridus ⁊ heredes mei gwarantizabimus predicto domino episcopo ⁊ ecclesie sue Linc' ⁊ successoribus suis .' predictum lundum ⁊ mensuram quatuor pedum terre . ⁊ predictum obulum de redditu pro predicto seruicio . sicut prenominatum est .' contra omnes homines in perpetuum . Pro hac autem donacione . concessione . ⁊ quieta clamantia dedit michi dominus episcopus unam marcam in geresumam . Et ut hec mea donatio ⁊ concessio ratam ⁊ perpetuam optineat stabilitatem . eam sigilli mei munimine roboraui . Hiis testibus . Johanne de mercato . Thoma Malherb . Rogero Malherb . Ricardo clerico . Willelmo filio Thome . Ricardo filio Walteri . Petro de Aluingham . Rogero Ducti ⁊ aliis.

Endorsed: (1) Luda (13 cent.). (2) .iij. (13 cent.). (3) Carta Galfridi clerici de Lud' (13 cent.).

Seal on tag—round, 1 inch, cream, conventional device.

+ **SIGILL' GALFR'**

Size: 7 x 4 inches.

Text: MS—Orig. Dij/83/1/3.

Var. R.: .I. *sic.*

Note: Grosseteste was bishop 1235–1253. The *lund* is probably a grove from Scandinavian *lundr*, a sacred wood.

ADD. CHART.

1740. Quitclaim by John son of Christian of Louth, to Robert [Grosseteste], bishop of Lincoln, of the messuage in Louth which he had of the gift of Christian his father. (1245.)

Omnibus sancte matris ecclesie filiis . has litteras uisuris . uel audituris .' Johannes filius Christiani de Luda .' salutem eternam in domino . Nouerit uniuersitas uestra me reddidisse . ⁊ quietum clamasse . domino . Roberto . dei gracia Lincoln' episcopo 7 successoribus suis . 7 ecclesie sue Lincoln' inperpetuum . totum mesuagium illud . cum omnibus pertinentiis suis . quod habui de dono Christiani patris mei in uilla de Luda . quod quidem mesuagium .' iacet inter terram que fuit Vmfridi Wÿther ex vna parte 7 terram que fuit Gileberti Gille ex altera . Tenend' 7 habend' predicto episcopo . 7 successoribus suis . 7 ecclesie sue predicte . solutum . 7 quietum . de me . 7 de heredibus meis . in liberam puram . 7 perpetuam elemosinam .' inperpetuum . In cuius rei testimonium .' huic scripto sigillum meum apposui . Hiis testibus . dominis Willelmo de Cursun tunc vicecomite Linc' . Henrico de Lekeburn' . Willelmo de Engelby . militibus . Galfrido de Swaleweclíu' . Stephano de Grafham . Johanne de Cateby . Petro de Wÿhum . Johanne de Oxecumbe . Rogero Mene . Galfrido de Huchendon' . tunc balliuo de Luda . 7 aliis.

Endorsed: (1) Carta Johannis filii Christiani de Lud' (13 cent.). (2) xix (13 cent.). (3) Luda (13 cent.).
Fragment of seal on tag, green, probably round, conventional device.

. . . NS FIL'IH . . .

Size: 5¾ x 2½ inches.
Text: MS—Orig. Dij/83/1/5.
Note: William de Curzon was sheriff in 1245 (*Lincs. N and Q*, xxiv, p. 7).

ADD. CHART.

1741. Agreement between Robert [Grosseteste], bishop of Lincoln, and Thomas Barfoth of Louth and Alice his wife, by which they gave the bishop fourteen selions containing five acres of land in the fields of Louth, in exchange for eighteen selions containing five acres also in the fields of Louth. (1235–1253.)

Indented

CYROGRAPHVM

Noscant vniuersi presens scriptum visuri uel audituri quod hec est conuencio facta inter dominum Robertum dei [gratia] Lincoln' episcopum ex vna parte .' 7 Thomam Barfoth de Luda 7 Aliciam vxorem eius ex altera . videlicet quod predicti Thomas 7 Alicia concesserunt . remiserunt . 7 quietas clamauerunt de se 7 heredibus suis in perpetuum .' predicto domino episcopo 7 successoribus suis . ecclesieque sue Lincoln' quatuordecim selliones terre cum pertinenciis in campis Lude continentes in se quinque acras . scilicet tres selliones jacentes uersus bercariam dicti domini . episcopi abuttantes super cornerium gardini . Item duos selliones abuttantes super warderobam eiusdem domini . Item tres selliones abuttantes super portam eiusdem . Item tres selliones uersus Folmethorp' jacentes inter culturas eiusdem domini . 7 tres selliones in quarentena ex orientali parte uie de

Grimmesb' uersus Twagrend' . Habend' ⁊ tenend' predicto domino episcopo . ⁊ successoribus suis . ecclesieque sue Linc' in liberam . puram . ⁊ perpetuam elemosinam . Quas eciam quinque acras terre cum pertinenciis .' dicti Thomas ⁊ Alicia ⁊ heredes ipsius Alicie prefato domino episcopo . ⁊ successoribus suis . ⁊ ecclesie sue Linc' tanquam puram ⁊ perpetuam elemosinam contra omnes gentes warantizabunt in perpetuum . Pro hac autem concessione . remissione . quietaclamancia . ⁊ warantizacione .' predictus dominus episcopus dedit ⁊ concessit predictis Thome ⁊ Alicie in escambium .' octodecim selliones jacentes in quarentena jam dicta uersus Twagrend' continentes in se quinque acras . Habend' ⁊ tenend' predictis Thome ⁊ Alicie ⁊ heredibus eiusdem Alicie de predicto domino episcopo ⁊ successoribus suis ⁊ ecclesia sua Linc' jure hereditario in perpetuum .' faciendo ei ⁊ successoribus suis pro dicta terra ⁊ pro altera terra quam prius tenuerunt .' seruicium quantum facere consueuerunt . Quas etiam quinque acras terre dictus dominus episcopus ⁊ successores sui predictis Thome . ⁊ Alicie ⁊ heredibus ipsius Alicie contra omnes gentes warantizabunt . Et ut hec conuencio rata . stabilis . ⁊ inconcussa semper permaneat .' huic scripto modo cyrographi confecto .' sigilla parcium mutuo sunt apposita . Hiis testibus . dominis Roberto de Welle . Radulpho de Normanneb' . Gilberto de Coniesholm' . Johanne de Somerchoth' . ⁊ Ranulpho de Brakinberewe militibus . Geruasio de Thorp' . Johanne de Kokerinton' . Johanne filio Ade de Luda . Willelmo filio Thome . Ricardo clerico . Johanne filio Thome . Jordano clerico . Thoma Duthy de eadem .' ⁊ aliis.

Endorsed: (1) Cyrographum de escambio terre apud Lud' (13 cent.).
Two tags for seals. Size: 6¼ x 5¾ inches.
Text: MS—Orig. Dij/83/1/7.
Note: The dates given are those of Robert Grosseteste as bishop. Rannulf of Brackenborough and Robert de Well held land in 1242–3 (*Book of Fees* ii, pp. 1053, 1058). Gervase of Thorp and John of Cockerington were jurors for the wapentake of Louthesk in that year (*ibid.*, p. 1053). The latter was sheriff in 1257 (*Lincs. N. and Q*, xxiv, p. 7).

ADD. CHART.

1742. Quitclaim by Roger de Somerby [? Somersby in Hill wapentake], to Richard [Gravesend] bishop of Lincoln, of all his right and claim in the lands and tenements of Thomas Gosepol his kinsman in Louth. (20th April, 1270–18th December, 1279.)

Omnibus Christi fidelibus ad quos presens scriptum peruenerit Rogerus de Sumerby manens in Teffordia salutem in domino . Noueritis me remisisse ⁊ quietum clamasse pro me ⁊ heredibus meis Ricardo dei gratia Lincoln' episcopo

7 successoribus suis inperpetuum totum ius 7 clamium meum quod habui uel quocunque modo habere potui in omnibus terris 7 tenementis que quondam fuerunt Thome de Gosepol consanguinei mei in Luda . Ita quod nec ego nec heredes mei nec aliquis nomine nostro in predictis terris 7 tenementis aliquid iuris uel clamii de cetero exigere poterimus uel vendicare Et si contingat dictum episcopum uel successores suos de dictis terris 7 [tene[1]]mentis per aliquos quocumque modo inplacitari . ego Rogerus 7 heredes mei predicto episcopo 7 successoribus suis terras 7 tenementa predicta contra omnes homines 7 feminas warantizabimus inperpetuum . In cuius rei testimonium huic scripto sigillum meum apposui . Hiis testibus . dominis Johanne de Wydington' 7 Waltero de Kersinton' canonicis Lincoln' . Willelmo filio Johannis de Luda . Symone de Aluingeham de eadem . Roberto Sturmy de eadem . Ricardo Weltecart de eadem . Thoma de Ouneby . 7 aliis.

Endorsed: (1) Luda (13 cent.). (2) .vj. (13 cent.).
Tag for seal. Size: 7½ x 4⅛ inches.
Text: MS—Orig. Dij/85/1/2.
Var. R.: [1] *supplied conjecturally*: *there is a hole in the charter.*
Note: John de Wydington and Walter of Carsington witness a charter together in April, 1270 (L.R.S., xx, p. 262): the former is described as a canon, but the latter is not. This quitclaim is therefore probably later than 1270, but must be earlier than 18th December, 1279, when Gravesend died.

ADD. CHART.

1743. Quitclaim by Roger de Somerby [? Somersby in Hill wapentake], dwelling in Tetford, to Richard [Gravesend] bishop of Lincoln, of his right and claim in the lands and tenements formerly of Thomas de Gosepol, his kinsman, in Louth. (20th April, 1270–18th December, 1279.)

Omnibus Christi fidelibus ad quos presens scriptum peruenerit ∴ Rogerus de Sumerby manens in Tefford salutem in domino . Noueritis me remisisse 7 quietum clamasse pro me 7 heredibus meis Ricardo dei gratia Linc' episcopo 7 successoribus suis inperpetuum totum ius 7 clamium meum quod habui uel quocunque modo habere potui in omnibus terris 7 tenementis que quondam fuerunt Thome de Gosepol consanguinei mei in Luda . Ita quod nec ego nec heredes mei nec aliquis nostro nomine in predictis terris 7 tenementis aliquid iuris uel clamii decetero exigere poterimus uel vendicare . In cuius rei testimonium huic presenti scripto sigillum meum apposui . Hiis testibus dominis Johanne de Wydington' 7 Waltero de Kersinton' canonicis Linc' . Willelmo filio Johannis de Luda . Symone de Aluingeham de eadem .

Roberto Sturmy de eadem . Ricardo Weltecart de eadem . Thoma de Ouneby . et aliis.

Endorsed : (1) Luda (13 cent.). (2) .vj. (13 cent.). (3) vij (13 cent.).
Fragment of seal on tag.
Size : 7⅜ x 4¼ inches.
Text : MS—Orig. Dij/83/1/4.

ADD. CHART.

1744. Grant by Alfred of Horncastle, to Henry of Lincoln, of land with buildings in Louth to be held of the lord bishop in free burgage for a yearly rent of twopence. (Henry III.)

Sciant presentes 7 futuri quod ego Aufredus de Hornecaster mane[ns] . . . . [con]silio 7 assensu S . . . . carta mea confirmaui Henrico de Lincolnia 7 heredibus suis uel cui [7 qua]ndo assignare voluer[it] . . . . ibus insuper fundatis 7 cum omnibus pertinenciis suis 7 eysiamentis . jacentem Ex . . . . quondam . Radulfi de Elkynton ex West parte . 7 terram que f[uit q]uondam Radulfi . . . . duarum perticarum . 7 in longitudine tenet in se mensuram [qua]tuor perticar[um] . . . . [H]enricus michi dedit premanibus in negociis meis . Habend' 7 tenend' . sibi . 7 heredibus suis in libero burgagio de [domino] episcopo . . . . . . Reddendo inde annuatim domino episcopo Lincol' 7 successoribus suis duos denarios argenti ad quatuor anni termi[nos unum obolum ad Nat]ale domini vnum obulum ad Pa[sc]ha . vnum . obulum . ad festum sancti Botulfi vnum obulum ad festum sancti Michaelis . . . . filio Petri Haldan 7 heredibus suis sexdecim denarios argenti ad quatuor anni terminos prescriptos . . . . [qua]tuor denarios pro omnibus terrenis consuetudinibus 7 demandis . Et ego Aufredus cum predicto consi[lio] . . . . meorum gwarantizabimus defendemus 7 de omnibus acquietabimus predictam partem terre cum . . . . pertinenciis suis cum tota latitudine 7 longitudine quam in se tenet predicto Henrico 7 heredibus suis . . . . Pro predicto seruicio faciente . sicut prenominatum est contra omnes homines in perpetuum . Hiis [testibus] . . . . filio Thome . Willelmo filio Johannis . Johanne filio Thome . Herberto filio Johannis . Ricardo filio Walteri Jordano clerico . Radulfo . . . .

Endorsed : (1) Luda (late 13 cent.). (2) .xj. (late 13 cent.). (3) .xxx (late 13 cent.).

Tag for seal. Size: circa 7 x $3\frac{3}{4}$ inches.
Text: MS—Orig. Dij/83/1/12.
Note: John son of Thomas and Jordan the clerk both witness no. 1746 below which is *temp.* Grosseteste.

ADD. CHART.

1745. Agreement between master John of Lindsey, canon of Lincoln and rector of the prebendal church of Louth, and William, the abbot, and the convent of Tupholme, by which it was provided that the abbey should pay three shillings yearly to the rector in respect of the tithe of the young of animals in the grange of Felmethorpe, to which both the parties had laid claim. (Pentecost, 1273.)

Indented

CIROGRAPHVM

Memorandum quod exorta quouis materia inter magistrum Johannem de Lyndes' canonicum Linc' ecclesie rectorem ecclesie prebendalis de Luda ex parte vna 7 religiosum virum fratrem Willelmum de . . . .[1] permissione diuina abbatem de Tupholm' 7 eiusdem loci conuentum ex altera super iure 7 possessione percipiendi decimas de nutrimentis animalium de grangia de Folmethorp' infra limites parochie eiusdem prebendalis ecclesie sita .ʻ ac ex parte predictorum abbatis 7 conuentus fuisset in medio exhibitum transcriptum priuilegii in quo continebatur quod nemo ab eis huiusmodi decimas exigere uel extorquere auderet propos[itum est[1]] a parte aduersa illud priuilegium non valere eo quod contra idem priuilegium venientes de predictis decimis satisfecerunt . vnde amicabili con[uencione . . . . .[1] i]nter eos conuenit quod predicti abbas 7 conuentus soluent predicto rectori . suis temporibus singulis annis pro bono pacis 7 la . . . . . .[1] evitandis tres solidos . argenti ad festum apostolorum Philippi 7 Jacobẏ . Ita etiam quod nec iidem abbas 7 conuentus animalibus ibidem . . .[1] existentibus minus soluere nec predictus rector amplius suis temporibus aliqua occasione possit exigere . predicta conuencione post tempora eiusdem rectoris nemini preiudicante . Et si in solucione predicte pecunie dicti abbas 7 conuentus aliquo termino cessauerint . liceat prefato rectori uel eius vices gerenti ipsos ad plenariam eiusdem pecunie solucionem per censuram ecclesiasticam compellere . In cuius rei testoimonium huic scripto bipartito partes alternatim sigilla sua apposuerunt . Actum ad festum Pentecosten anno domino . M° . CC° . lxx° tercio.

Endorsed: .ij. scripta tangentia prebende de Buggeden' 7 de Luda (query by Q2).
Tag for seal. Size: $7\frac{3}{4}$ x $4\frac{7}{8}$ inches.
Var. R.: [1] *There are two holes in the charter.*
Text: MS—Orig. Dij/83/1/21.
Note: The grange of Folmethorpe or Fanthorpe is now represented by Fanthorpe Lawn and certain cottages near the boundary of South Elkington. (See L.R.S. xix, p. lv.)

COCKERINGTON

ADD. CHART.

1746. Grant by Roger Malherbe of Louth, to Robert [Grosseteste], bishop of Lincoln, of eight acres of meadow in Cockerington. (1235–1253.)

Omnibus Christi fidelibus presentem cartam inspecturis vel audituris :· Rogerus Malherbe de Luda salutem in domino. Nouerit vniuersitas vestra me concessisse . dedisse . 7 hac presenti carta mea confirmasse deo 7 ecclesie beate Marie Lincoln' venerabilique patri 7 domino meo Roberto dei gratia Lincolniensi episcopo . octo acras prati in Kokerinton' in loco qui vocatur Cudailes infra pratum quod vocatur Houedailes . Tenendas 7 habendas dicto domino episcopo 7 successoribus suis . ecclesieque sue predicte in liberam . puram . 7 perpetuam elemosinam quietam ab omni seruicio seculari . Et ego Rogerus 7 heredes mei predictum pratum cum pertinenciis predicto domino episcopo 7 successoribus suis . ecclesie que sue Lincoln' tanquam liberam . puram . 7 perpetuam elemosinam :· contra omnes gentes warantizabimus . adquietabimus . 7 defendemus in perpetuum . Quod ut perpetuam optineat firmitatem presenti carte sigillum meum feci apponi . Hiis testibus . dominis Roberto de Welle . Radulpho de Normanneb' . Gilberto de Coniisholm . Johanne de Somerchoth' . 7 Ranulpho de Brakinberewe . militibus . Geruasio de Thorp' . Johanne de Kokerinton' . Johanne filio Ade de Luda . Willelmo filio Thome . Ricardo clerico . Johanne filio Thome . Jordano clerico . Thoma Duty de eadem :· 7 aliis.

Endorsed: (1) Carta Rogeri Malherbe de Luda de .viii. acris prati (contemporary). (2) Luda (late 13 cent.). (3) .x. (late 13 cent.).
Four holes for a cord for the seal.
Size: $6\frac{1}{2}$ x $3\frac{3}{4}$ inches.
Text: MS—Orig. Dij/83/1/8.
Note: The date is probably the same as no. 1741, above: the witnesses are the same.

KELSTERN

ADD. CHART.

1747. *Inspeximus* by William [Lexington], the dean, and the chapter of Lincoln, of a charter of Richard [Gravesend], bishop of Lincoln, to W. the abbot and the convent of Thornton by which he allowed them to appropriate the church of Kelstern on the death or cession of the rector, since they were about to rebuild their conventual church to the honour of the Virgin Mary. One hundred shillings was to be reserved for the vicarage. 20th September, 1268.

Vniuersis sancte matris ecclesie filiis ad quos presens scriptum peruenerit . Willelmus decanus ⁊ capitulum Lincoln' ecclesie salutem in domino . Litteras venerabilis patris domini Ricardi dei gratia Lincoln' episcopi non cancellatas non abolitas nec in aliqua sui parte uiciatas sed signo auctentico suo signatas inspeximus in hec uerba . Ricardus miseracione diuina Lincoln' episcopus dilectis in Christo filiis .W. dei gratia Abbati de Thorenton' ⁊ eiusdem loci conuentui salutem . gratiam ⁊ benediccionem . Cum ecclesiam uestram in honorem sancte dei genitricis Marie edificare inceperitis opere magnifico ⁊ quam plurimum sumptuoso ⁊ ad consummacionem tanti operis ⁊ ad suscepcionem hospitum ⁊ pauperum cui diligenter intenditis ac alia uobis incumbencia onera sustinenda iuxta multorum fidedignorum assercionem vestre non sufficiant facultates ut tanto studiosius ⁊ deuocius diuino vacetis obsequio quanto deputatus ad id locus decencior efficitur cuius decencia infirmos animos ad pietatis affectum frequenter inducit . ⁊ ut ad perfeccionem operis supradicti ⁊ alia misericordie opera excercenda copisius sufficere valeatis vobis ⁊ successoribus vestris damus concedimus . et auctoritate pontificali confirmamus fructus ⁊ prouentus ecclesie de Kelesterne . que de vestro est patronatu in usus uestros ad construccionem operis memorati ⁊ ad conseruacionem ipsius cum constructum fuerit . Volentes ut cedente vel decedente eiusdem rectore possitis absque nostra uel successorum nostrorum contradiccione ipsos fructus ⁊ prouentus vobis ⁊ monasterio vestro applicare . ⁊ in vsus predictos perpetuis temporibus retinere . Salua porcione centum solidorum de prouentibus antedictis ad sustentacionem vicarii ministraturi in eadem ecclesia . Saluis eciam episcopalibus ⁊ archidiaconalibus consuetudinibus . ⁊ Lincoln' ecclesie dignitate . Et ut hec nostra donacio . concessio . ⁊ confirmacio robur optineat perpetue firmitatis ./ presenti scripto sigillum nostrum fecimus apponi ./ Datum apud Grimesby septimo idus augusti . Anno domini millesimo . ducentesimo . sexagesimo . octauo . Nos igitur predictis donacioni . concessioni . ⁊ confirmacioni de fructibus et prouentibus ecclesie predicte factis de fratrum nostrorum vnanimi voluntate quantum ad nos pertinet nostrum confirmatorium prebemus assensum . Saluis in omnibus Lincoln' ecclesie iure et dignitate . In cuius rei testimonium presentibus sigillum commune capituli nostri fecimus apponi . Datum Lincoln' . duodecimo kalendas Octobris . anno domini superius annotato.

Endorsed: (1) Confirmacio ecclesie de Kelsterne per Willelmum decanum ⁊ capitulum Lincoln' (14 cent.). (2) Stephanus (14 cent.). (3) . 29 . (query 15 cent.). (4) On the fold—Kelsterne (contemp.).

The charter is torn where the seal tag should be.

Size: 11 x 7 inches.

Text: MS—Orig. 73/1/4*a*.

INDEX OF PERSONS AND PLACES

INDEX OF COUNTIES AND COUNTRIES

(EXTINCT PLACES ARE PRINTED IN ITALICS)

NORTHAMPTONSHIRE

NORTHUMBERLAND

NOTTINGHAMSHIRE

OXFORDSHIRE

SOMERSET

INDEX OF SUBJECTS